Shojo Beat

OTOMEN

Story & Art by
Aya Kanno

Volume
THIRTEEN

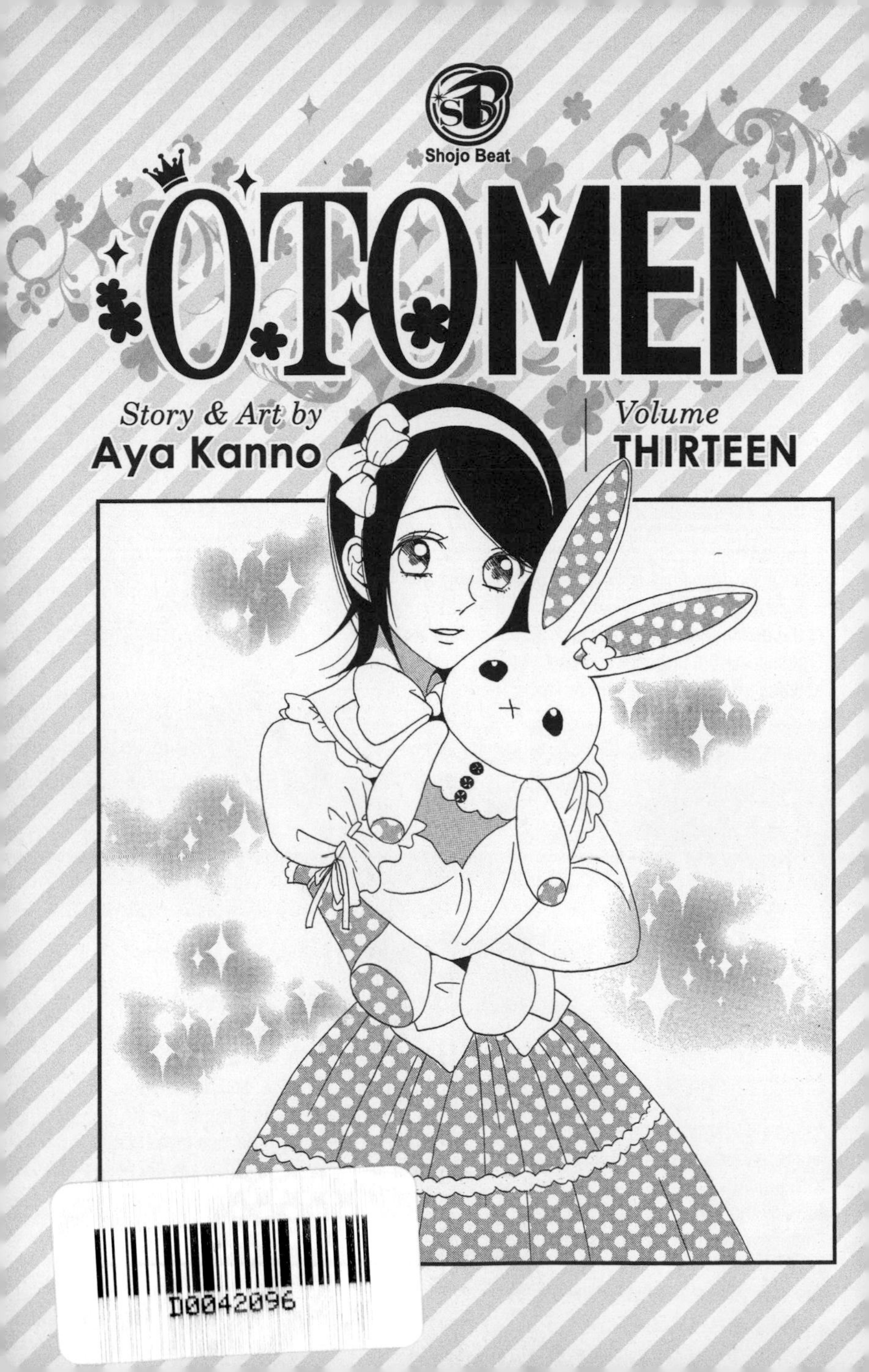

OTOMEN Characters & Story

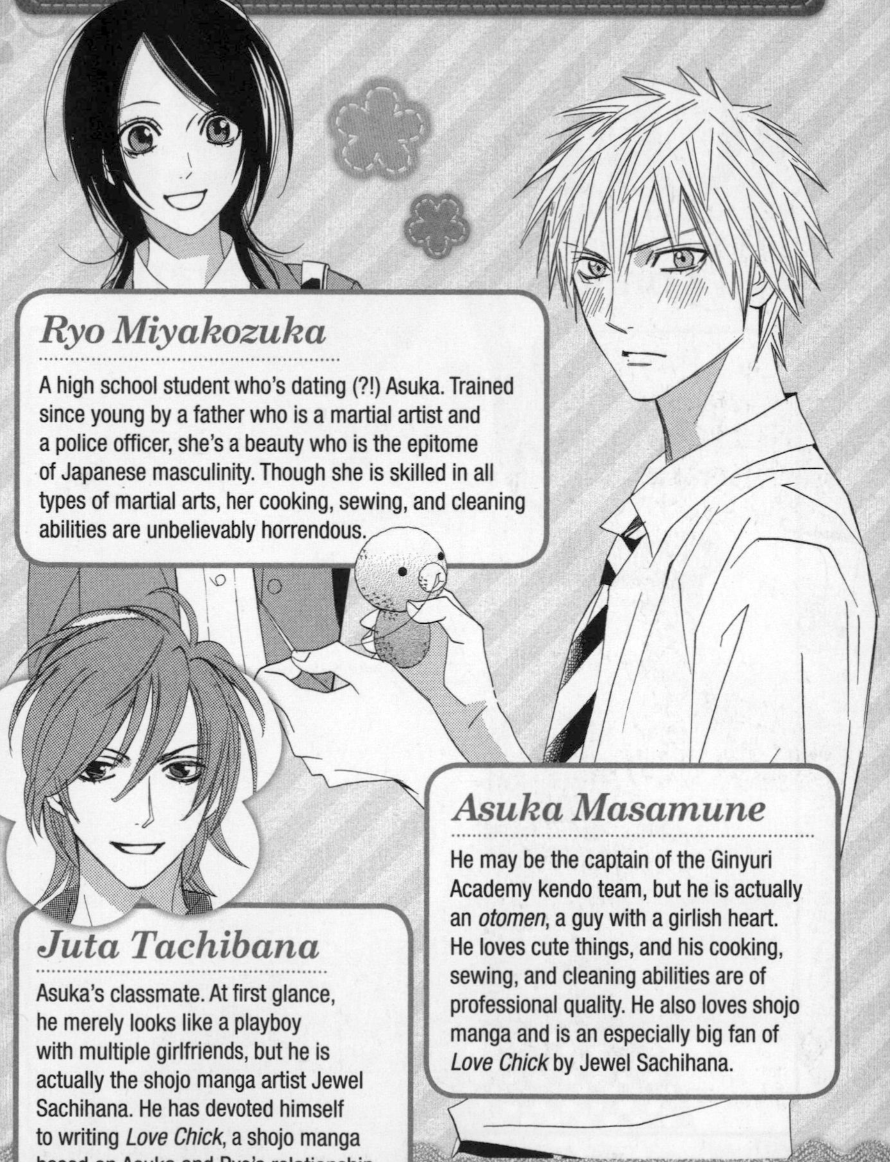

Ryo Miyakozuka

A high school student who's dating (?!) Asuka. Trained since young by a father who is a martial artist and a police officer, she's a beauty who is the epitome of Japanese masculinity. Though she is skilled in all types of martial arts, her cooking, sewing, and cleaning abilities are unbelievably horrendous.

Asuka Masamune

He may be the captain of the Ginyuri Academy kendo team, but he is actually an *otomen*, a guy with a girlish heart. He loves cute things, and his cooking, sewing, and cleaning abilities are of professional quality. He also loves shojo manga and is an especially big fan of *Love Chick* by Jewel Sachihana.

Juta Tachibana

Asuka's classmate. At first glance, he merely looks like a playboy with multiple girlfriends, but he is actually the shojo manga artist Jewel Sachihana. He has devoted himself to writing *Love Chick*, a shojo manga based on Asuka and Ryo's relationship.

STORY

Asuka's anti-*otomen* mother, Kiyomi, allows him to attend a baking class for men at Patisserie Violet. There, he deepens his friendship with Hiromi, the chef who runs the class. Asuka is mistaken for a Patisserie Violet employee and is kidnapped. Because of that, Hiromi ends up revealing that he is actually Asuka's father, and the two of them are reunited as father and son.

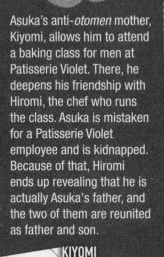

KIYOMI MASAMUNE

HIROMI YOSHINO

DON'T YOU LAY A FINGER...

...ON MY SON!

TWO OTOMEN ARE REUNITED AS FATHER AND SON! ♥

OTHER OTOMEN

Hajime Tonomine

The captain of the Kinbara High School kendo team, he considers Asuka his sworn rival. He is actually an *otomen* who is good with cosmetics.

Yamato Ariake

He is younger than Asuka and looks like a cute girl. He is a delusional *otomen* who admires manliness.

Kitora Kurokawa

Asuka's classmate. A man who is captivated by the beauty of flowers. He is an obsessed *otomen* who wants to cover the world in flowers.

OTOMEN

volume 13
CONTENTS

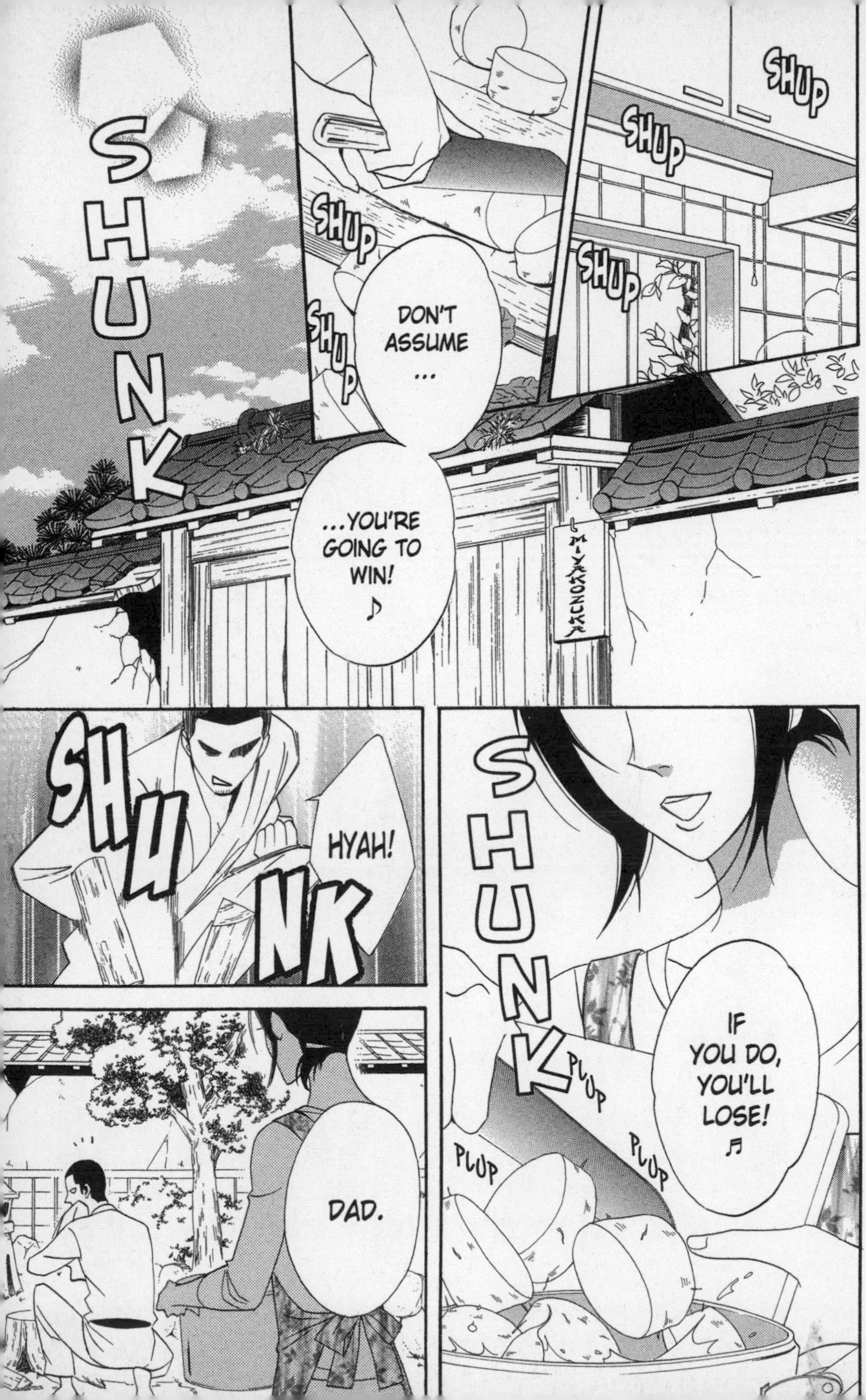
SHUP
SHUP
SHUP
SHUP
SHUP
SHUNK
DON'T ASSUME ...
...YOU'RE GOING TO WIN! ♪
MIYAKOZUKA
SHUNK
IF YOU DO, YOU'LL LOSE! ♬
PLUP
PLUP
PLUP
HYAH!
SHUNK
DAD.

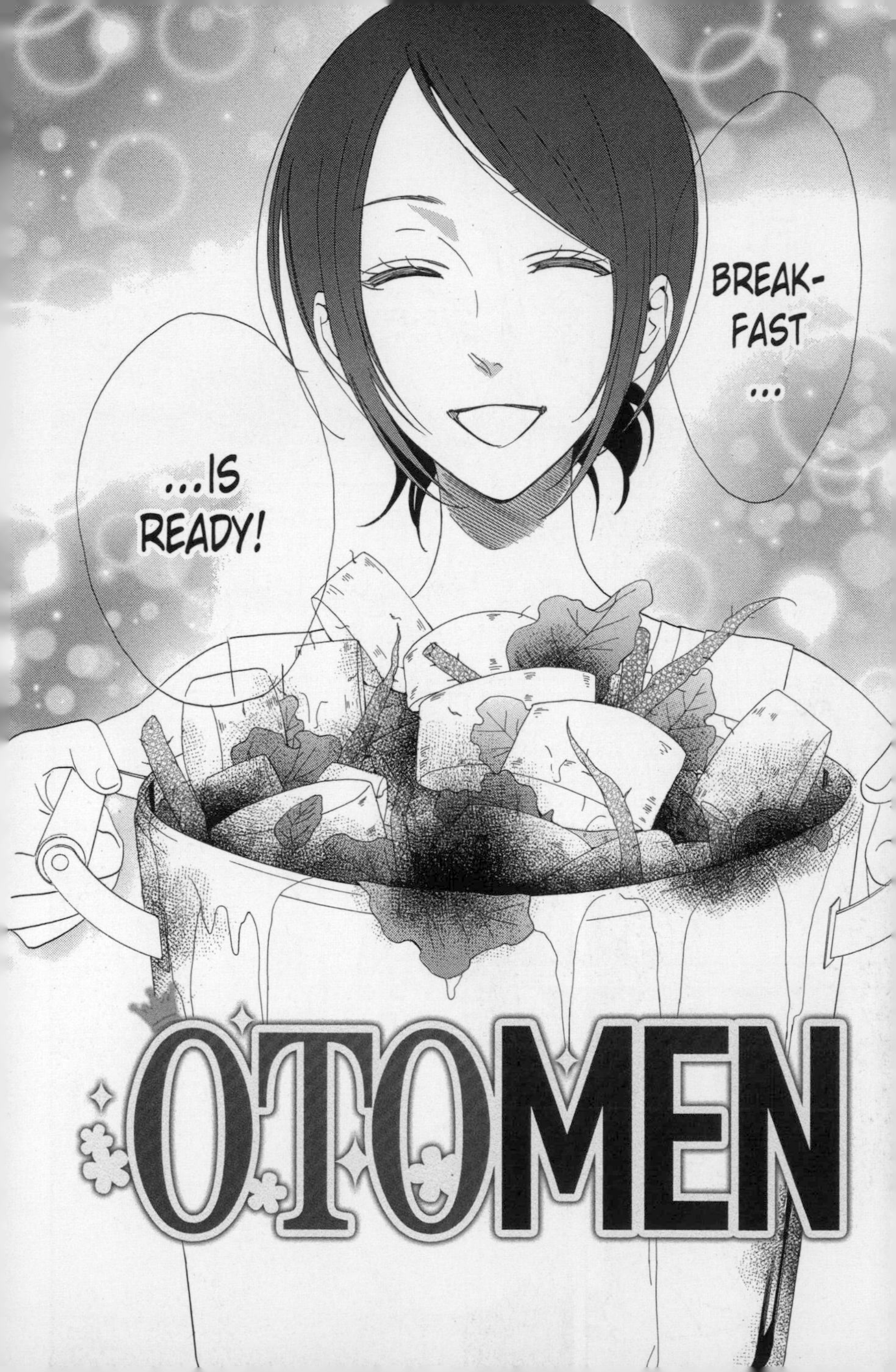
BREAK-
FAST
...
...IS
READY!
OTOMEN

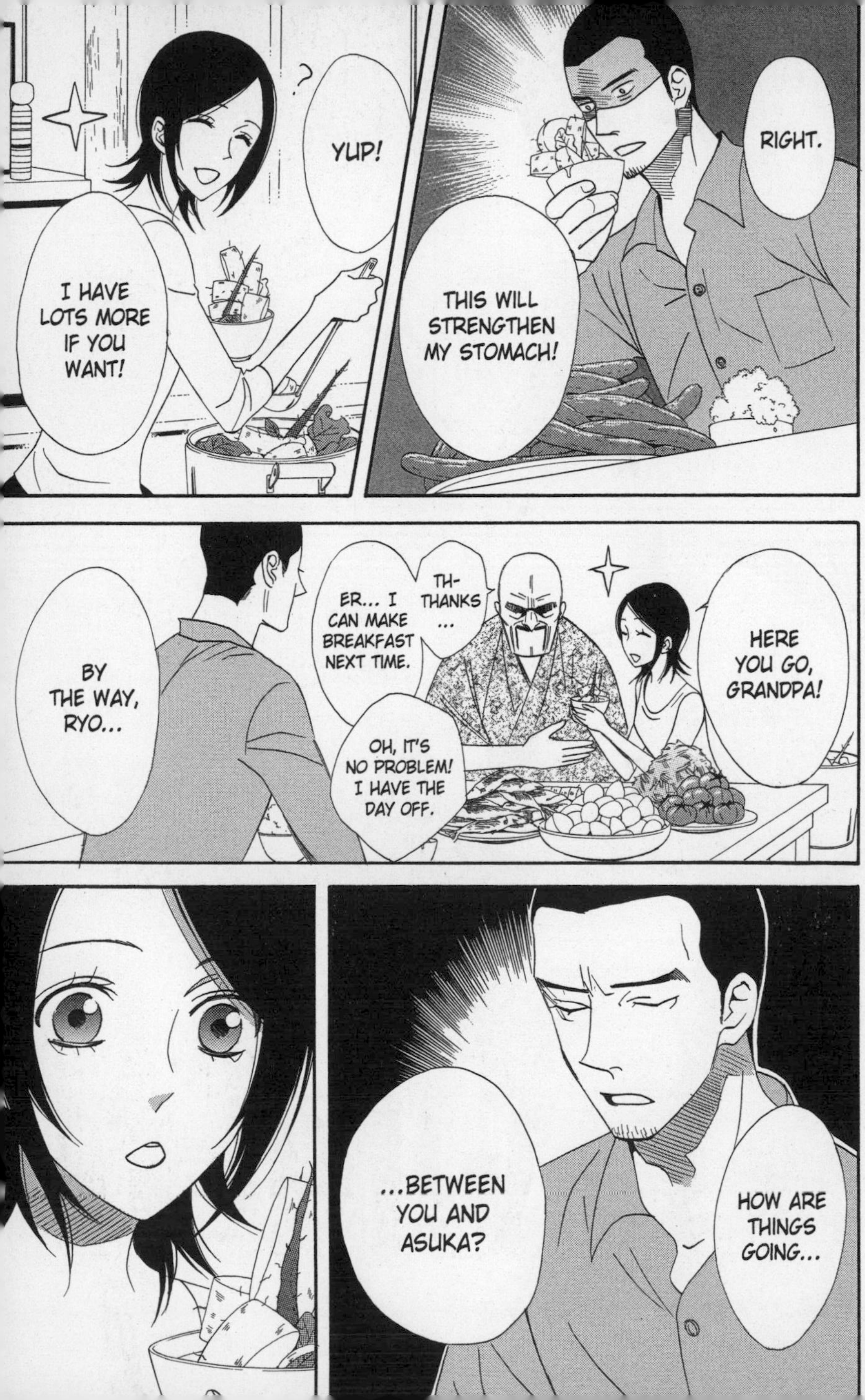
RIGHT.
THIS WILL STRENGTHEN MY STOMACH!
YUP!
I HAVE LOTS MORE IF YOU WANT!
HERE YOU GO, GRANDPA!
TH-THANKS ...
ER... I CAN MAKE BREAKFAST NEXT TIME.
OH, IT'S NO PROBLEM! I HAVE THE DAY OFF.
BY THE WAY, RYO...
HOW ARE THINGS GOING...
...BETWEEN YOU AND ASUKA?

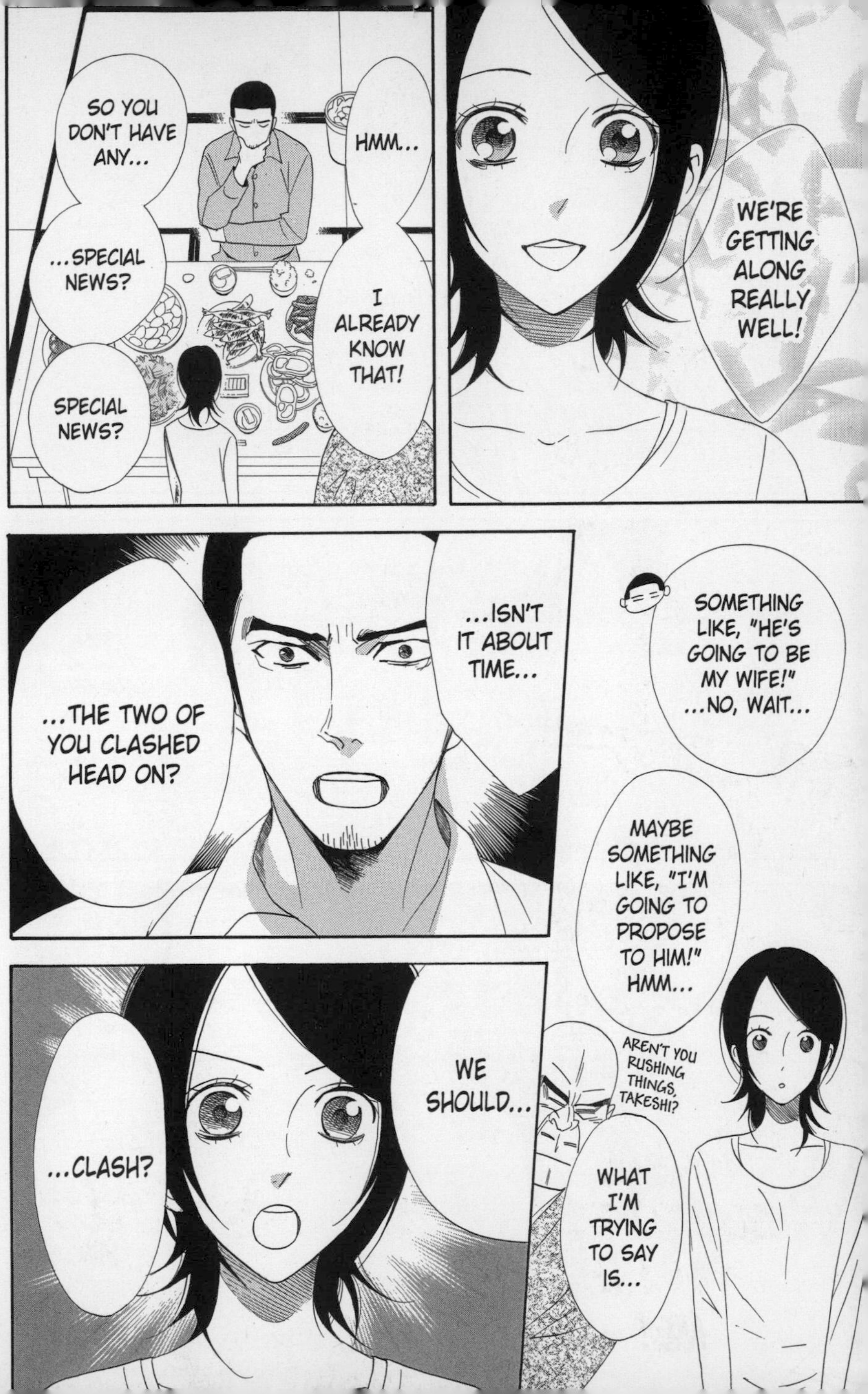
WE'RE GETTING ALONG REALLY WELL!
HMM...
I ALREADY KNOW THAT!
SO YOU DON'T HAVE ANY...
...SPECIAL NEWS?
SPECIAL NEWS?
SOMETHING LIKE, "HE'S GOING TO BE MY WIFE!" ...NO, WAIT...
...ISN'T IT ABOUT TIME...
...THE TWO OF YOU CLASHED HEAD ON?
MAYBE SOMETHING LIKE, "I'M GOING TO PROPOSE TO HIM!" HMM...
AREN'T YOU RUSHING THINGS, TAKESHI?
WHAT I'M TRYING TO SAY IS...
WE SHOULD...
...CLASH?

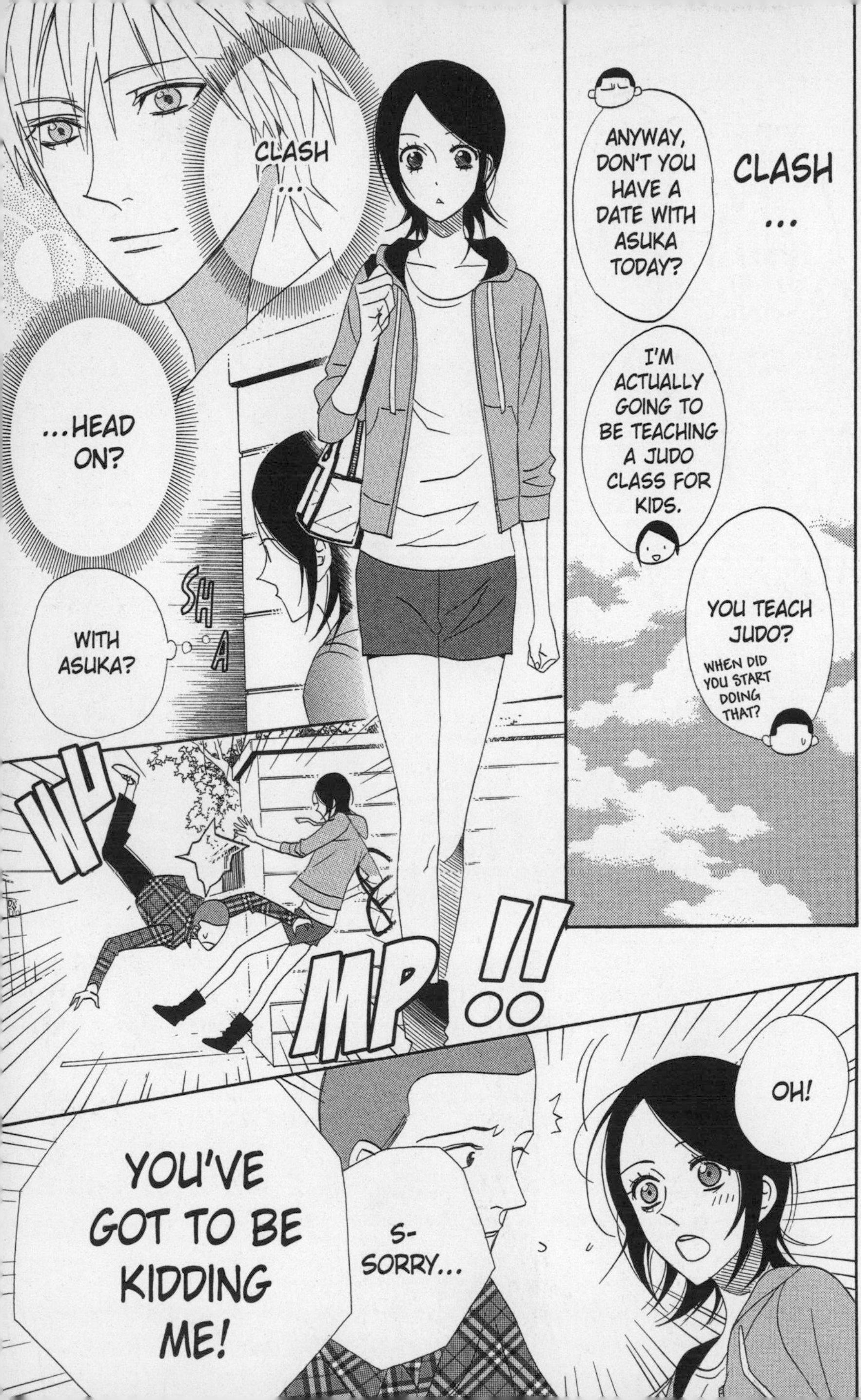
CLASH ...
ANYWAY, DON'T YOU HAVE A DATE WITH ASUKA TODAY?
I'M ACTUALLY GOING TO BE TEACHING A JUDO CLASS FOR KIDS.
YOU TEACH JUDO?
WHEN DID YOU START DOING THAT?
CLASH ...
...HEAD ON?
SHA
WITH ASUKA?
WU
MP!!
OH!
S-SORRY...
YOU'VE GOT TO BE KIDDING ME!

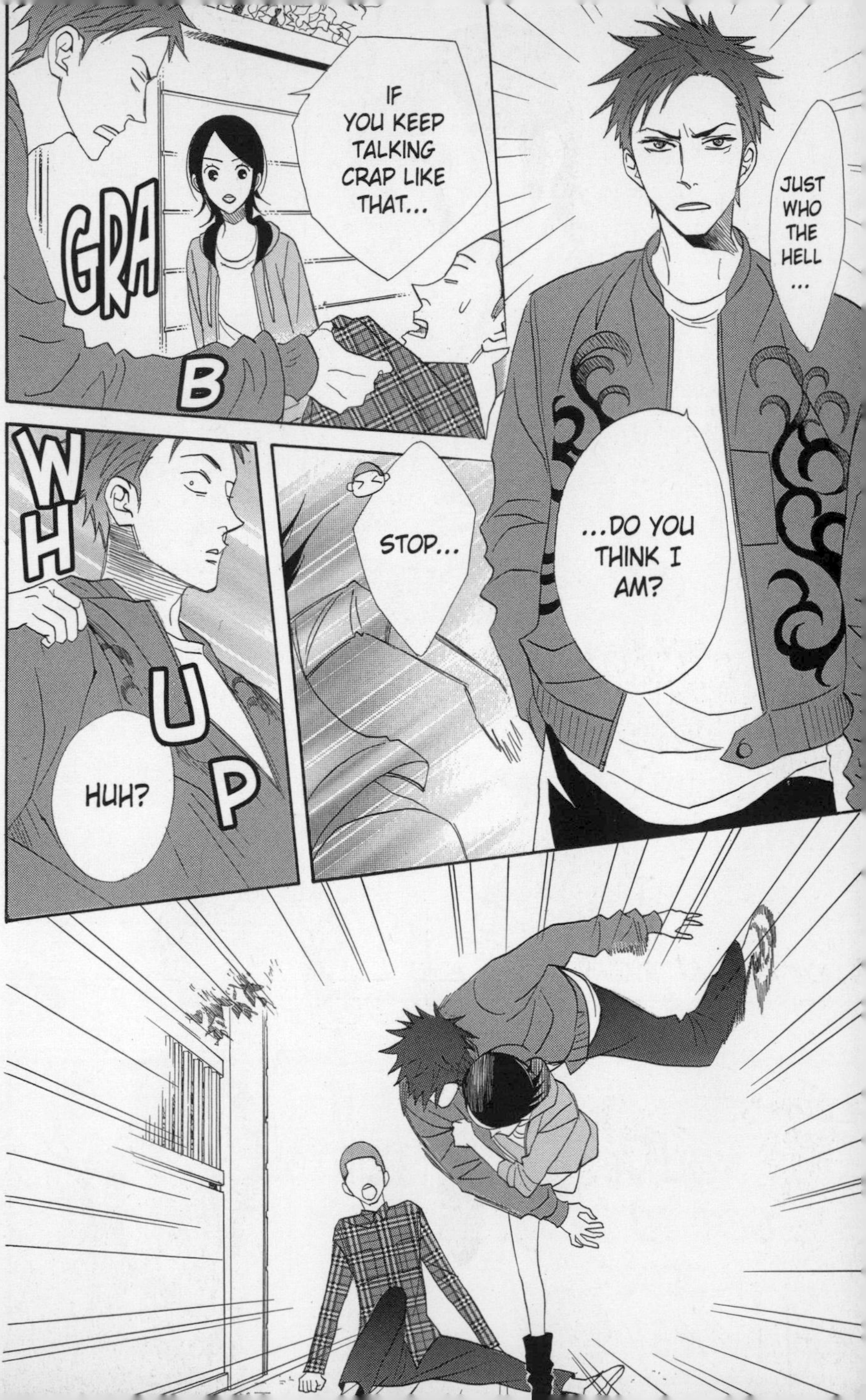

JUST WHO THE HELL ...
...DO YOU THINK I AM?
IF YOU KEEP TALKING CRAP LIKE THAT...
GRAB
STOP...
WHUP
HUH?

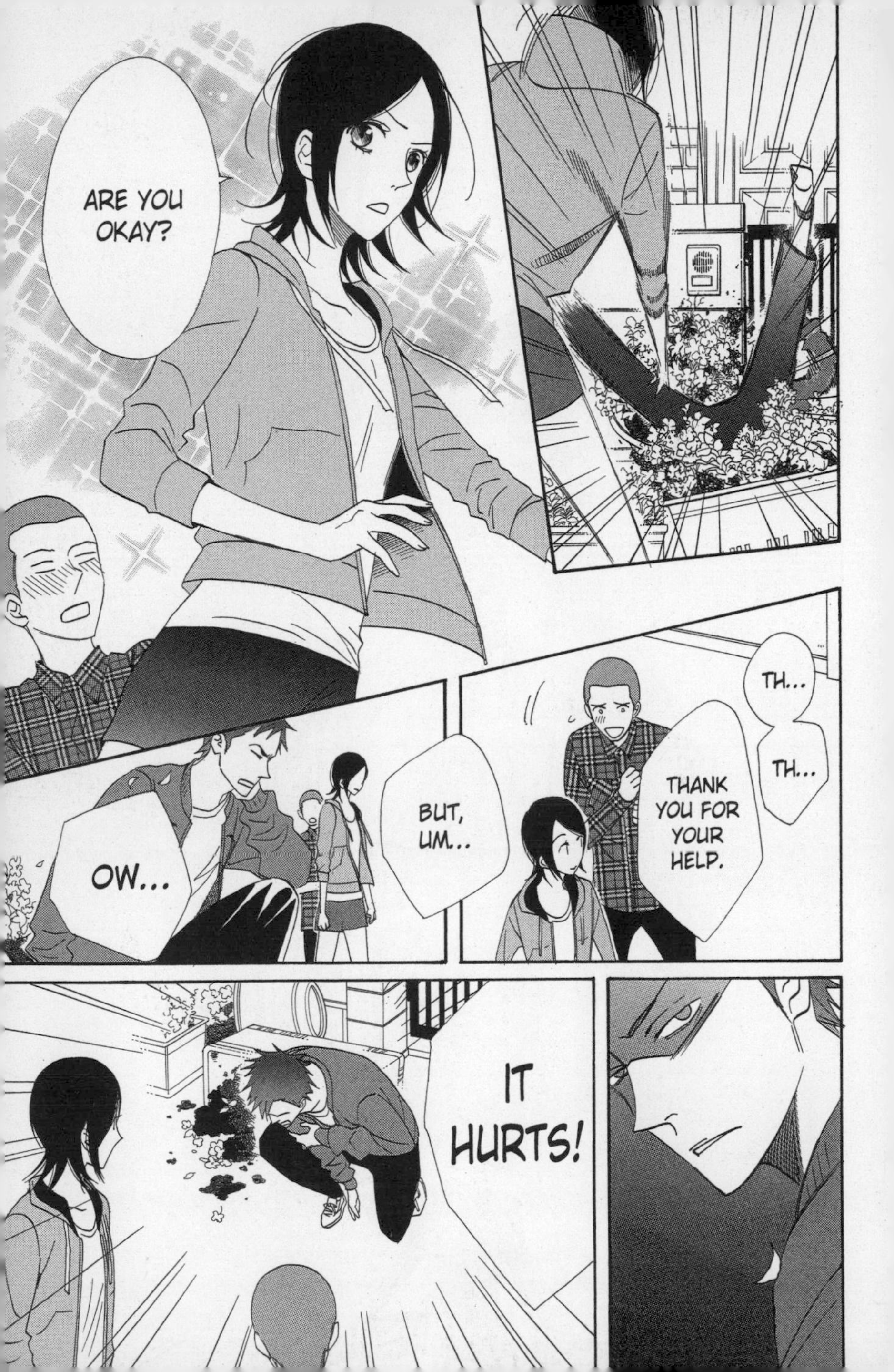
ARE YOU OKAY?
TH...
TH...
THANK YOU FOR YOUR HELP.
BUT, UM...
OW...
IT HURTS!

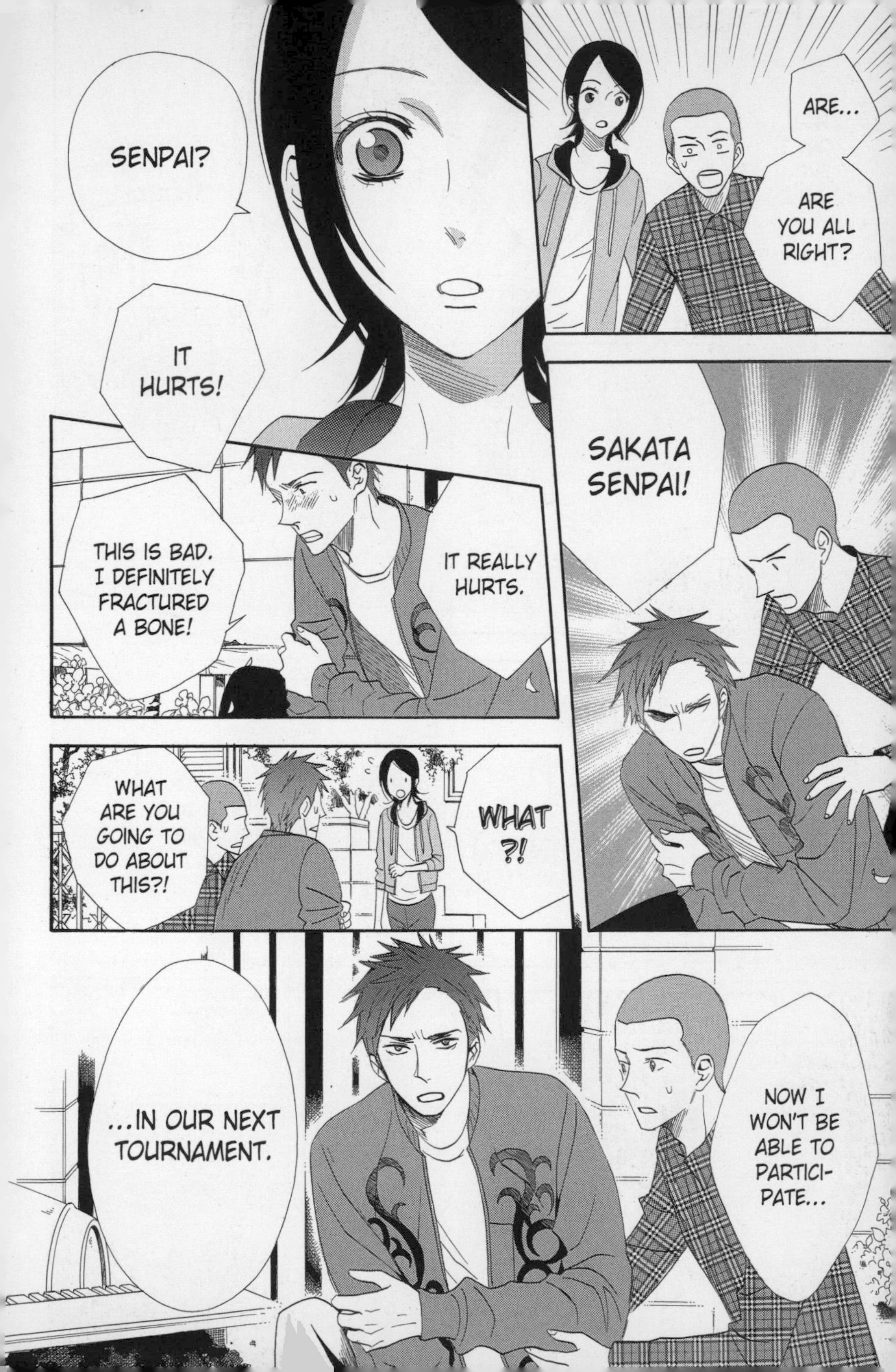
ARE...
ARE YOU ALL RIGHT?
SENPAI?
SAKATA SENPAI!
IT HURTS!
IT REALLY HURTS.
THIS IS BAD. I DEFINITELY FRACTURED A BONE!
WHAT ?!
WHAT ARE YOU GOING TO DO ABOUT THIS?!
NOW I WON'T BE ABLE TO PARTICI-PATE...
...IN OUR NEXT TOURNAMENT.

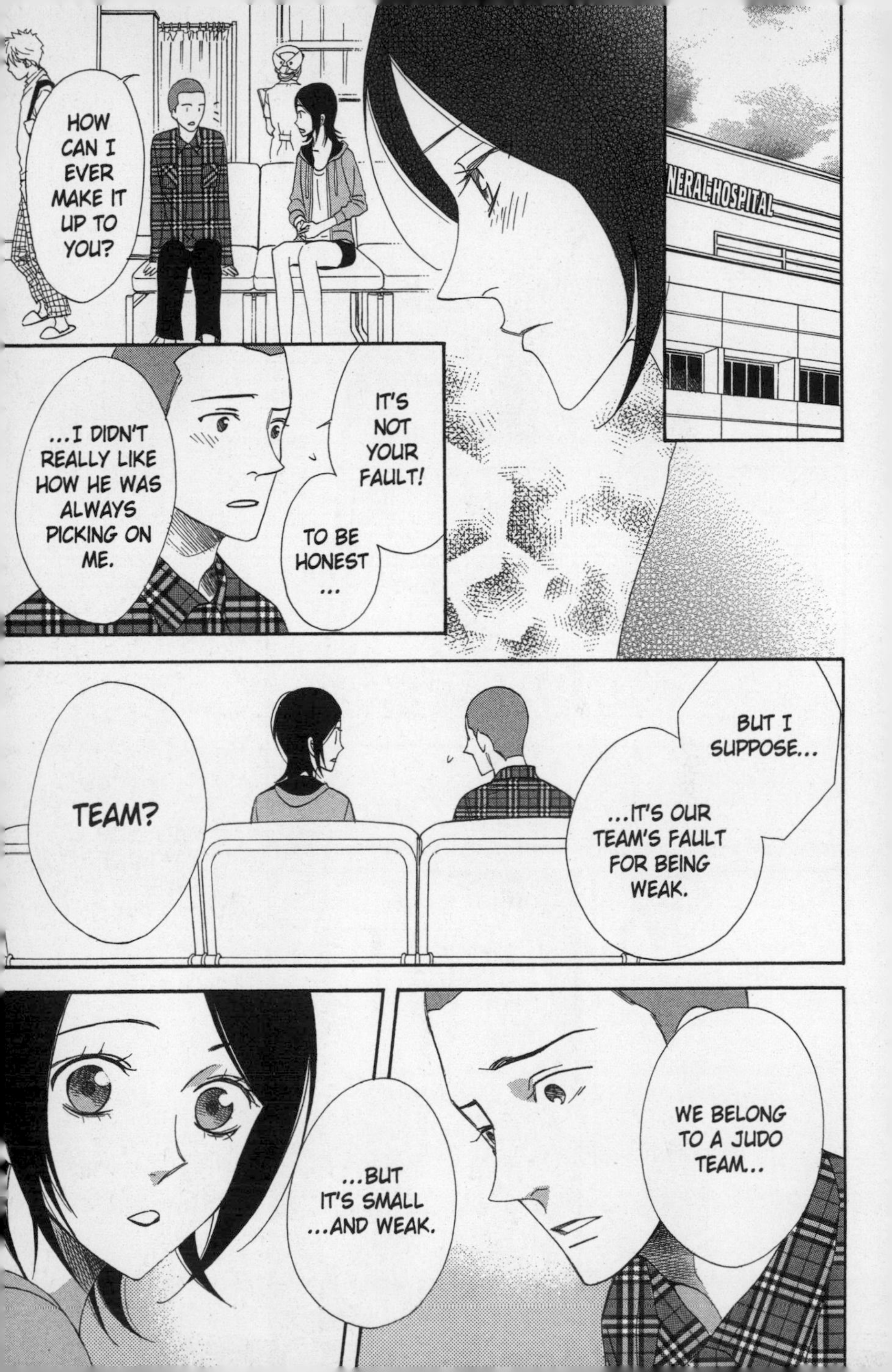
NERAL-HOSPITAL
HOW CAN I EVER MAKE IT UP TO YOU?
IT'S NOT YOUR FAULT!
TO BE HONEST ...
...I DIDN'T REALLY LIKE HOW HE WAS ALWAYS PICKING ON ME.
BUT I SUPPOSE...
...IT'S OUR TEAM'S FAULT FOR BEING WEAK.
TEAM?
WE BELONG TO A JUDO TEAM...
...BUT IT'S SMALL ...AND WEAK.

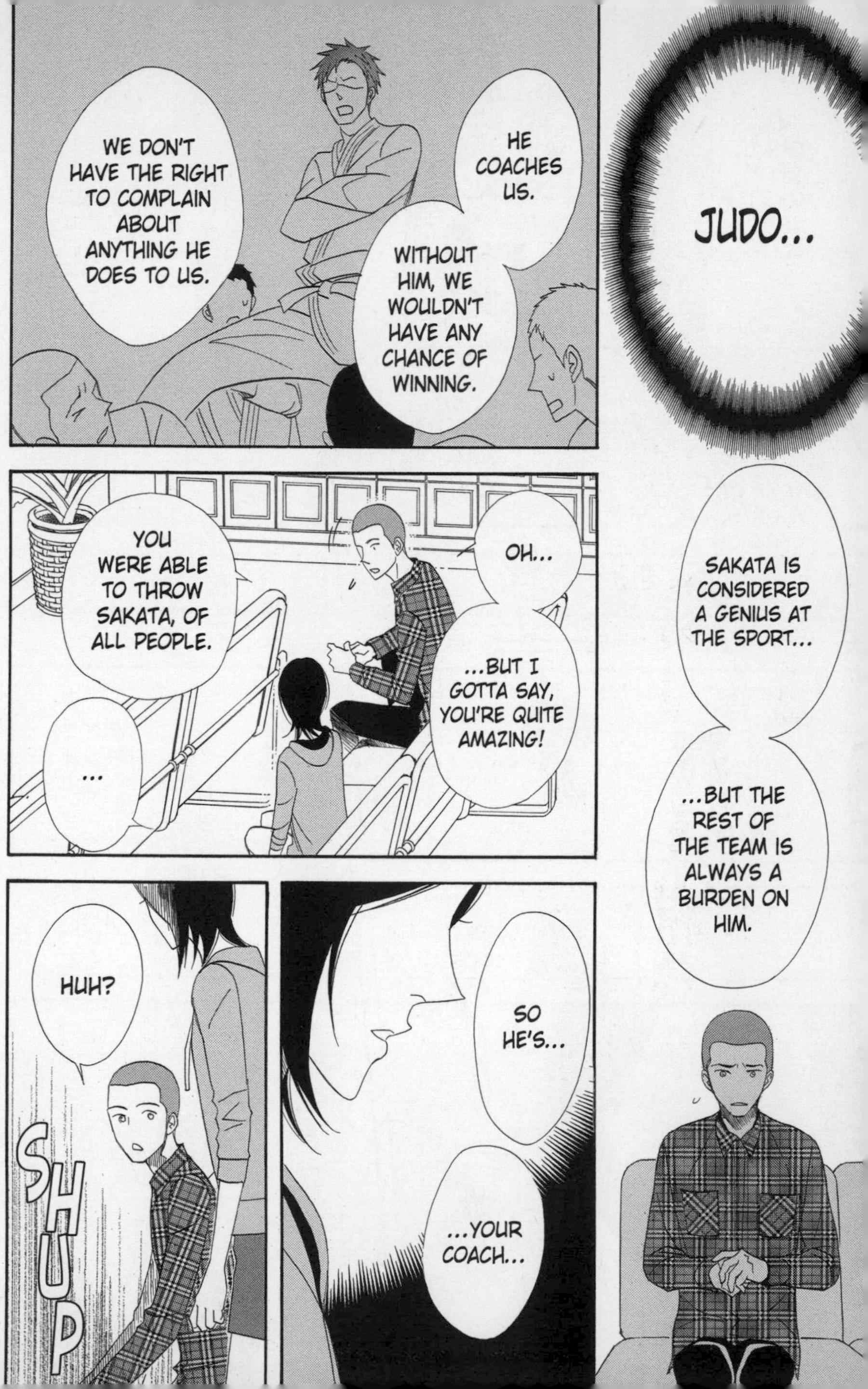
JUDO...
SAKATA IS CONSIDERED A GENIUS AT THE SPORT...
...BUT THE REST OF THE TEAM IS ALWAYS A BURDEN ON HIM.
HE COACHES US.
WITHOUT HIM, WE WOULDN'T HAVE ANY CHANCE OF WINNING.
WE DON'T HAVE THE RIGHT TO COMPLAIN ABOUT ANYTHING HE DOES TO US.
OH...
...BUT I GOTTA SAY, YOU'RE QUITE AMAZING!
YOU WERE ABLE TO THROW SAKATA, OF ALL PEOPLE.
...
SO HE'S...
...YOUR COACH...
HUH?
SHUP

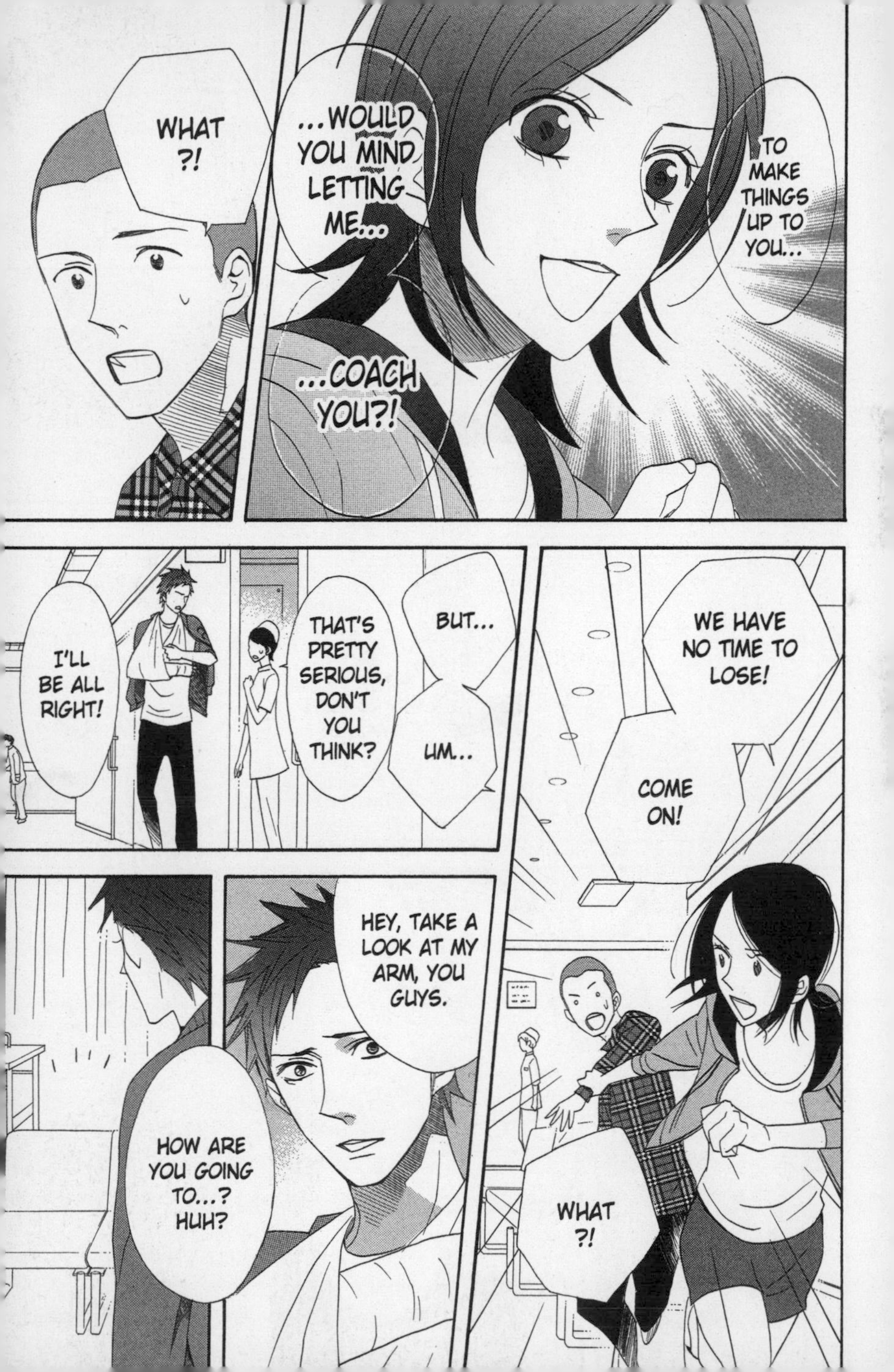
TO MAKE THINGS UP TO YOU...
...WOULD YOU MIND LETTING ME...
...COACH YOU?!
WHAT ?!
WE HAVE NO TIME TO LOSE!
COME ON!
WHAT ?!
BUT...
UM...
THAT'S PRETTY SERIOUS, DON'T YOU THINK?
I'LL BE ALL RIGHT!
HEY, TAKE A LOOK AT MY ARM, YOU GUYS.
HOW ARE YOU GOING TO...? HUH?

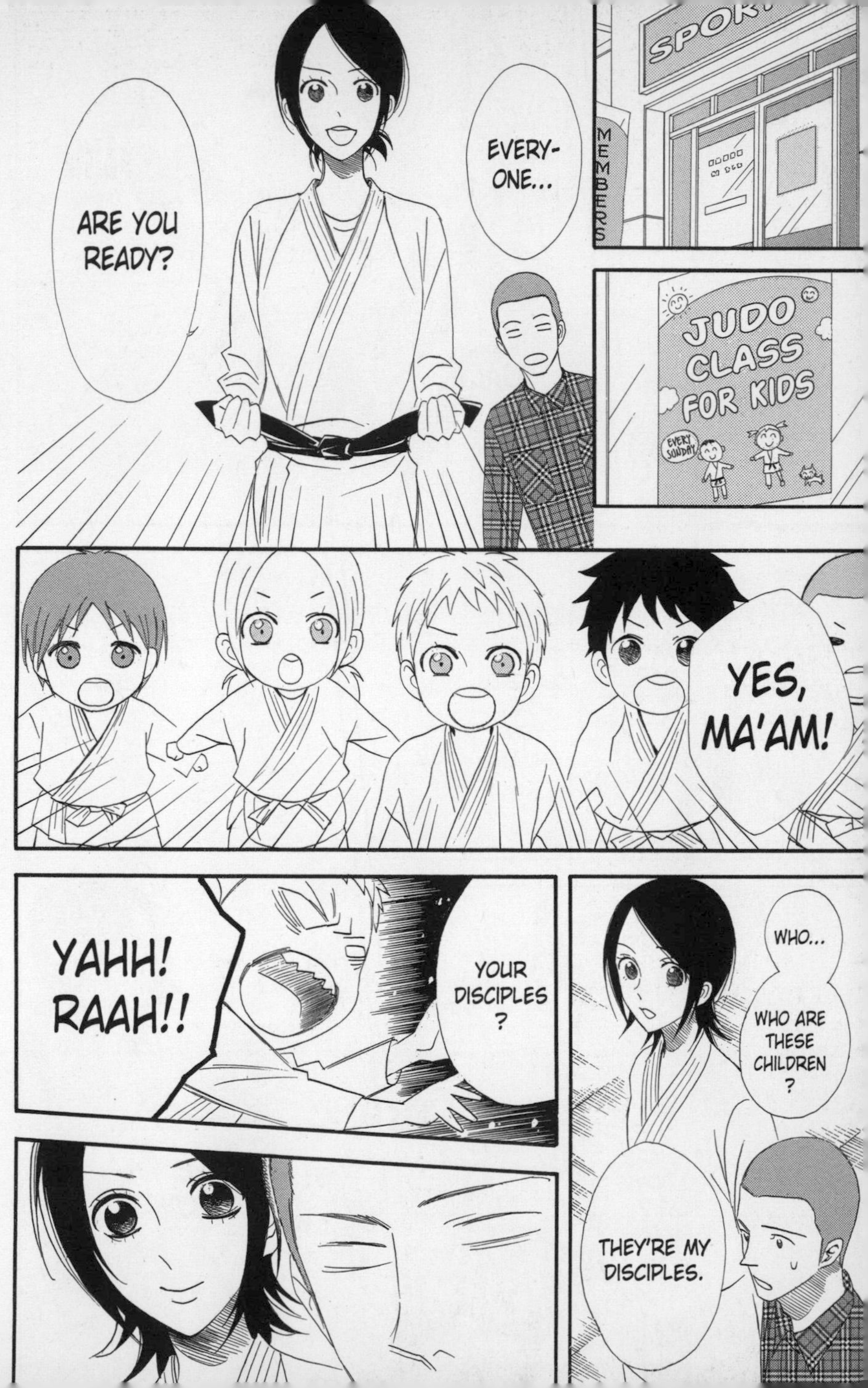
MEMBERS
JUDO CLASS FOR KIDS
EVERY SUNDAY
EVERY-ONE...
ARE YOU READY?
YES, MA'AM!
WHO...
WHO ARE THESE CHILDREN?
THEY'RE MY DISCIPLES.
YOUR DISCIPLES?
YAHH! RAAH!!

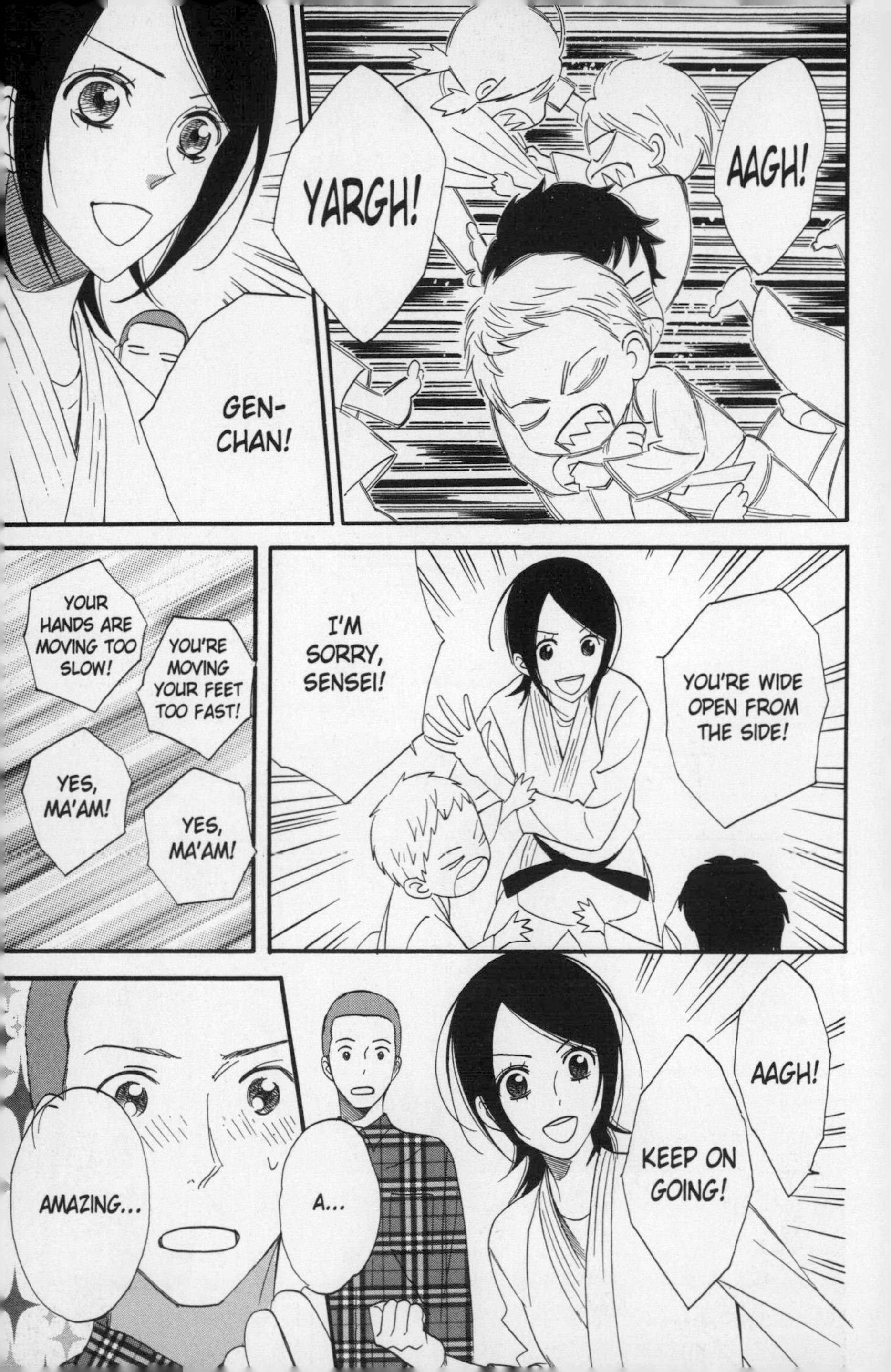
AAGH!
YARGH!
GEN-CHAN!
YOU'RE WIDE OPEN FROM THE SIDE!
I'M SORRY, SENSEI!
YOU'RE MOVING YOUR FEET TOO FAST!
YOUR HANDS ARE MOVING TOO SLOW!
YES, MA'AM!
YES, MA'AM!
AAGH!
KEEP ON GOING!
A...
AMAZING...

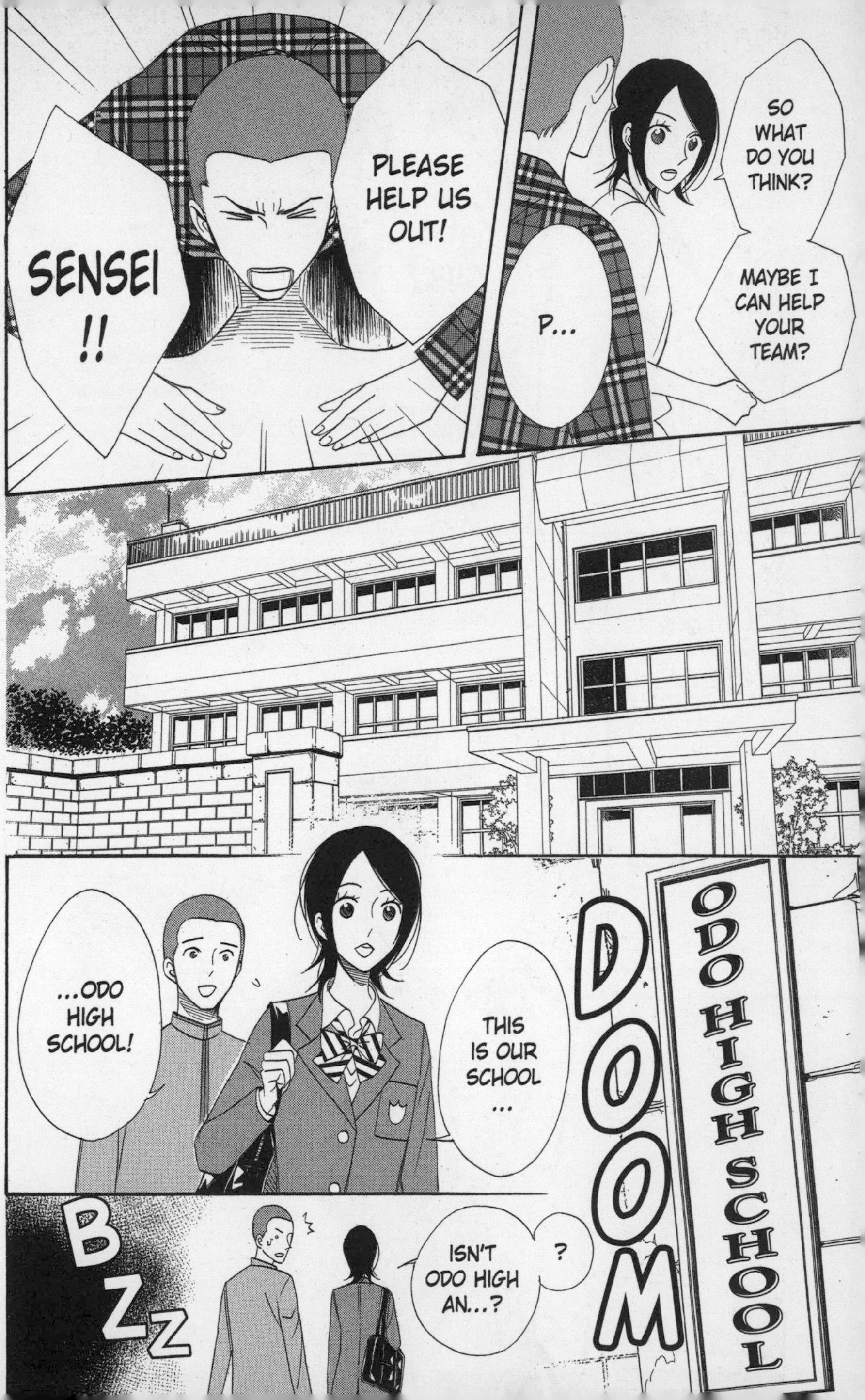
SO WHAT DO YOU THINK?
MAYBE I CAN HELP YOUR TEAM?
P...
PLEASE HELP US OUT!
SENSEI !!
ODO HIGH SCHOOL
DOOM
THIS IS OUR SCHOOL ...
...ODO HIGH SCHOOL!
?
ISN'T ODO HIGH AN...?
BZZ

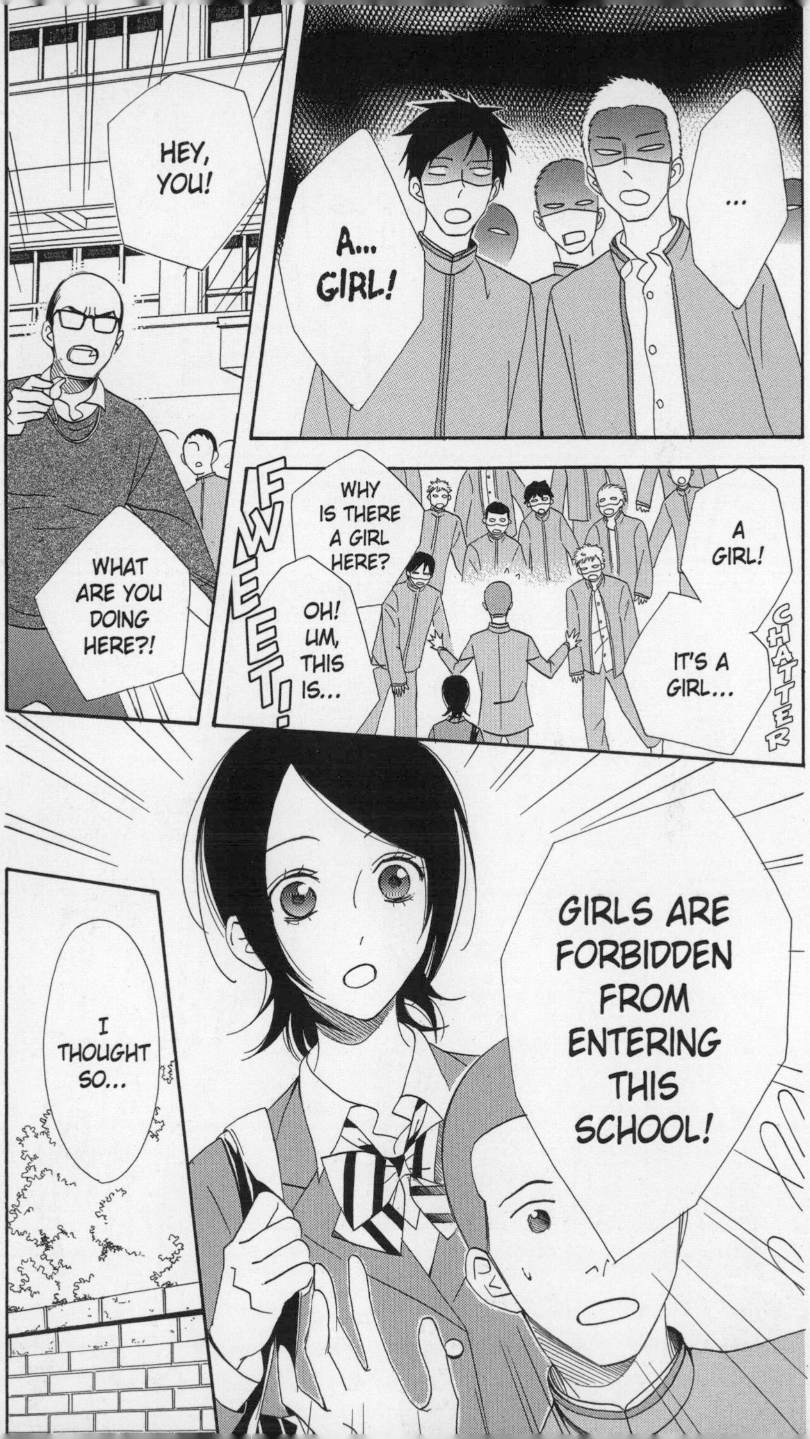
...
A... GIRL!
A GIRL!
CHATTER
IT'S A GIRL...
WHY IS THERE A GIRL HERE?
OH! UM, THIS IS...
FWEET!
HEY, YOU!
WHAT ARE YOU DOING HERE?!
GIRLS ARE FORBIDDEN FROM ENTERING THIS SCHOOL!
I THOUGHT SO...

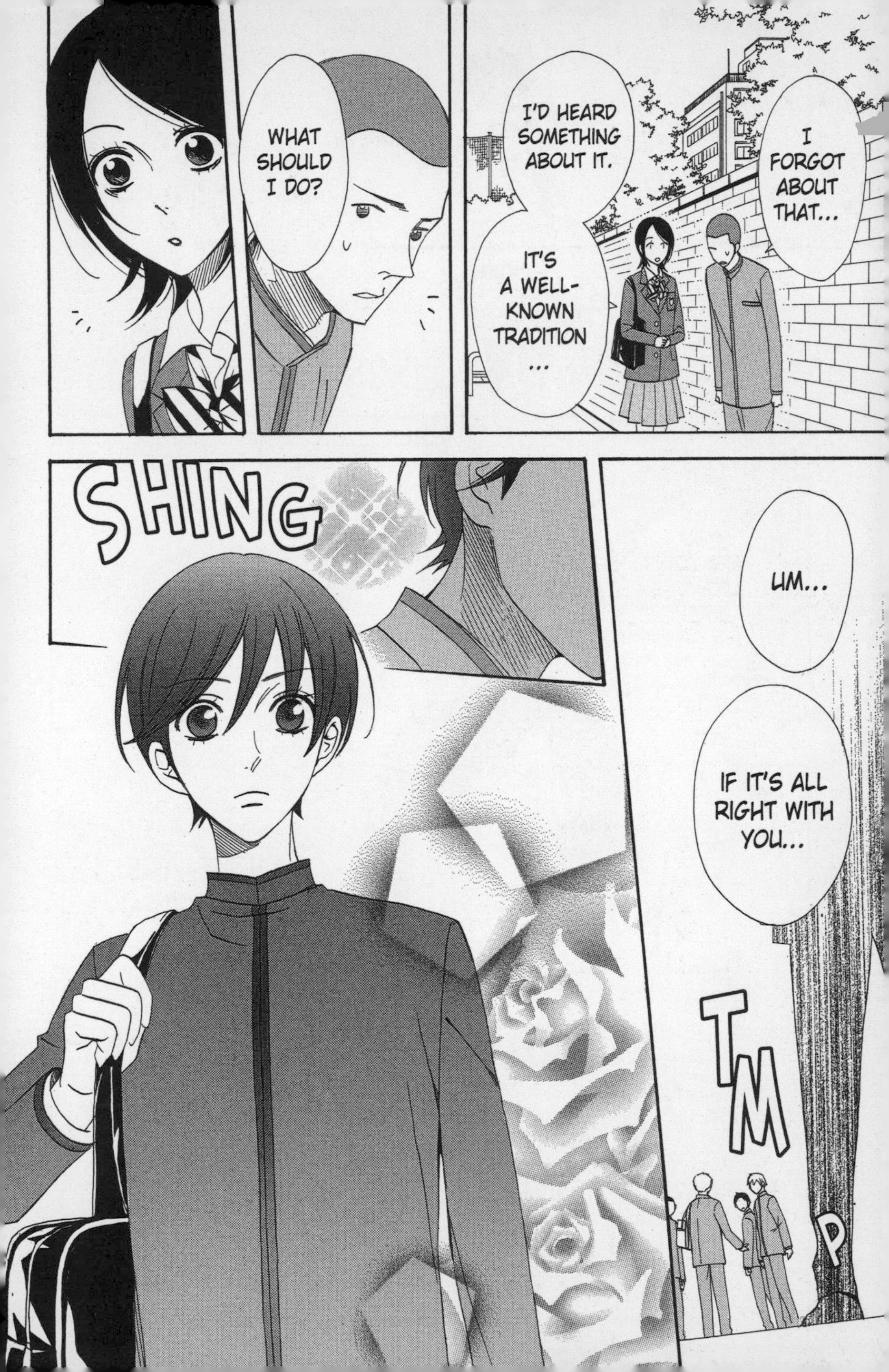
I FORGOT ABOUT THAT...
I'D HEARD SOMETHING ABOUT IT.
IT'S A WELL-KNOWN TRADITION...
WHAT SHOULD I DO?
UM...
IF IT'S ALL RIGHT WITH YOU...
TMP
SHING

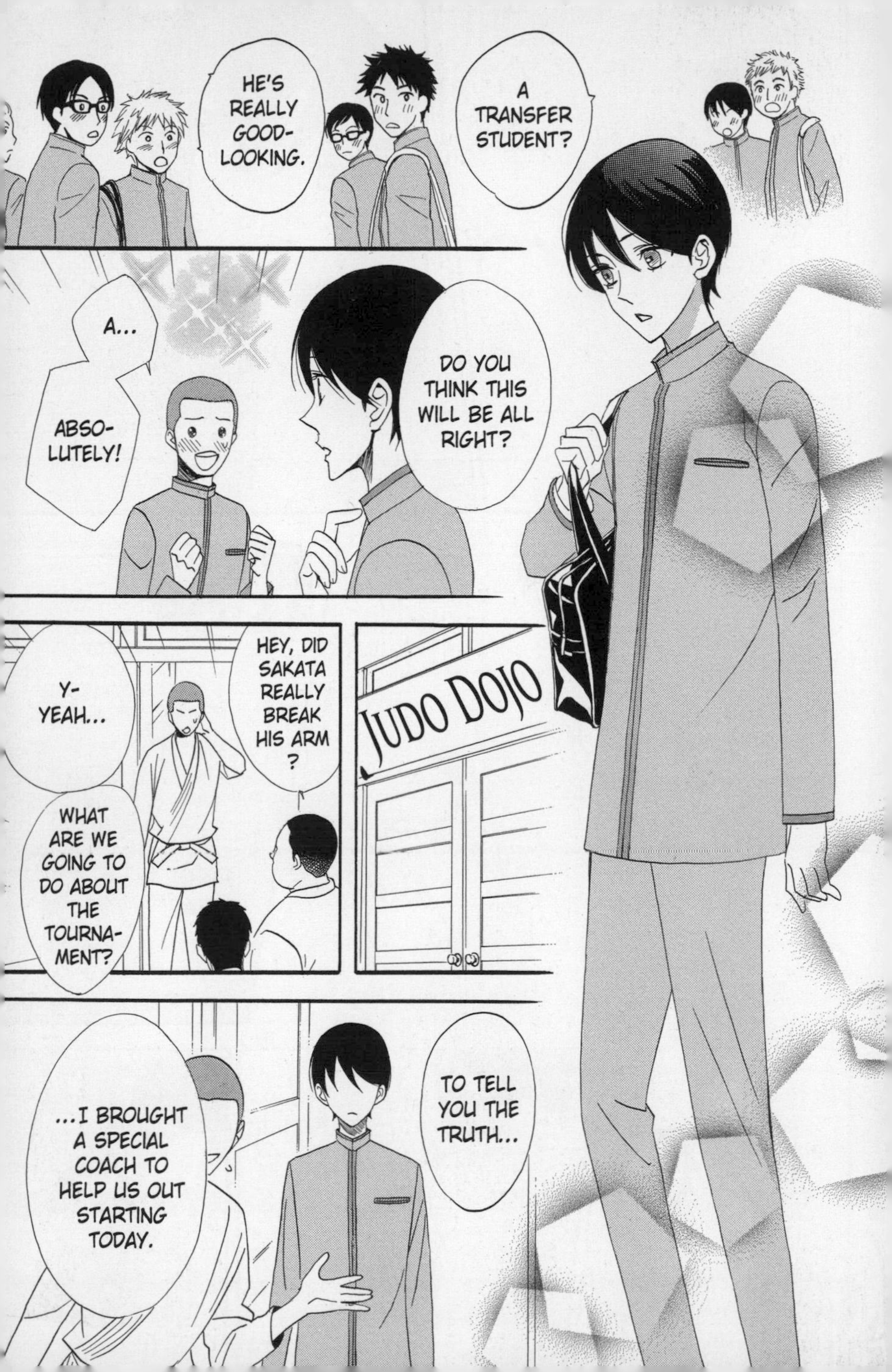
A TRANSFER STUDENT?
HE'S REALLY GOOD-LOOKING.
DO YOU THINK THIS WILL BE ALL RIGHT?
A...
ABSO-LUTELY!
JUDO DOJO
HEY, DID SAKATA REALLY BREAK HIS ARM?
Y-YEAH...
WHAT ARE WE GOING TO DO ABOUT THE TOURNAMENT?
TO TELL YOU THE TRUTH...
...I BROUGHT A SPECIAL COACH TO HELP US OUT STARTING TODAY.

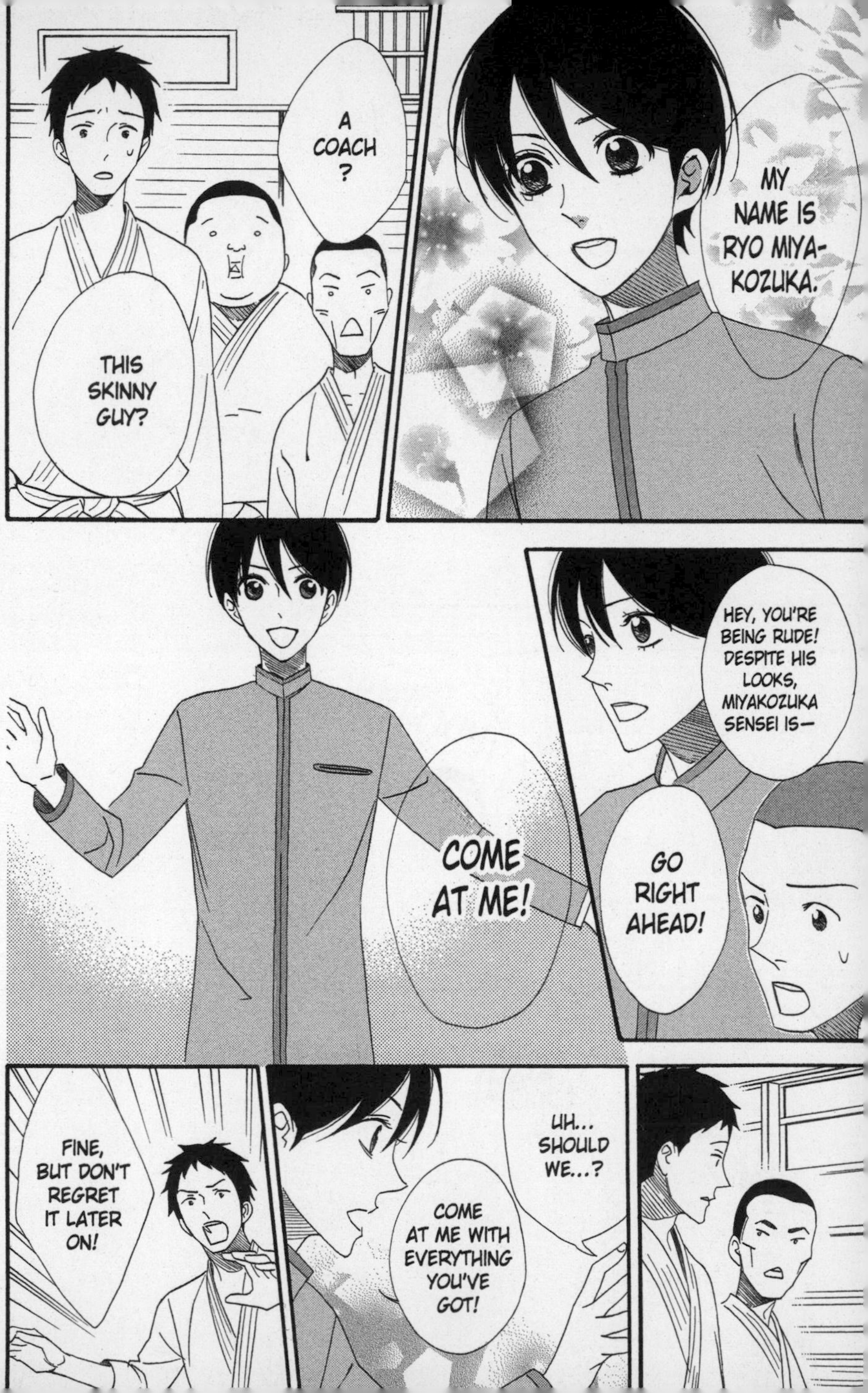
MY NAME IS RYO MIYA-KOZUKA.
A COACH?
THIS SKINNY GUY?
HEY, YOU'RE BEING RUDE! DESPITE HIS LOOKS, MIYAKOZUKA SENSEI IS—
GO RIGHT AHEAD!
COME AT ME!
UH... SHOULD WE...?
COME AT ME WITH EVERYTHING YOU'VE GOT!
FINE, BUT DON'T REGRET IT LATER ON!

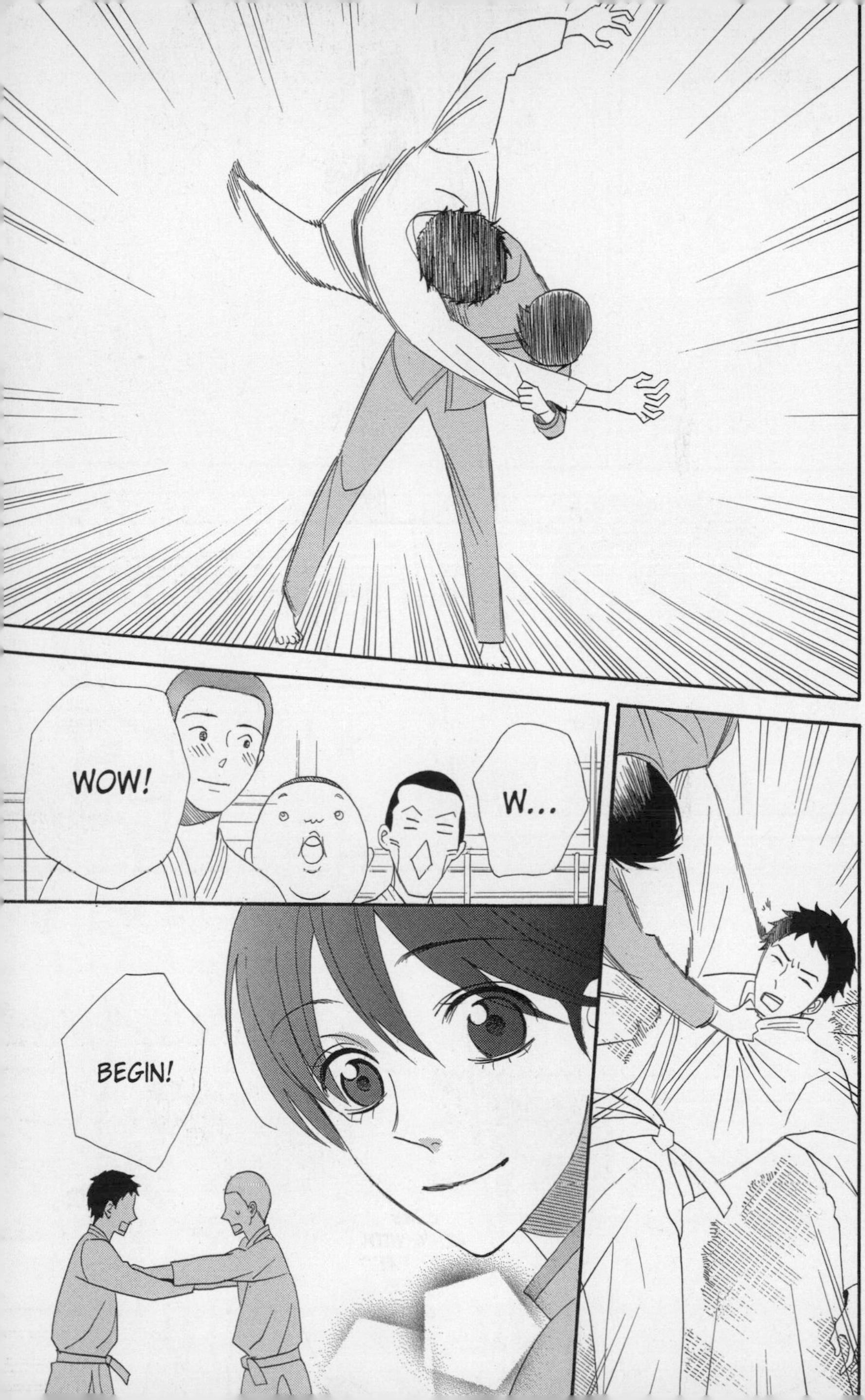
W...
WOW!
BEGIN!

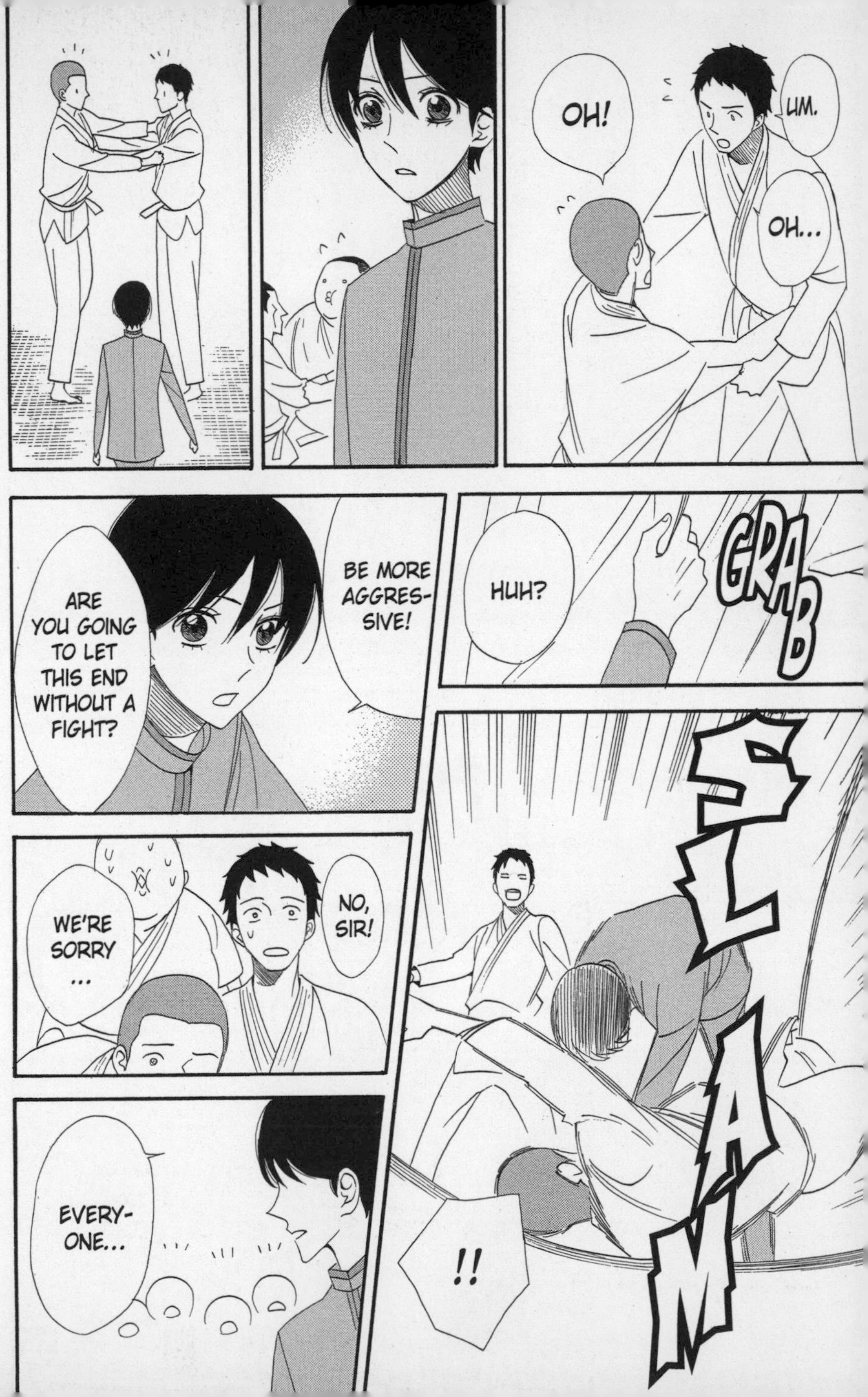
UM.
OH!
OH...
HUH?
GRAB
SLAM
!!
BE MORE AGGRES-SIVE!
ARE YOU GOING TO LET THIS END WITHOUT A FIGHT?
NO, SIR!
WE'RE SORRY ...
EVERY-ONE...

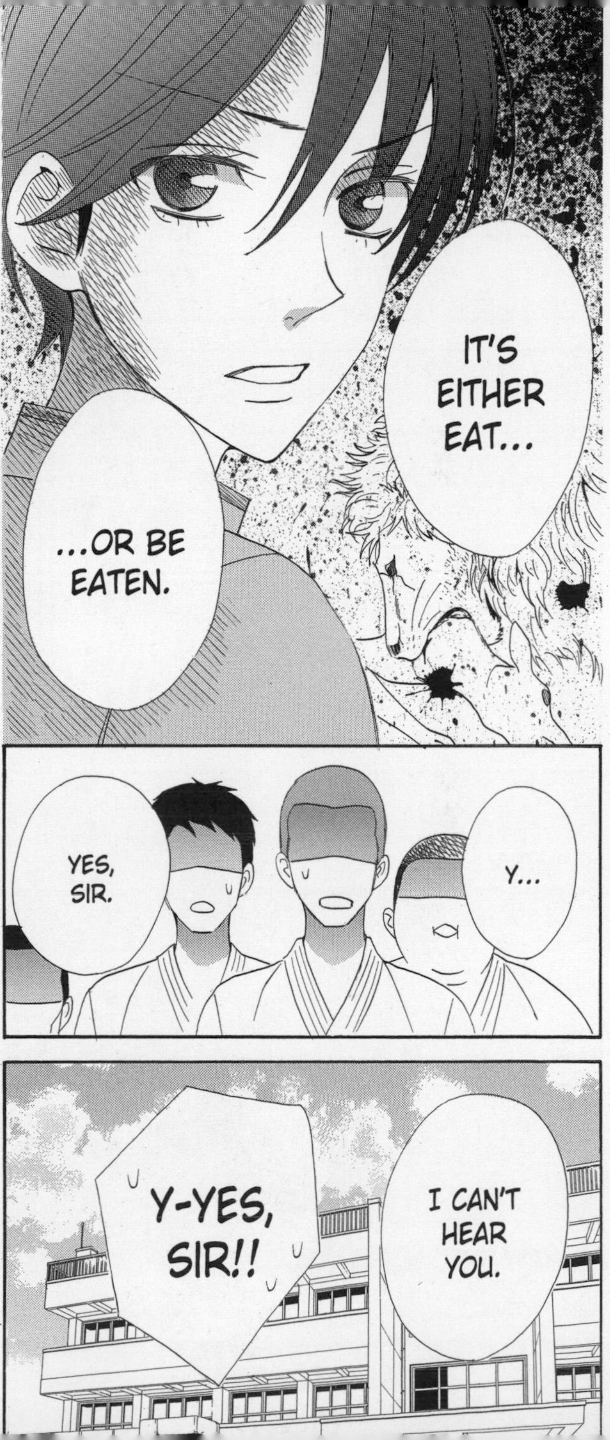
IT'S EITHER EAT...
...OR BE EATEN.
Y...
YES, SIR.
I CAN'T HEAR YOU.
Y-YES, SIR!!

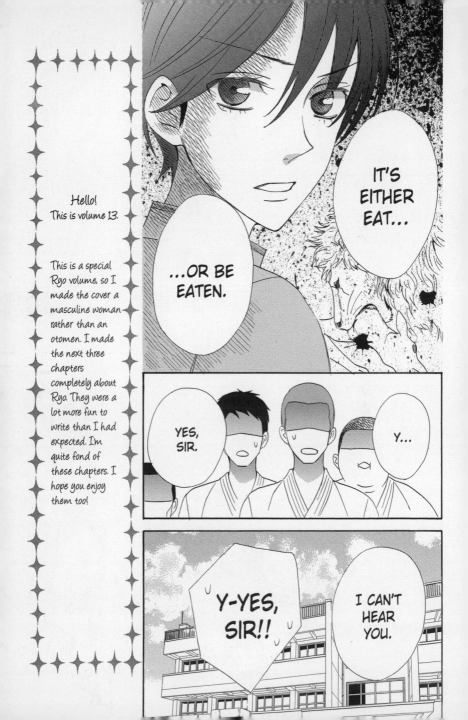

Hello!
This is volume 13.

This is a special Ryo volume, so I made the cover a masculine woman rather than an otomen. I made the next three chapters completely about Ryo. They were a lot more fun to write than I had expected. I'm quite fond of these chapters. I hope you enjoy them too!

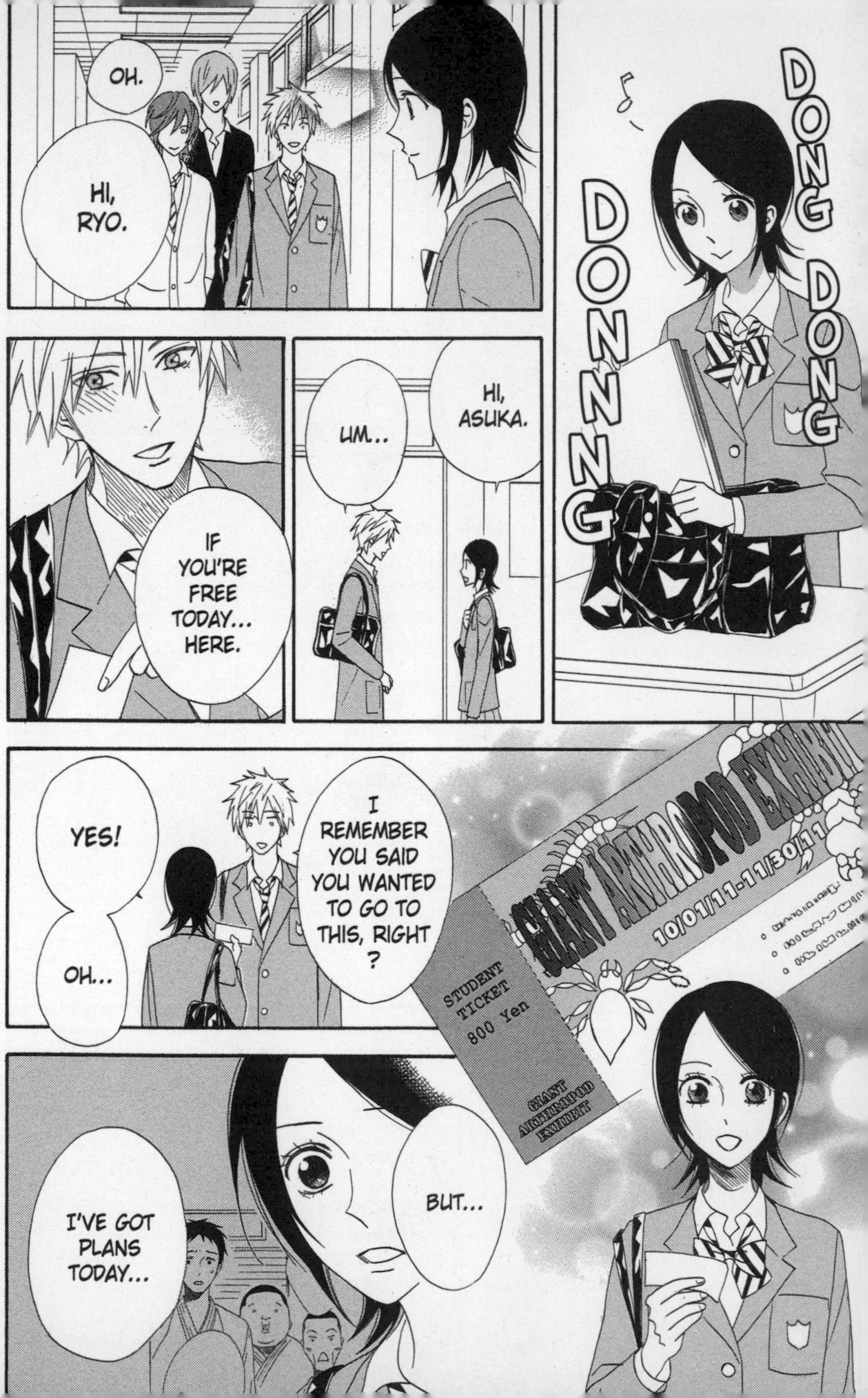
DONG DONG
DONNG
OH.
HI, RYO.
HI, ASUKA.
UM...
IF YOU'RE FREE TODAY... HERE.
GIANT ARTHROPOD EXHIBIT
10/01/11-11/30/11
STUDENT TICKET 800 Yen
GIANT ARTHROPOD EXHIBIT
I REMEMBER YOU SAID YOU WANTED TO GO TO THIS, RIGHT?
YES!
OH...
BUT...
I'VE GOT PLANS TODAY...

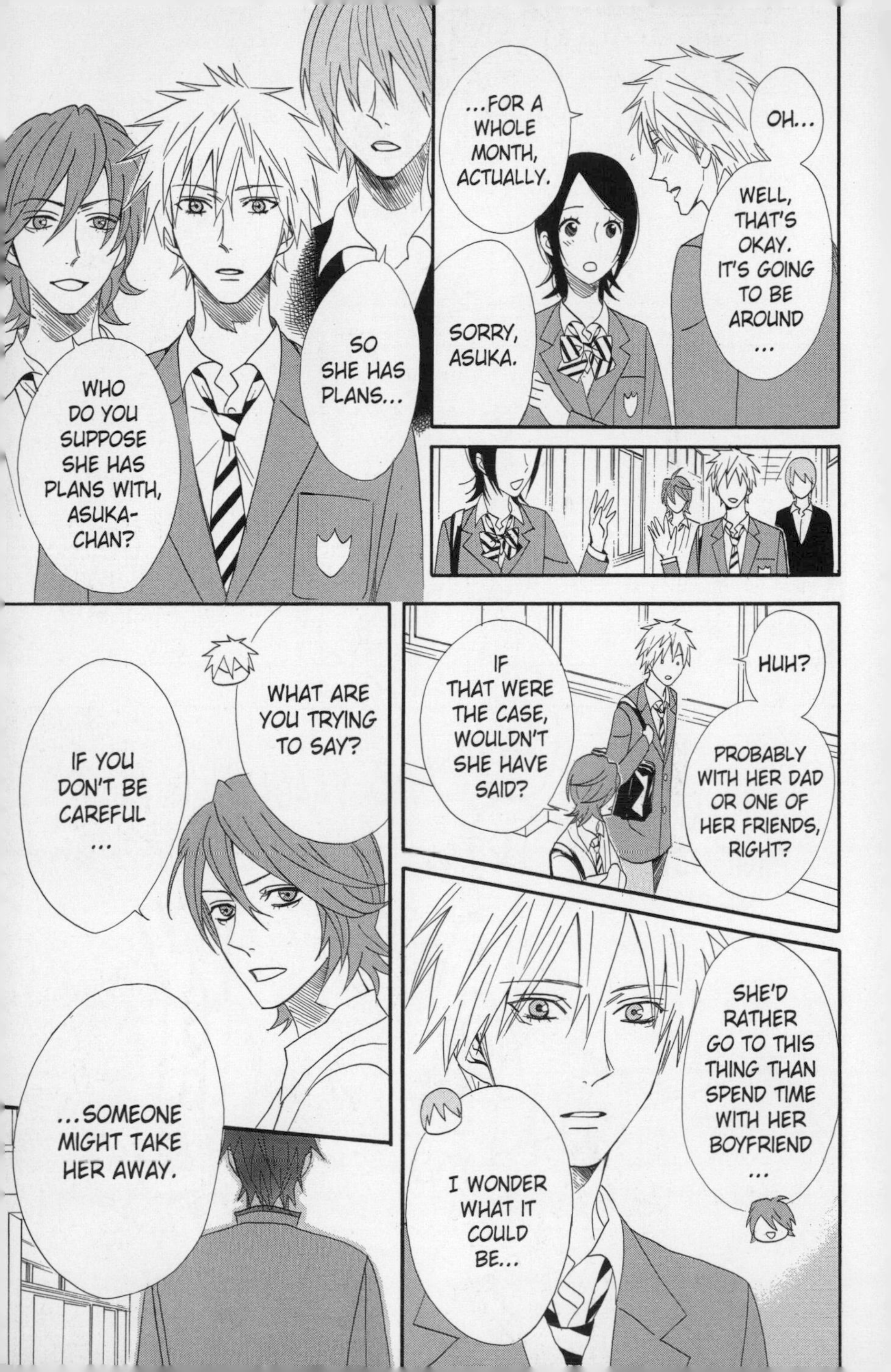
OH...
WELL, THAT'S OKAY. IT'S GOING TO BE AROUND ...
...FOR A WHOLE MONTH, ACTUALLY.
SORRY, ASUKA.
SO SHE HAS PLANS...
WHO DO YOU SUPPOSE SHE HAS PLANS WITH, ASUKA-CHAN?
HUH?
PROBABLY WITH HER DAD OR ONE OF HER FRIENDS, RIGHT?
IF THAT WERE THE CASE, WOULDN'T SHE HAVE SAID?
SHE'D RATHER GO TO THIS THING THAN SPEND TIME WITH HER BOYFRIEND ...
I WONDER WHAT IT COULD BE...
WHAT ARE YOU TRYING TO SAY?
IF YOU DON'T BE CAREFUL ...
...SOMEONE MIGHT TAKE HER AWAY.

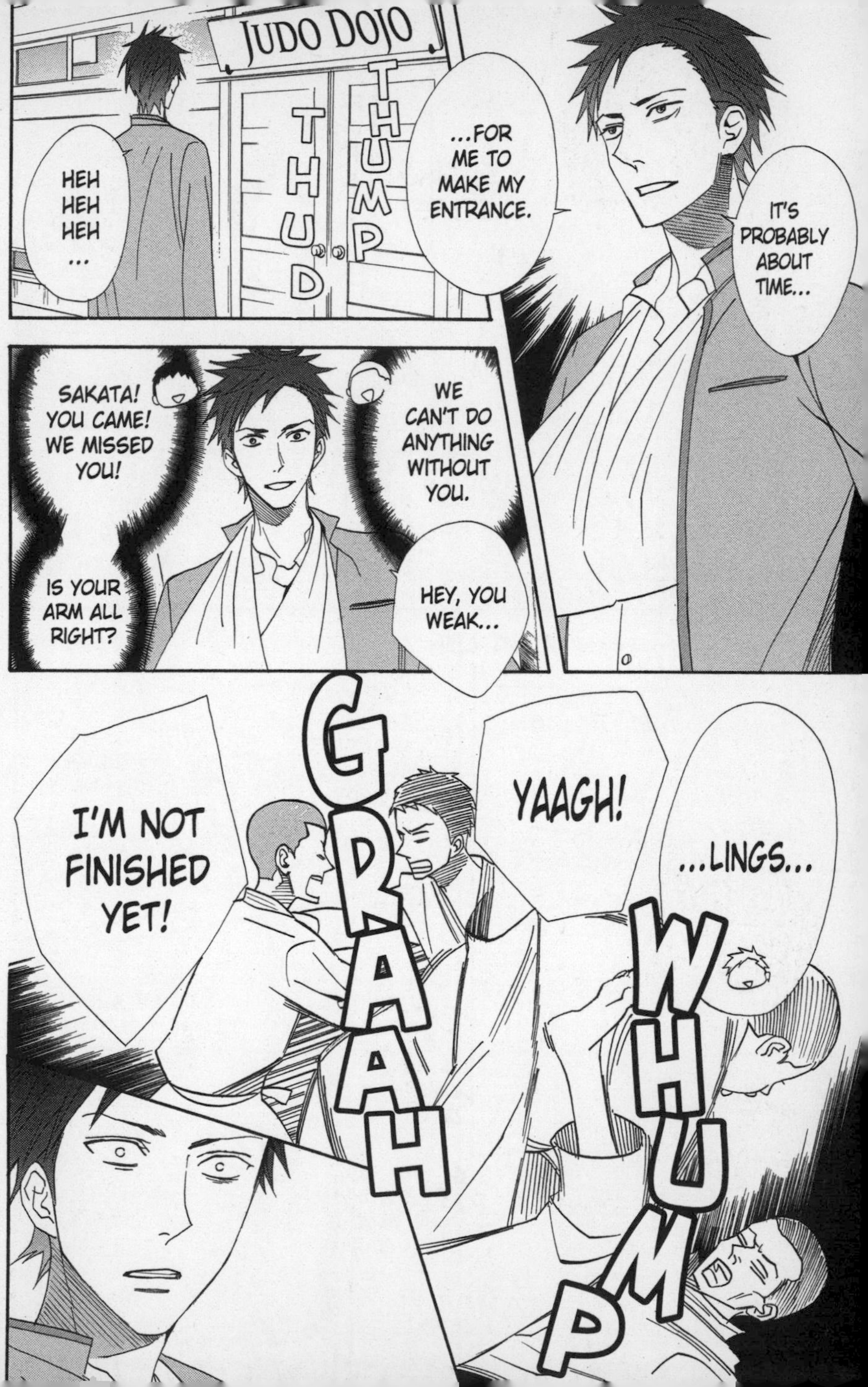
IT'S PROBABLY ABOUT TIME...
...FOR ME TO MAKE MY ENTRANCE.
JUDO DOJO
THUMP
THUD
HEH HEH HEH ...
WE CAN'T DO ANYTHING WITHOUT YOU.
SAKATA! YOU CAME! WE MISSED YOU!
HEY, YOU WEAK...
IS YOUR ARM ALL RIGHT?
...LINGS...
YAAGH!
WHUMP
GRAAH
I'M NOT FINISHED YET!

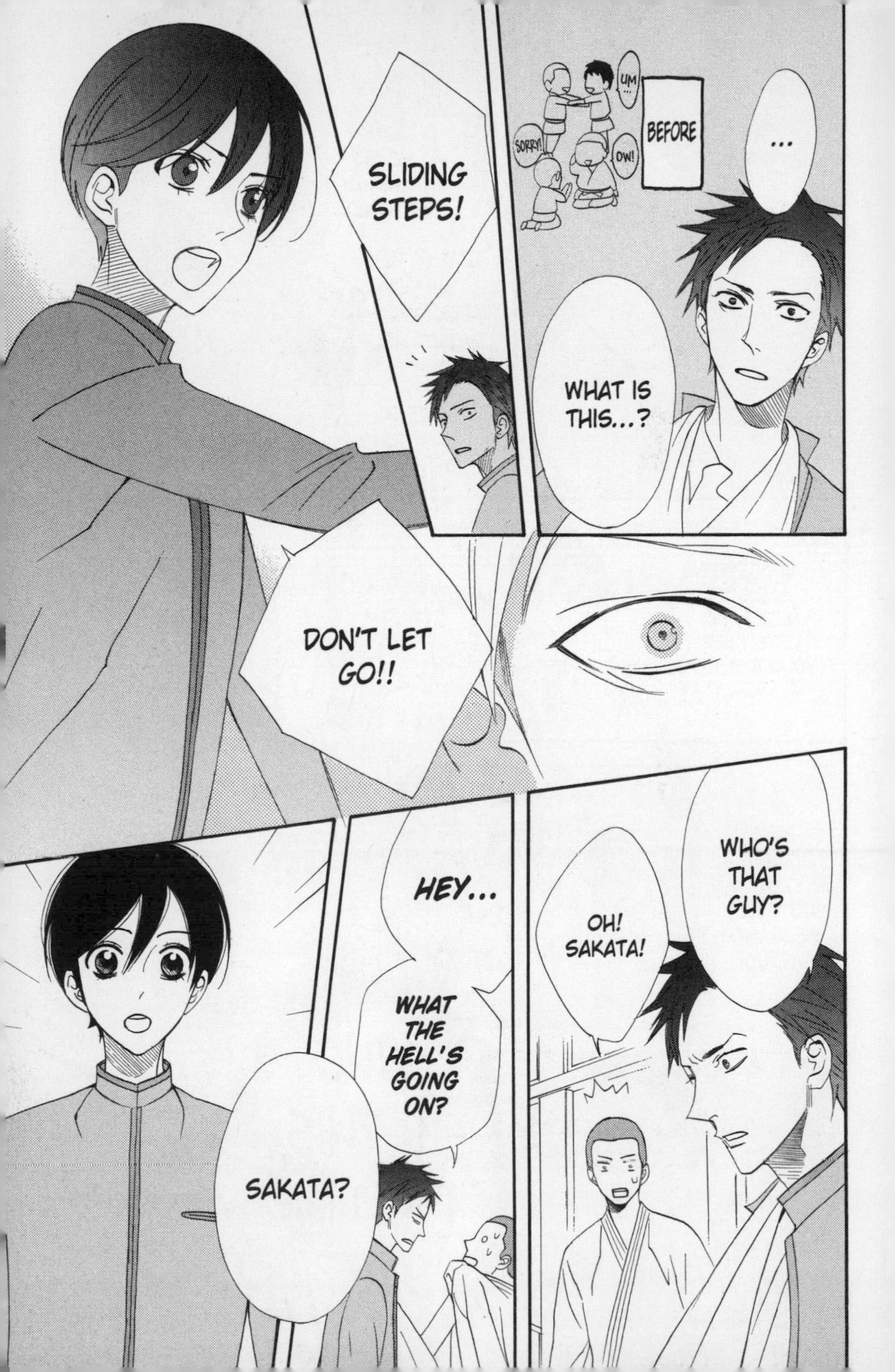
...
BEFORE
UM...
OW!
SORRY!
WHAT IS THIS...?
SLIDING STEPS!
DON'T LET GO!!
WHO'S THAT GUY?
OH! SAKATA!
HEY...
WHAT THE HELL'S GOING ON?
SAKATA?

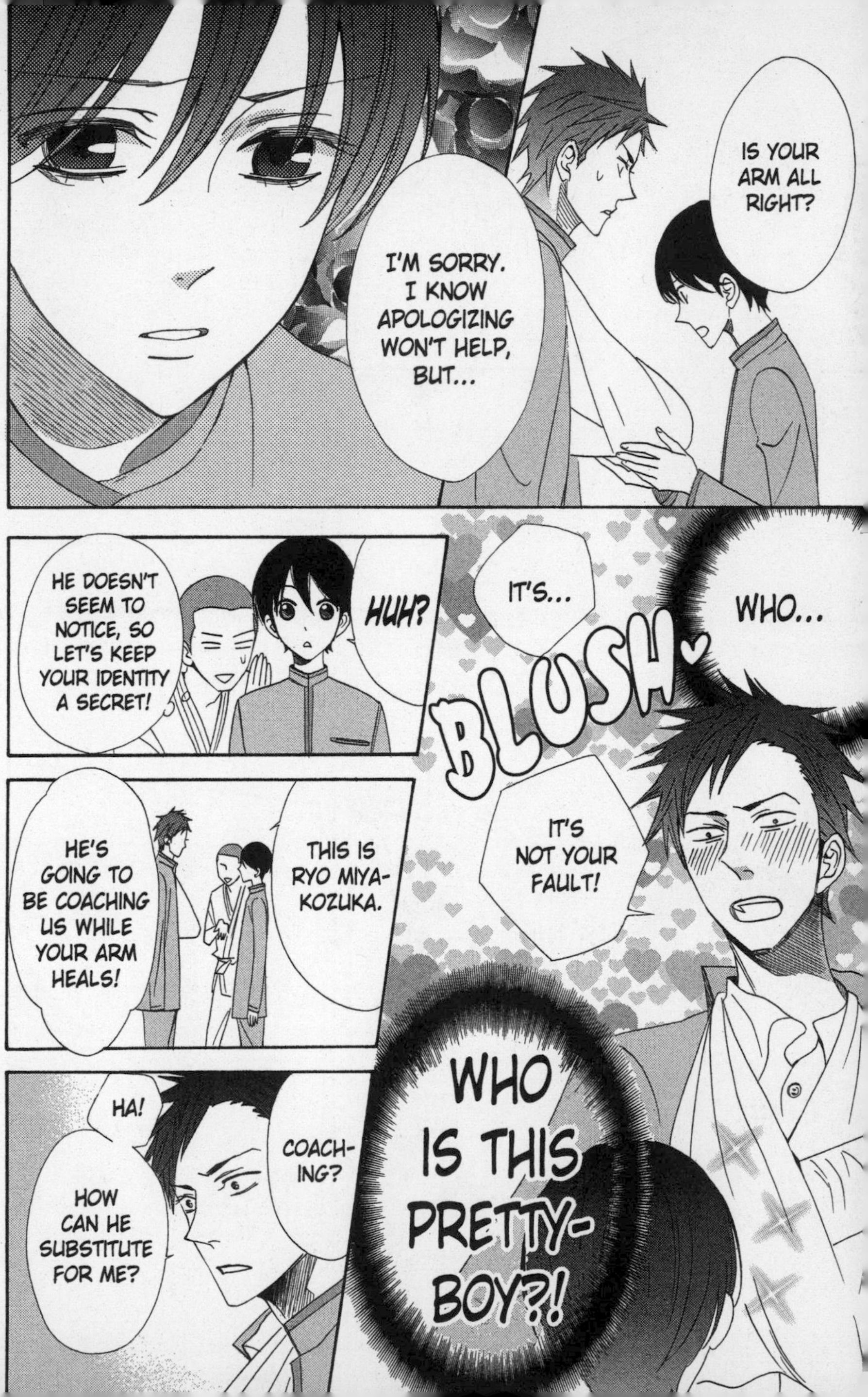
IS YOUR ARM ALL RIGHT?
I'M SORRY. I KNOW APOLOGIZING WON'T HELP, BUT...
WHO...
IT'S...
BLUSH
IT'S NOT YOUR FAULT!
WHO IS THIS PRETTY-BOY?!
HUH?
HE DOESN'T SEEM TO NOTICE, SO LET'S KEEP YOUR IDENTITY A SECRET!
THIS IS RYO MIYA-KOZUKA.
HE'S GOING TO BE COACHING US WHILE YOUR ARM HEALS!
COACH-ING?
HA!
HOW CAN HE SUBSTITUTE FOR ME?

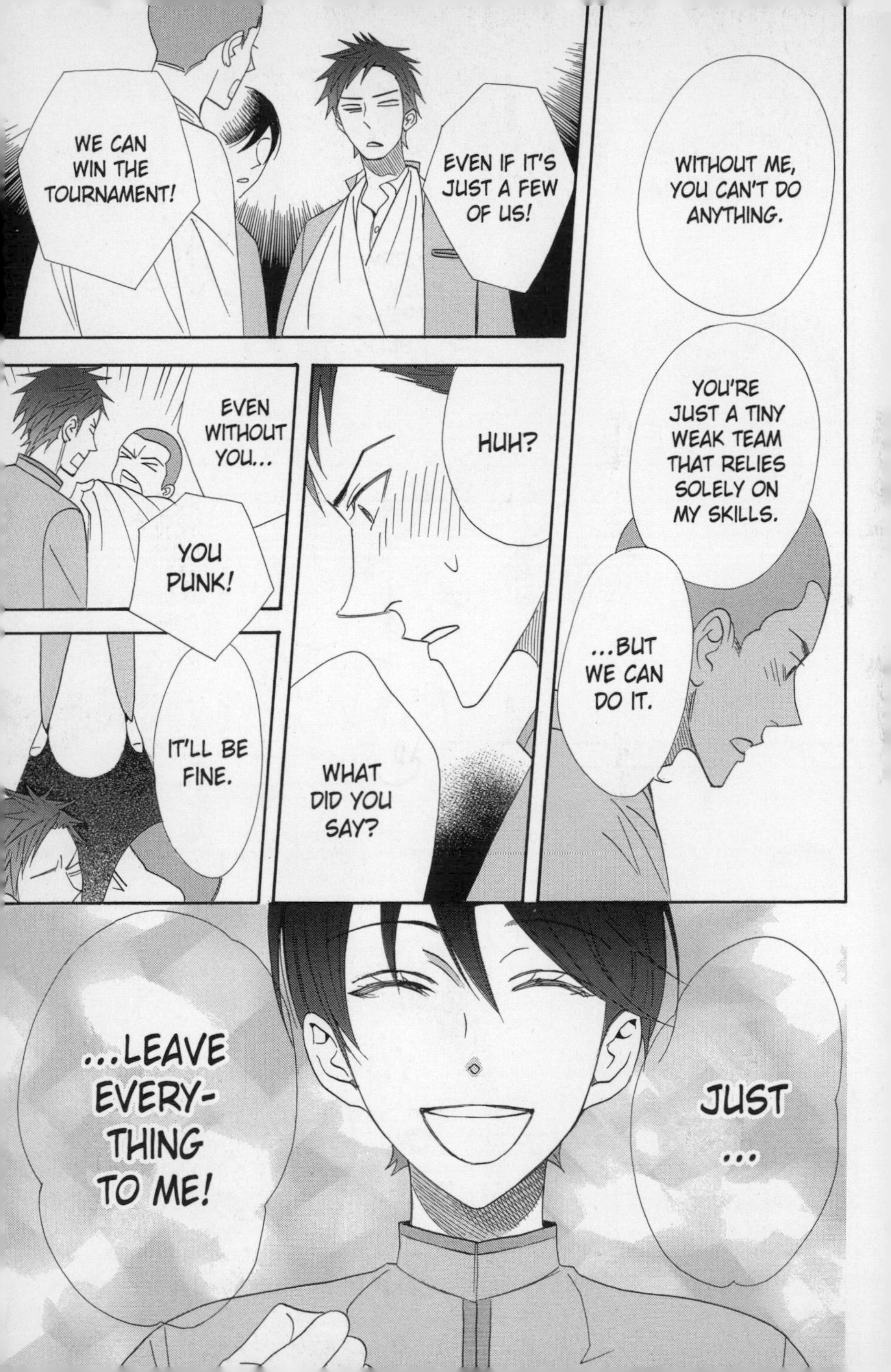
WITHOUT ME, YOU CAN'T DO ANYTHING.
YOU'RE JUST A TINY WEAK TEAM THAT RELIES SOLELY ON MY SKILLS.
...BUT WE CAN DO IT.
EVEN IF IT'S JUST A FEW OF US!
WE CAN WIN THE TOURNAMENT!
HUH?
WHAT DID YOU SAY?
EVEN WITHOUT YOU...
YOU PUNK!
IT'LL BE FINE.
JUST ...
...LEAVE EVERY-THING TO ME!

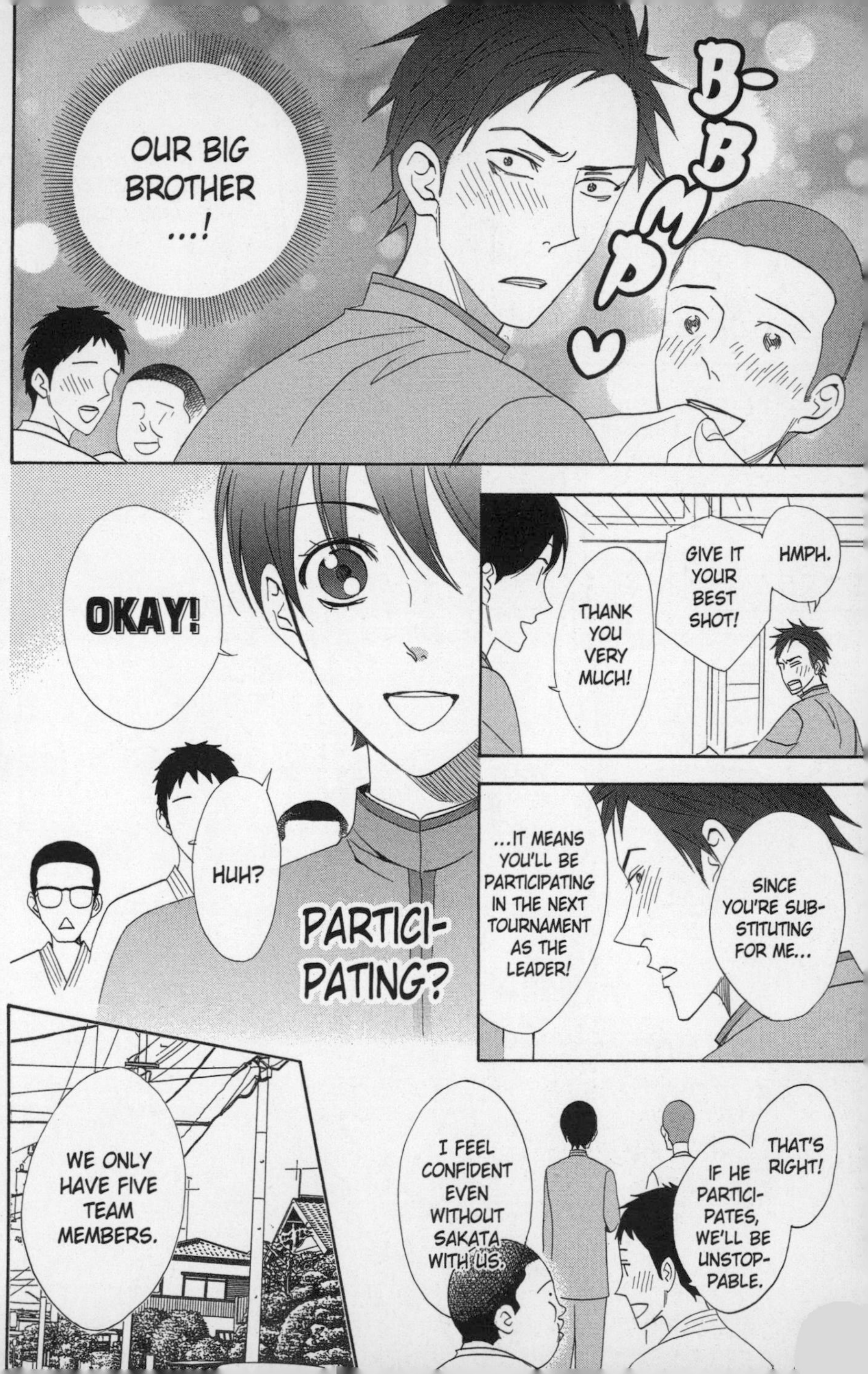
B-BMP ♥
OUR BIG BROTHER ...!
HMPH.
GIVE IT YOUR BEST SHOT!
THANK YOU VERY MUCH!
SINCE YOU'RE SUB-STITUTING FOR ME...
...IT MEANS YOU'LL BE PARTICIPATING IN THE NEXT TOURNAMENT AS THE LEADER!
OKAY!
HUH?
PARTICI-PATING?
THAT'S RIGHT!
IF HE PARTICI-PATES, WE'LL BE UNSTOP-PABLE.
I FEEL CONFIDENT EVEN WITHOUT SAKATA WITH US.
WE ONLY HAVE FIVE TEAM MEMBERS.

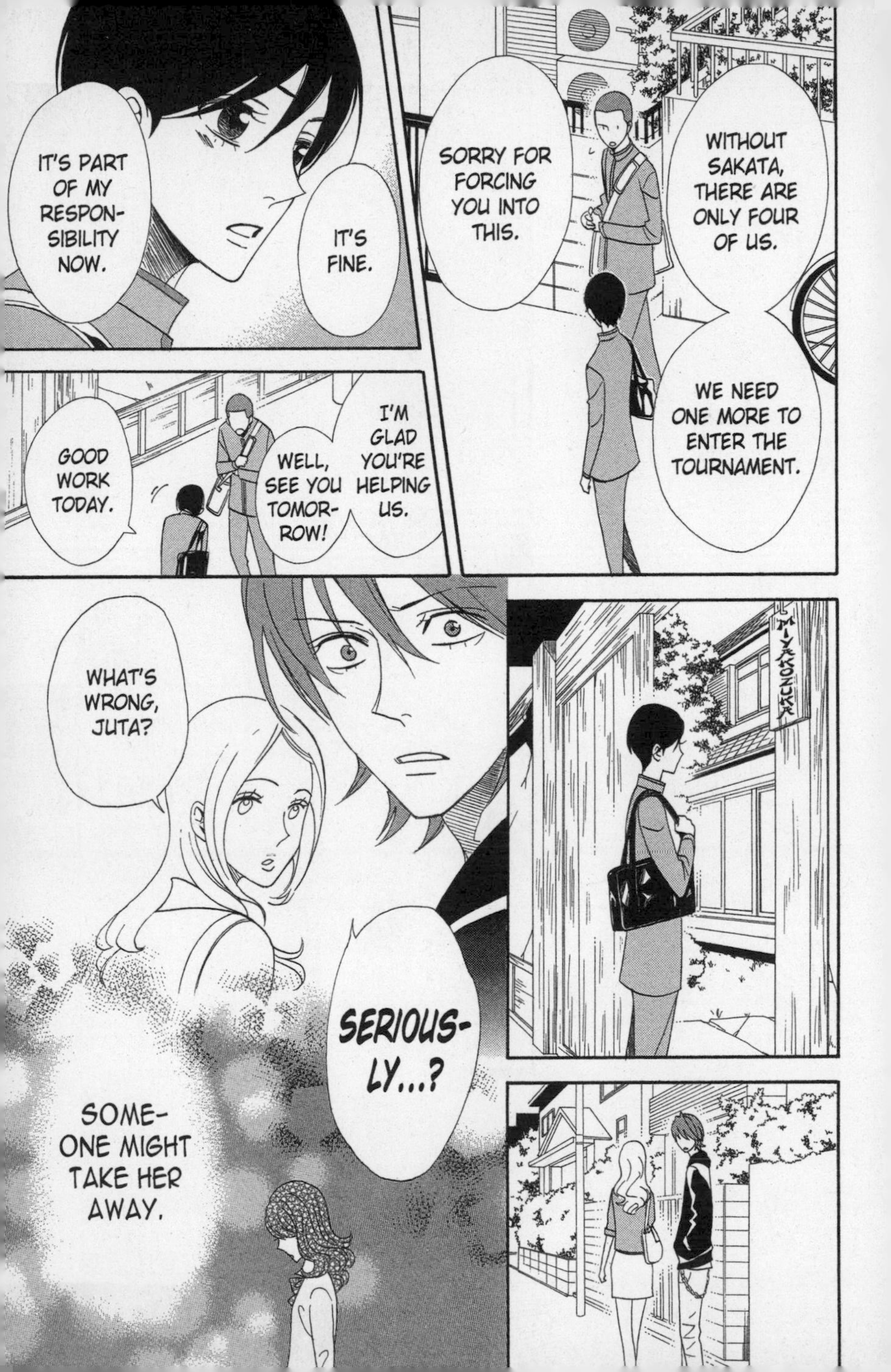
WITHOUT SAKATA, THERE ARE ONLY FOUR OF US.
WE NEED ONE MORE TO ENTER THE TOURNAMENT.
SORRY FOR FORCING YOU INTO THIS.
IT'S FINE.
IT'S PART OF MY RESPON-SIBILITY NOW.
I'M GLAD YOU'RE HELPING US.
WELL, SEE YOU TOMOR-ROW!
GOOD WORK TODAY.
MIYAKOZUKA
SERIOUS-LY...?
WHAT'S WRONG, JUTA?
SOME-ONE MIGHT TAKE HER AWAY.

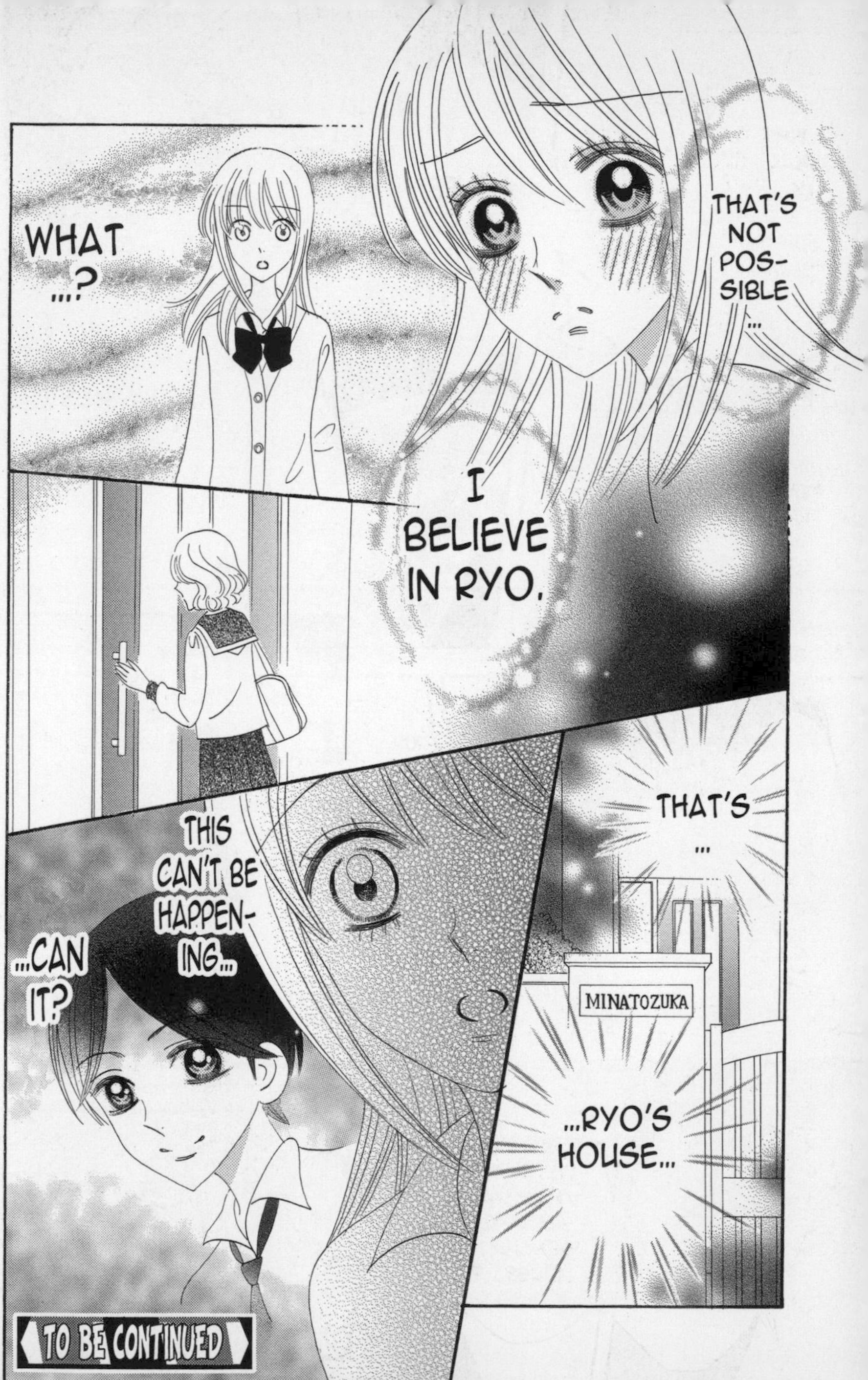
THAT'S NOT POS-SIBLE ...
I BELIEVE IN RYO.
WHAT ....?
THAT'S ...
...RYO'S HOUSE...
MINATOZUKA
THIS CAN'T BE HAPPEN-ING...
...CAN IT?
TO BE CONTINUED

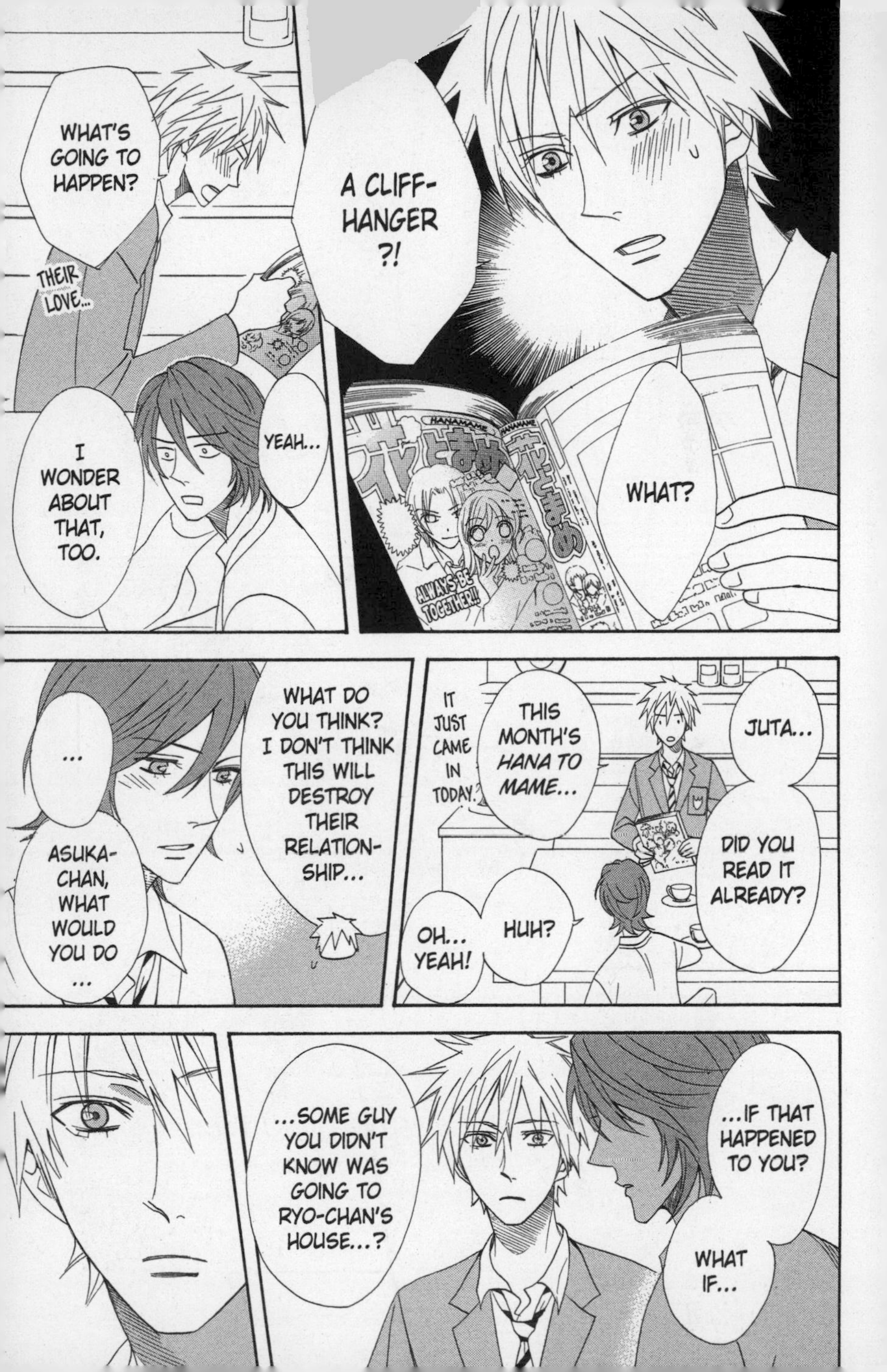
A CLIFF-HANGER ?!
WHAT?
HANAMAME
HANAMAME
ALWAYS BE TOGETHER!!
WHAT'S GOING TO HAPPEN?
THEIR LOVE...
YEAH...
I WONDER ABOUT THAT, TOO.
JUTA...
DID YOU READ IT ALREADY?
THIS MONTH'S *HANA TO MAME*...
IT JUST CAME IN TODAY.
HUH?
OH... YEAH!
WHAT DO YOU THINK? I DON'T THINK THIS WILL DESTROY THEIR RELATION-SHIP...
...
ASUKA-CHAN, WHAT WOULD YOU DO ...
...IF THAT HAPPENED TO YOU?
WHAT IF...
...SOME GUY YOU DIDN'T KNOW WAS GOING TO RYO-CHAN'S HOUSE...?

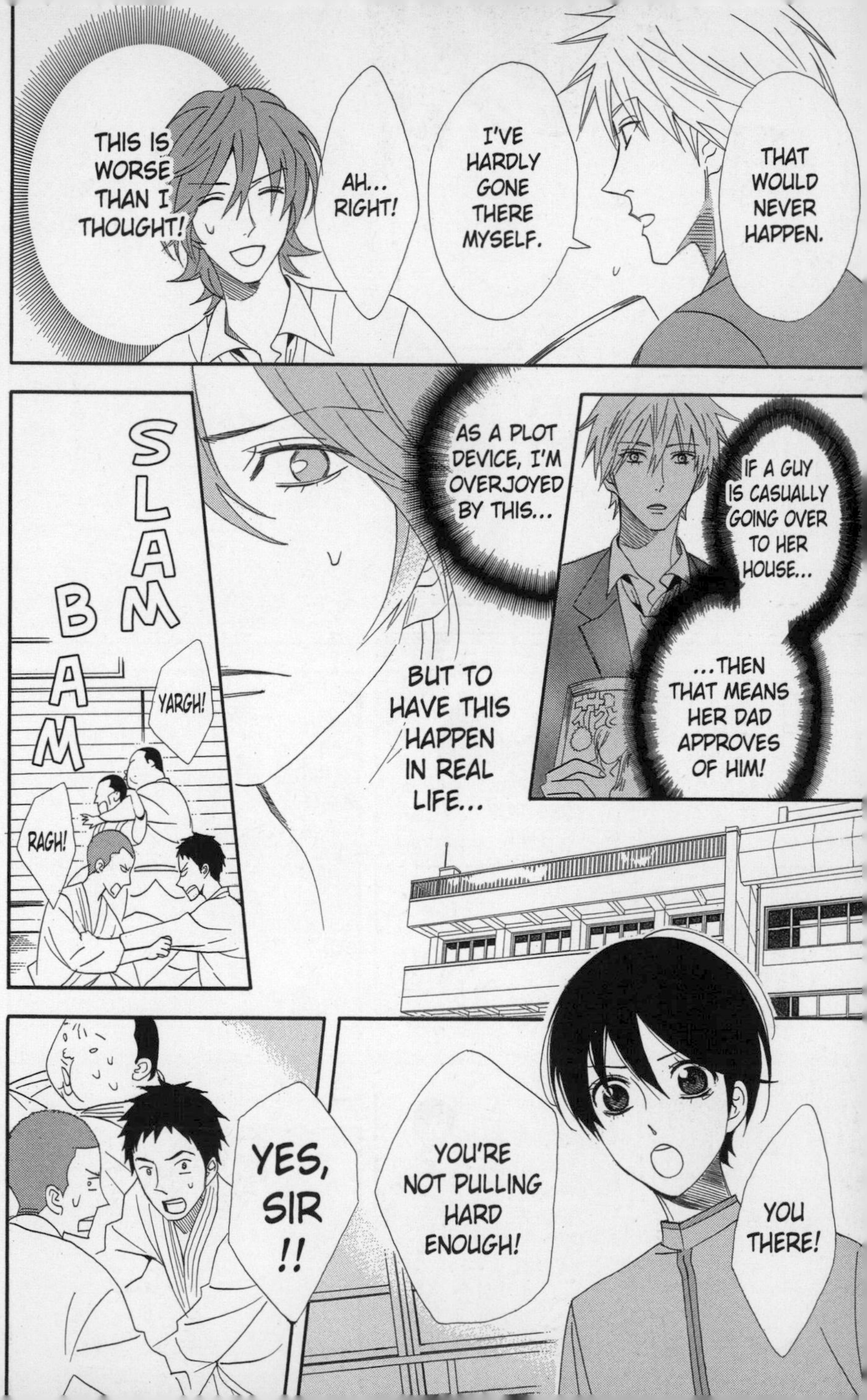
THAT WOULD NEVER HAPPEN.
I'VE HARDLY GONE THERE MYSELF.
AH... RIGHT!
THIS IS WORSE THAN I THOUGHT!
IF A GUY IS CASUALLY GOING OVER TO HER HOUSE...
...THEN THAT MEANS HER DAD APPROVES OF HIM!
AS A PLOT DEVICE, I'M OVERJOYED BY THIS...
BUT TO HAVE THIS HAPPEN IN REAL LIFE...
SLAM
BAM
YARGH!
RAGH!
YOU THERE!
YOU'RE NOT PULLING HARD ENOUGH!
YES, SIR!!

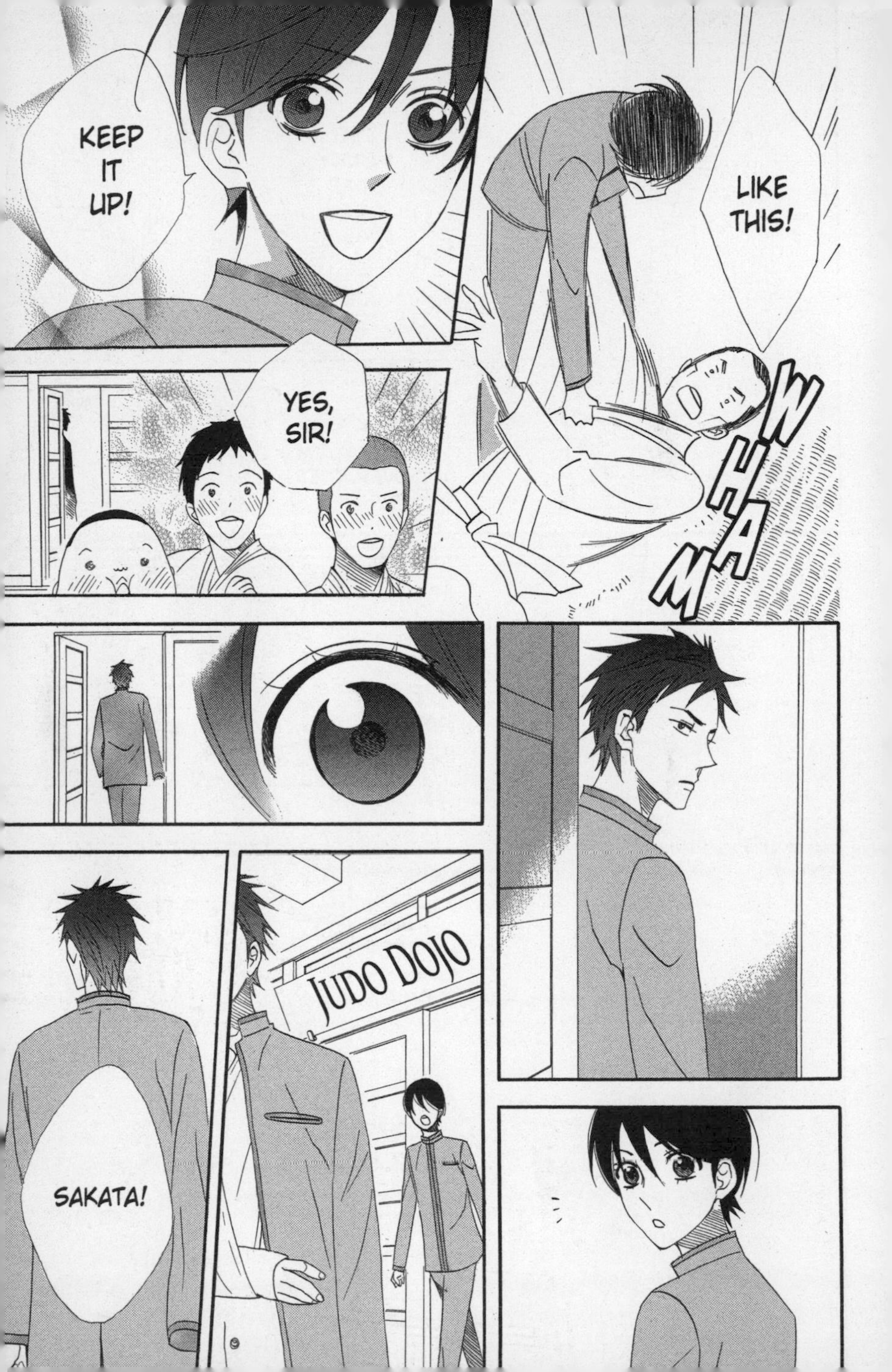
LIKE THIS!
WHAM
KEEP IT UP!
YES, SIR!
JUDO DOJO
SAKATA!

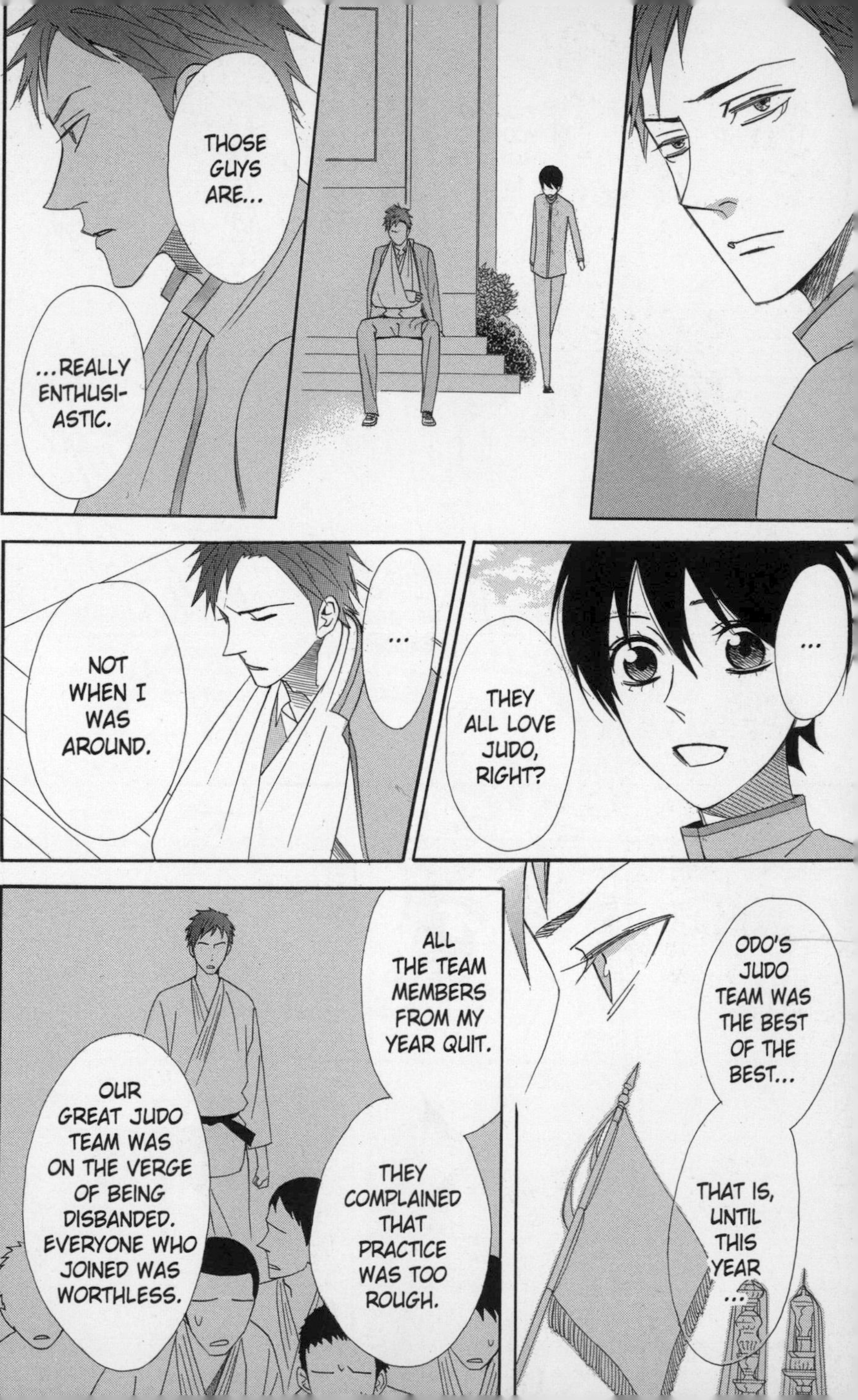
THOSE GUYS ARE...
...REALLY ENTHUSI-ASTIC.
...
THEY ALL LOVE JUDO, RIGHT?
...
NOT WHEN I WAS AROUND.
ODO'S JUDO TEAM WAS THE BEST OF THE BEST...
THAT IS, UNTIL THIS YEAR ...
ALL THE TEAM MEMBERS FROM MY YEAR QUIT.
THEY COMPLAINED THAT PRACTICE WAS TOO ROUGH.
OUR GREAT JUDO TEAM WAS ON THE VERGE OF BEING DISBANDED. EVERYONE WHO JOINED WAS WORTHLESS.

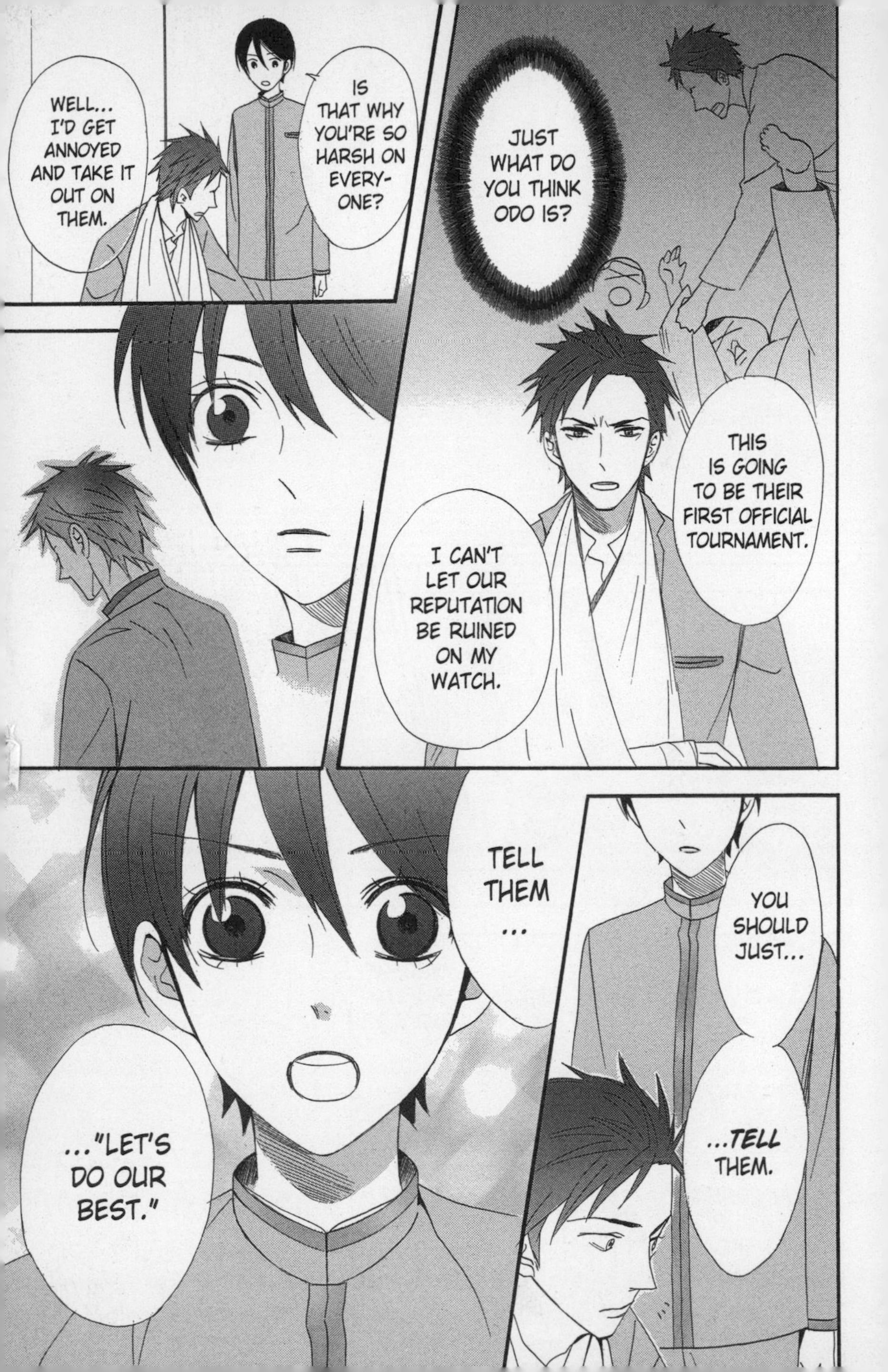
JUST WHAT DO YOU THINK ODO IS?
THIS IS GOING TO BE THEIR FIRST OFFICIAL TOURNAMENT.
I CAN'T LET OUR REPUTATION BE RUINED ON MY WATCH.
IS THAT WHY YOU'RE SO HARSH ON EVERY-ONE?
WELL... I'D GET ANNOYED AND TAKE IT OUT ON THEM.
YOU SHOULD JUST...
...*TELL* THEM.
TELL THEM ...
..."LET'S DO OUR BEST."

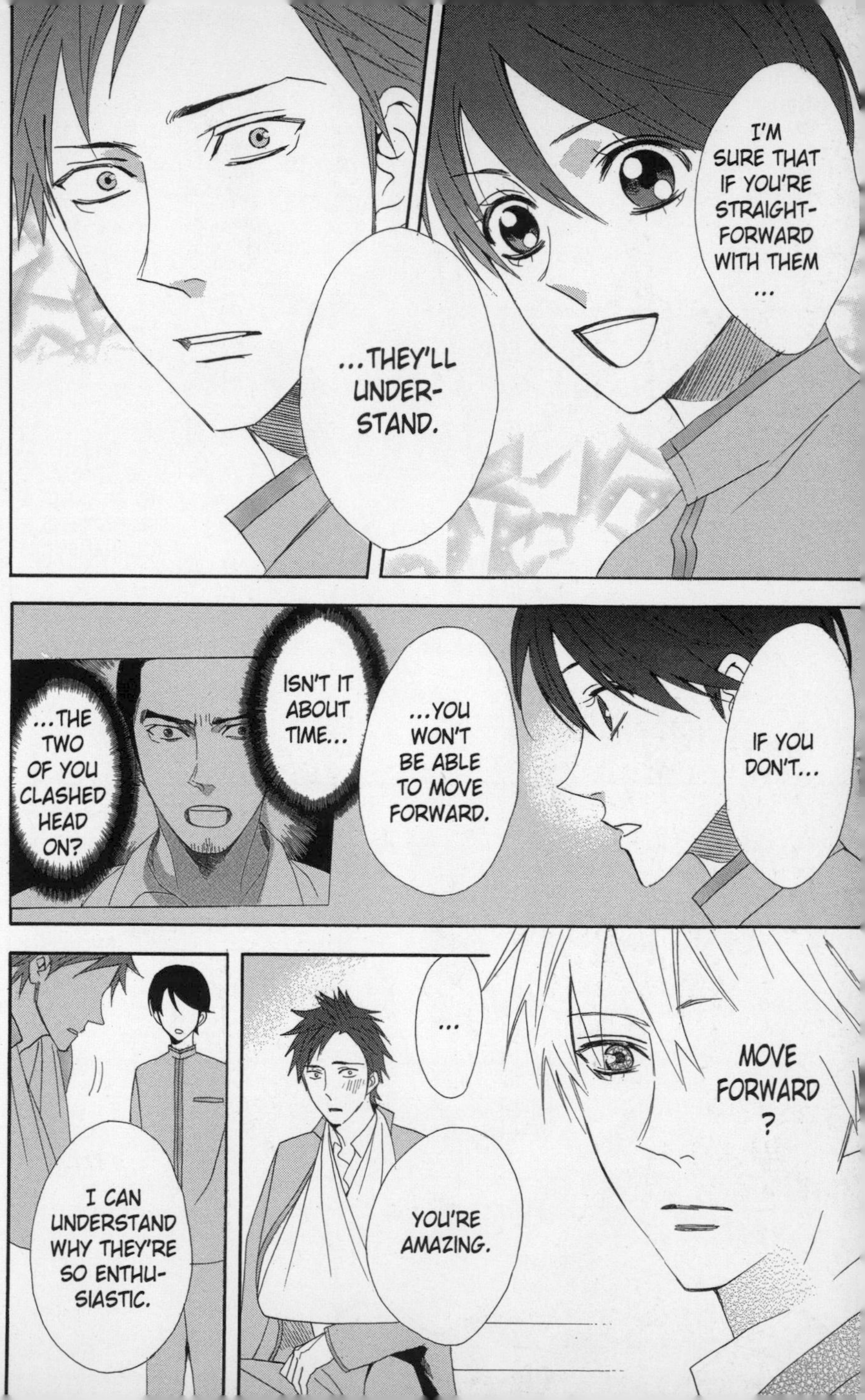
I'M SURE THAT IF YOU'RE STRAIGHT-FORWARD WITH THEM ...
...THEY'LL UNDER-STAND.
IF YOU DON'T...
...YOU WON'T BE ABLE TO MOVE FORWARD.
ISN'T IT ABOUT TIME...
...THE TWO OF YOU CLASHED HEAD ON?
MOVE FORWARD ?
...
YOU'RE AMAZING.
I CAN UNDERSTAND WHY THEY'RE SO ENTHU-SIASTIC.

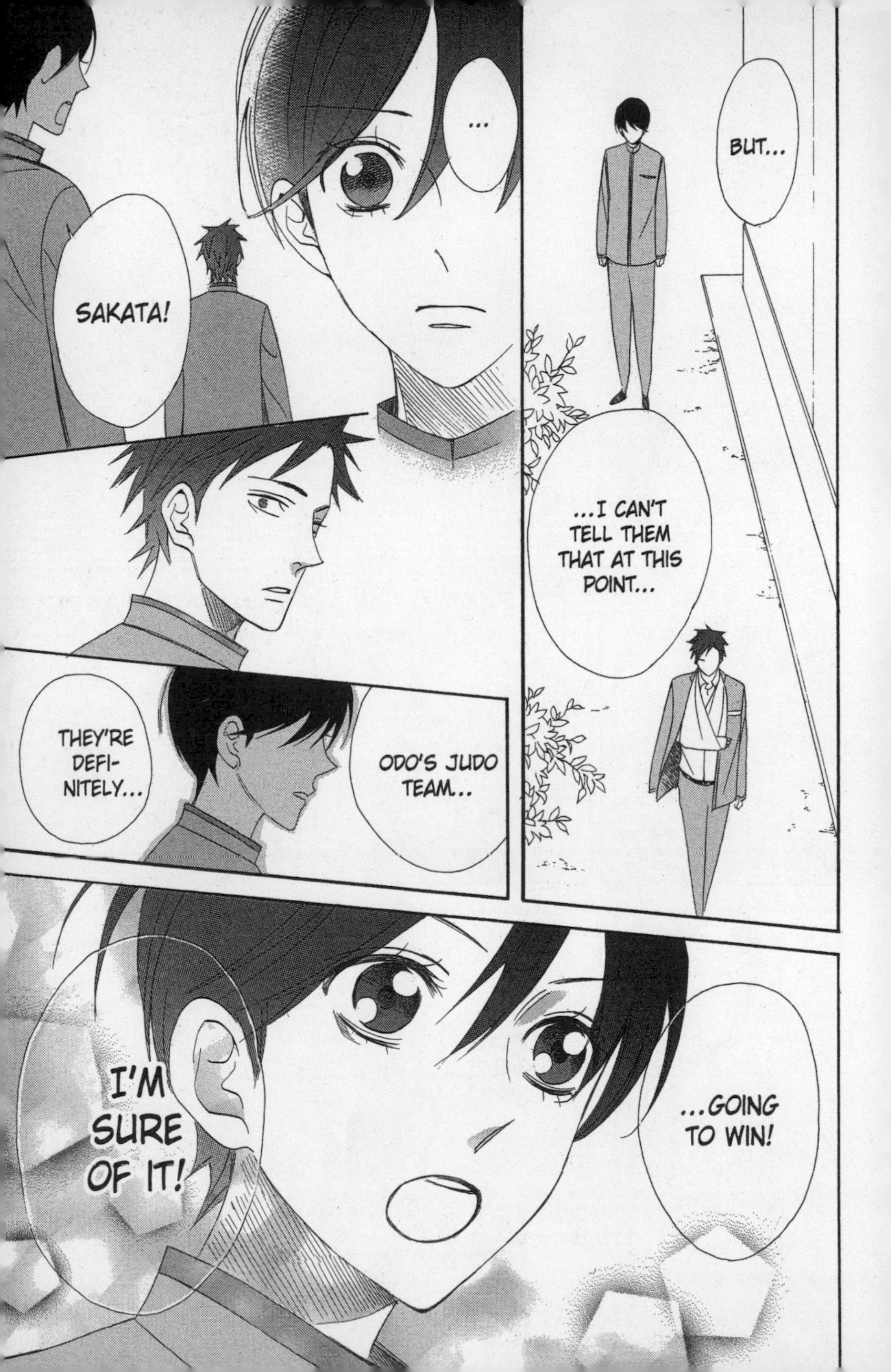

BUT...
...I CAN'T TELL THEM THAT AT THIS POINT...
...
SAKATA!
ODO'S JUDO TEAM...
THEY'RE DEFI-NITELY...
...GOING TO WIN!
I'M SURE OF IT!

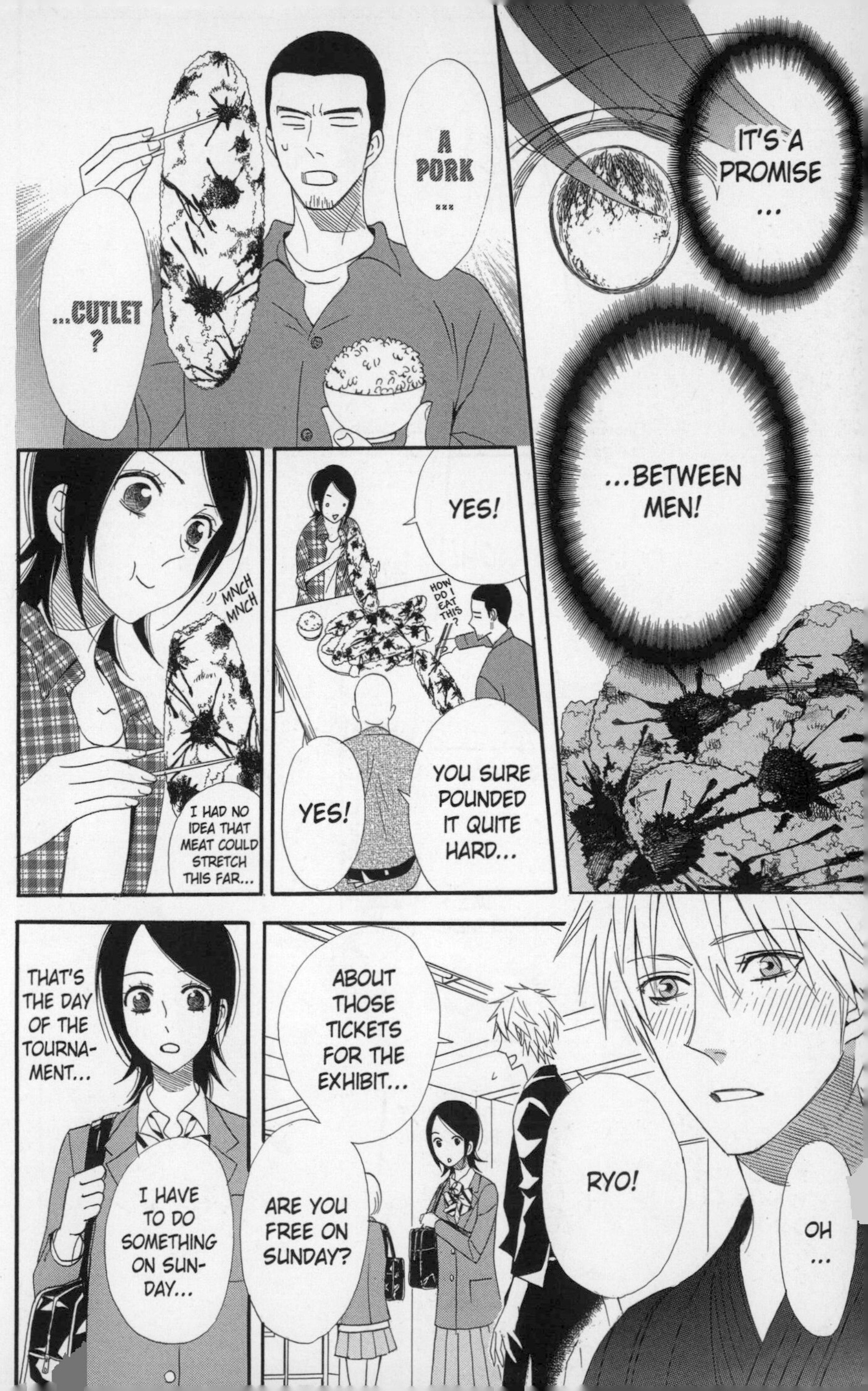

IT'S A PROMISE ...
...BETWEEN MEN!
A PORK ...
...CUTLET ?
YES!
HOW DO I EAT THIS?
YOU SURE POUNDED IT QUITE HARD...
YES!
MNCH MNCH
I HAD NO IDEA THAT MEAT COULD STRETCH THIS FAR...
OH ...
RYO!
ABOUT THOSE TICKETS FOR THE EXHIBIT...
ARE YOU FREE ON SUNDAY?
THAT'S THE DAY OF THE TOURNAMENT...
I HAVE TO DO SOMETHING ON SUNDAY...

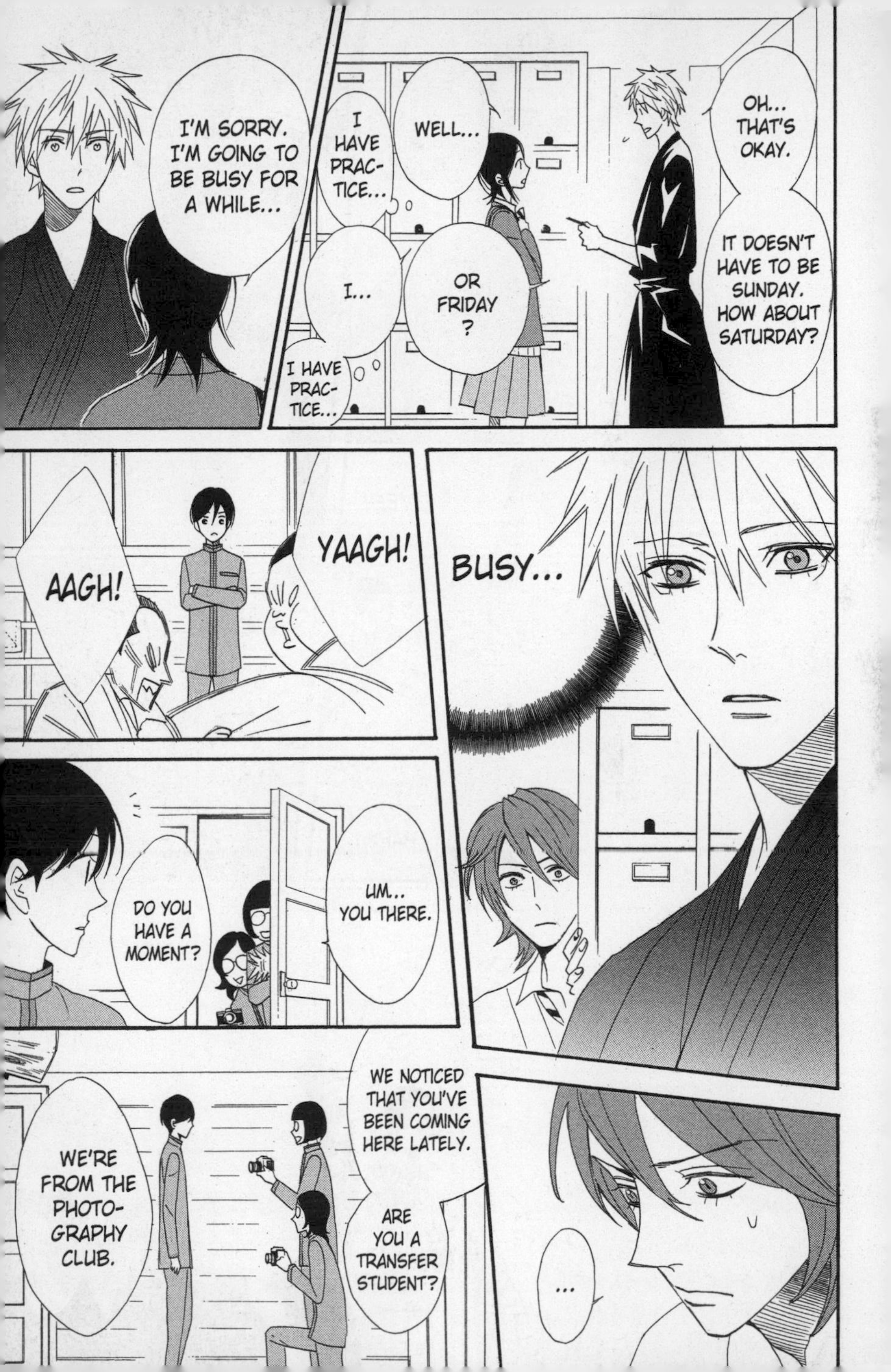
OH... THAT'S OKAY.
IT DOESN'T HAVE TO BE SUNDAY. HOW ABOUT SATURDAY?
WELL...
I HAVE PRAC-TICE...
OR FRIDAY ?
I...
I HAVE PRAC-TICE...
I'M SORRY. I'M GOING TO BE BUSY FOR A WHILE...
BUSY...
YAAGH!
AAGH!
UM.. YOU THERE.
DO YOU HAVE A MOMENT?
...
WE NOTICED THAT YOU'VE BEEN COMING HERE LATELY.
ARE YOU A TRANSFER STUDENT?
WE'RE FROM THE PHOTO-GRAPHY CLUB.

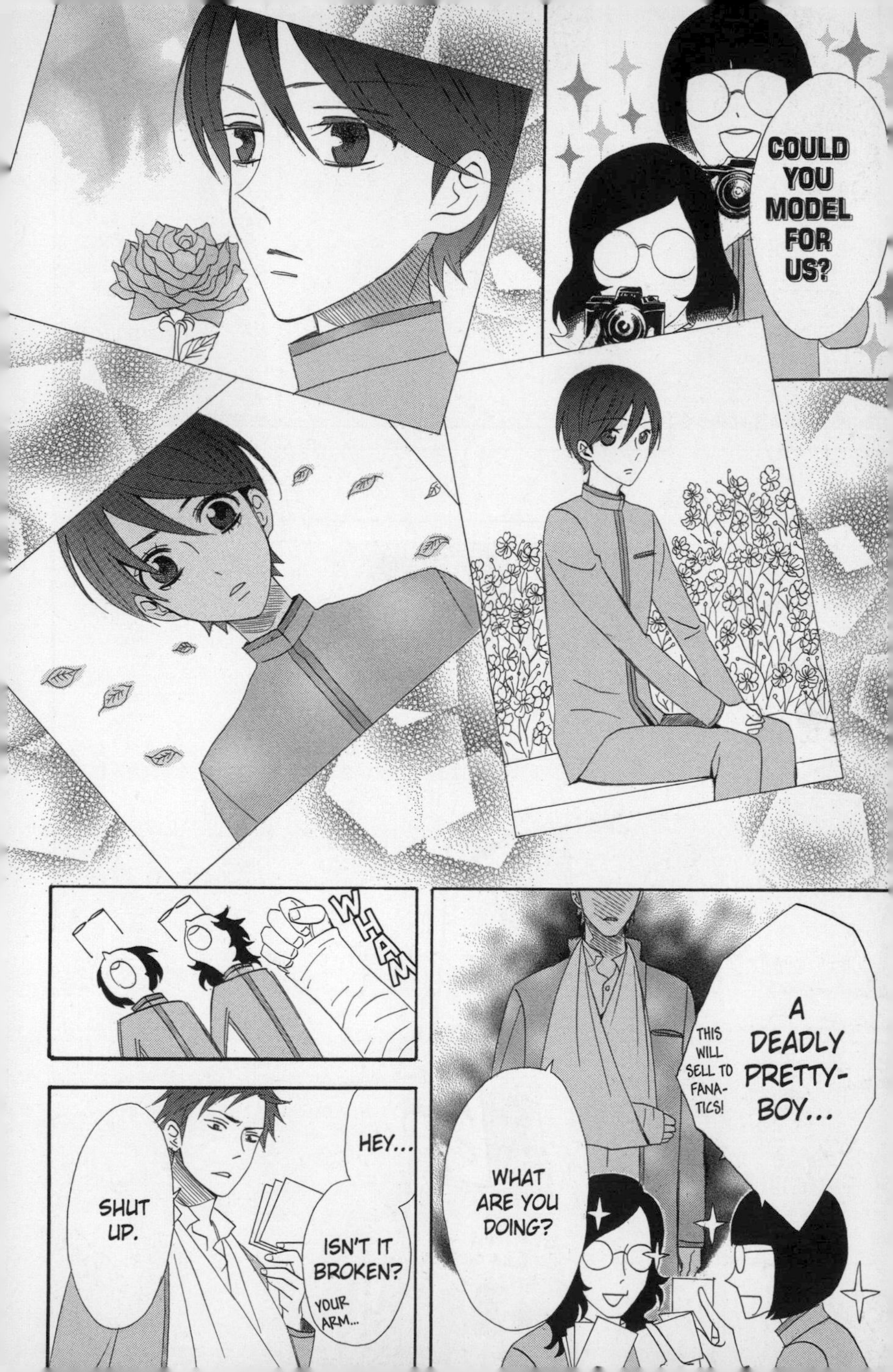
COULD YOU MODEL FOR US?
A DEADLY PRETTY-BOY...
THIS WILL SELL TO FANA-TICS!
WHAT ARE YOU DOING?
WHAM
HEY...
ISN'T IT BROKEN?
YOUR ARM...
SHUT UP.

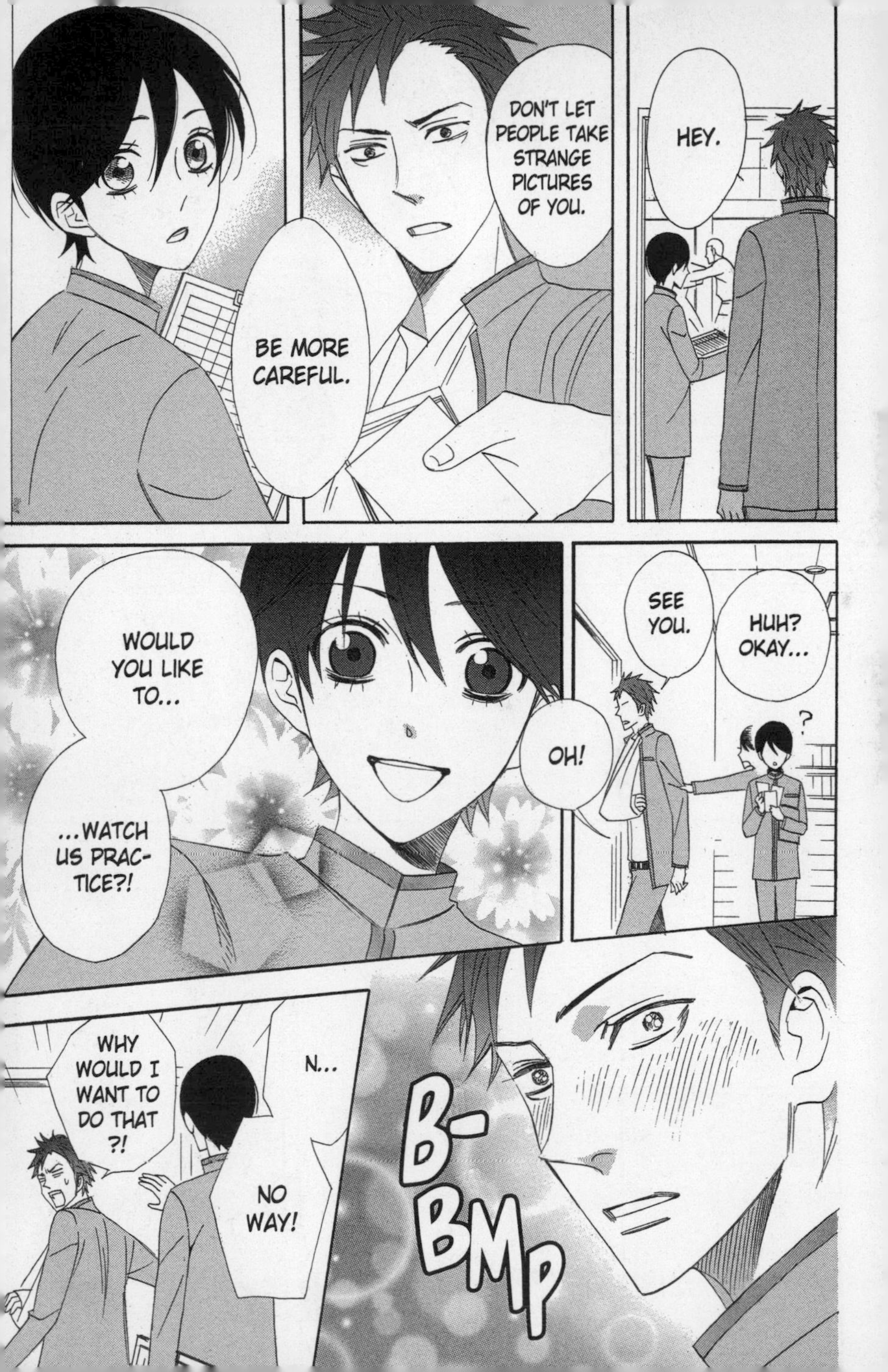
HEY.
DON'T LET PEOPLE TAKE STRANGE PICTURES OF YOU.
BE MORE CAREFUL.
SEE YOU.
HUH? OKAY...
?
OH!
WOULD YOU LIKE TO...
...WATCH US PRAC-TICE?!
B-BMP
N...
NO WAY!
WHY WOULD I WANT TO DO THAT ?!

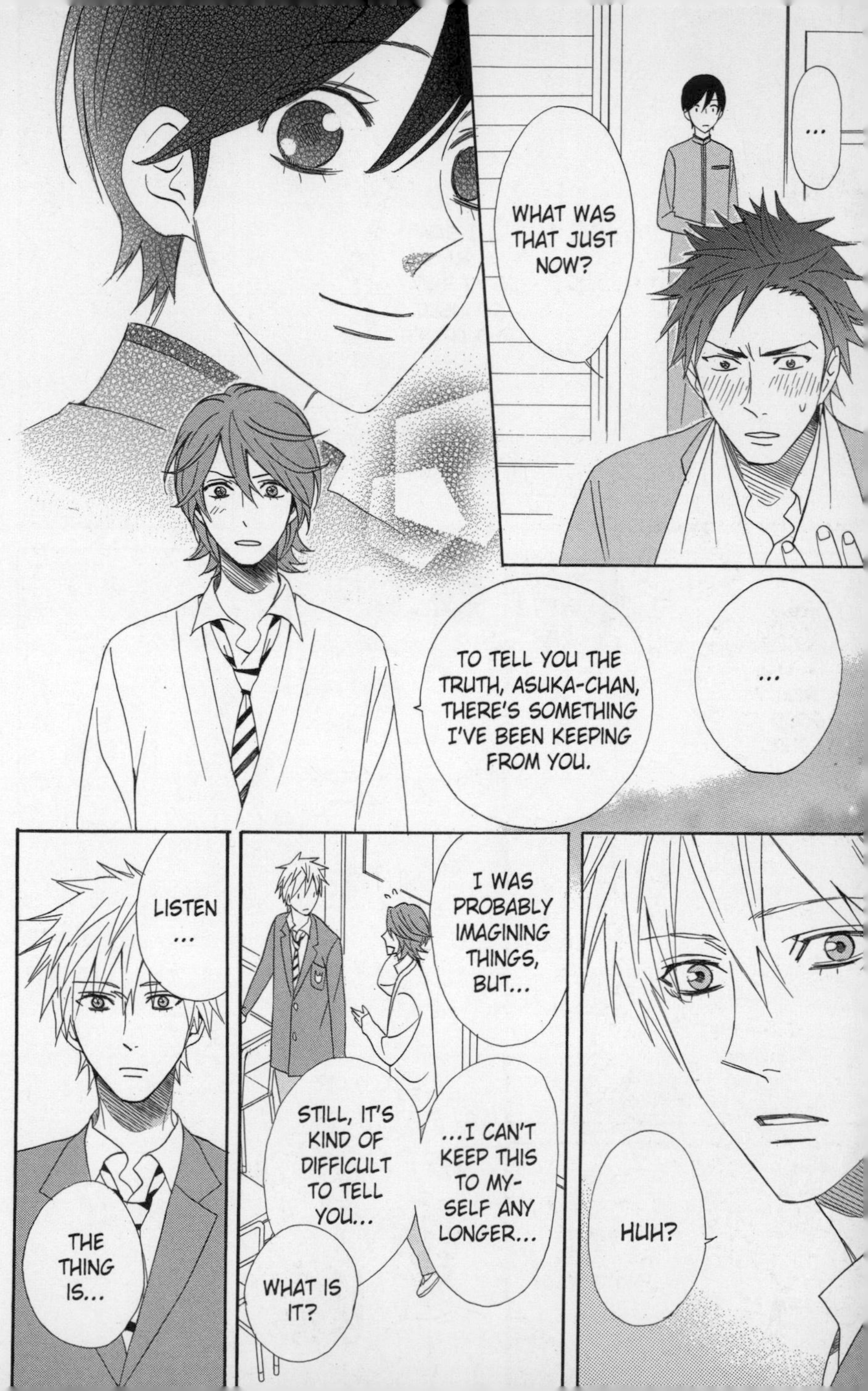
...
WHAT WAS THAT JUST NOW?
...
TO TELL YOU THE TRUTH, ASUKA-CHAN, THERE'S SOMETHING I'VE BEEN KEEPING FROM YOU.
HUH?
I WAS PROBABLY IMAGINING THINGS, BUT...
...I CAN'T KEEP THIS TO MY-SELF ANY LONGER...
STILL, IT'S KIND OF DIFFICULT TO TELL YOU...
WHAT IS IT?
LISTEN...
THE THING IS...

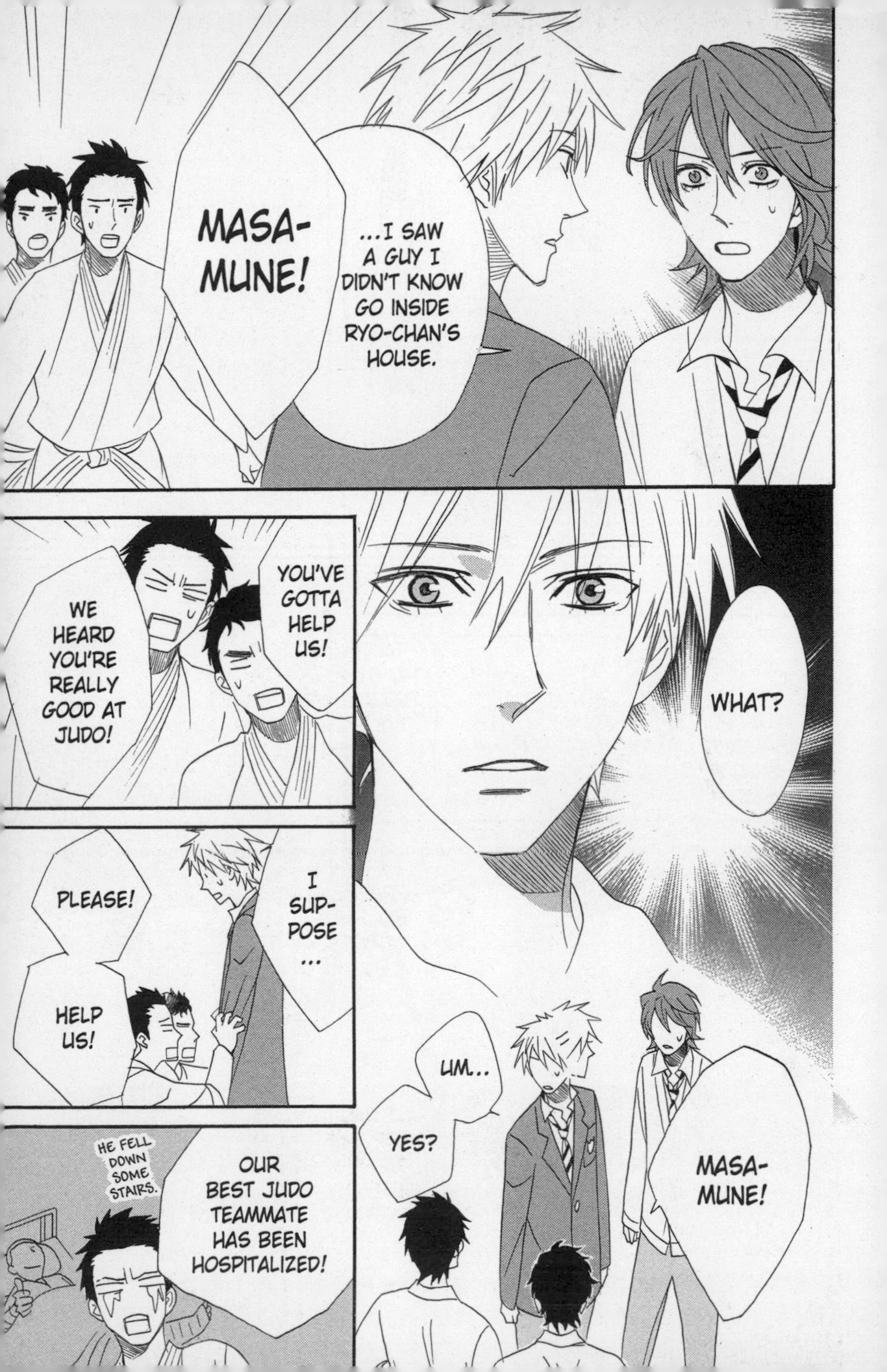
...I SAW A GUY I DIDN'T KNOW GO INSIDE RYO-CHAN'S HOUSE.
MASA-MUNE!
WHAT?
MASA-MUNE!
UM... YES?
YOU'VE GOTTA HELP US!
WE HEARD YOU'RE REALLY GOOD AT JUDO!
I SUP-POSE...
PLEASE!
HELP US!
OUR BEST JUDO TEAMMATE HAS BEEN HOSPITALIZED!
HE FELL DOWN SOME STAIRS.

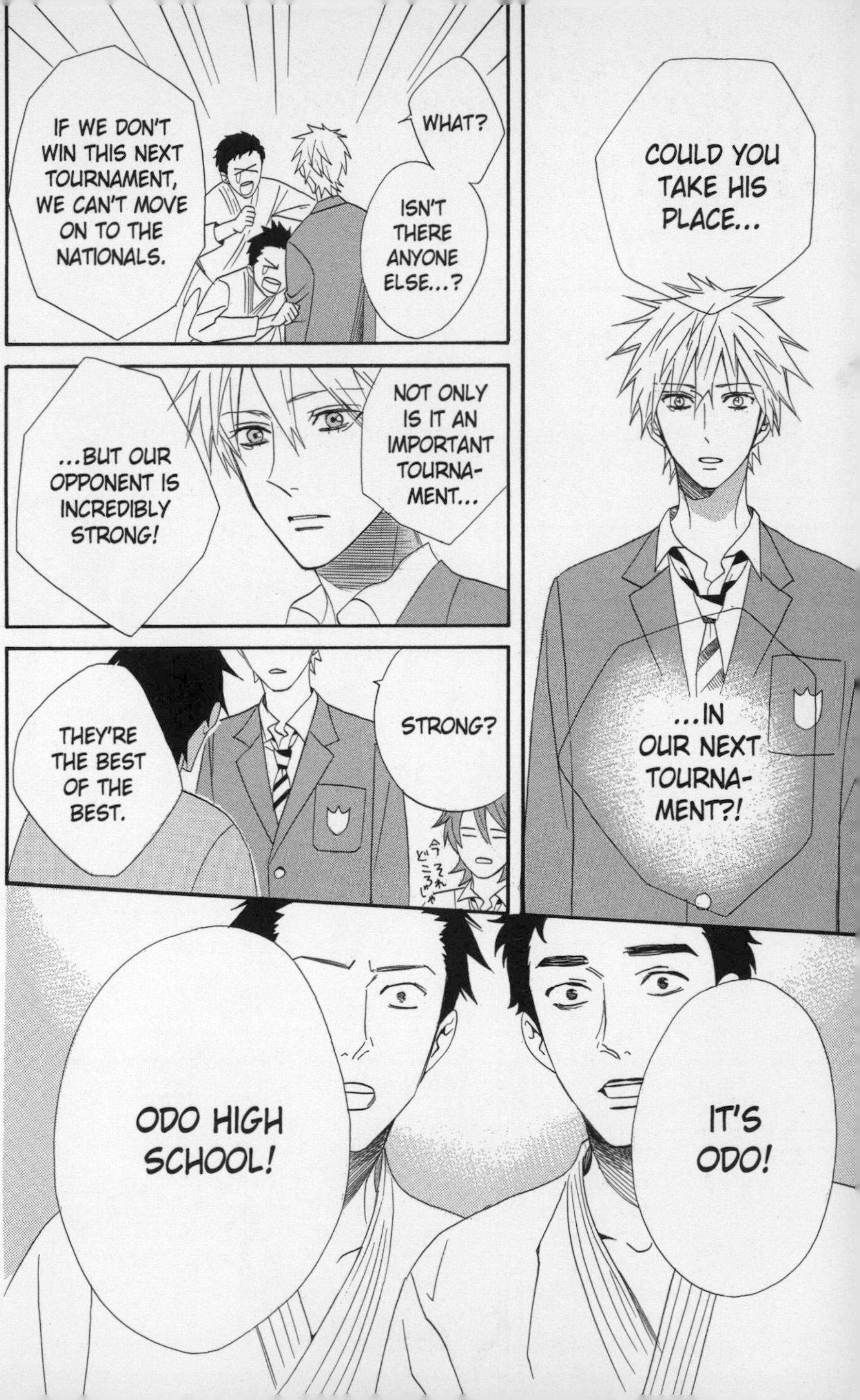
COULD YOU TAKE HIS PLACE...
...IN OUR NEXT TOURNAMENT?!
WHAT?
ISN'T THERE ANYONE ELSE...?
IF WE DON'T WIN THIS NEXT TOURNAMENT, WE CAN'T MOVE ON TO THE NATIONALS.
NOT ONLY IS IT AN IMPORTANT TOURNAMENT...
...BUT OUR OPPONENT IS INCREDIBLY STRONG!
STRONG?
今それどころじゃ
THEY'RE THE BEST OF THE BEST.
IT'S ODO!
ODO HIGH SCHOOL!

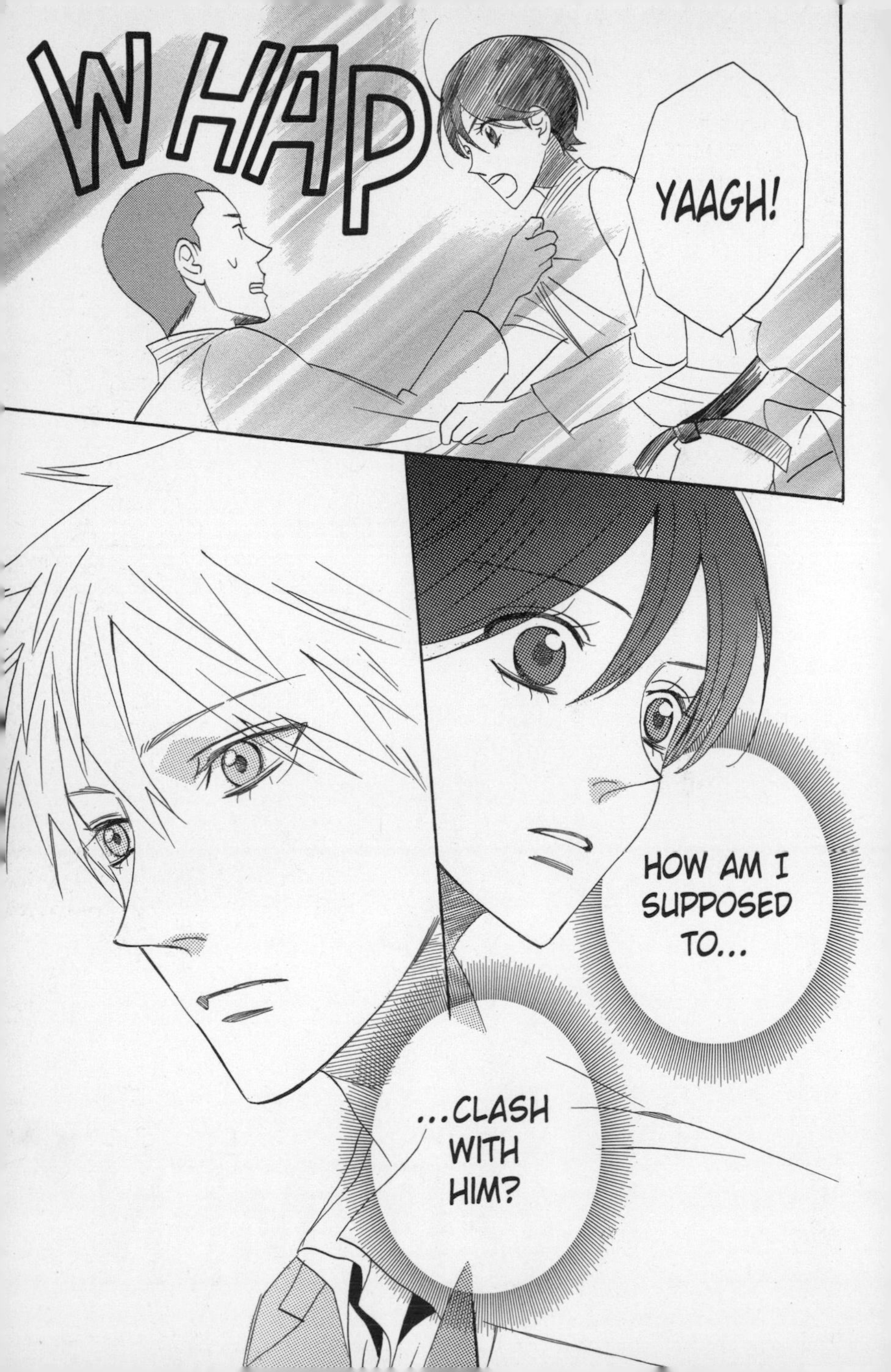
WHAP
YAAGH!
HOW AM I SUPPOSED TO...
...CLASH WITH HIM?

OTOMEN

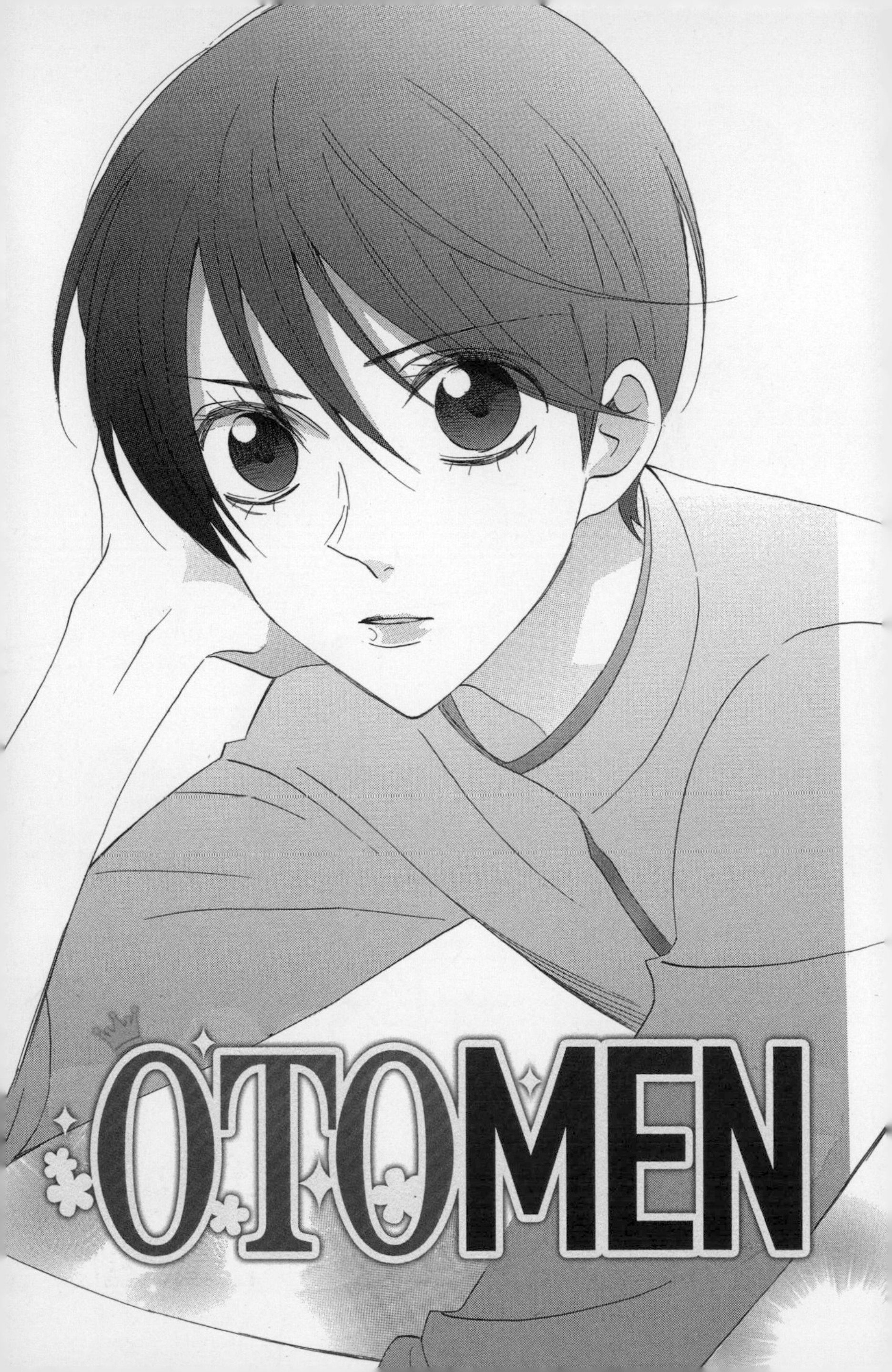
OTOMEN

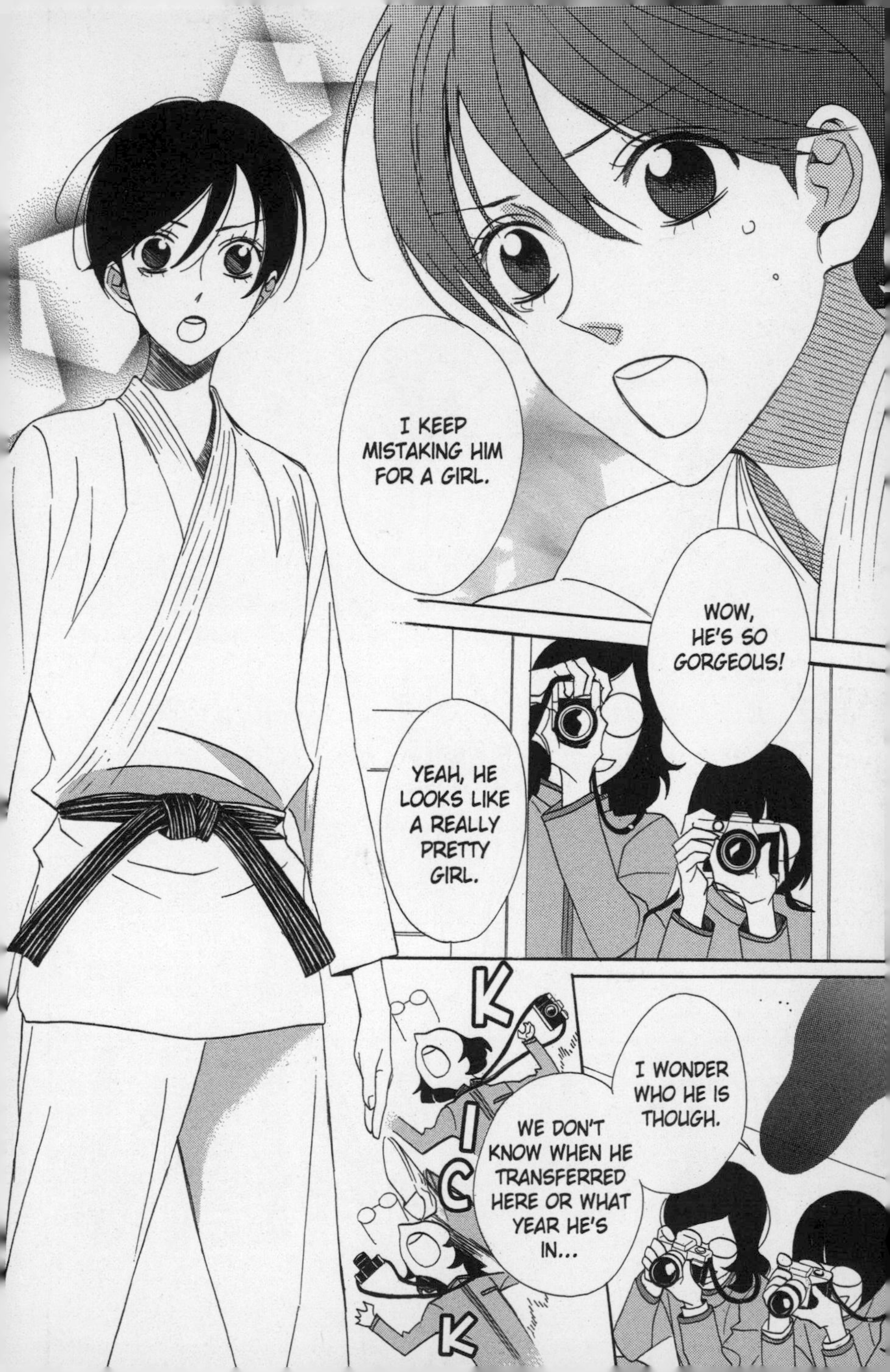
I KEEP MISTAKING HIM FOR A GIRL.
WOW, HE'S SO GORGEOUS!
YEAH, HE LOOKS LIKE A REALLY PRETTY GIRL.
I WONDER WHO HE IS THOUGH.
WE DON'T KNOW WHEN HE TRANSFERRED HERE OR WHAT YEAR HE'S IN...
KICK

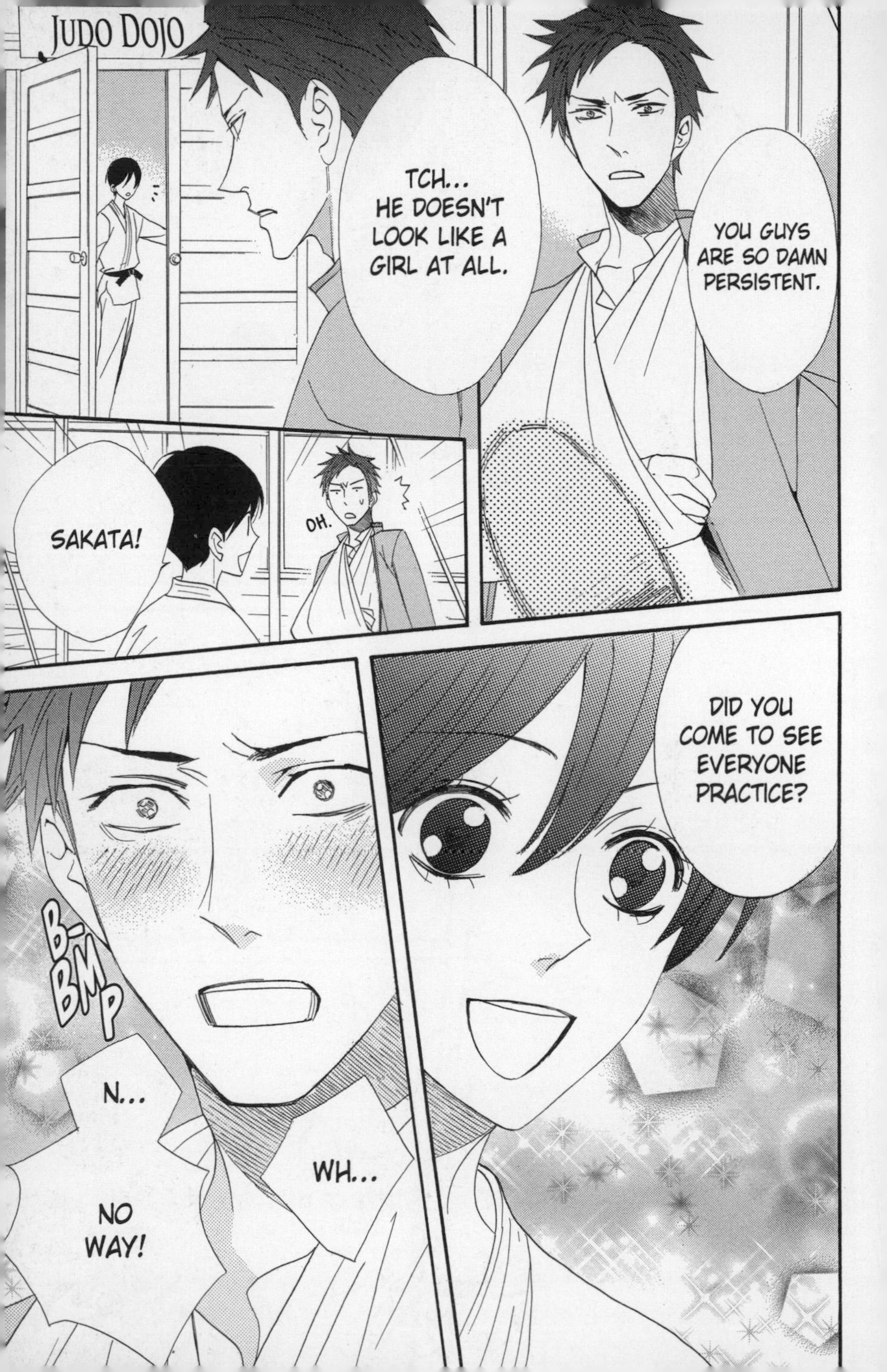
JUDO DOJO
YOU GUYS ARE SO DAMN PERSISTENT.
TCH... HE DOESN'T LOOK LIKE A GIRL AT ALL.
OH.
SAKATA!
DID YOU COME TO SEE EVERYONE PRACTICE?
B-BMP
WH...
N...
NO WAY!

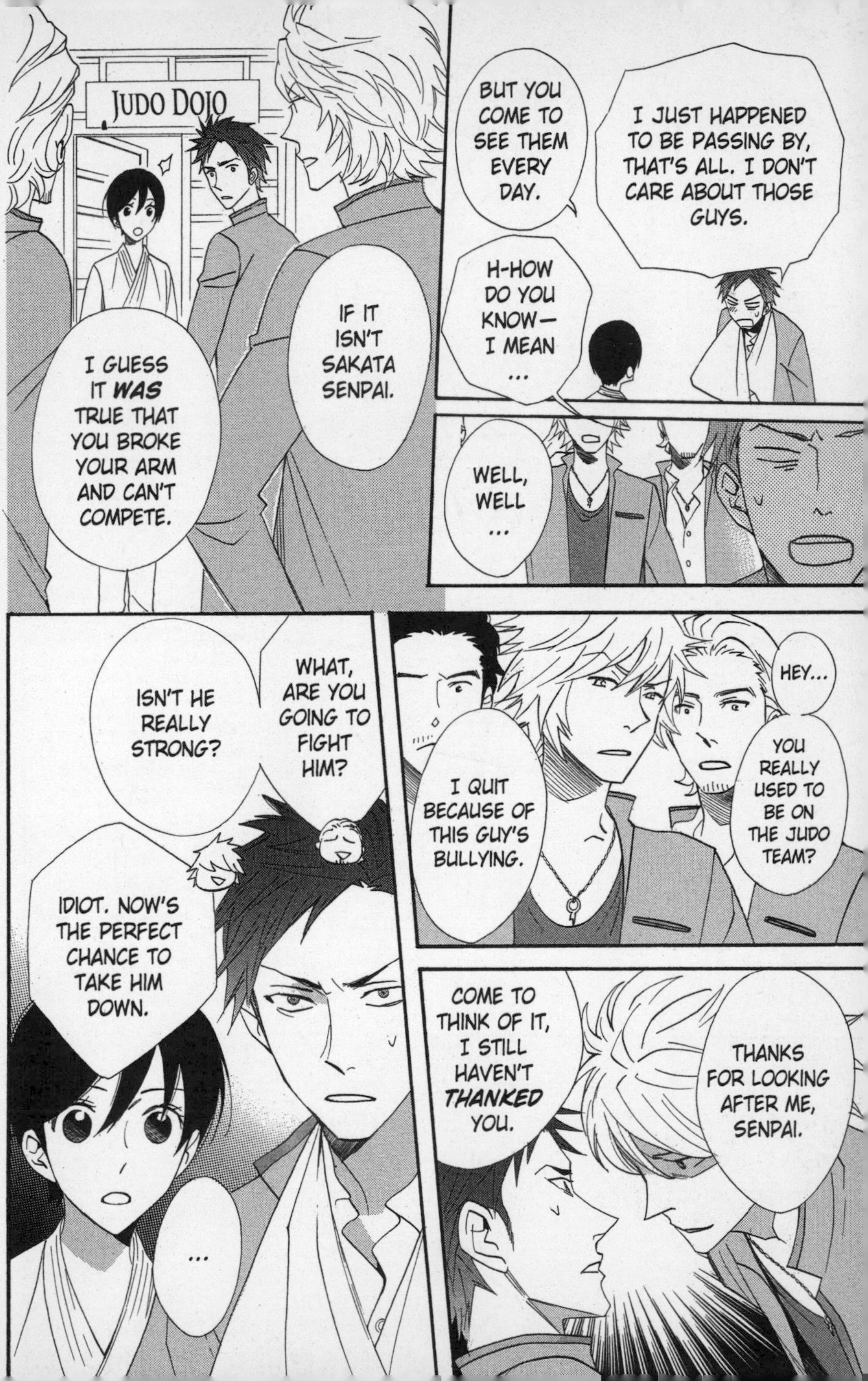
I JUST HAPPENED TO BE PASSING BY, THAT'S ALL. I DON'T CARE ABOUT THOSE GUYS.
BUT YOU COME TO SEE THEM EVERY DAY.
H-HOW DO YOU KNOW— I MEAN ...
WELL, WELL ...
JUDO DOJO
IF IT ISN'T SAKATA SENPAI.
I GUESS IT *WAS* TRUE THAT YOU BROKE YOUR ARM AND CAN'T COMPETE.
HEY...
YOU REALLY USED TO BE ON THE JUDO TEAM?
I QUIT BECAUSE OF THIS GUY'S BULLYING.
THANKS FOR LOOKING AFTER ME, SENPAI.
COME TO THINK OF IT, I STILL HAVEN'T *THANKED* YOU.
WHAT, ARE YOU GOING TO FIGHT HIM?
ISN'T HE REALLY STRONG?
IDIOT. NOW'S THE PERFECT CHANCE TO TAKE HIM DOWN.
...

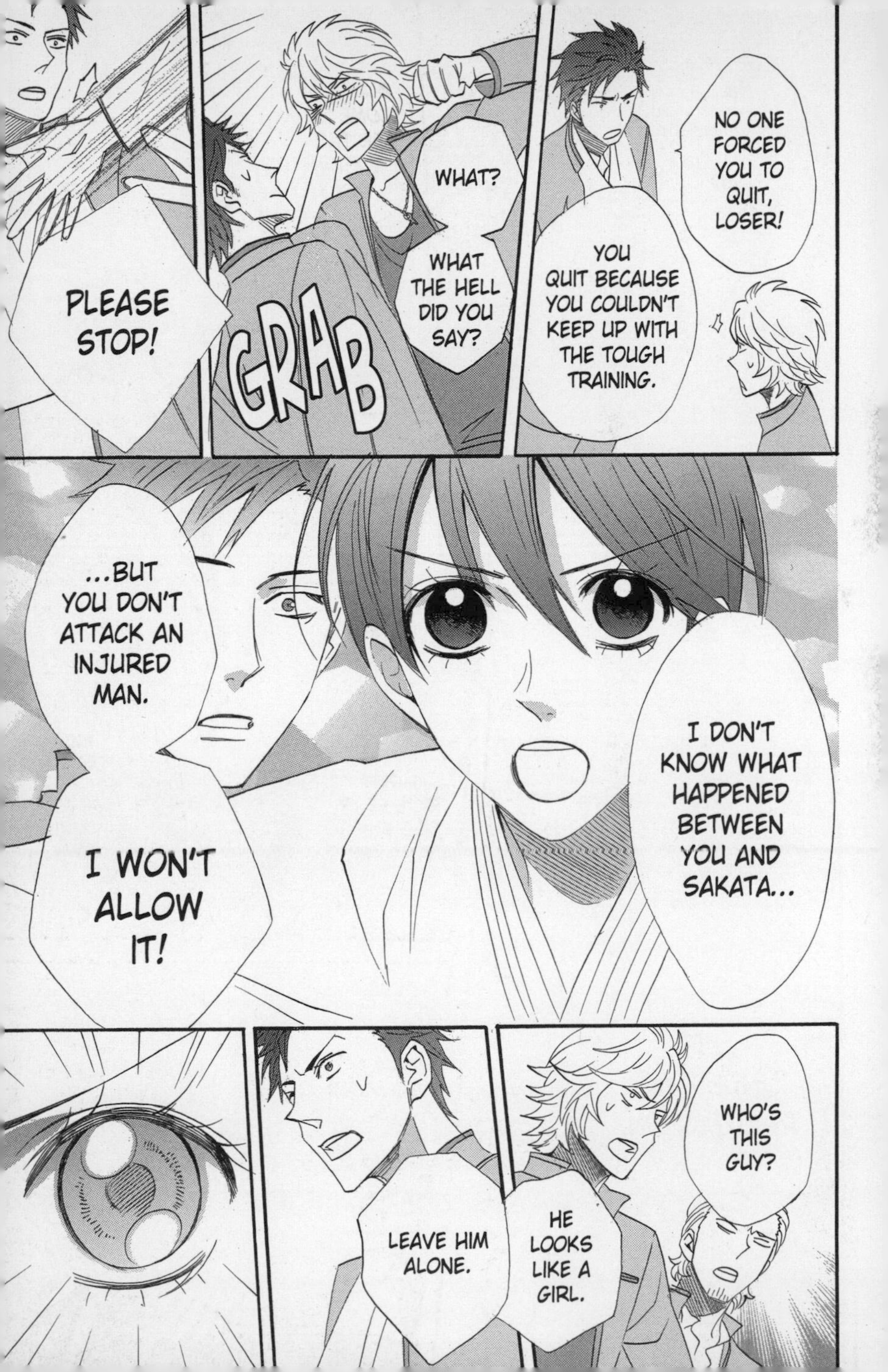
NO ONE FORCED YOU TO QUIT, LOSER!
YOU QUIT BECAUSE YOU COULDN'T KEEP UP WITH THE TOUGH TRAINING.
WHAT?
WHAT THE HELL DID YOU SAY?
GRAB
PLEASE STOP!
I DON'T KNOW WHAT HAPPENED BETWEEN YOU AND SAKATA...
...BUT YOU DON'T ATTACK AN INJURED MAN.
I WON'T ALLOW IT!
WHO'S THIS GUY?
HE LOOKS LIKE A GIRL.
LEAVE HIM ALONE.

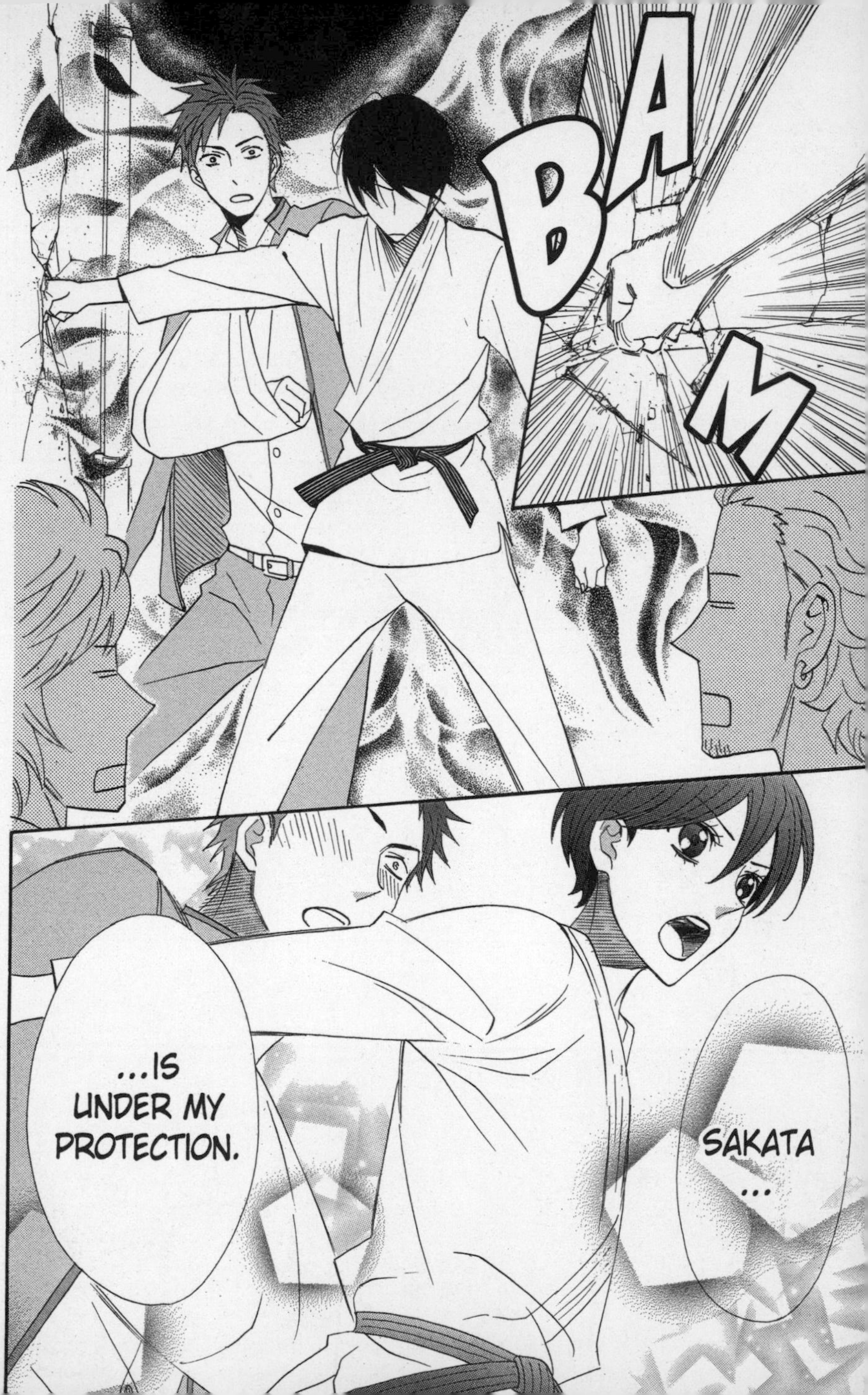
BAM
SAKATA ...
...IS UNDER MY PROTECTION.

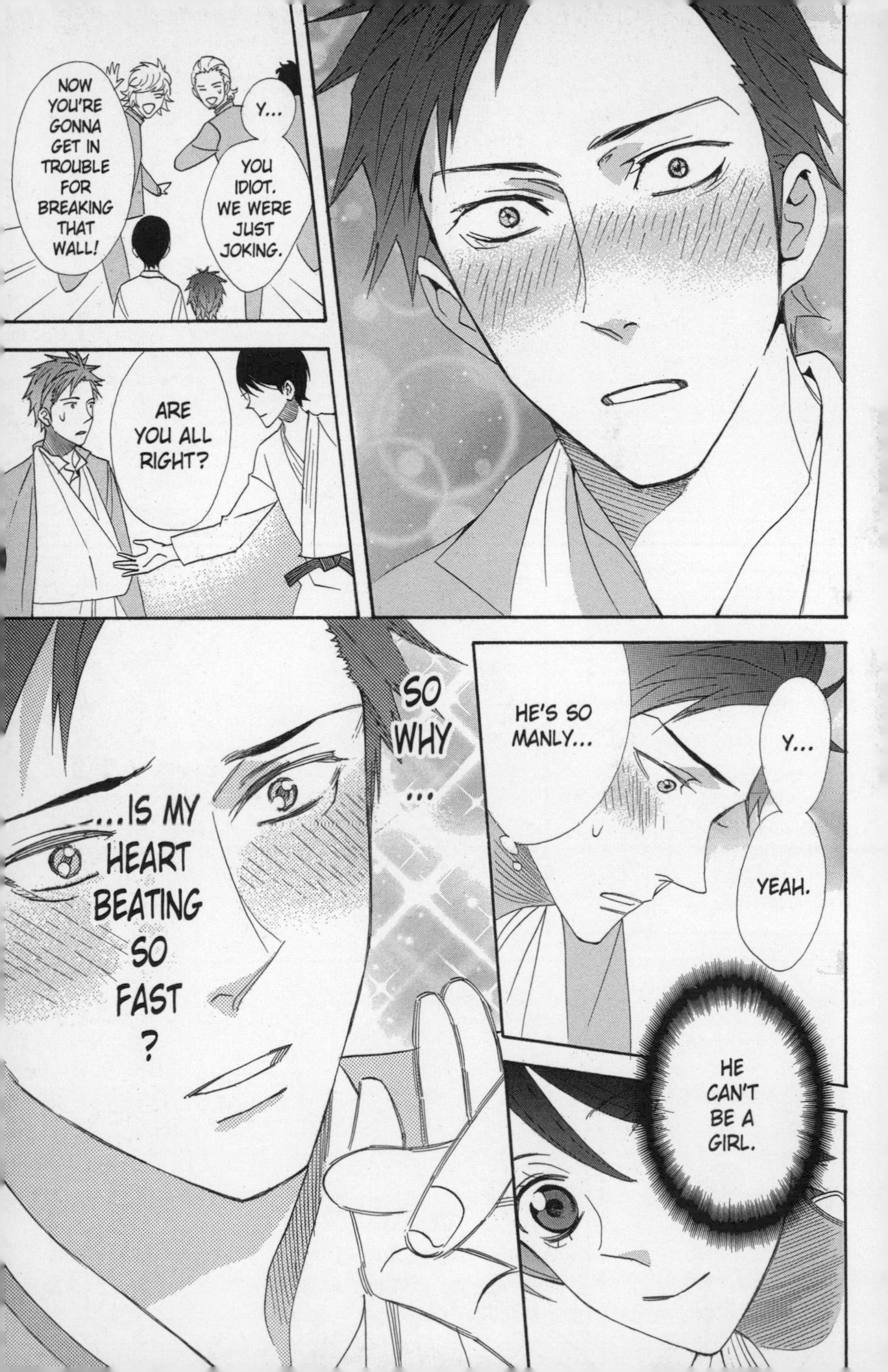
Y...
YOU IDIOT. WE WERE JUST JOKING.
NOW YOU'RE GONNA GET IN TROUBLE FOR BREAKING THAT WALL!
ARE YOU ALL RIGHT?
Y...
HE'S SO MANLY...
YEAH.
HE CAN'T BE A GIRL.
SO WHY...
...IS MY HEART BEATING SO FAST?

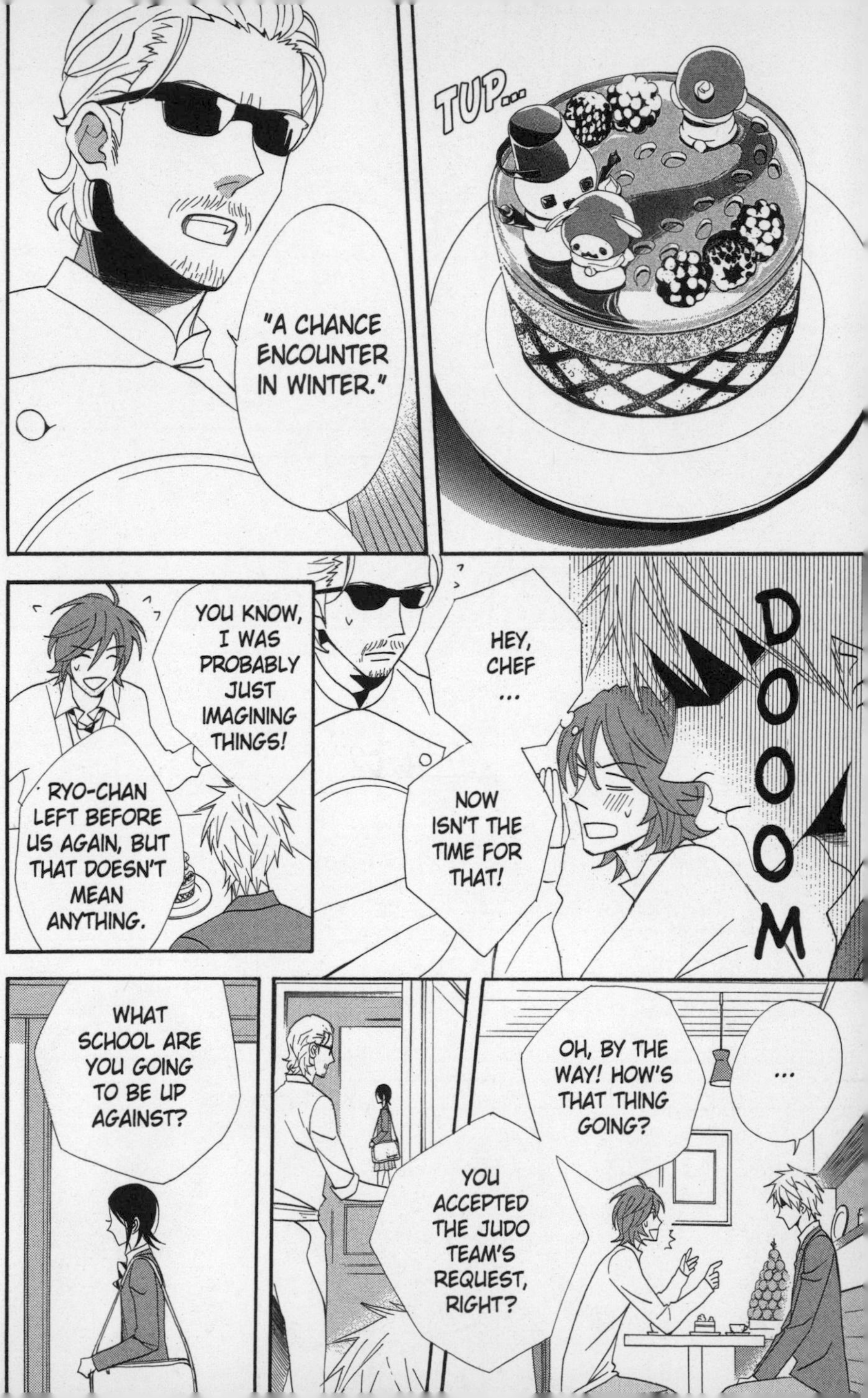
TUP...
"A CHANCE ENCOUNTER IN WINTER."
DOOOM
HEY, CHEF ...
NOW ISN'T THE TIME FOR THAT!
YOU KNOW, I WAS PROBABLY JUST IMAGINING THINGS!
RYO-CHAN LEFT BEFORE US AGAIN, BUT THAT DOESN'T MEAN ANYTHING.
...
OH, BY THE WAY! HOW'S THAT THING GOING?
YOU ACCEPTED THE JUDO TEAM'S REQUEST, RIGHT?
WHAT SCHOOL ARE YOU GOING TO BE UP AGAINST?

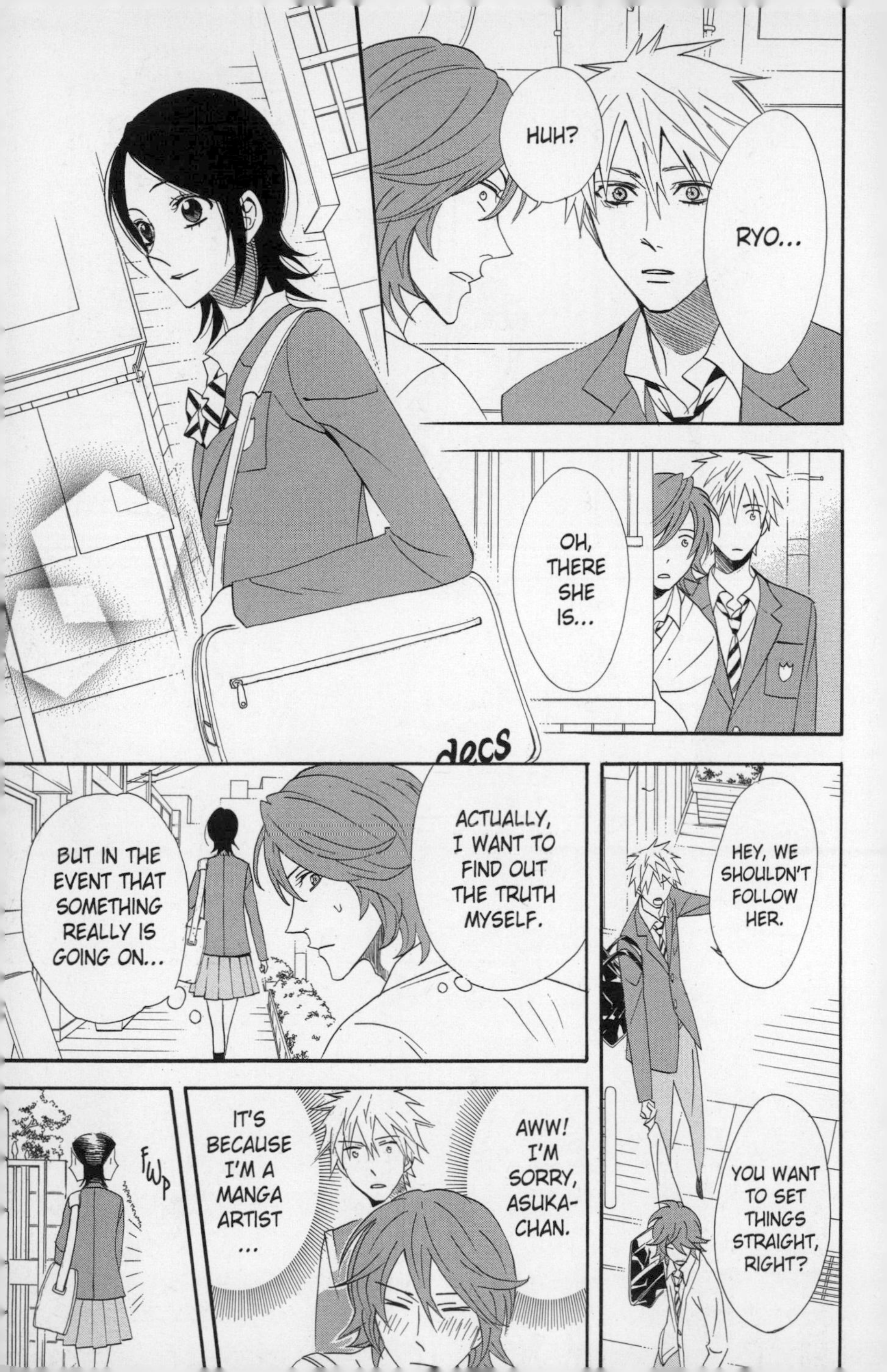
RYO...
HUH?
OH, THERE SHE IS...
decs
HEY, WE SHOULDN'T FOLLOW HER.
YOU WANT TO SET THINGS STRAIGHT, RIGHT?
ACTUALLY, I WANT TO FIND OUT THE TRUTH MYSELF.
BUT IN THE EVENT THAT SOMETHING REALLY IS GOING ON...
AWW! I'M SORRY, ASUKA-CHAN.
IT'S BECAUSE I'M A MANGA ARTIST ...
FWP

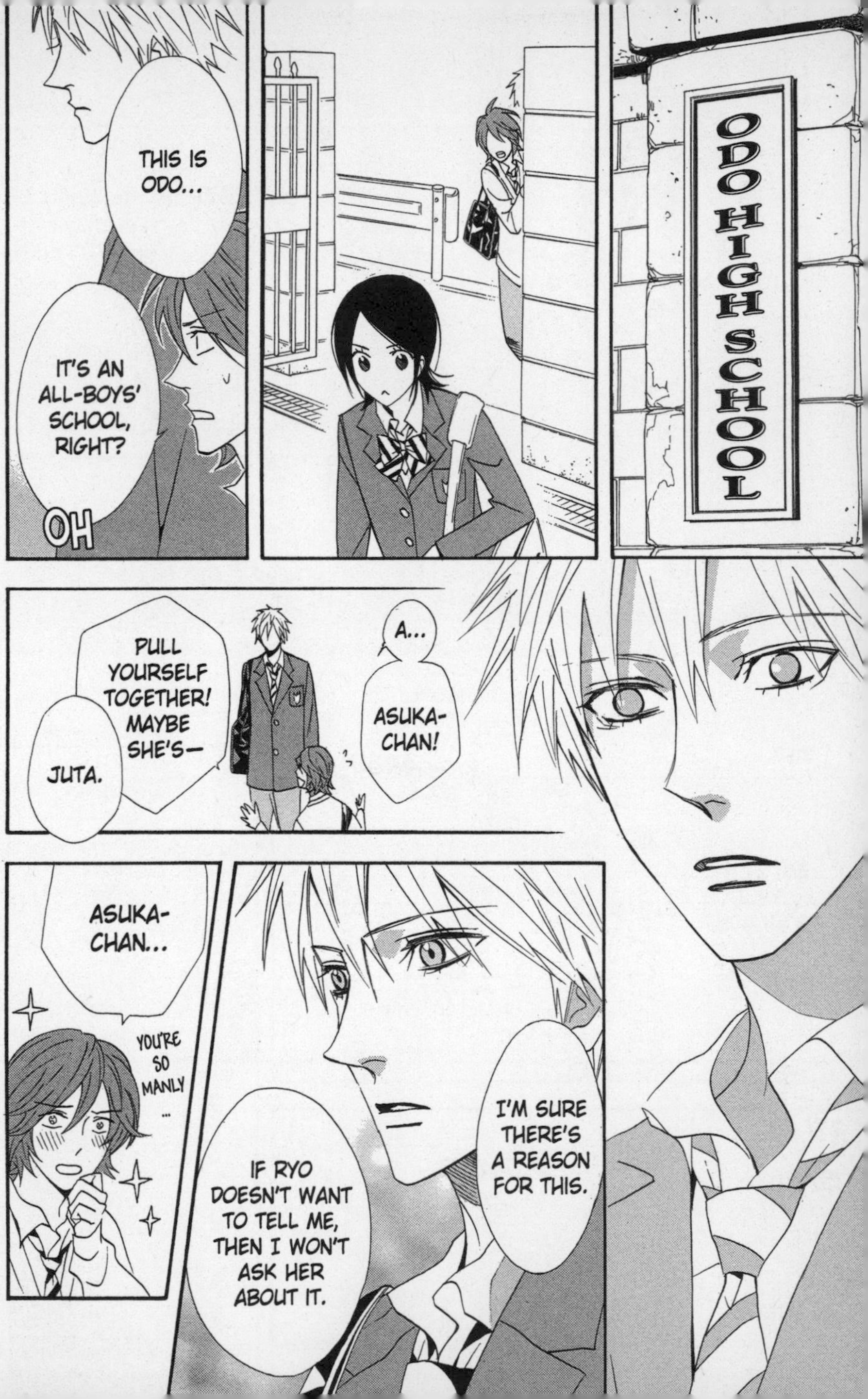
ODO HIGH SCHOOL
THIS IS ODO...
IT'S AN ALL-BOYS' SCHOOL, RIGHT?
OH
A... ASUKA-CHAN!
PULL YOURSELF TOGETHER! MAYBE SHE'S—
JUTA.
I'M SURE THERE'S A REASON FOR THIS.
IF RYO DOESN'T WANT TO TELL ME, THEN I WON'T ASK HER ABOUT IT.
ASUKA-CHAN...
YOU'RE SO MANLY ...

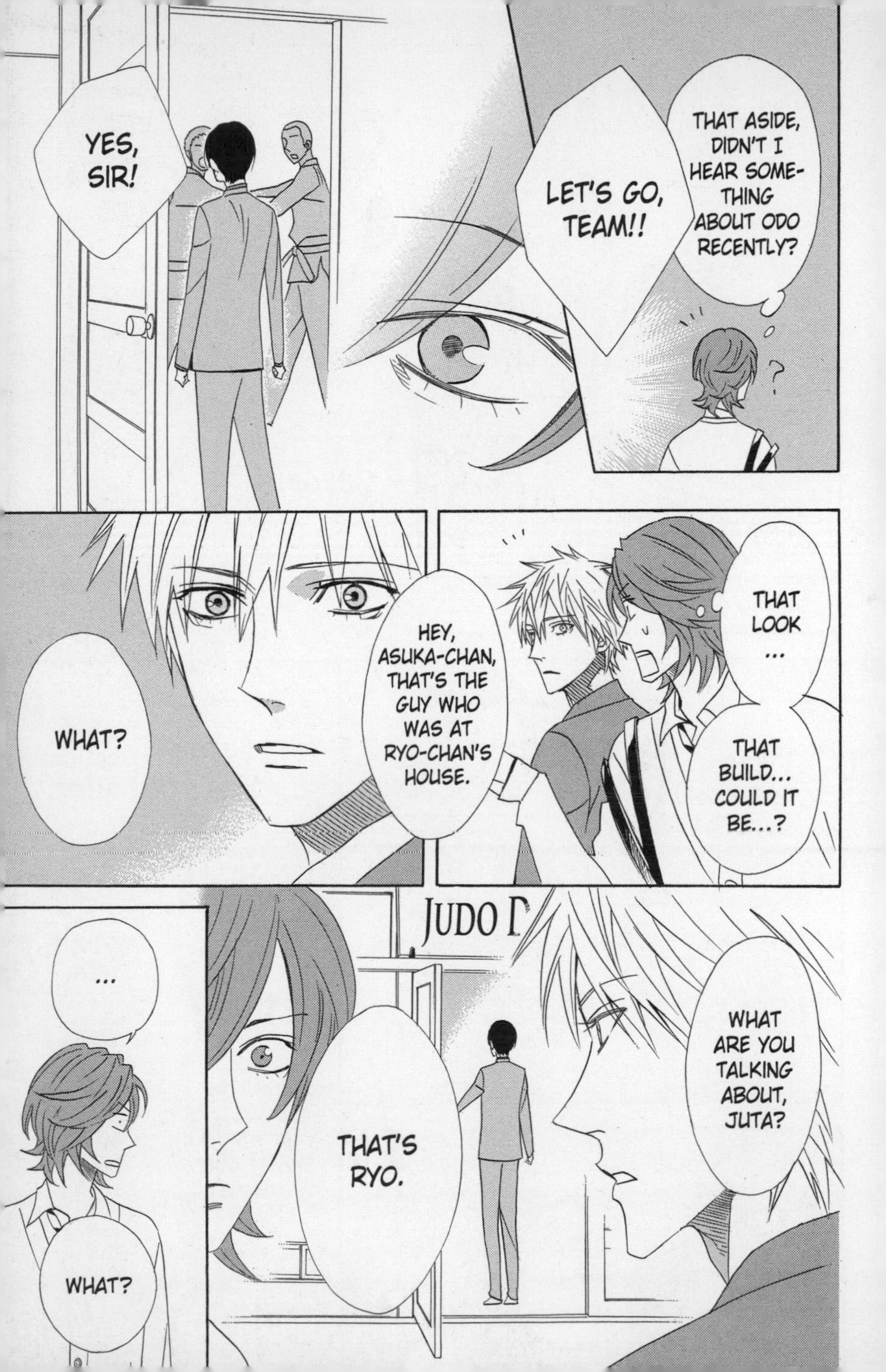
THAT ASIDE, DIDN'T I HEAR SOME-THING ABOUT ODO RECENTLY?
LET'S GO, TEAM!!
YES, SIR!
THAT LOOK ...
THAT BUILD... COULD IT BE...?
HEY, ASUKA-CHAN, THAT'S THE GUY WHO WAS AT RYO-CHAN'S HOUSE.
WHAT?
WHAT ARE YOU TALKING ABOUT, JUTA?
JUDO D
THAT'S RYO.
...
WHAT?

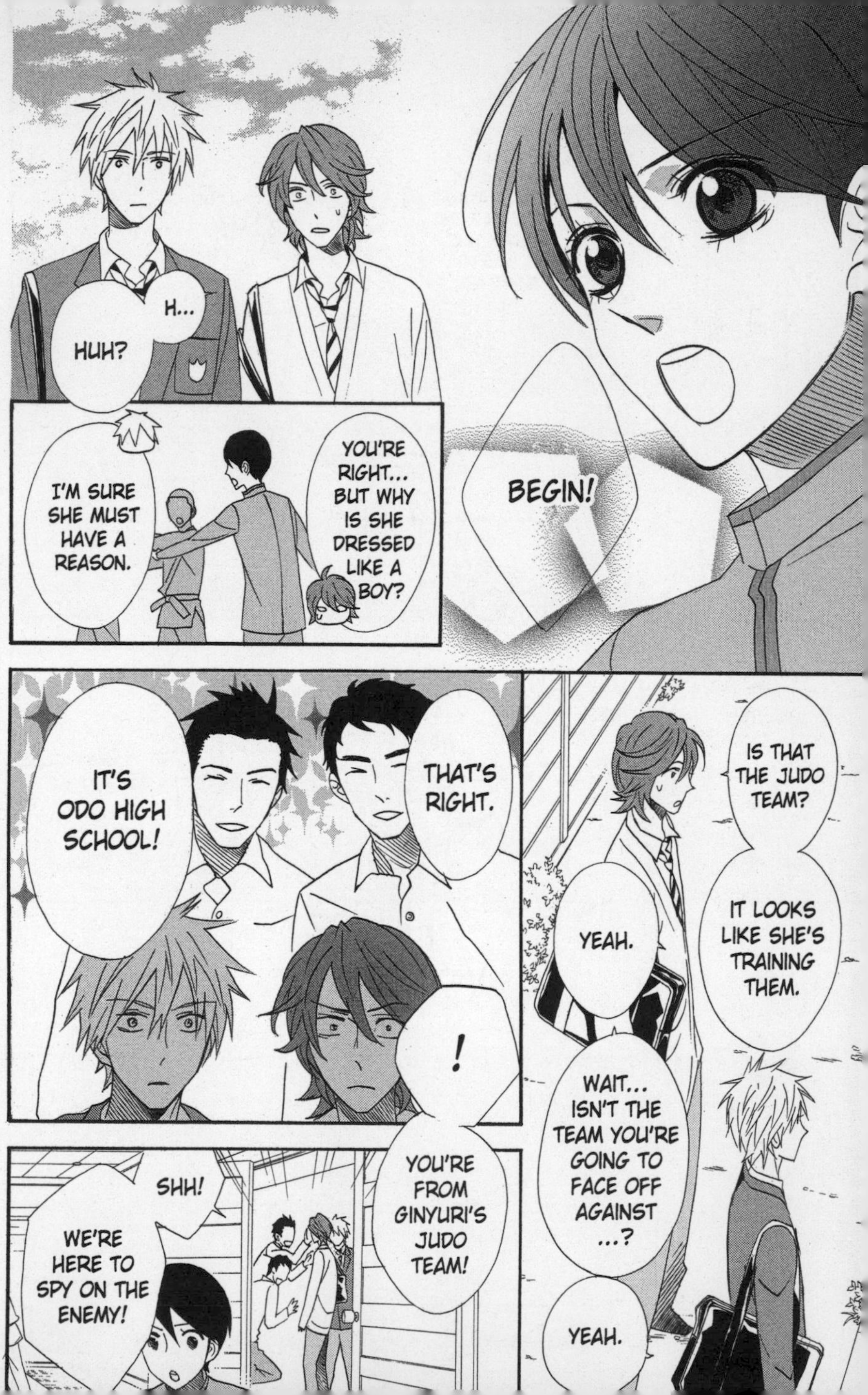
BEGIN!
H...
HUH?
YOU'RE RIGHT... BUT WHY IS SHE DRESSED LIKE A BOY?
I'M SURE SHE MUST HAVE A REASON.
IS THAT THE JUDO TEAM?
IT LOOKS LIKE SHE'S TRAINING THEM.
YEAH.
WAIT... ISN'T THE TEAM YOU'RE GOING TO FACE OFF AGAINST ...?
YEAH.
THAT'S RIGHT.
IT'S ODO HIGH SCHOOL!
!
YOU'RE FROM GINYURI'S JUDO TEAM!
SHH!
WE'RE HERE TO SPY ON THE ENEMY!

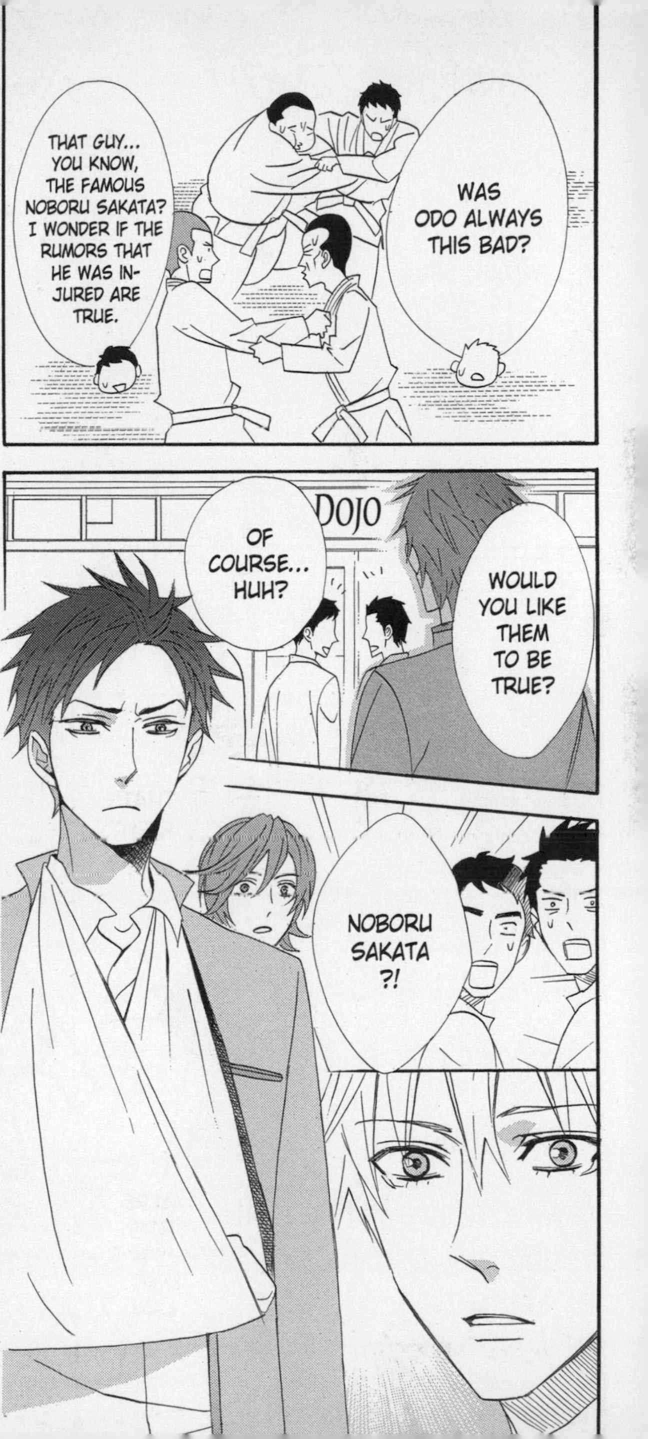
WAS ODO ALWAYS THIS BAD?
THAT GUY... YOU KNOW, THE FAMOUS NOBORU SAKATA? I WONDER IF THE RUMORS THAT HE WAS INJURED ARE TRUE.
WOULD YOU LIKE THEM TO BE TRUE?
DOJO
OF COURSE... HUH?
NOBORU SAKATA ?!

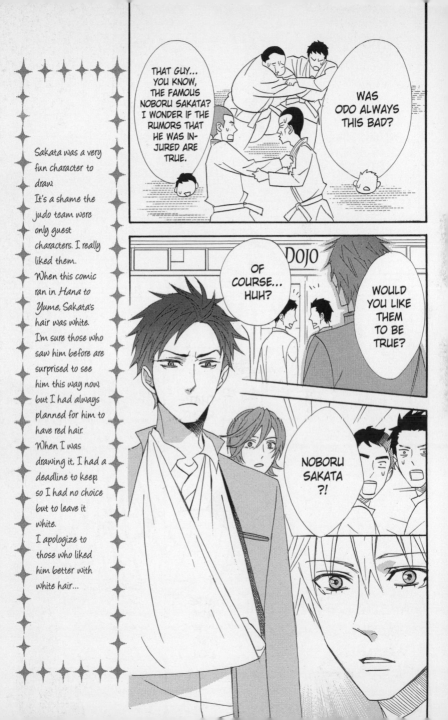

Sakata was a very fun character to draw.
It's a shame the judo team were only guest characters. I really liked them.
When this comic ran in *Hana to Yume*, Sakata's hair was white. I'm sure those who saw him before are surprised to see him this way now, but I had always planned for him to have red hair. When I was drawing it, I had a deadline to keep, so I had no choice but to leave it white.
I apologize to those who liked him better with white hair...

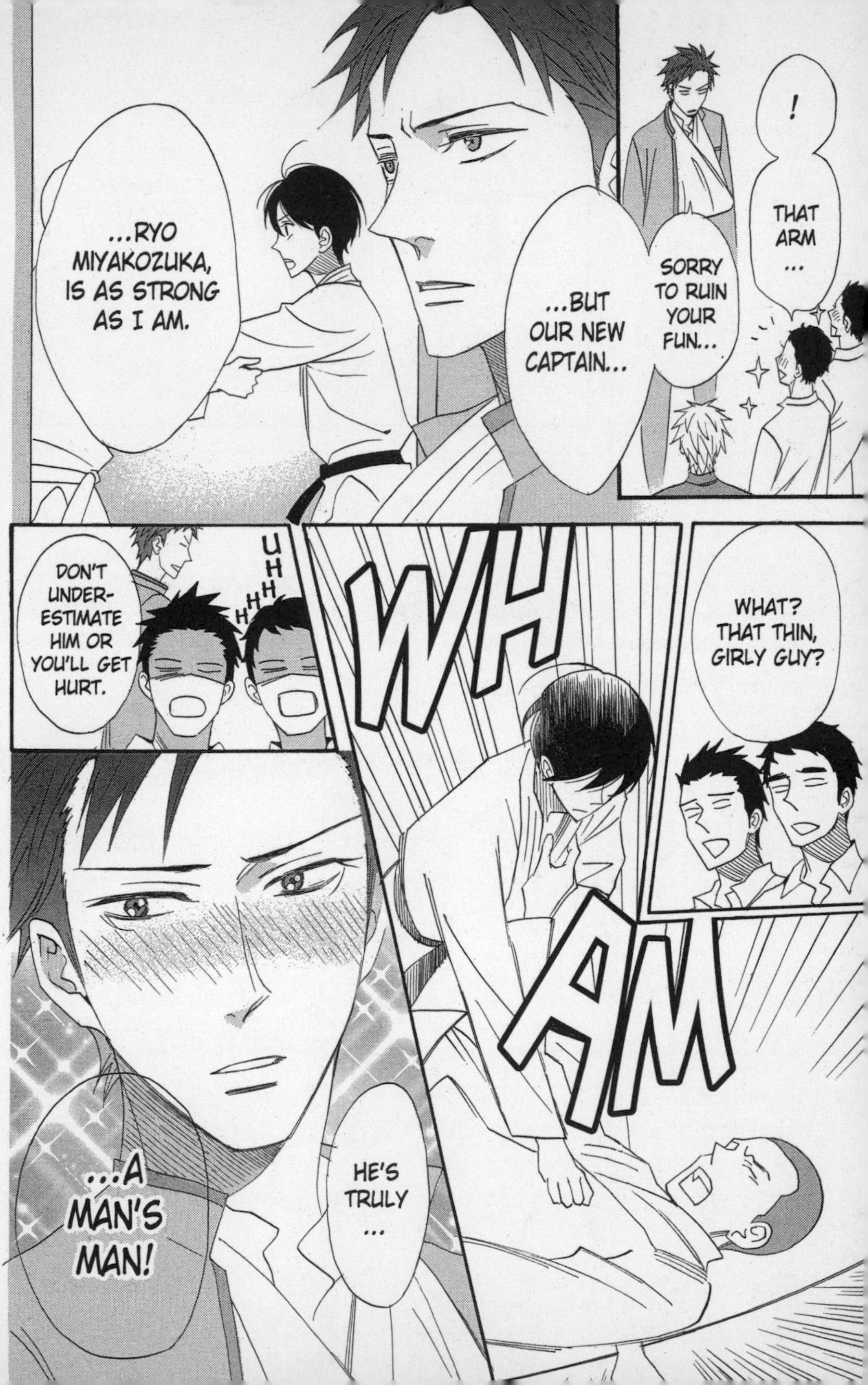

!
THAT ARM ...
SORRY TO RUIN YOUR FUN...
...BUT OUR NEW CAPTAIN...
...RYO MIYAKOZUKA, IS AS STRONG AS I AM.
WHAT? THAT THIN, GIRLY GUY?
WHAM
UHHHH
DON'T UNDER-ESTIMATE HIM OR YOU'LL GET HURT.
HE'S TRULY ...
...A MAN'S MAN!

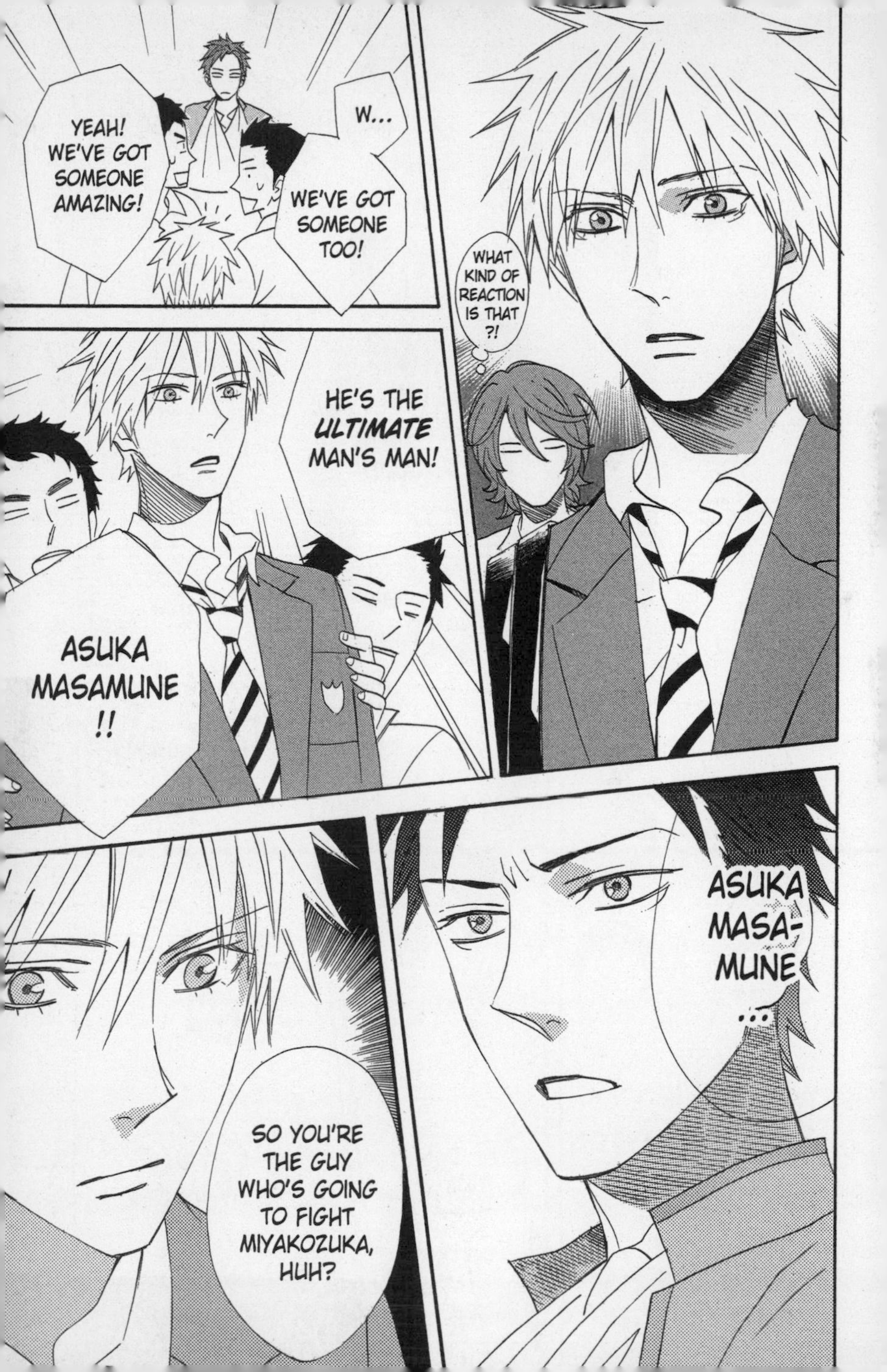

WHAT KIND OF REACTION IS THAT?!
YEAH! WE'VE GOT SOMEONE AMAZING!
W...
WE'VE GOT SOMEONE TOO!
HE'S THE *ULTIMATE* MAN'S MAN!
ASUKA MASAMUNE!!
ASUKA MASA-MUNE...
SO YOU'RE THE GUY WHO'S GOING TO FIGHT MIYAKOZUKA, HUH?

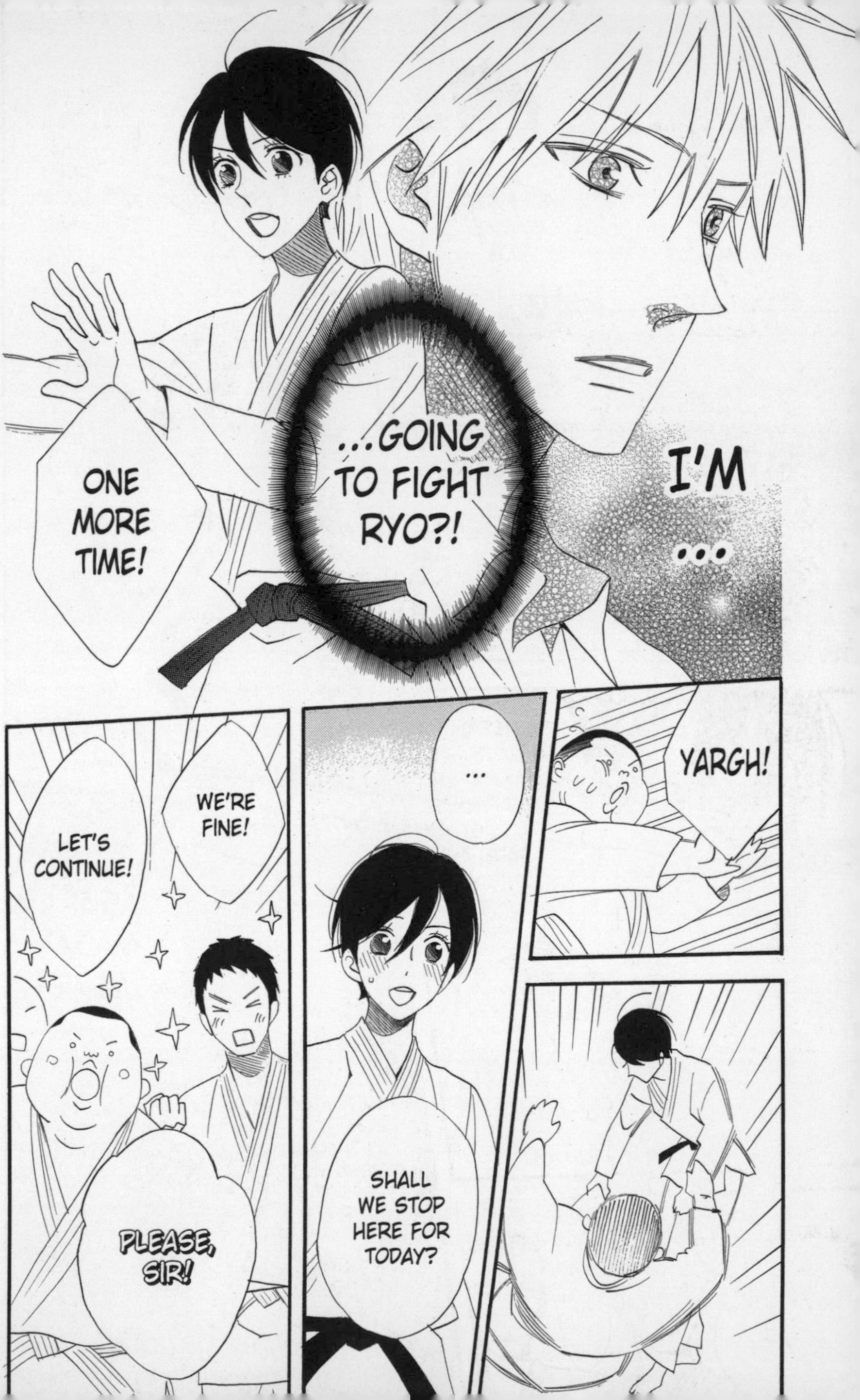
I'M ...
...GOING TO FIGHT RYO?!
ONE MORE TIME!
YARGH!
...
SHALL WE STOP HERE FOR TODAY?
WE'RE FINE!
LET'S CONTINUE!
PLEASE, SIR!

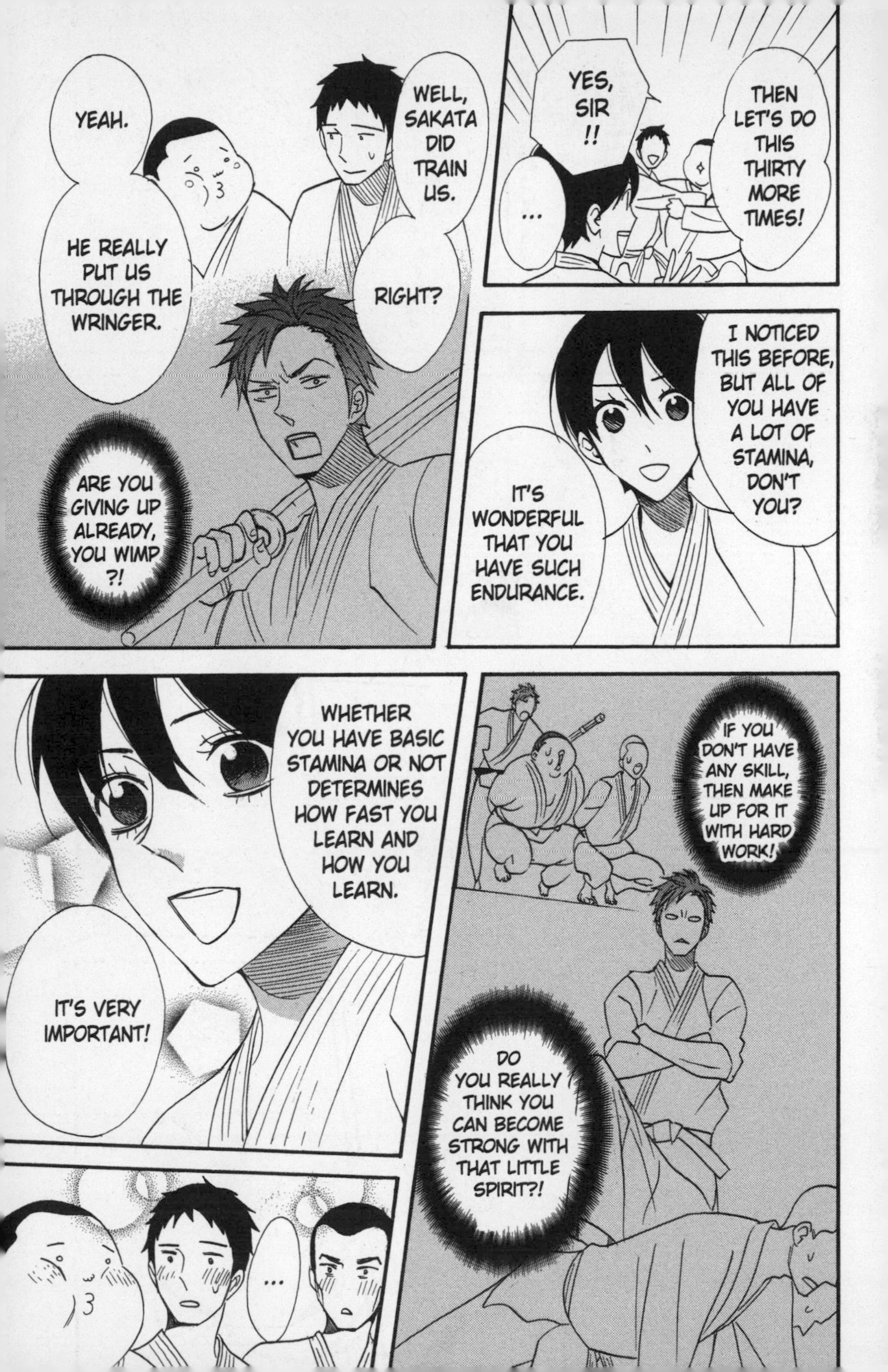
THEN LET'S DO THIS THIRTY MORE TIMES!
YES, SIR!!
...
I NOTICED THIS BEFORE, BUT ALL OF YOU HAVE A LOT OF STAMINA, DON'T YOU?
IT'S WONDERFUL THAT YOU HAVE SUCH ENDURANCE.
WELL, SAKATA DID TRAIN US.
YEAH.
RIGHT?
HE REALLY PUT US THROUGH THE WRINGER.
ARE YOU GIVING UP ALREADY, YOU WIMP?!
IF YOU DON'T HAVE ANY SKILL, THEN MAKE UP FOR IT WITH HARD WORK!
DO YOU REALLY THINK YOU CAN BECOME STRONG WITH THAT LITTLE SPIRIT?!
WHETHER YOU HAVE BASIC STAMINA OR NOT DETERMINES HOW FAST YOU LEARN AND HOW YOU LEARN.
IT'S VERY IMPORTANT!
...

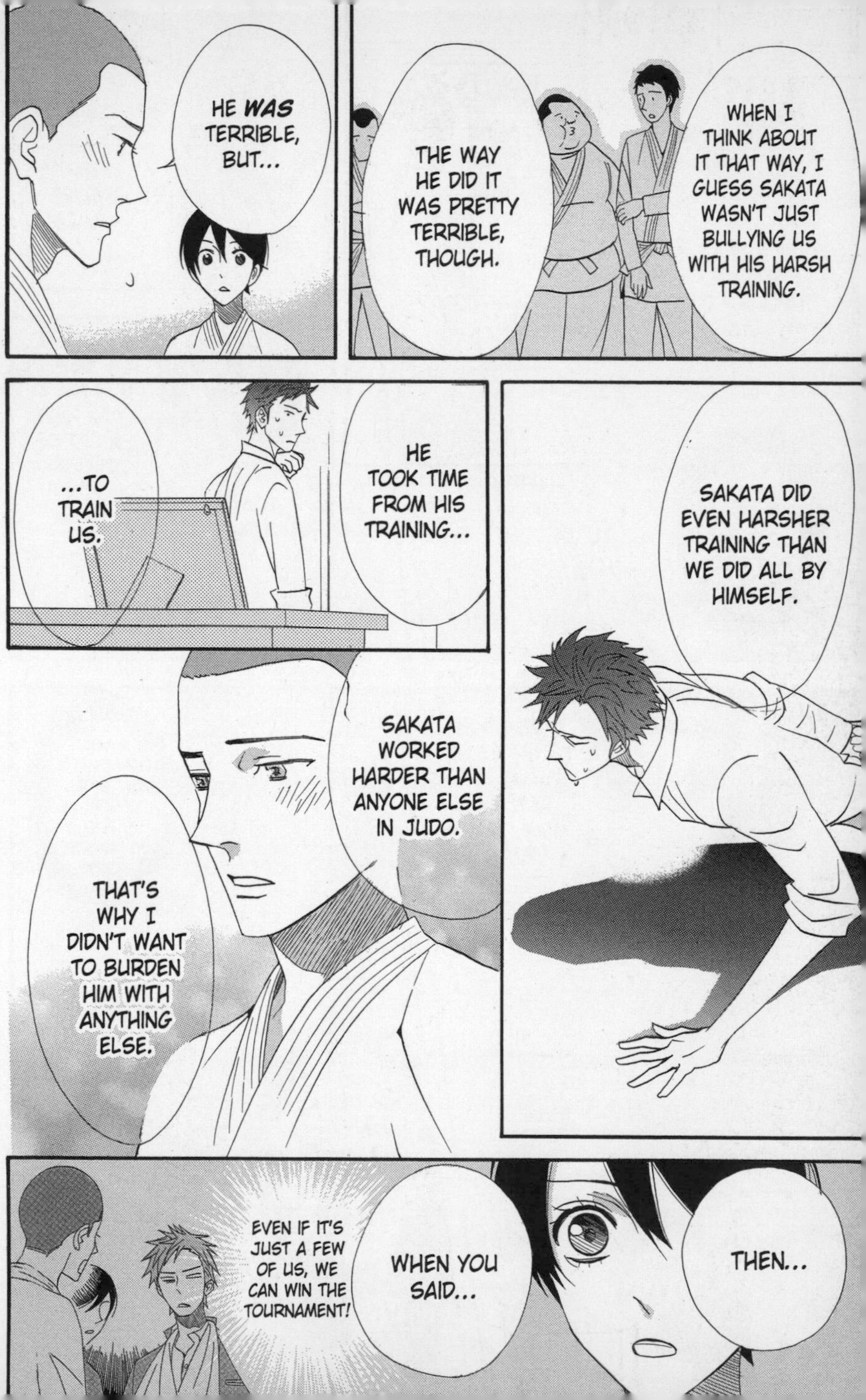

WHEN I THINK ABOUT IT THAT WAY, I GUESS SAKATA WASN'T JUST BULLYING US WITH HIS HARSH TRAINING.
THE WAY HE DID IT WAS PRETTY TERRIBLE, THOUGH.
HE *WAS* TERRIBLE, BUT...
SAKATA DID EVEN HARSHER TRAINING THAN WE DID ALL BY HIMSELF.
HE TOOK TIME FROM HIS TRAINING...
...TO TRAIN US.
SAKATA WORKED HARDER THAN ANYONE ELSE IN JUDO.
THAT'S WHY I DIDN'T WANT TO BURDEN HIM WITH ANYTHING ELSE.
THEN...
WHEN YOU SAID...
EVEN IF IT'S JUST A FEW OF US, WE CAN WIN THE TOURNAMENT!

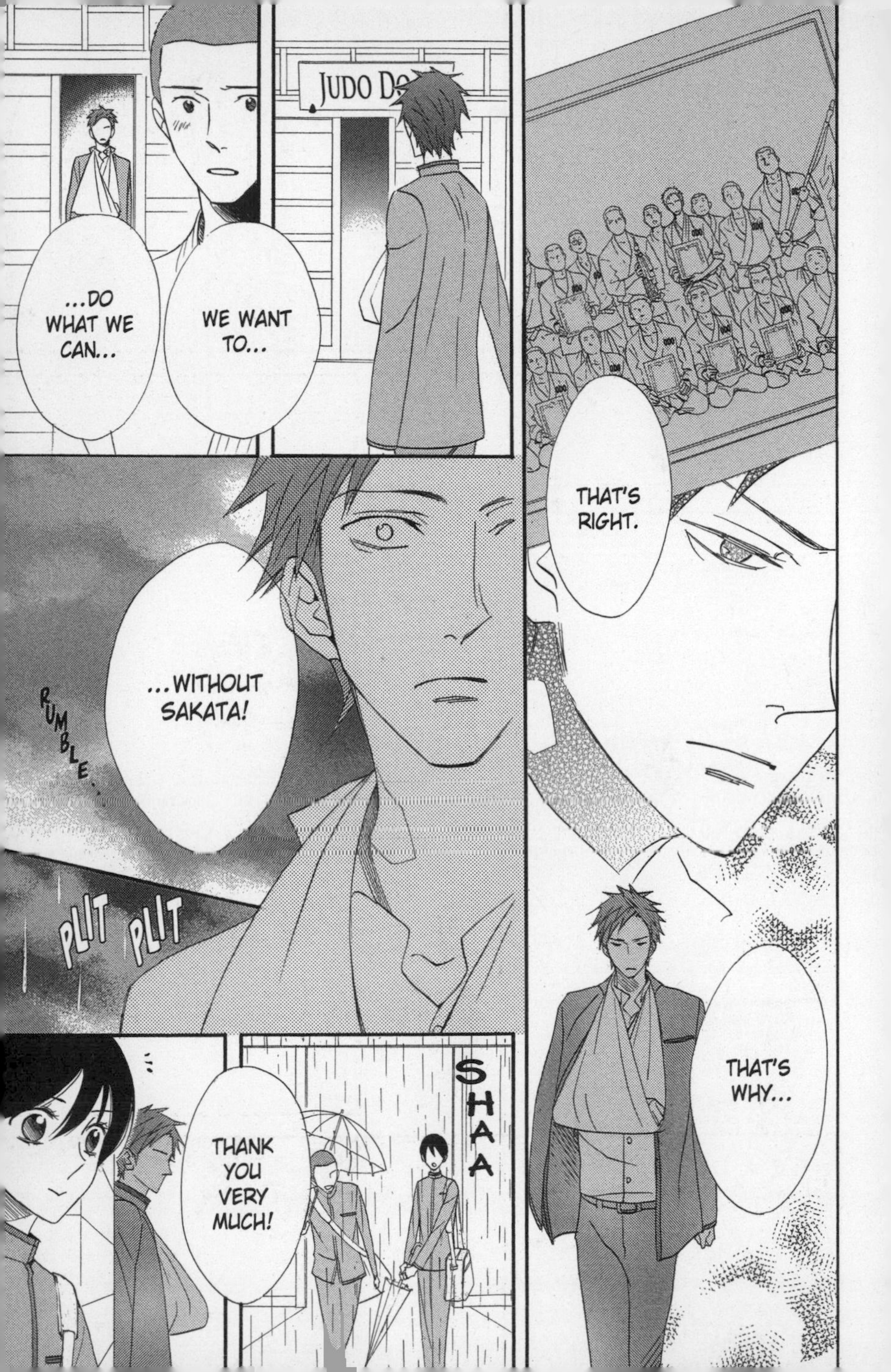
THAT'S RIGHT.
THAT'S WHY...
JUDO DO
WE WANT TO...
...DO WHAT WE CAN...
RUMBLE...
...WITHOUT SAKATA!
PLIT PLIT
SHAA
THANK YOU VERY MUCH!

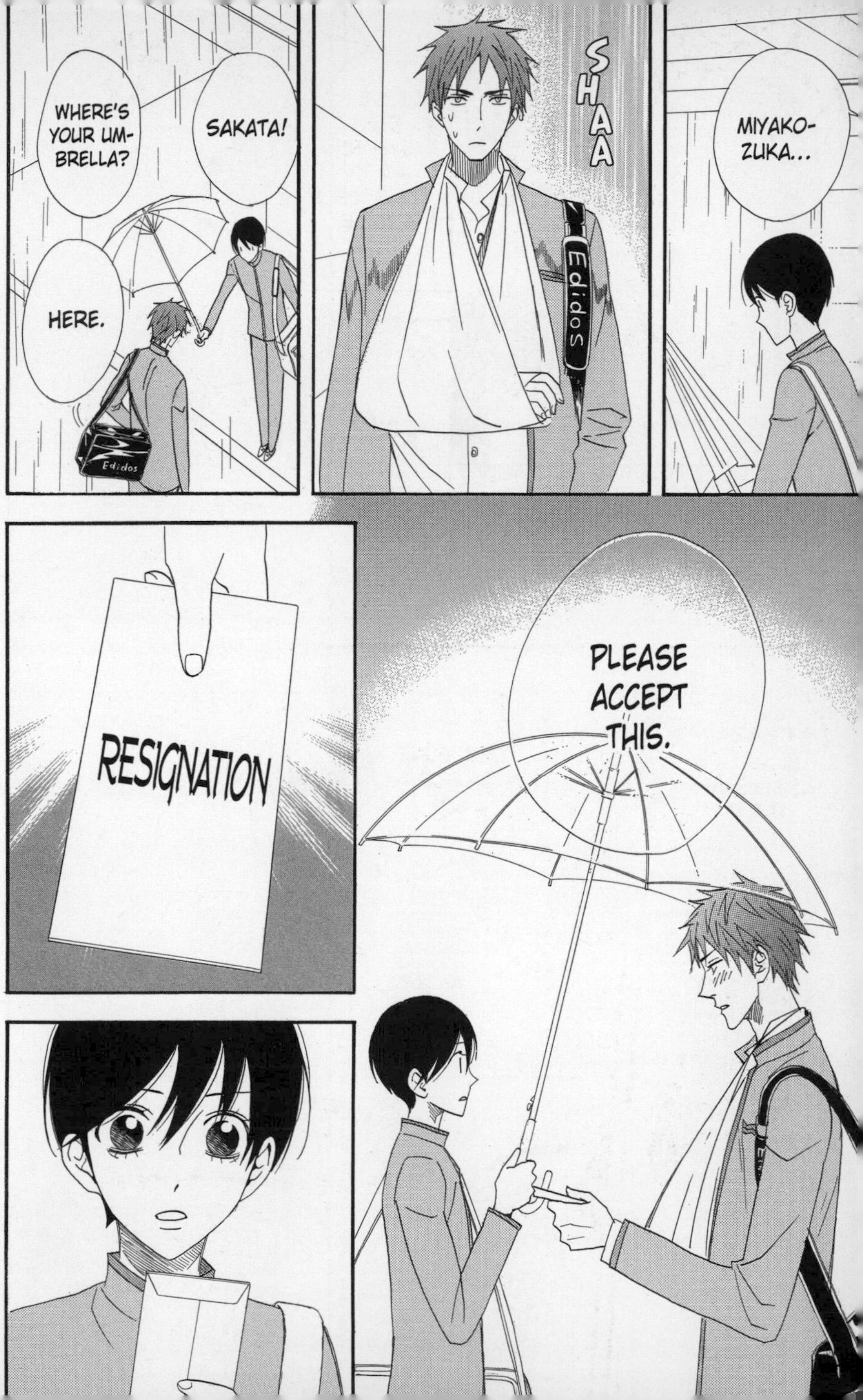
MIYAKO-ZUKA...
SHAA
Edidos
SAKATA!
WHERE'S YOUR UM-BRELLA?
HERE.
Edidos
PLEASE ACCEPT THIS.
RESIGNATION

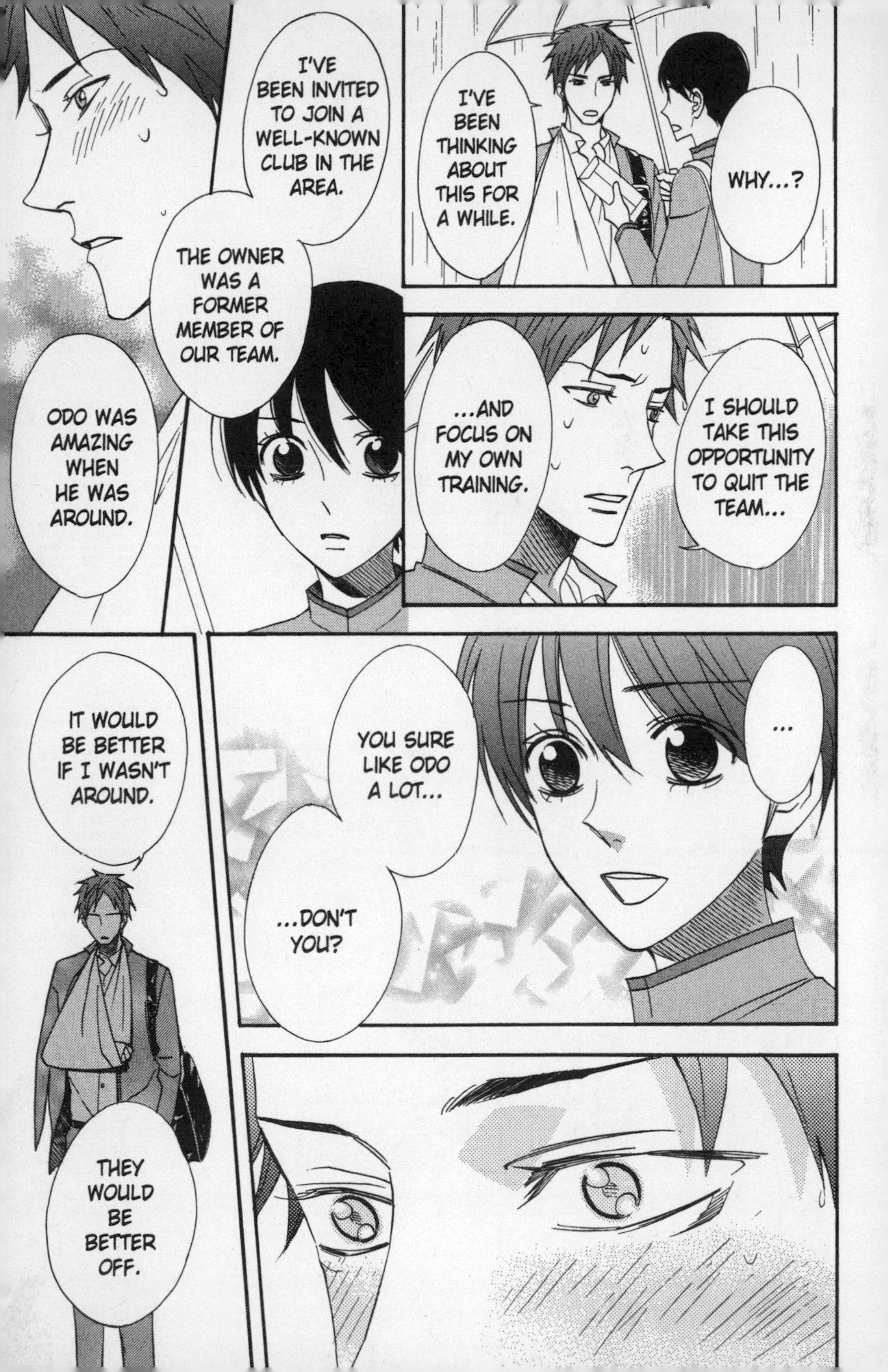
WHY...?
I'VE BEEN THINKING ABOUT THIS FOR A WHILE.
I SHOULD TAKE THIS OPPORTUNITY TO QUIT THE TEAM...
...AND FOCUS ON MY OWN TRAINING.
I'VE BEEN INVITED TO JOIN A WELL-KNOWN CLUB IN THE AREA.
THE OWNER WAS A FORMER MEMBER OF OUR TEAM.
ODO WAS AMAZING WHEN HE WAS AROUND.
...
YOU SURE LIKE ODO A LOT...
...DON'T YOU?
IT WOULD BE BETTER IF I WASN'T AROUND.
THEY WOULD BE BETTER OFF.

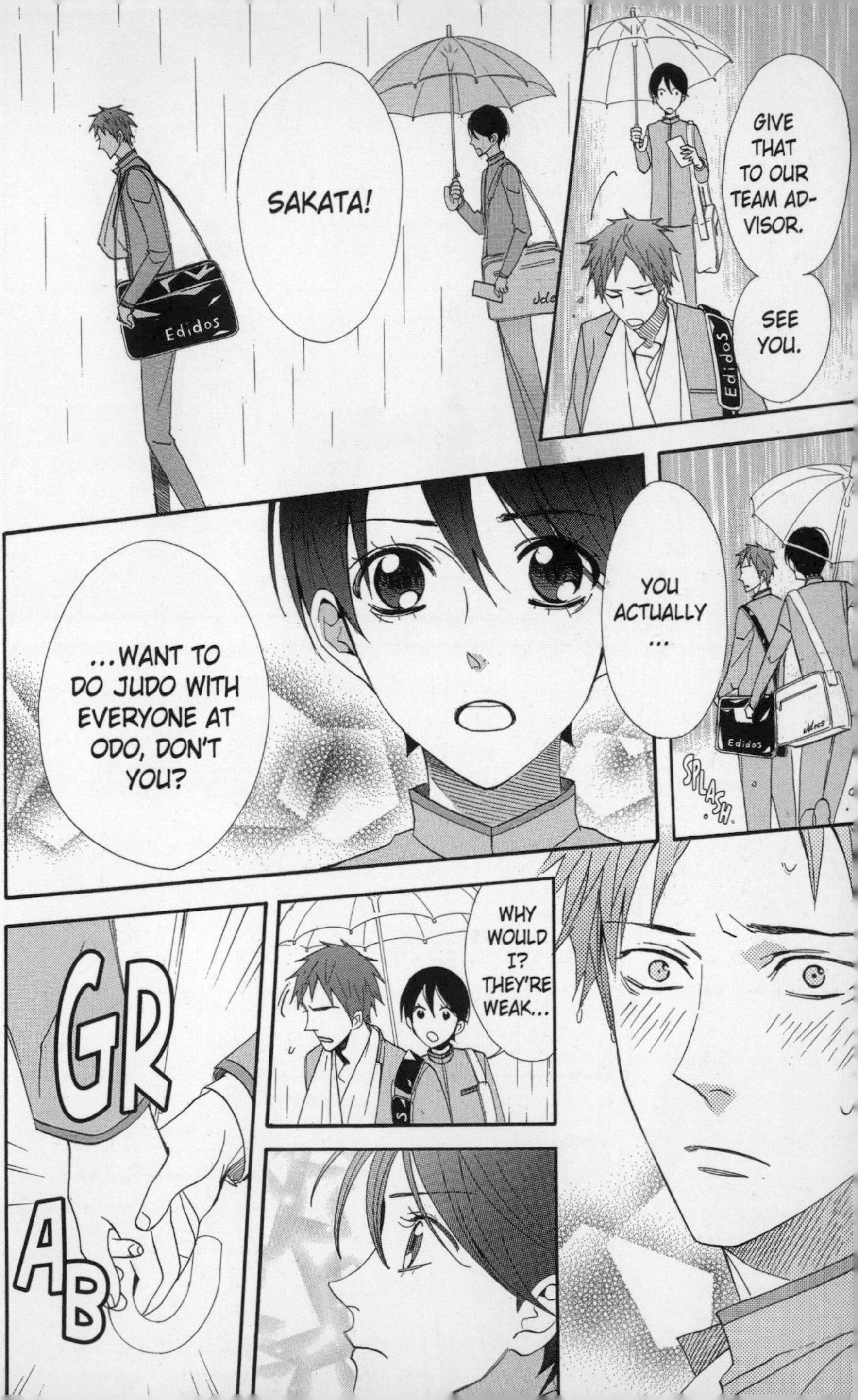
GIVE THAT TO OUR TEAM AD-VISOR.
SEE YOU.
SAKATA!
YOU ACTUALLY ...
SPLASH
...WANT TO DO JUDO WITH EVERYONE AT ODO, DON'T YOU?
WHY WOULD I? THEY'RE WEAK...
GRAB

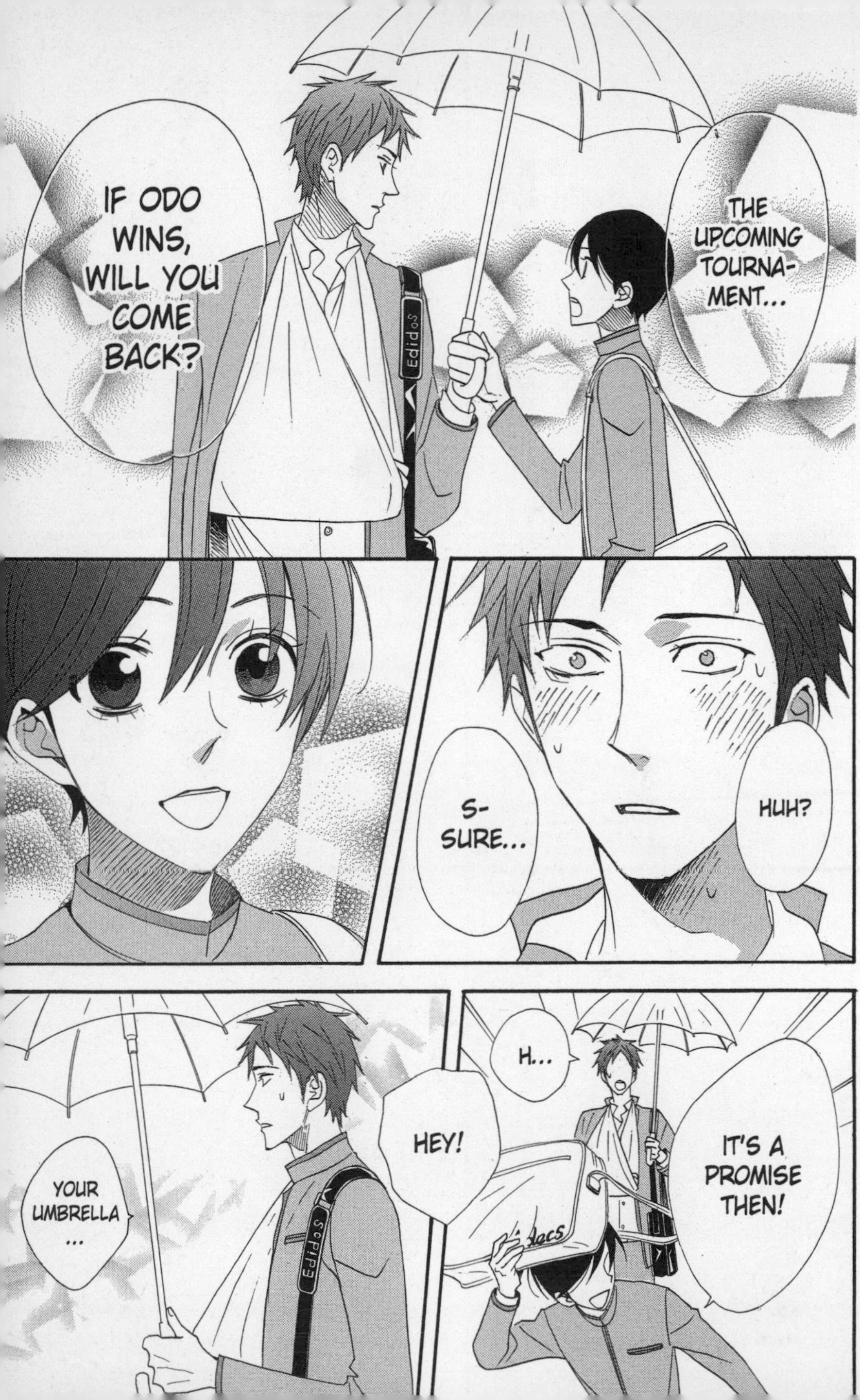
THE UPCOMING TOURNAMENT...
IF ODO WINS, WILL YOU COME BACK?
HUH?
S-SURE...
IT'S A PROMISE THEN!
H...
HEY!
YOUR UMBRELLA ...

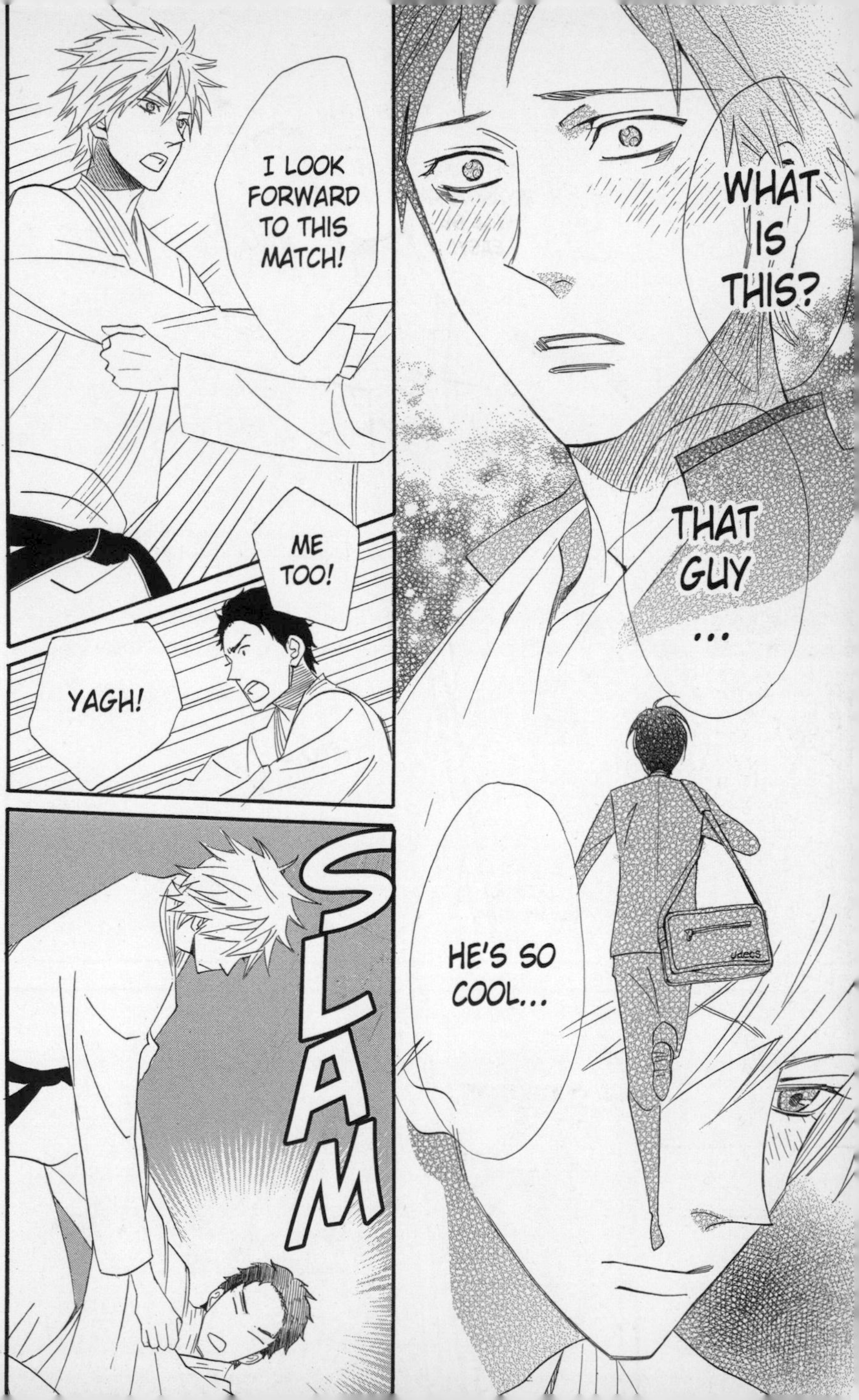
WHAT IS THIS?
THAT GUY...
HE'S SO COOL...
I LOOK FORWARD TO THIS MATCH!
ME TOO!
YAGH!
SLAM

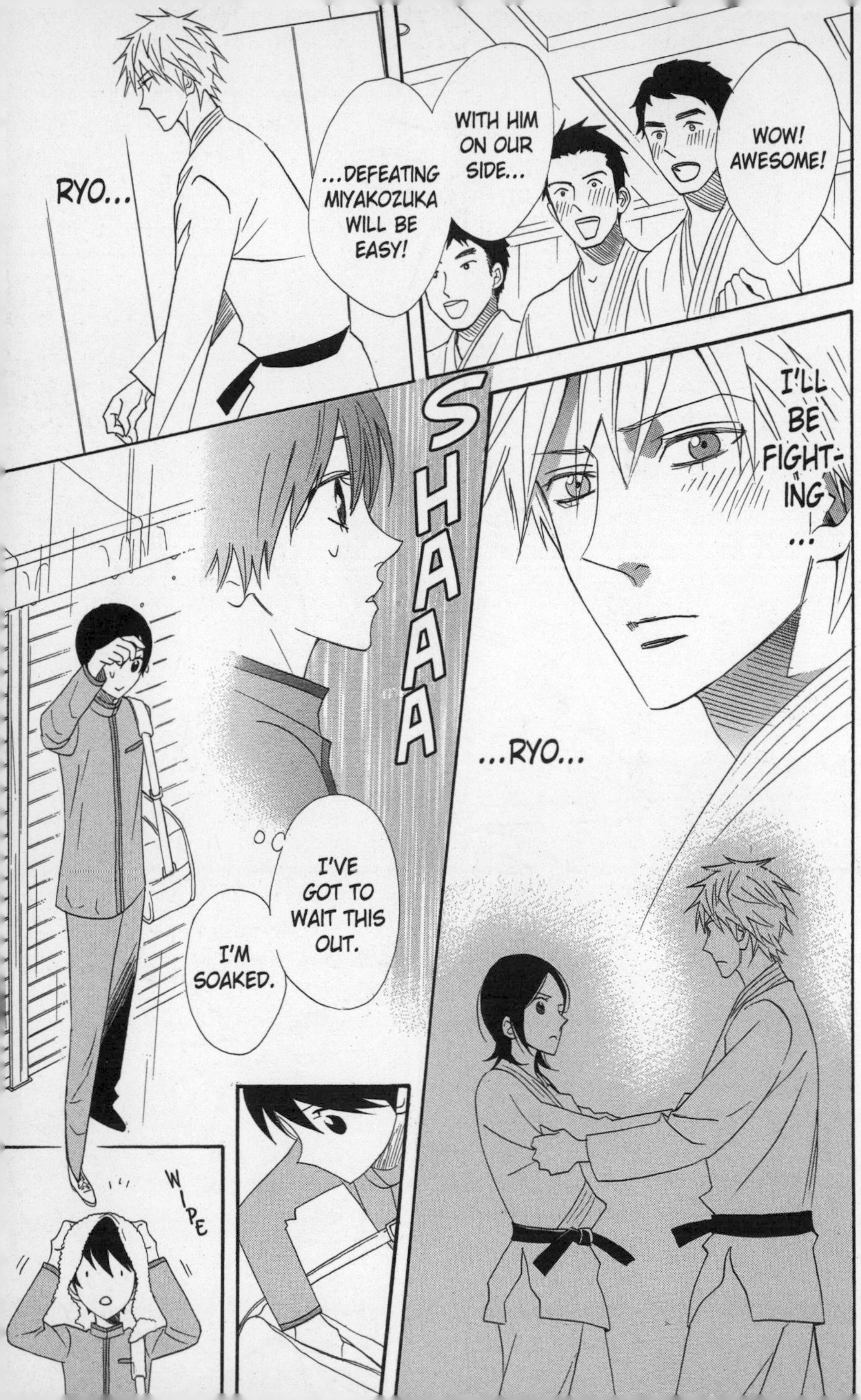
WOW! AWESOME!
WITH HIM ON OUR SIDE...
...DEFEATING MIYAKOZUKA WILL BE EASY!
RYO...
I'LL BE FIGHTING...
...RYO...
SHAAAA
I'VE GOT TO WAIT THIS OUT.
I'M SOAKED.
WIPE

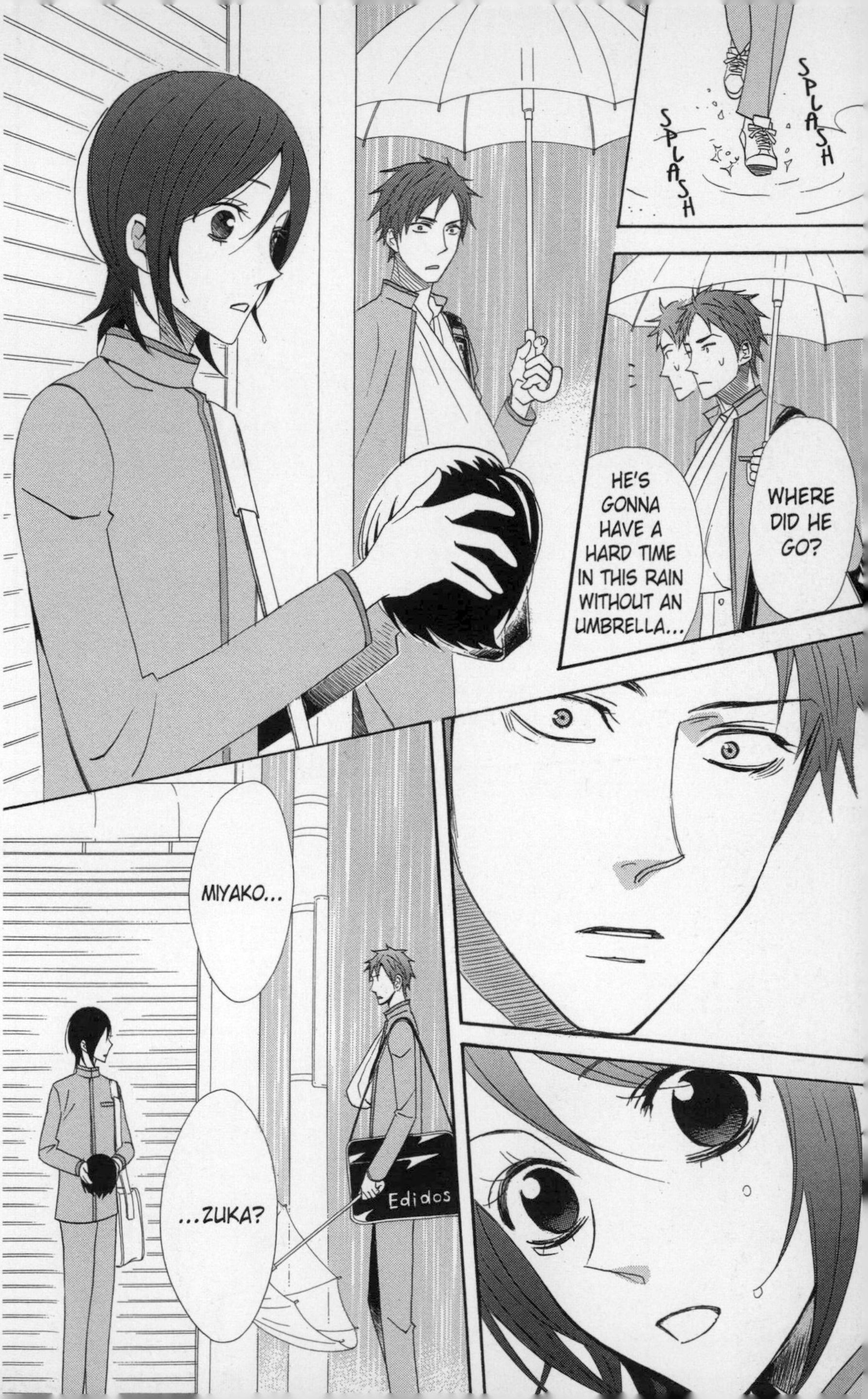
SPLASH
SPLASH
WHERE DID HE GO?
HE'S GONNA HAVE A HARD TIME IN THIS RAIN WITHOUT AN UMBRELLA...
MIYAKO...
Edidos
...ZUKA?

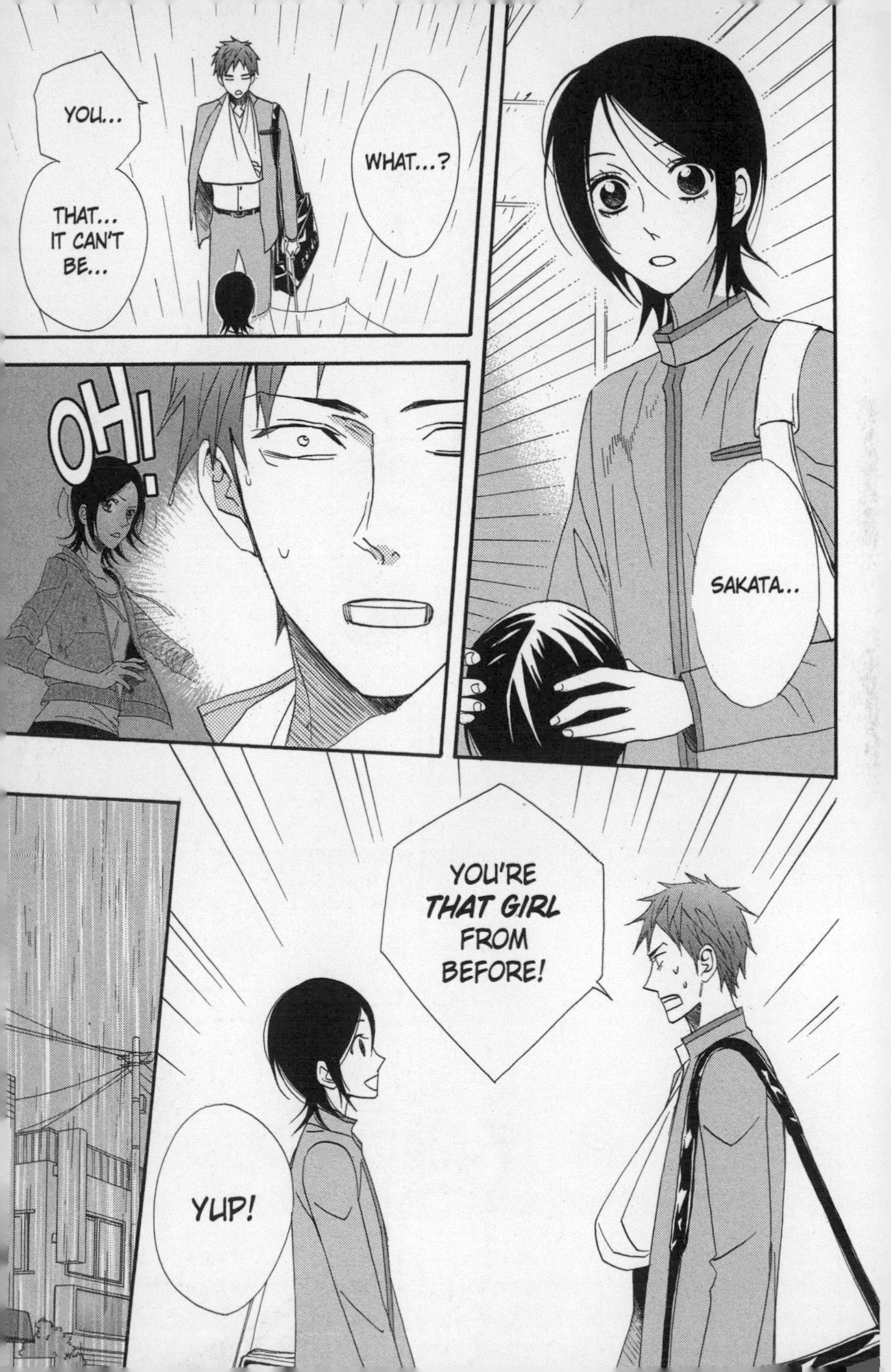
SAKATA...
WHAT...?
YOU...
THAT... IT CAN'T BE...
OH!
YOU'RE *THAT GIRL* FROM BEFORE!
YUP!

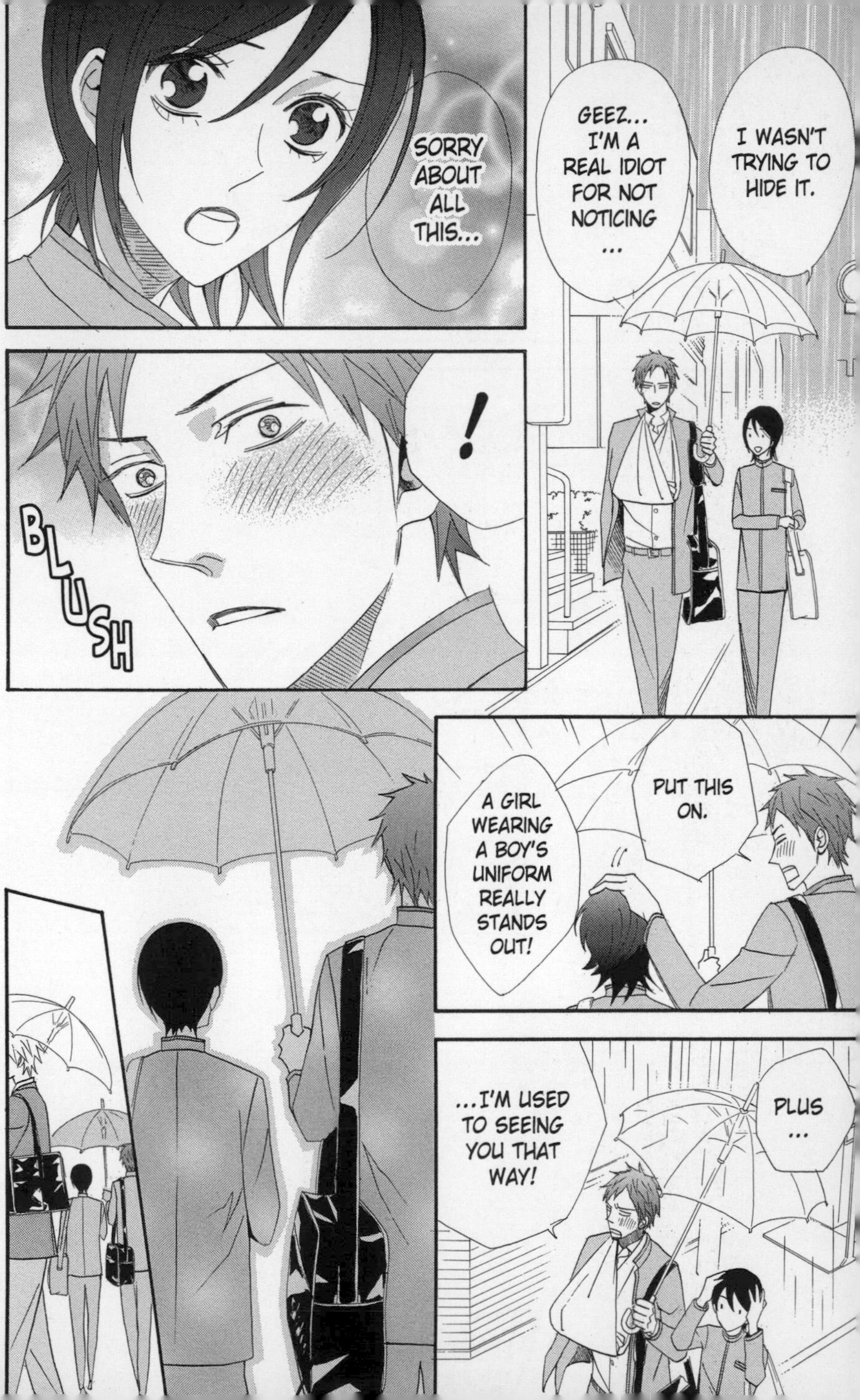
I WASN'T TRYING TO HIDE IT.
GEEZ... I'M A REAL IDIOT FOR NOT NOTICING...
SORRY ABOUT ALL THIS...
!
BLUSH
PUT THIS ON.
A GIRL WEARING A BOY'S UNIFORM REALLY STANDS OUT!
PLUS...
...I'M USED TO SEEING YOU THAT WAY!

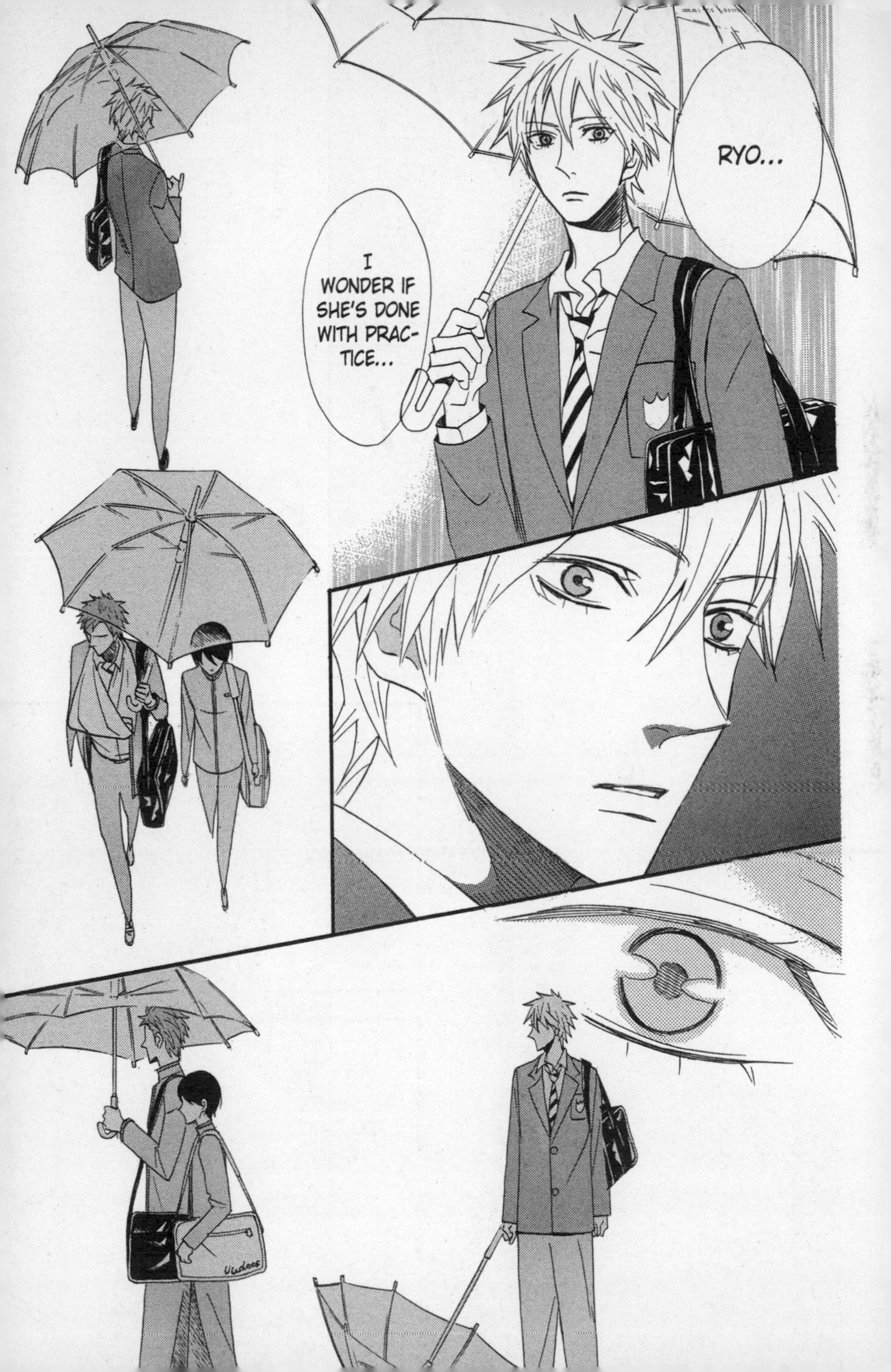
RYO...
I WONDER IF SHE'S DONE WITH PRAC-TICE...

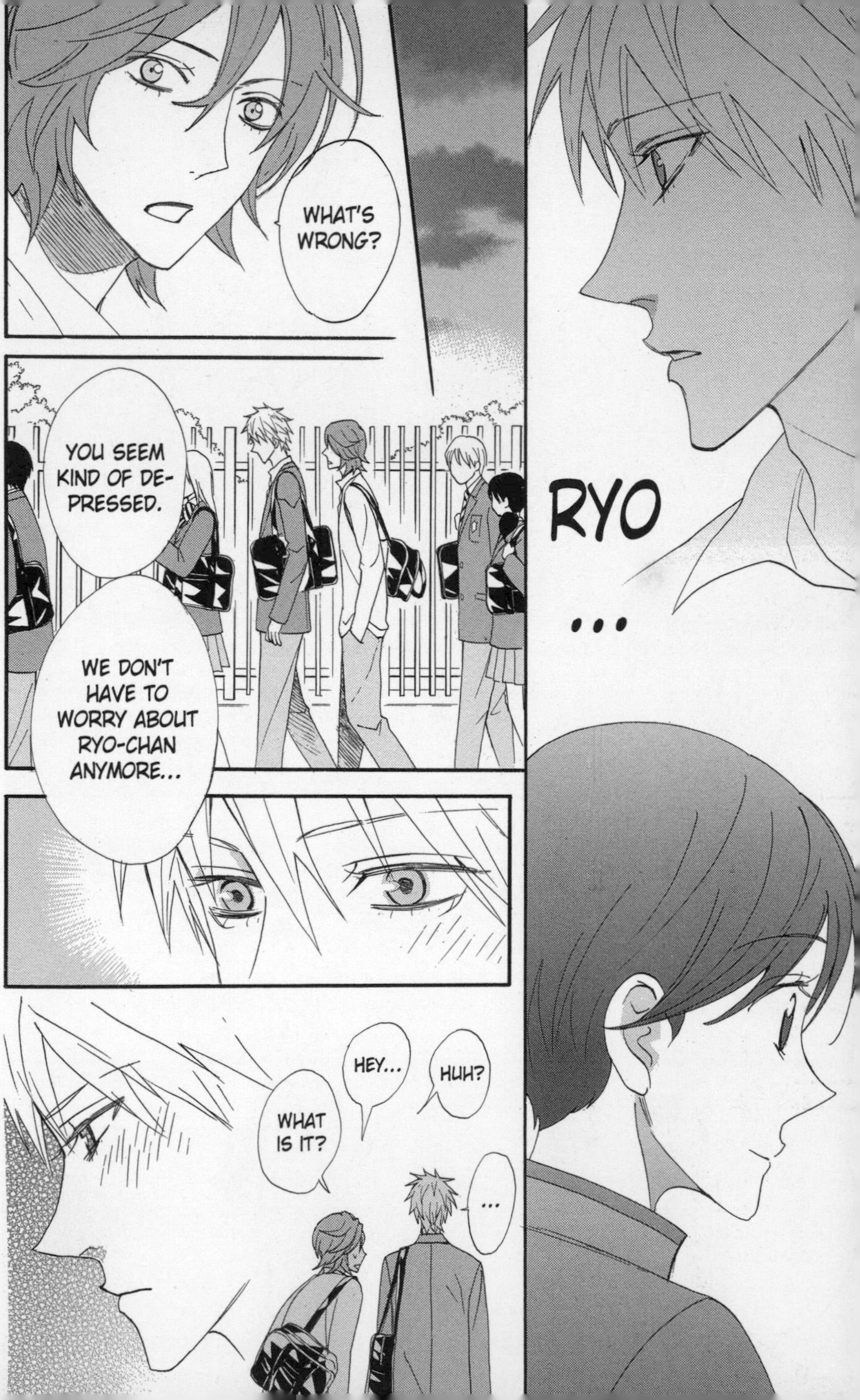
RYO
...
WHAT'S WRONG?
YOU SEEM KIND OF DE-PRESSED.
WE DON'T HAVE TO WORRY ABOUT RYO-CHAN ANYMORE...
HEY...
HUH?
WHAT IS IT?
...

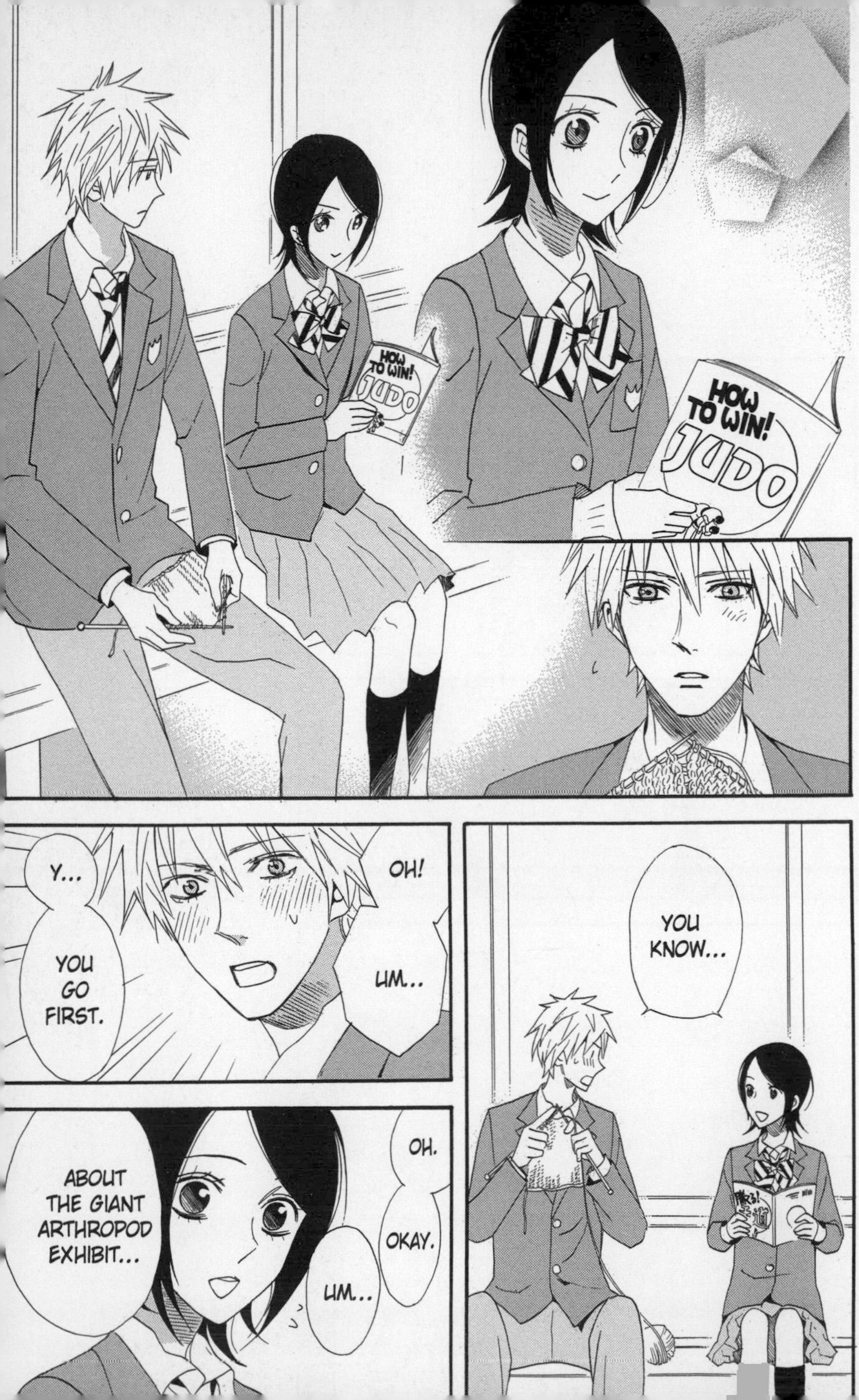
HOW TO WIN! JUDO
HOW TO WIN! JUDO
YOU KNOW...
OH!
UM...
Y...
YOU GO FIRST.
OH.
OKAY.
UM...
ABOUT THE GIANT ARTHROPOD EXHIBIT...

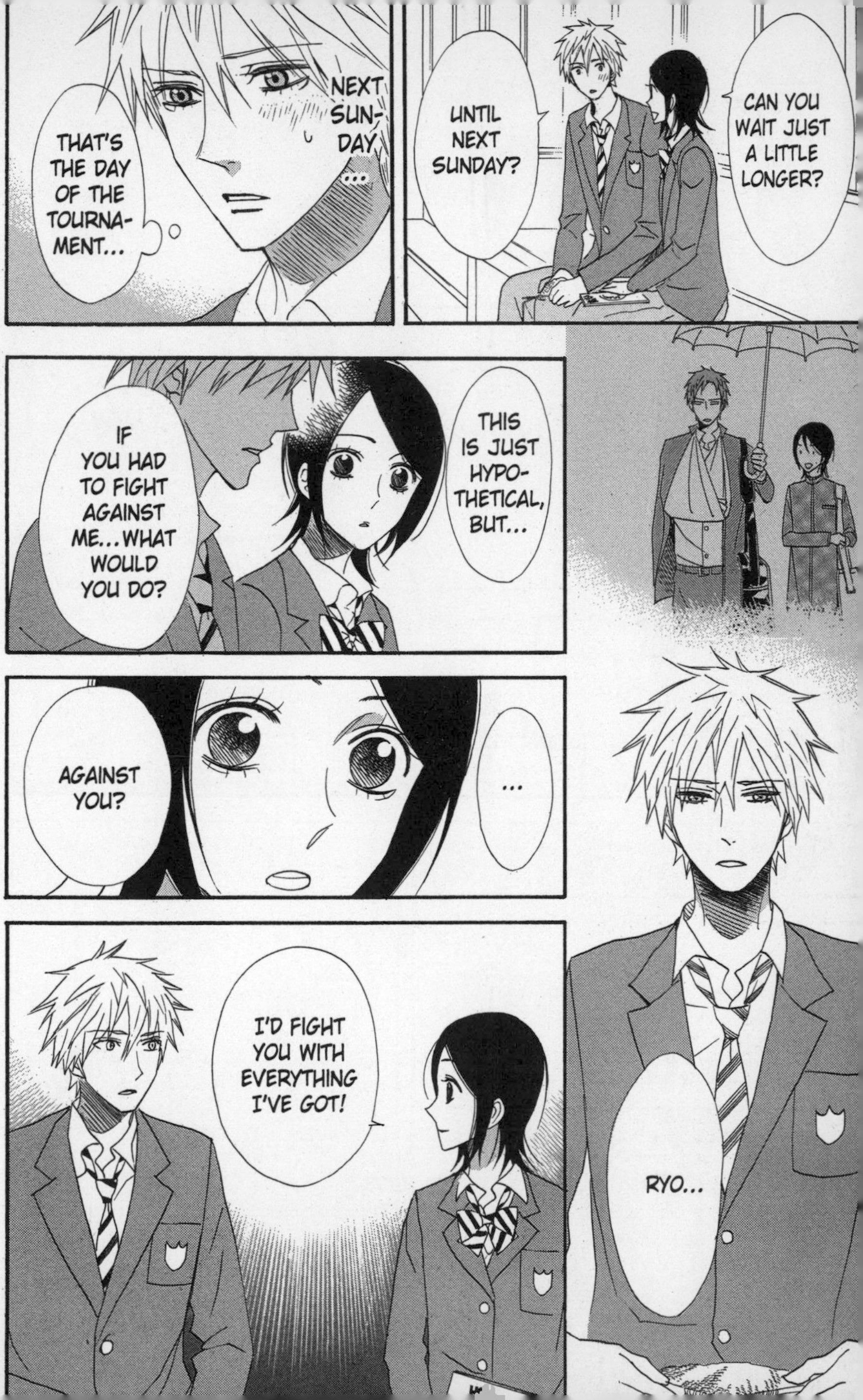
CAN YOU WAIT JUST A LITTLE LONGER?
UNTIL NEXT SUNDAY?
NEXT SUN-DAY...
THAT'S THE DAY OF THE TOURNA-MENT...
THIS IS JUST HYPO-THETICAL, BUT...
IF YOU HAD TO FIGHT AGAINST ME...WHAT WOULD YOU DO?
RYO...
...
AGAINST YOU?
I'D FIGHT YOU WITH EVERYTHING I'VE GOT!

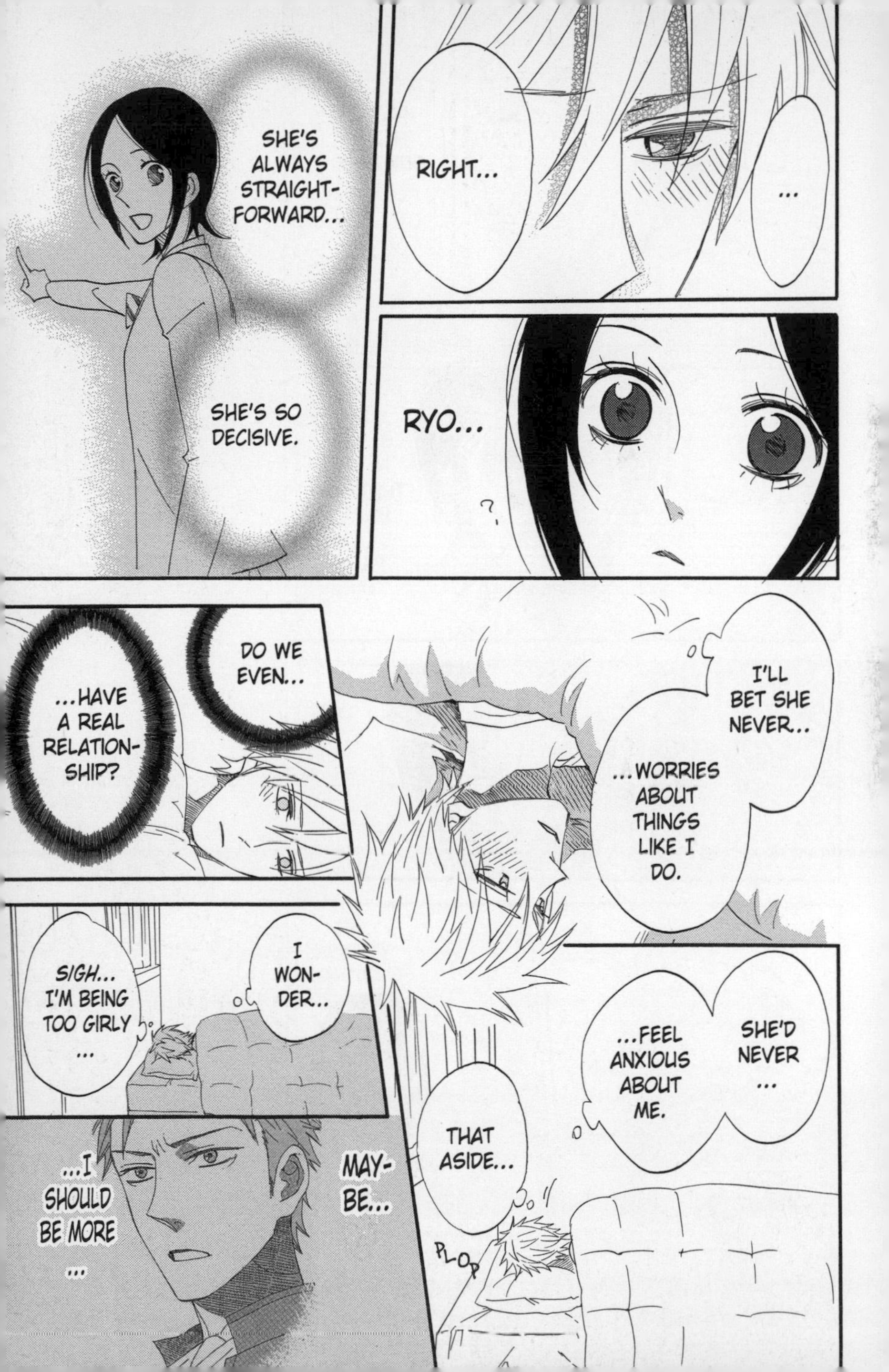
...
RIGHT...
RYO...
?
SHE'S ALWAYS STRAIGHT-FORWARD...
SHE'S SO DECISIVE.
I'LL BET SHE NEVER...
...WORRIES ABOUT THINGS LIKE I DO.
DO WE EVEN...
...HAVE A REAL RELATION-SHIP?
SHE'D NEVER...
...FEEL ANXIOUS ABOUT ME.
THAT ASIDE...
PLOP
I WON-DER...
SIGH... I'M BEING TOO GIRLY...
MAY-BE...
...I SHOULD BE MORE...

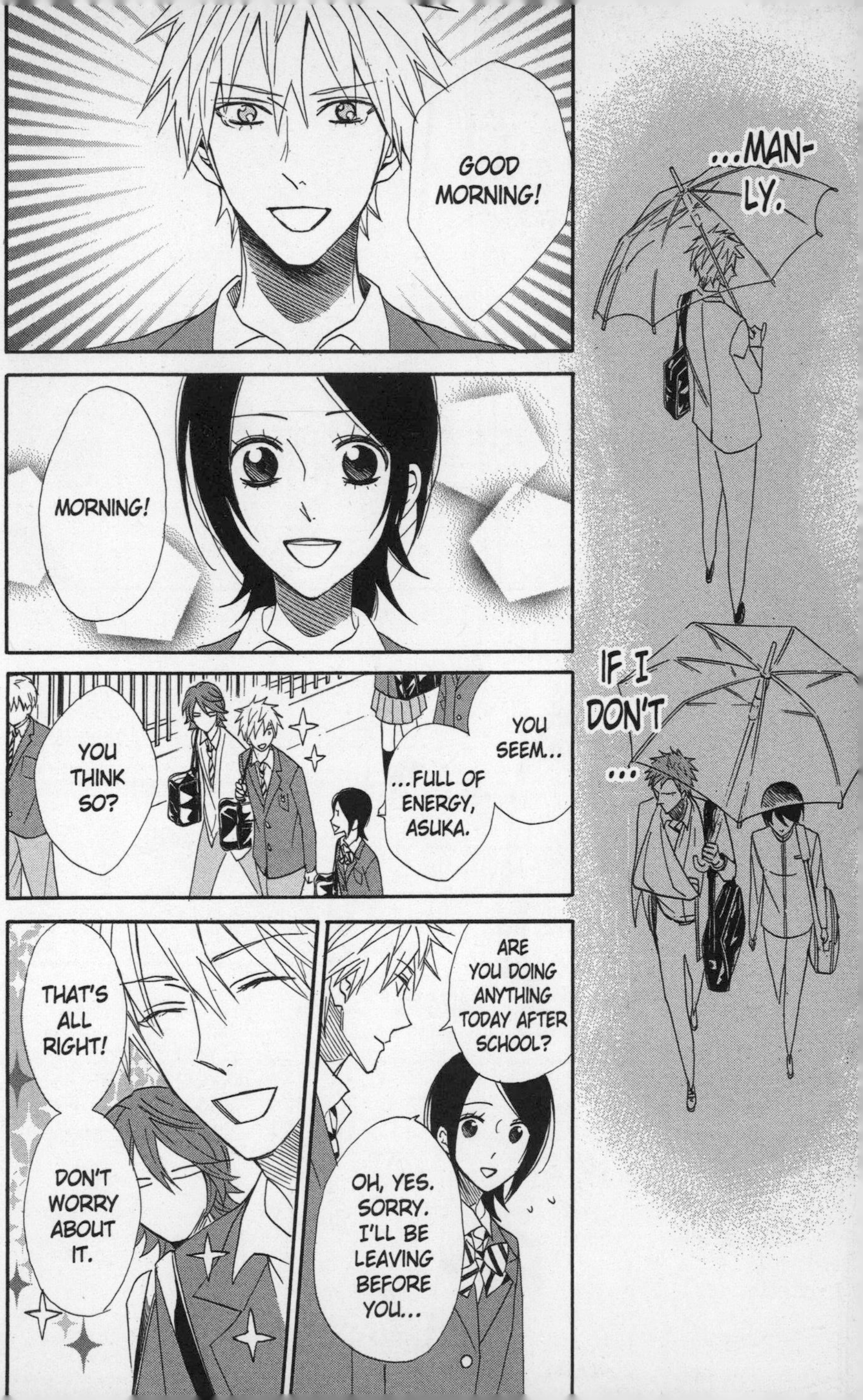

...MAN-LY.
IF I DON'T ...
GOOD MORNING!
MORNING!
YOU SEEM...
...FULL OF ENERGY, ASUKA.
YOU THINK SO?
ARE YOU DOING ANYTHING TODAY AFTER SCHOOL?
OH, YES. SORRY. I'LL BE LEAVING BEFORE YOU...
THAT'S ALL RIGHT!
DON'T WORRY ABOUT IT.

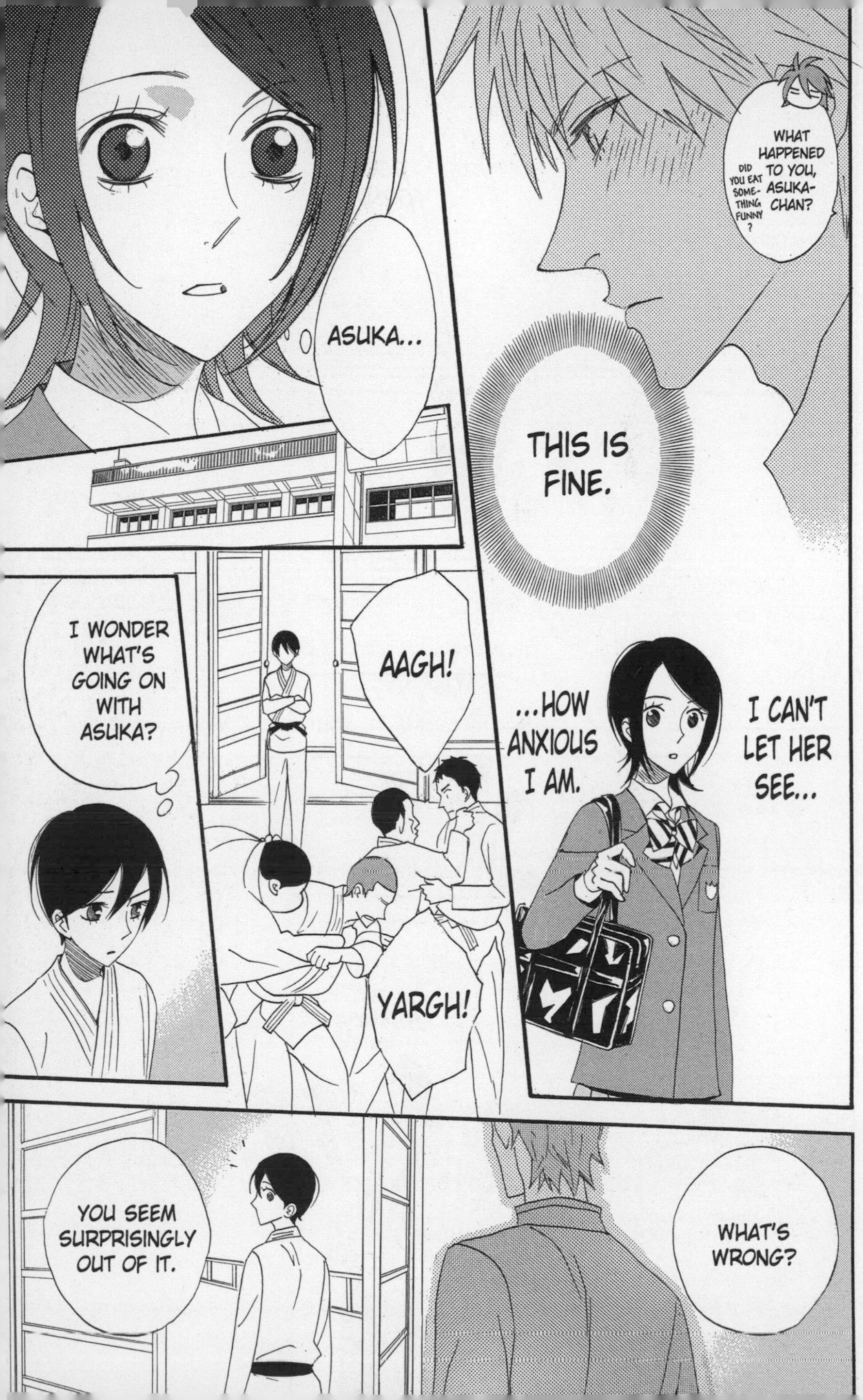

WHAT HAPPENED TO YOU, ASUKA-CHAN?
DID YOU EAT SOMETHING FUNNY?
THIS IS FINE.
ASUKA...
I CAN'T LET HER SEE...
...HOW ANXIOUS I AM.
AAGH!
YARGH!
I WONDER WHAT'S GOING ON WITH ASUKA?
WHAT'S WRONG?
YOU SEEM SURPRISINGLY OUT OF IT.

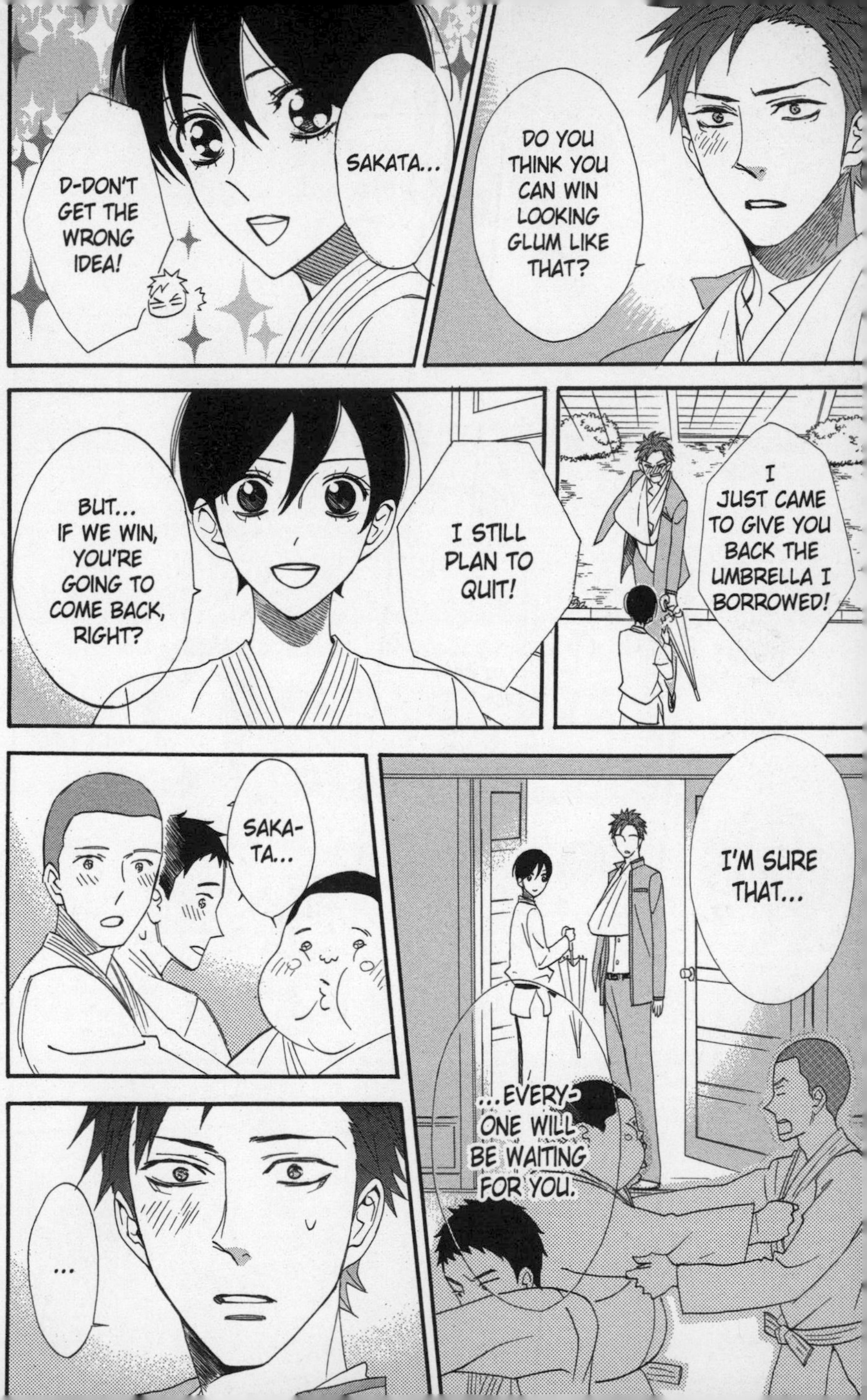
DO YOU THINK YOU CAN WIN LOOKING GLUM LIKE THAT?
SAKATA...
D-DON'T GET THE WRONG IDEA!
I JUST CAME TO GIVE YOU BACK THE UMBRELLA I BORROWED!
I STILL PLAN TO QUIT!
BUT... IF WE WIN, YOU'RE GOING TO COME BACK, RIGHT?
I'M SURE THAT...
...EVERY-ONE WILL BE WAITING FOR YOU.
SAKA-TA...
...

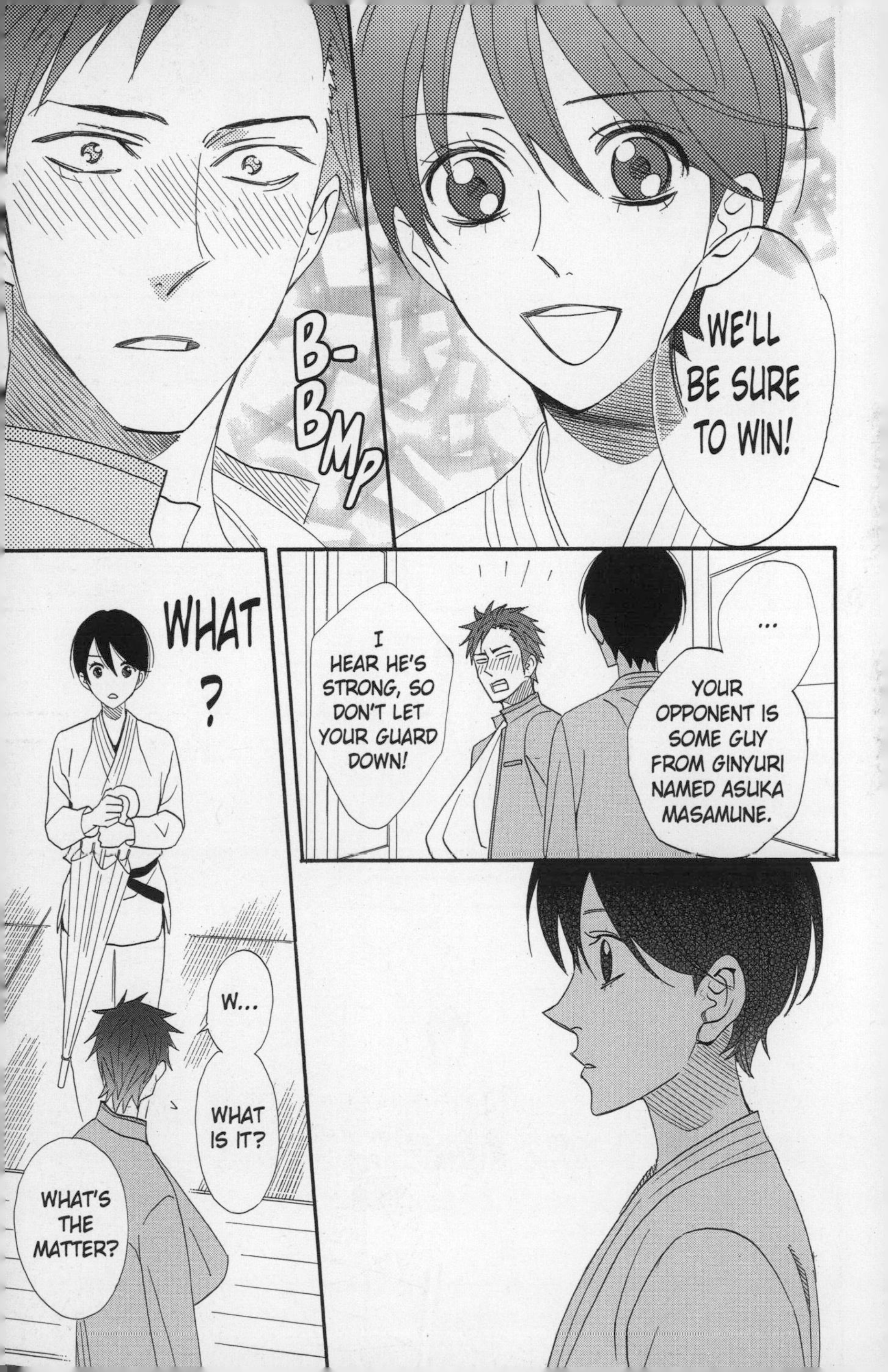
WE'LL BE SURE TO WIN!
B-BMP
...
YOUR OPPONENT IS SOME GUY FROM GINYURI NAMED ASUKA MASAMUNE.
I HEAR HE'S STRONG, SO DON'T LET YOUR GUARD DOWN!
WHAT ?
W...
WHAT IS IT?
WHAT'S THE MATTER?

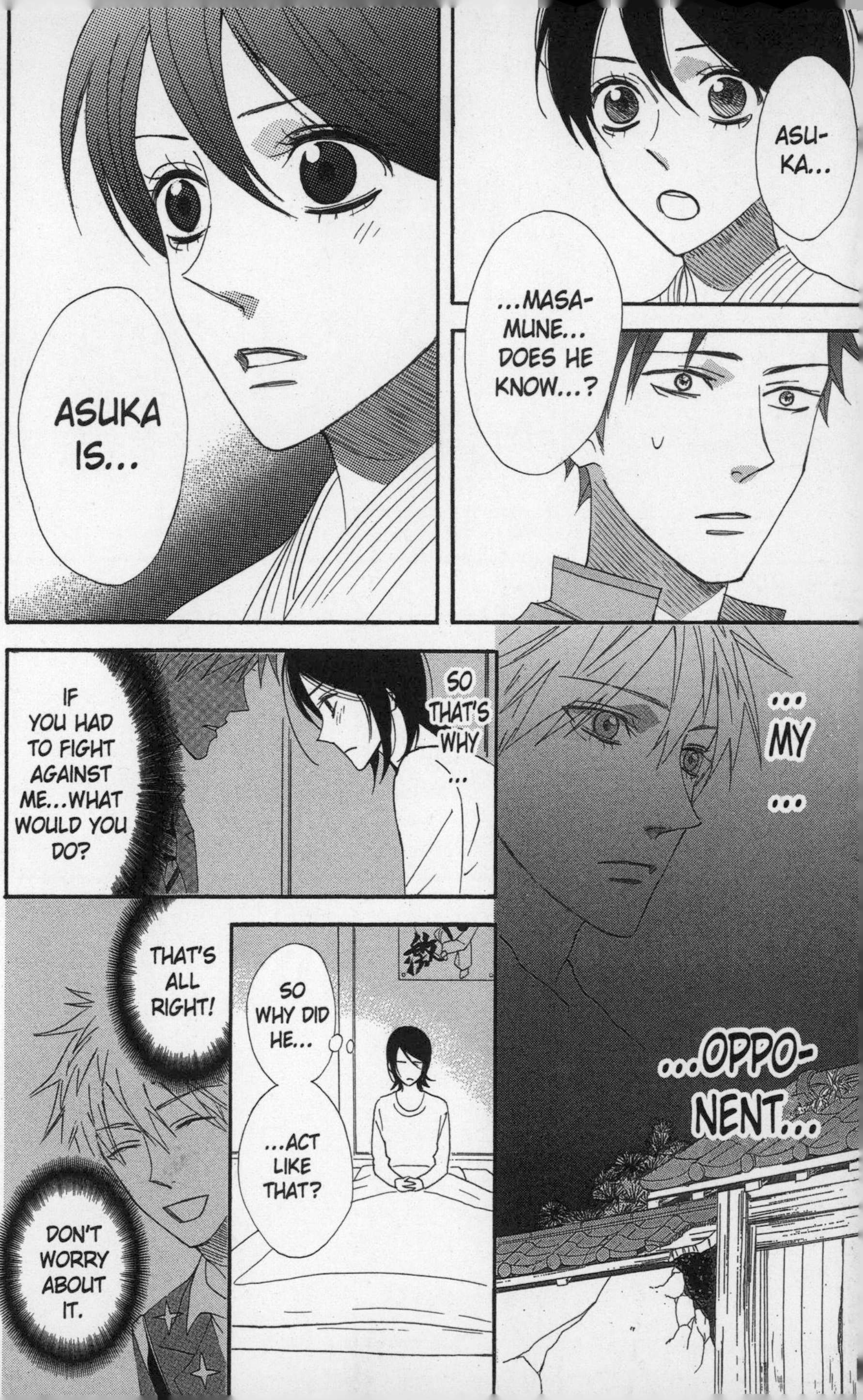
ASU-KA...
...MASA-MUNE... DOES HE KNOW...?
ASUKA IS...
...MY...
...OPPO-NENT...
SO THAT'S WHY...
IF YOU HAD TO FIGHT AGAINST ME...WHAT WOULD YOU DO?
SO WHY DID HE...
...ACT LIKE THAT?
THAT'S ALL RIGHT!
DON'T WORRY ABOUT IT.

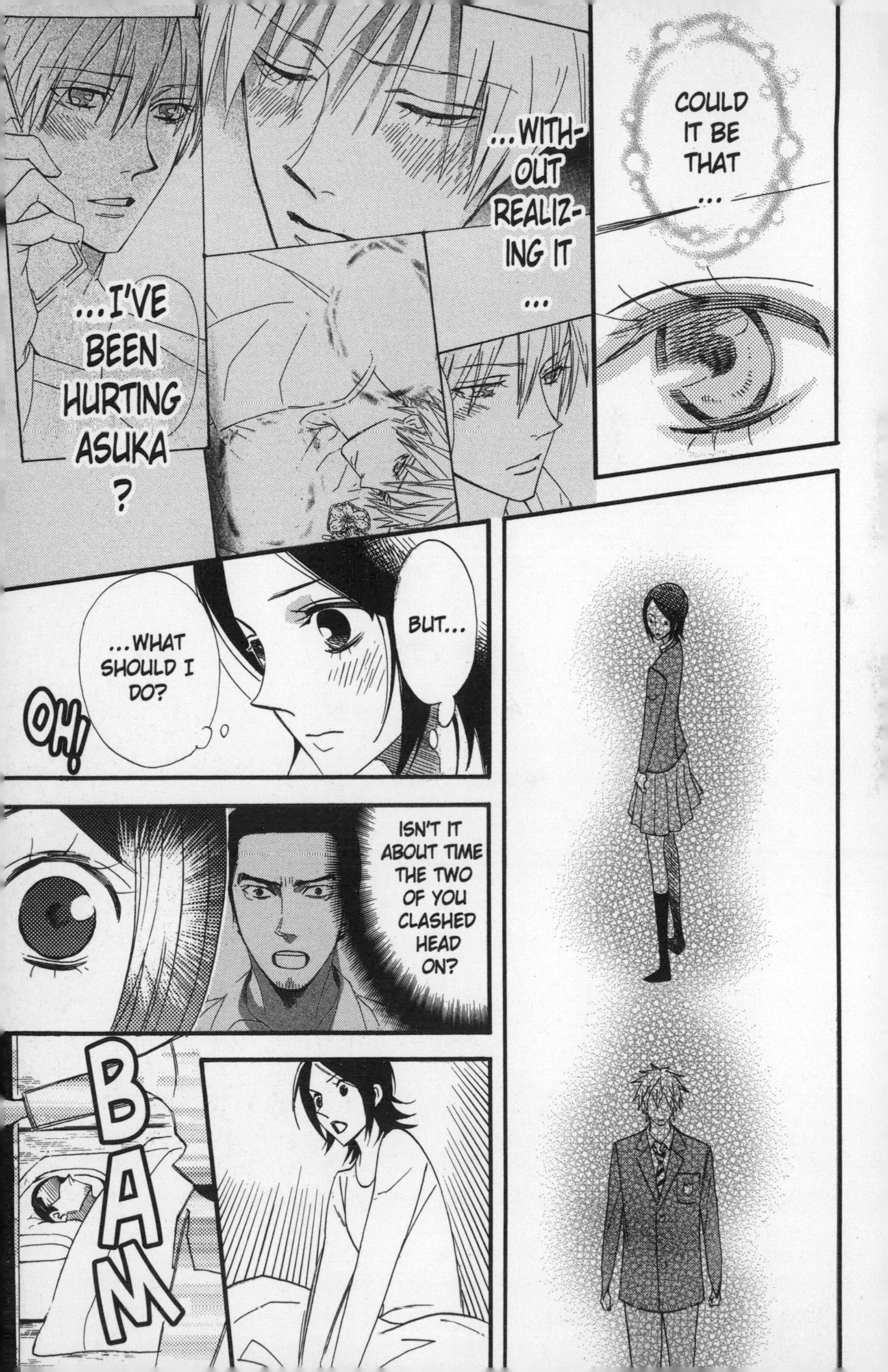
COULD IT BE THAT ...
...WITHOUT REALIZING IT ...
...I'VE BEEN HURTING ASUKA ?
BUT...
...WHAT SHOULD I DO?
OH!
ISN'T IT ABOUT TIME THE TWO OF YOU CLASHED HEAD ON?
BAM

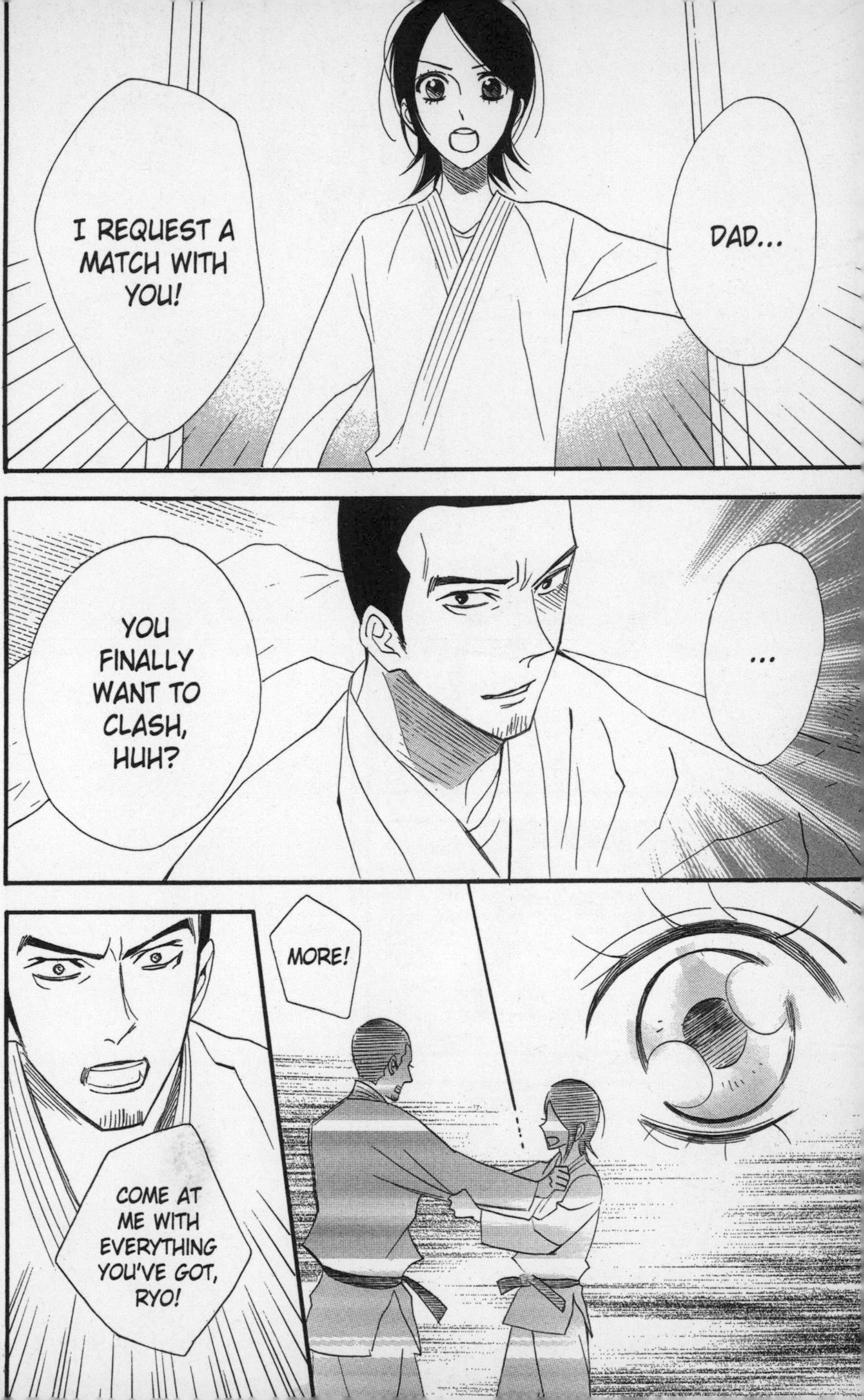
DAD...
I REQUEST A MATCH WITH YOU!
...
YOU FINALLY WANT TO CLASH, HUH?
MORE!
COME AT ME WITH EVERYTHING YOU'VE GOT, RYO!

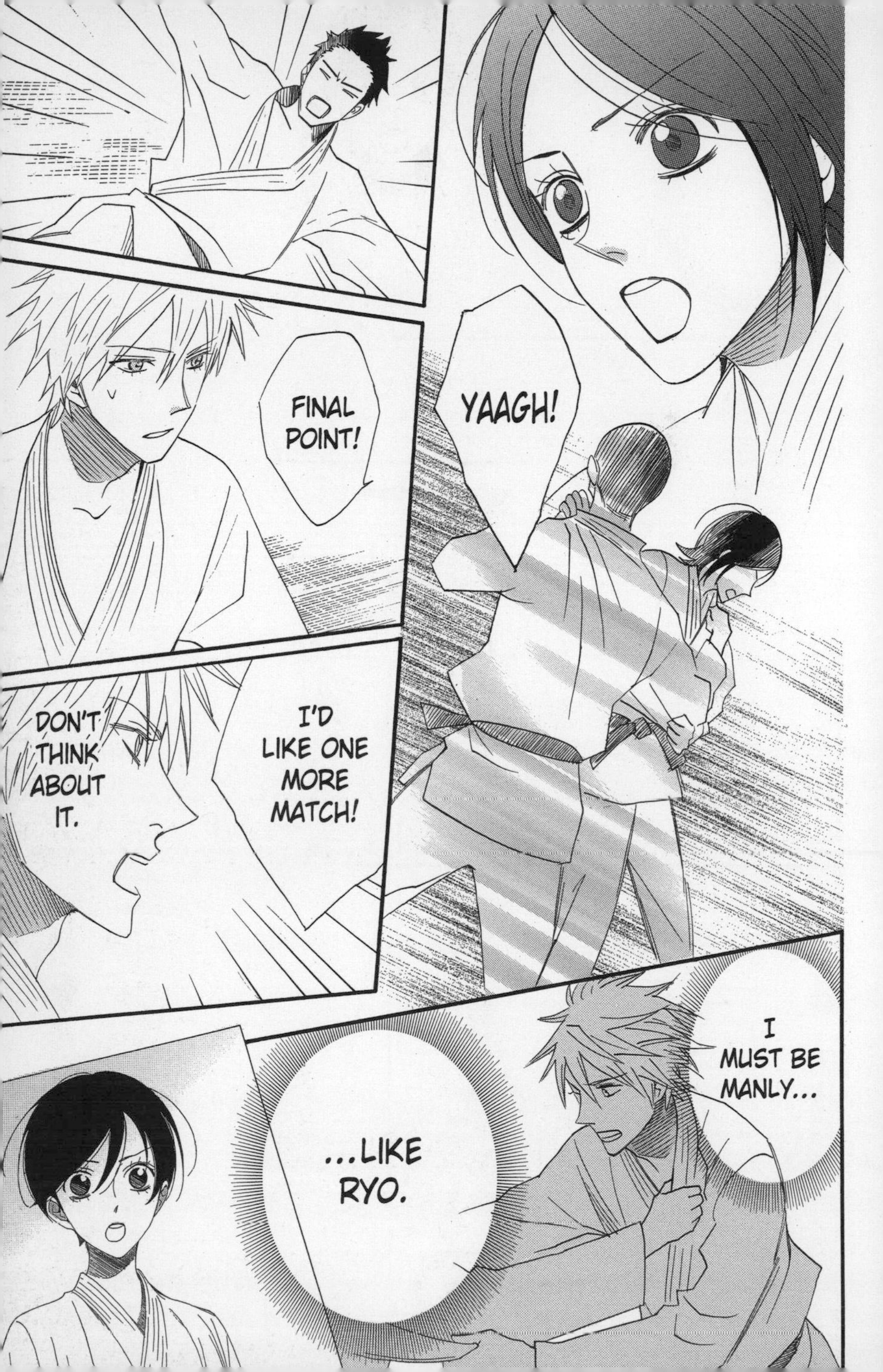
YAAGH!
FINAL POINT!
I'D LIKE ONE MORE MATCH!
DON'T THINK ABOUT IT.
I MUST BE MANLY...
...LIKE RYO.

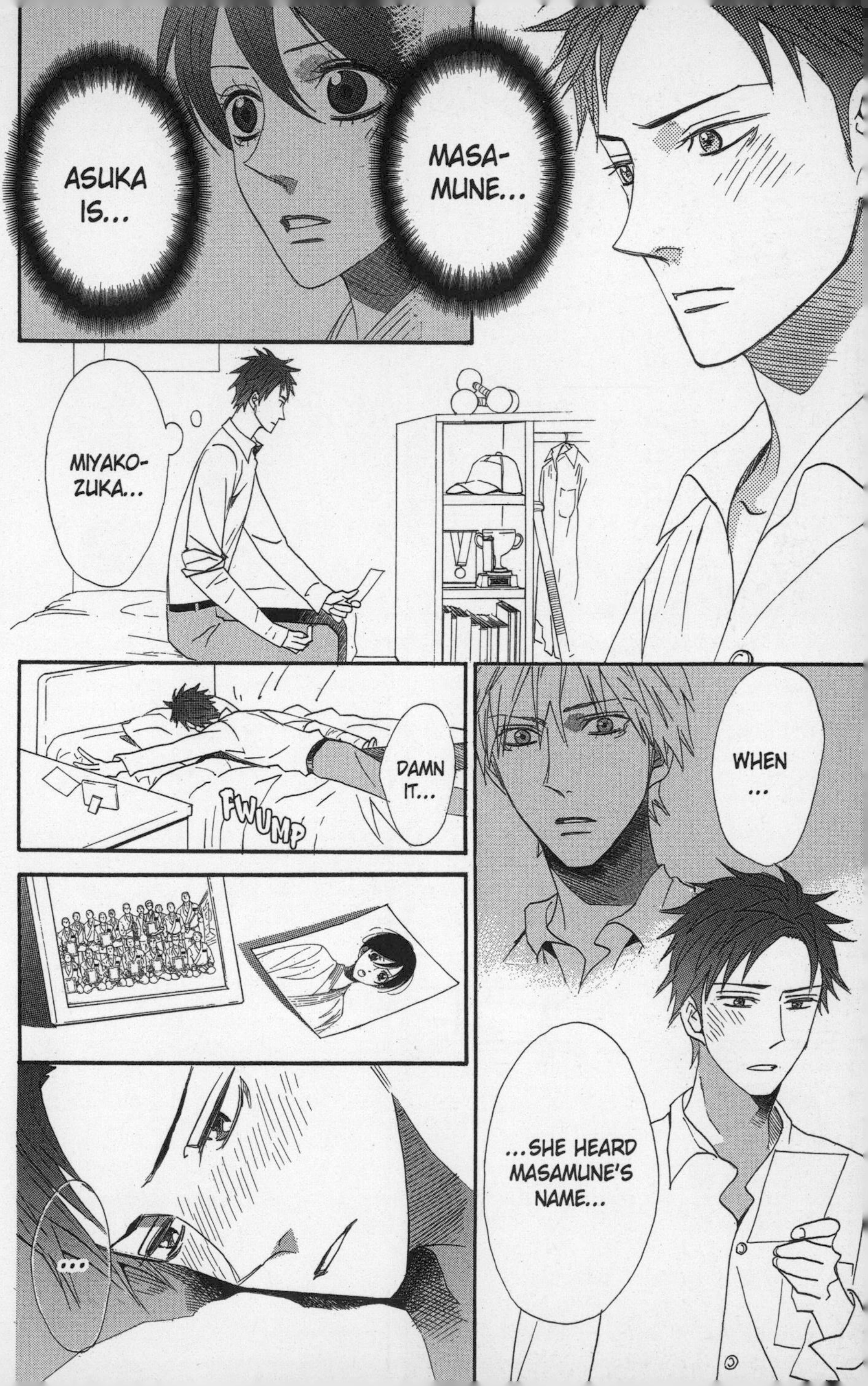
MASA-MUNE...
ASUKA IS...
MIYAKO-ZUKA...
WHEN ...
...SHE HEARD MASAMUNE'S NAME...
DAMN IT...
FWUMP
...

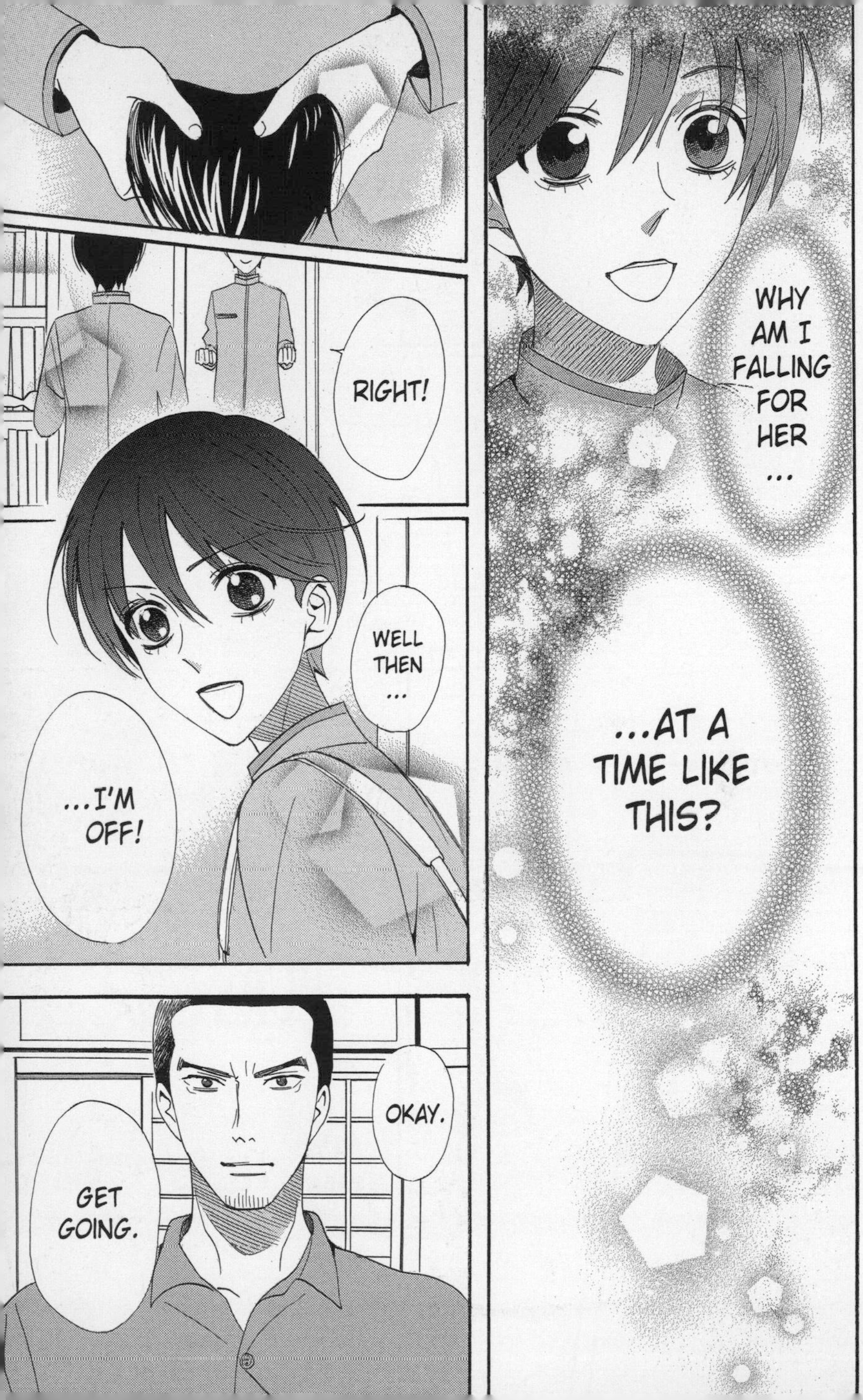
WHY AM I FALLING FOR HER ...
...AT A TIME LIKE THIS?
RIGHT!
WELL THEN ...
...I'M OFF!
OKAY.
GET GOING.

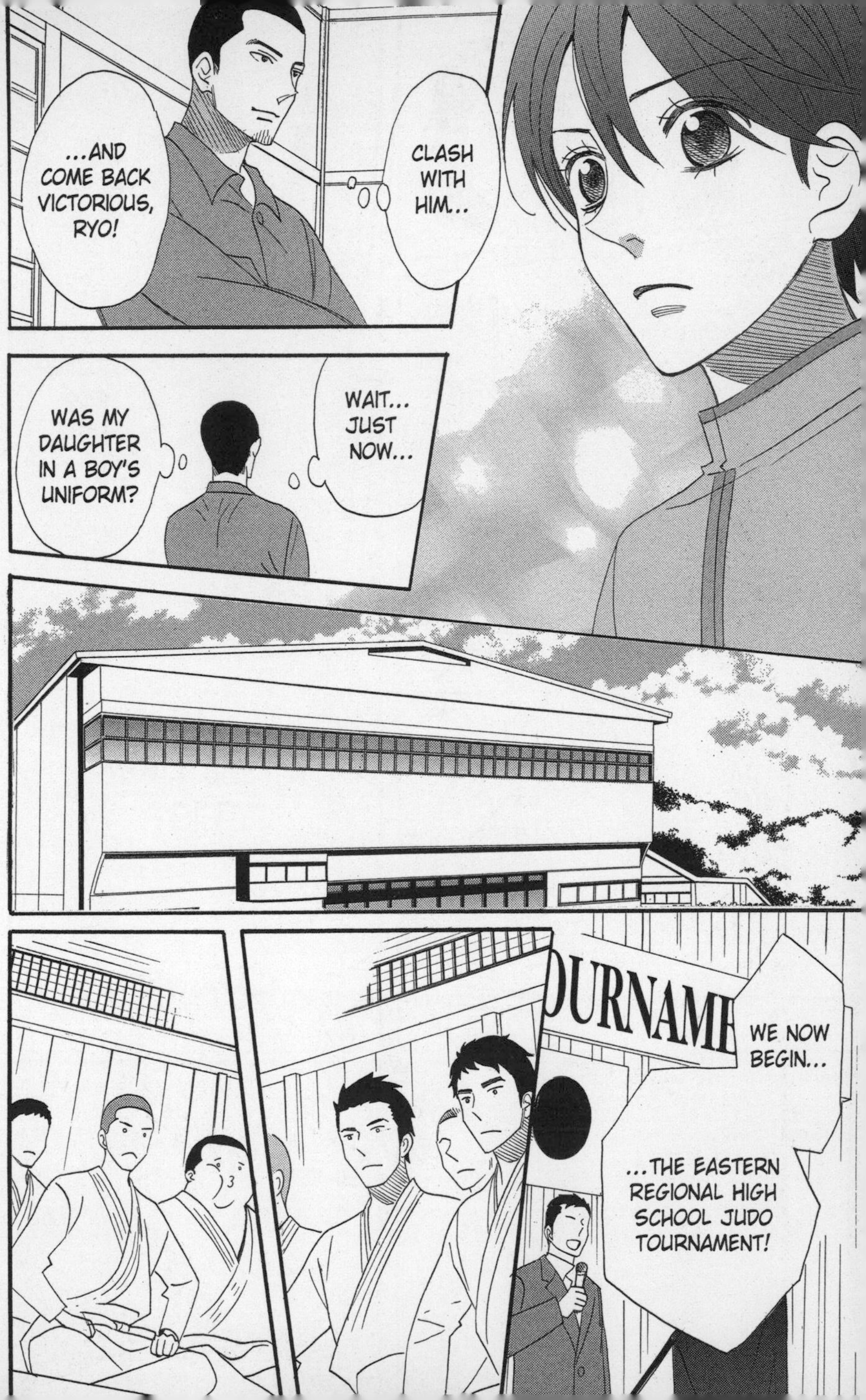
CLASH WITH HIM...
...AND COME BACK VICTORIOUS, RYO!
WAIT... JUST NOW...
WAS MY DAUGHTER IN A BOY'S UNIFORM?
OURNAME
WE NOW BEGIN...
...THE EASTERN REGIONAL HIGH SCHOOL JUDO TOURNAMENT!

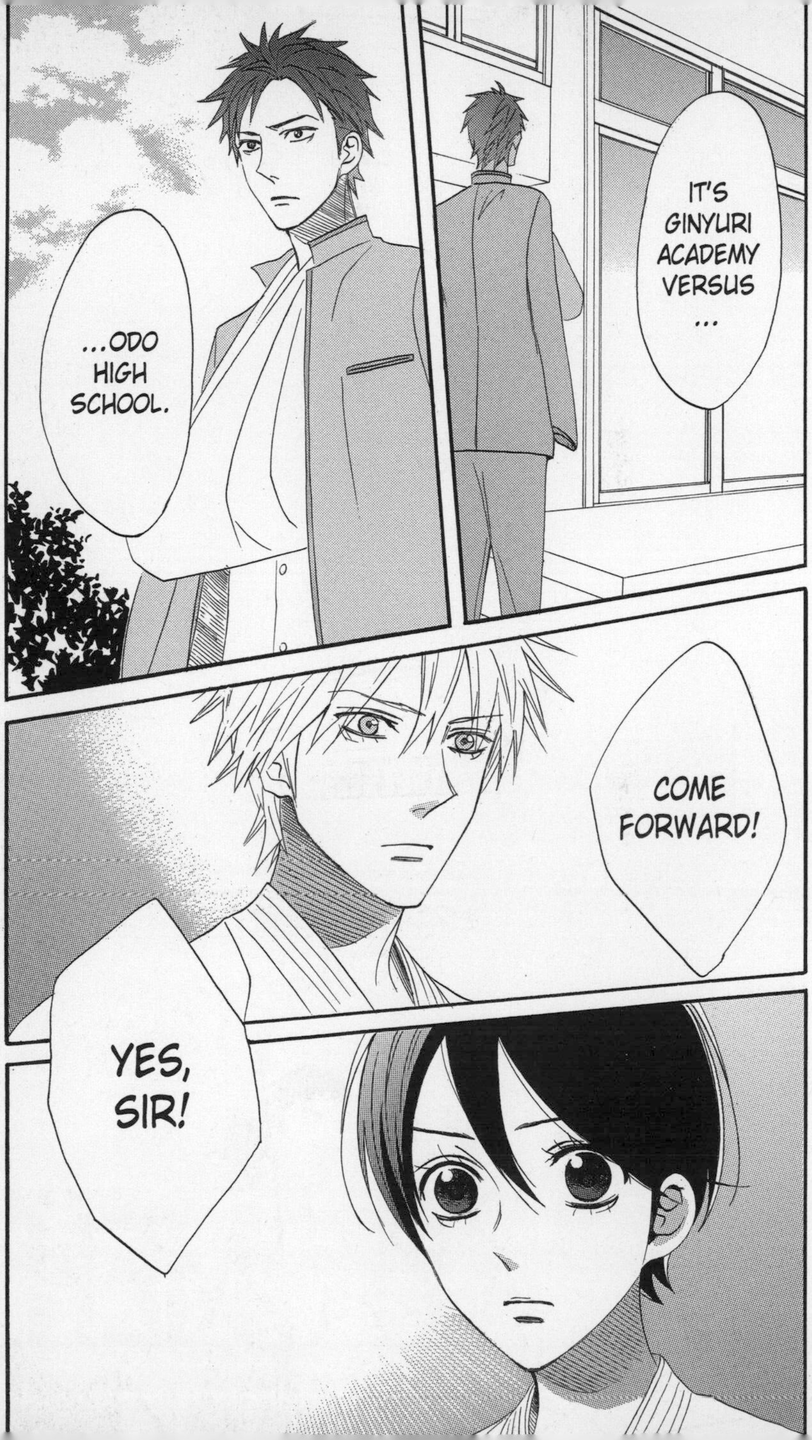
IT'S GINYURI ACADEMY VERSUS ...
...ODO HIGH SCHOOL.
COME FORWARD!
YES, SIR!

OTOMEN

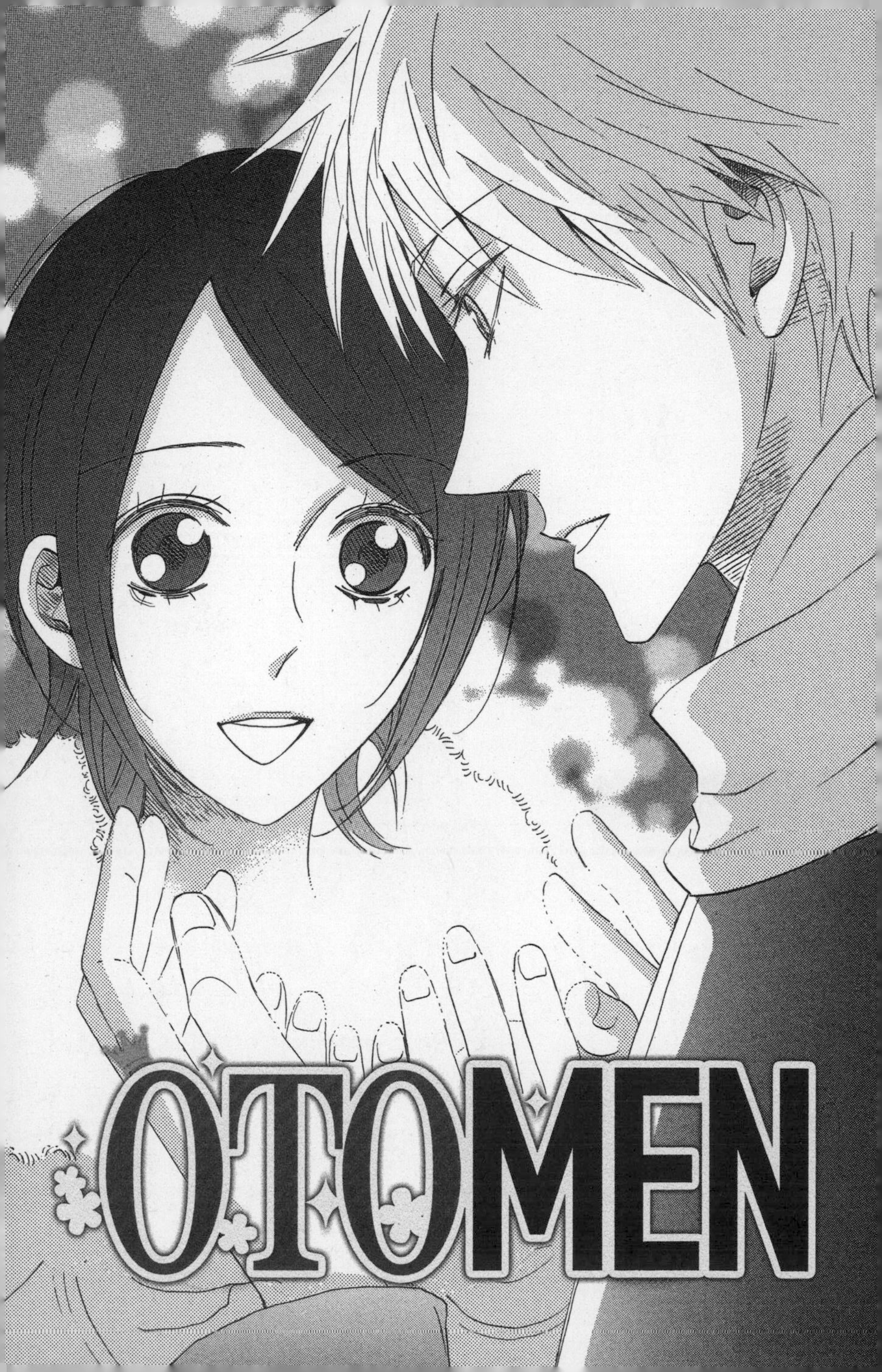
OTOMEN

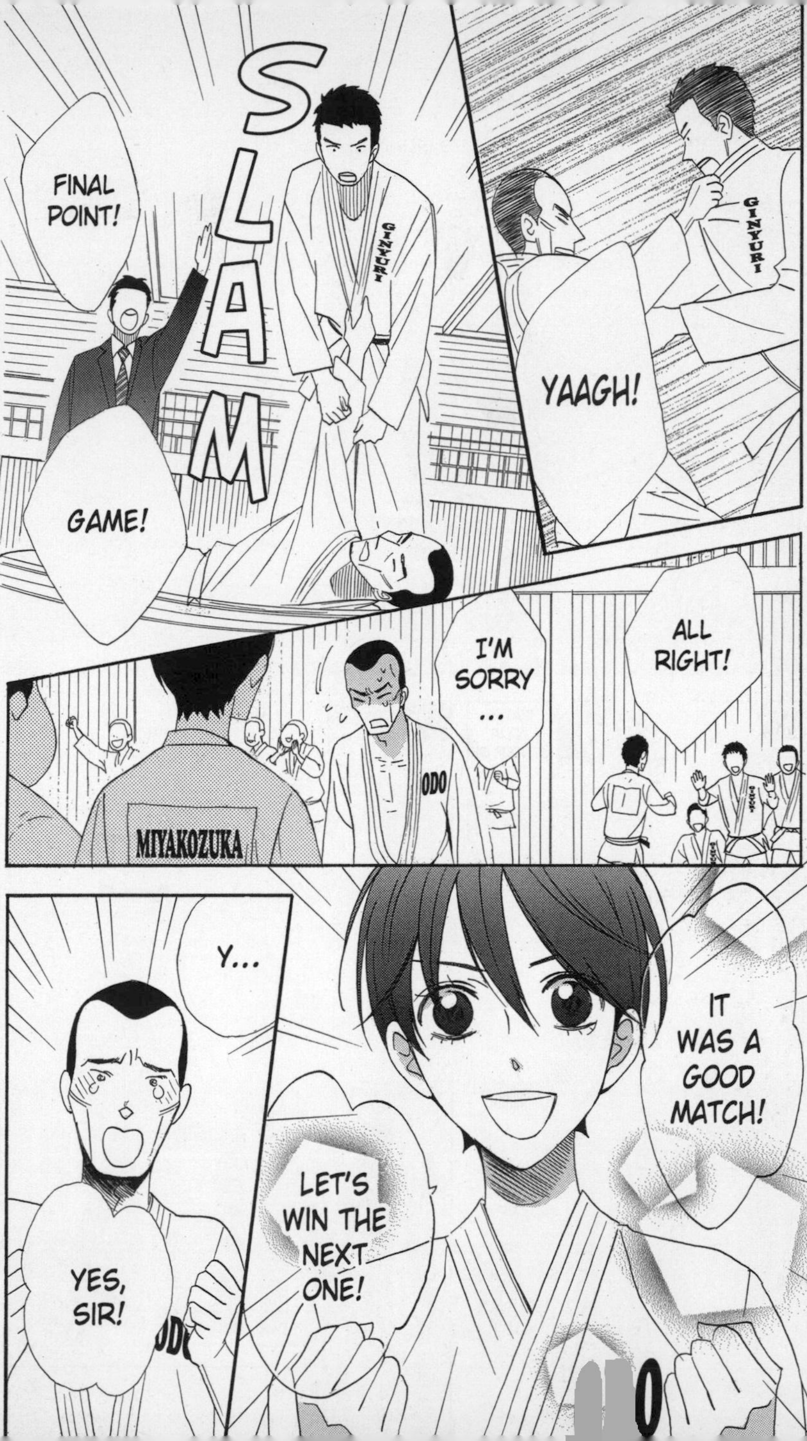
GINYURI
YAAGH!
SLAM
GINYURI
FINAL POINT!
GAME!
ALL RIGHT!
I'M SORRY ...
ODO
MIYAKOZUKA
IT WAS A GOOD MATCH!
LET'S WIN THE NEXT ONE!
Y...
YES, SIR!

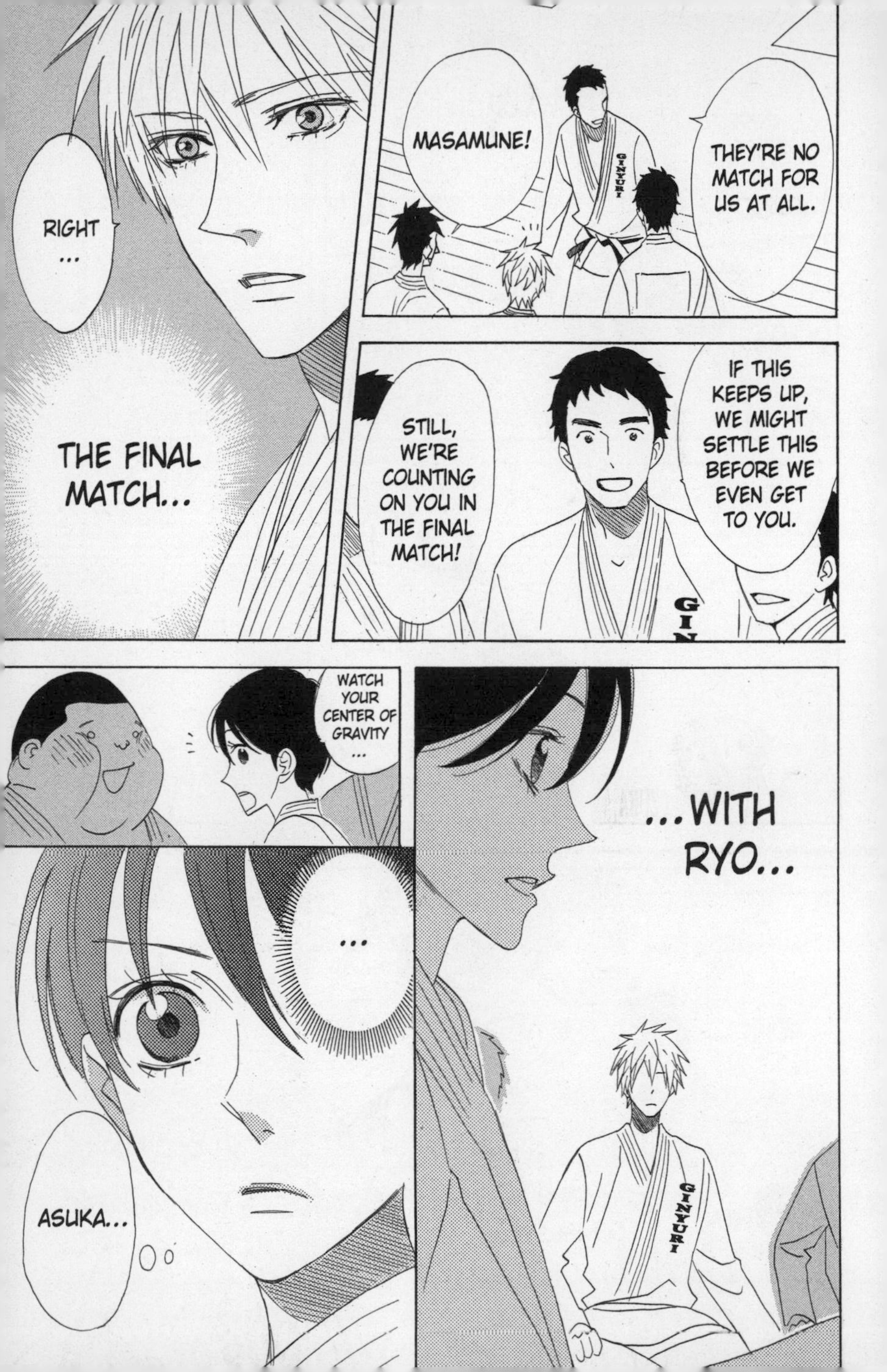
THEY'RE NO MATCH FOR US AT ALL.
MASAMUNE!
IF THIS KEEPS UP, WE MIGHT SETTLE THIS BEFORE WE EVEN GET TO YOU.
STILL, WE'RE COUNTING ON YOU IN THE FINAL MATCH!
RIGHT ...
THE FINAL MATCH...
...WITH RYO...
WATCH YOUR CENTER OF GRAVITY ...
...
ASUKA...

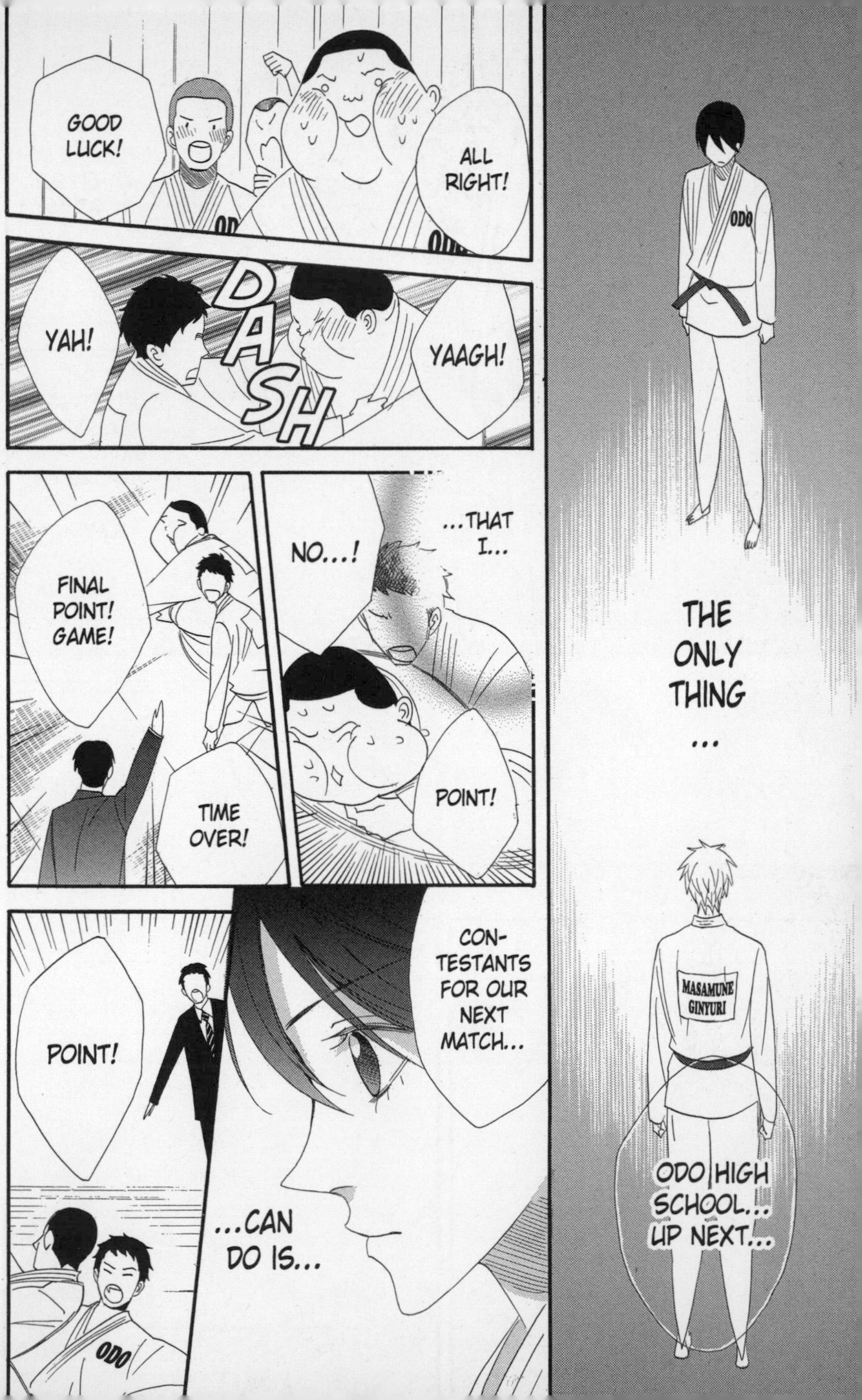
THE ONLY THING ...
ODO HIGH SCHOOL... UP NEXT...
ODO
MASAMUNE GINYURI
ALL RIGHT!
GOOD LUCK!
ODO
YAAGH!
DASH
YAH!
...THAT I...
NO...!
POINT!
FINAL POINT! GAME!
TIME OVER!
CON-TESTANTS FOR OUR NEXT MATCH...
...CAN DO IS...
POINT!
ODO

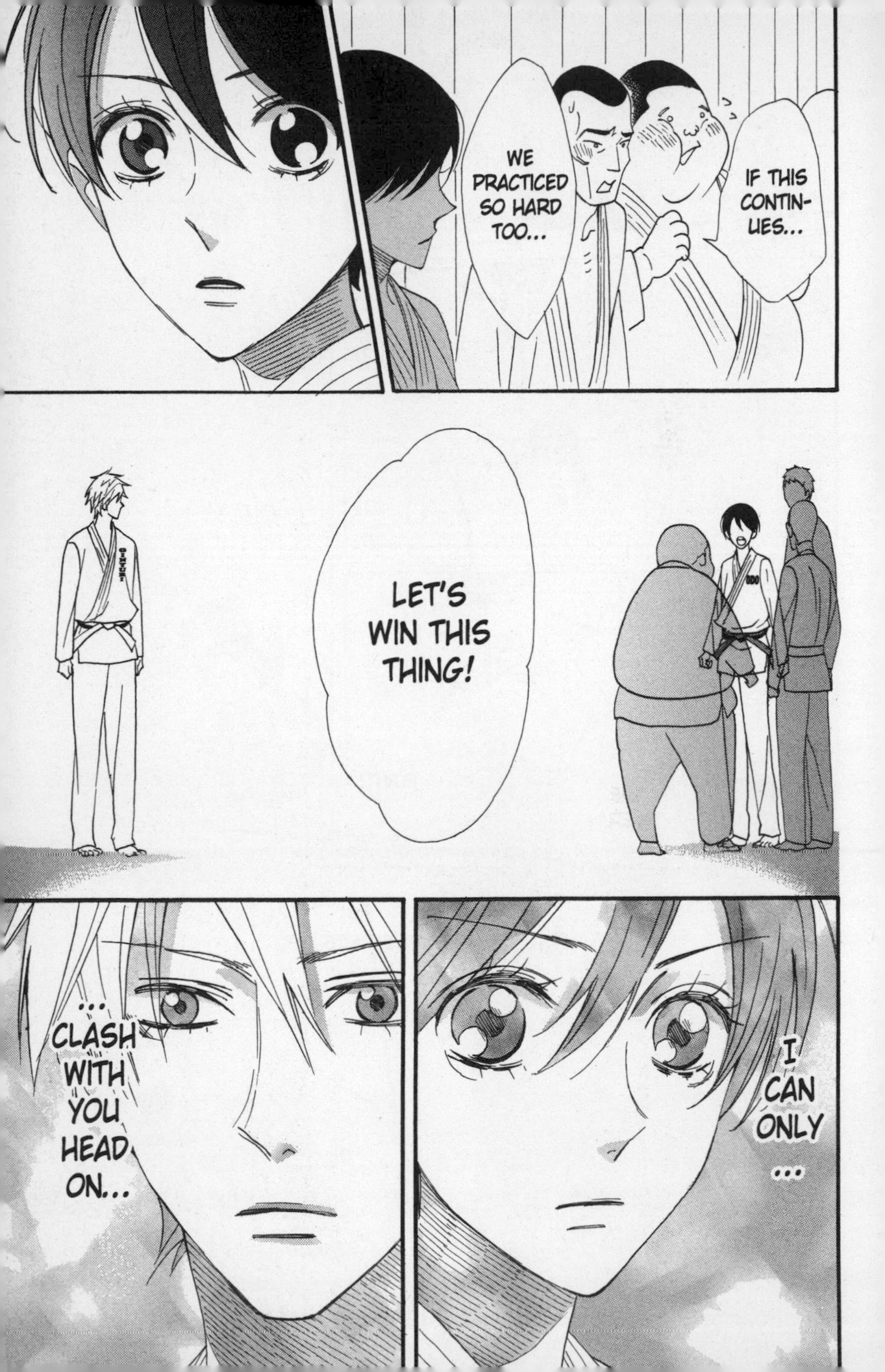
IF THIS CONTIN-UES...
WE PRACTICED SO HARD TOO...
LET'S WIN THIS THING!
I CAN ONLY ...
...CLASH WITH YOU HEAD ON...

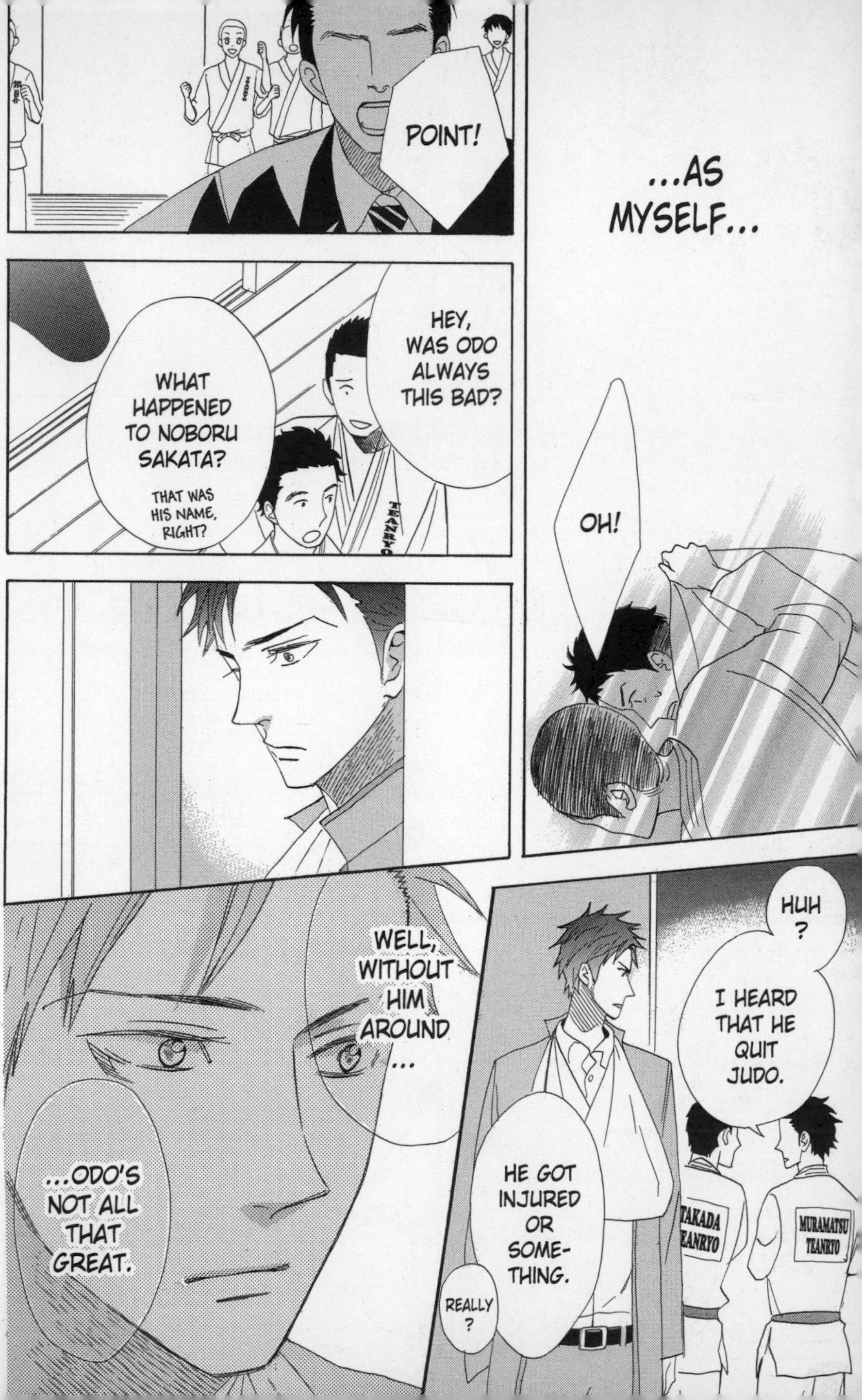
...AS MYSELF...
OH!
POINT!
HEY, WAS ODO ALWAYS THIS BAD?
WHAT HAPPENED TO NOBORU SAKATA?
THAT WAS HIS NAME, RIGHT?
TEANRYO
HUH?
I HEARD THAT HE QUIT JUDO.
HE GOT INJURED OR SOME-THING.
REALLY?
TAKADA
MURAMATSU TEANRYO
WELL, WITHOUT HIM AROUND...
...ODO'S NOT ALL THAT GREAT.

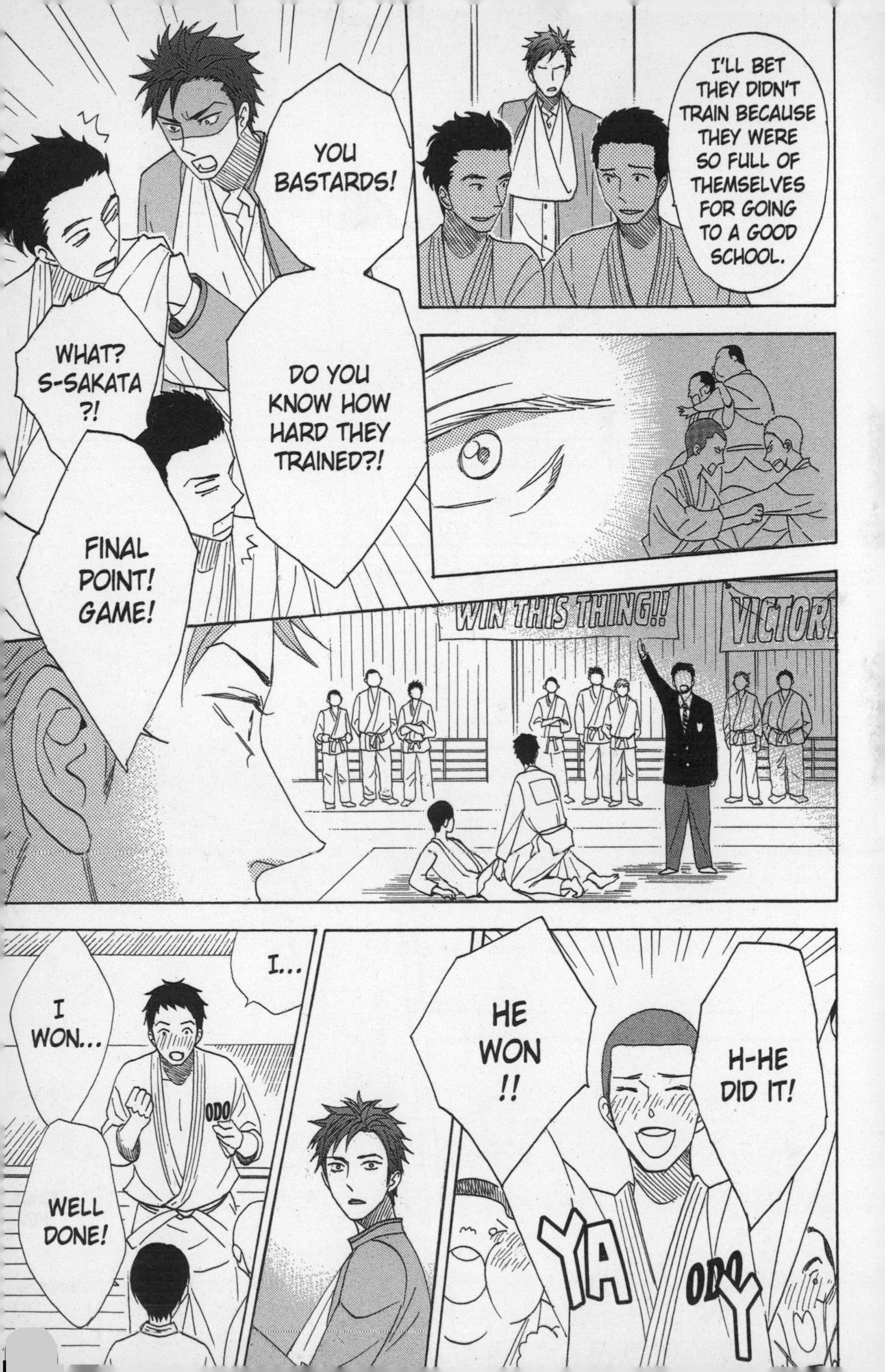
I'LL BET THEY DIDN'T TRAIN BECAUSE THEY WERE SO FULL OF THEMSELVES FOR GOING TO A GOOD SCHOOL.
YOU BASTARDS!
WHAT? S-SAKATA ?!
DO YOU KNOW HOW HARD THEY TRAINED?!
FINAL POINT! GAME!
WIN THIS THING!!
VICTORI
H-HE DID IT!
HE WON !!
YAY
ODO
I...
I WON...
ODO
WELL DONE!

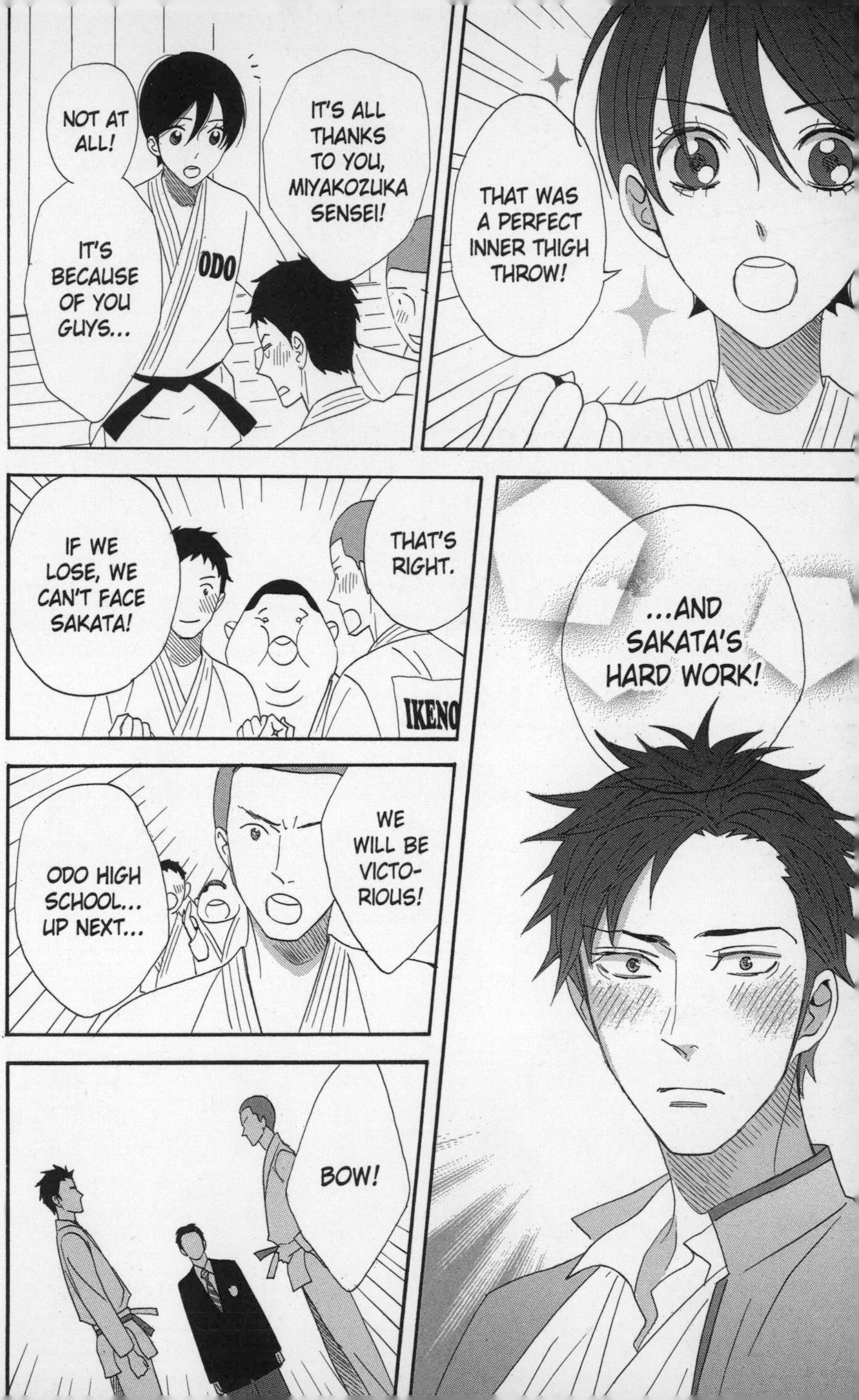
THAT WAS A PERFECT INNER THIGH THROW!
IT'S ALL THANKS TO YOU, MIYAKOZUKA SENSEI!
NOT AT ALL!
IT'S BECAUSE OF YOU GUYS...
ODO
...AND SAKATA'S HARD WORK!
THAT'S RIGHT.
IF WE LOSE, WE CAN'T FACE SAKATA!
IKENO
WE WILL BE VICTORIOUS!
ODO HIGH SCHOOL... UP NEXT...
BOW!

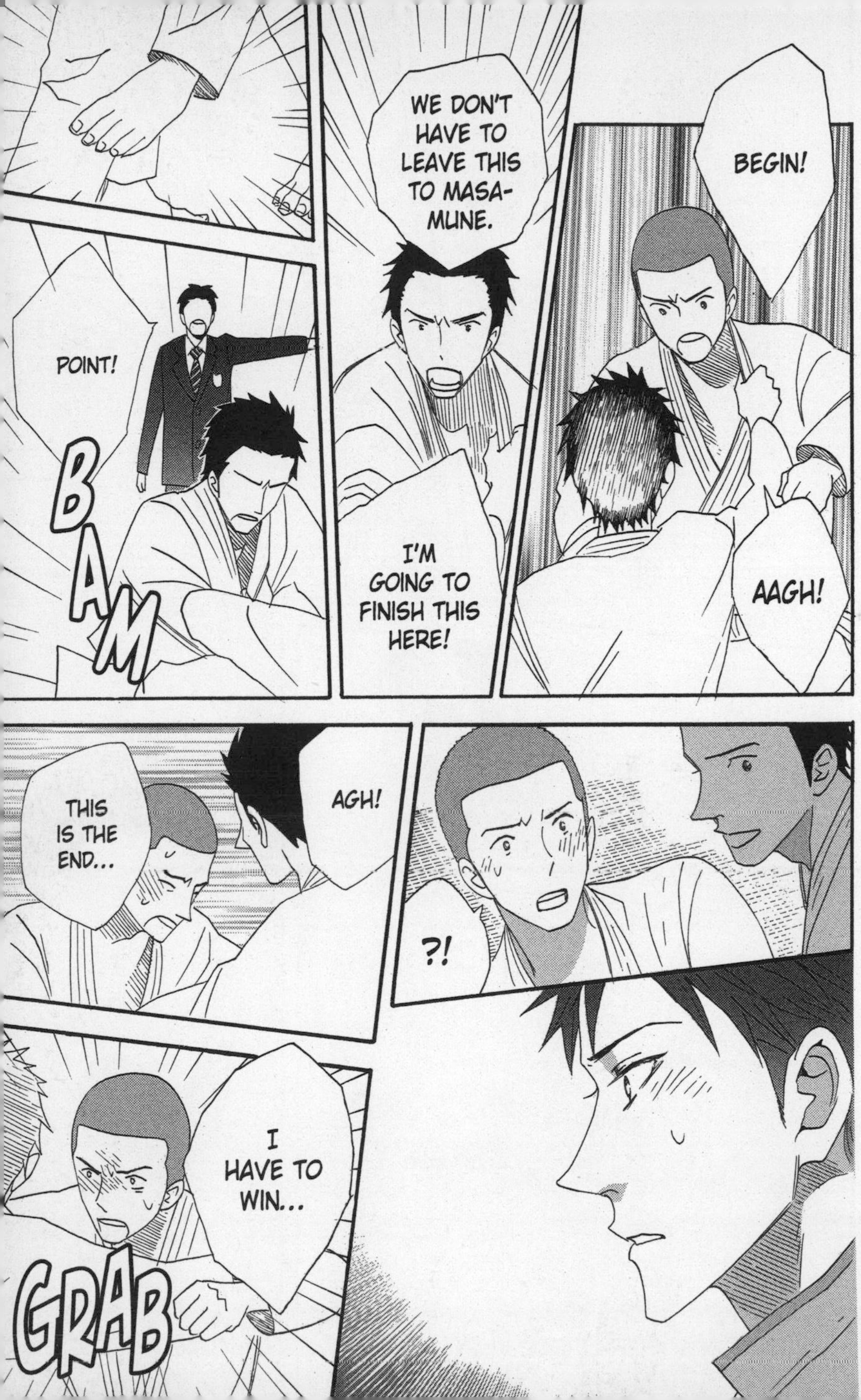
BEGIN!
AAGH!
WE DON'T HAVE TO LEAVE THIS TO MASA-MUNE.
I'M GOING TO FINISH THIS HERE!
POINT!
BAM
?!
AGH!
THIS IS THE END...
I HAVE TO WIN...
GRAB

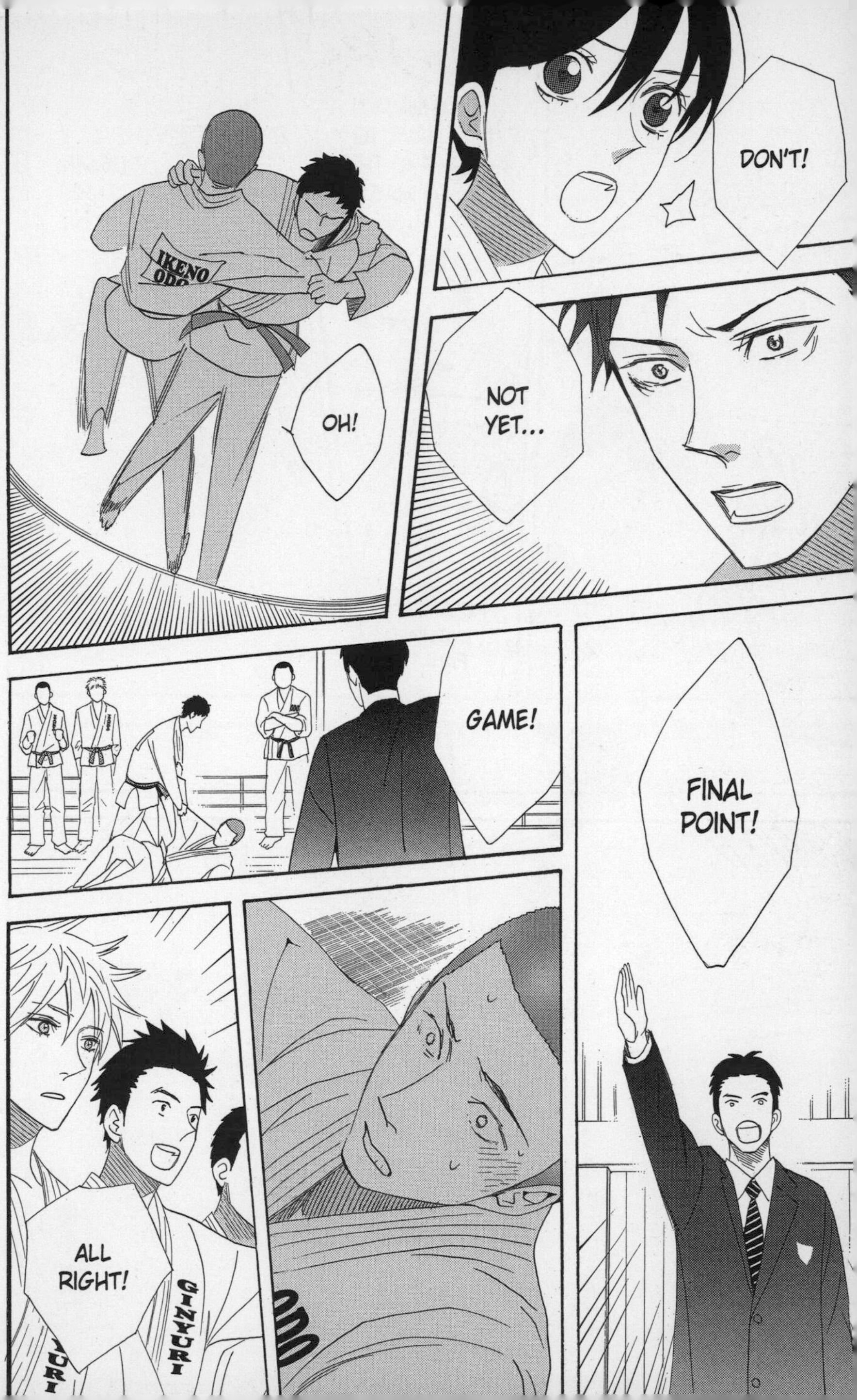
DON'T!
NOT YET...
OH!
IKENO
FINAL POINT!
GAME!
ALL RIGHT!
GINYURI

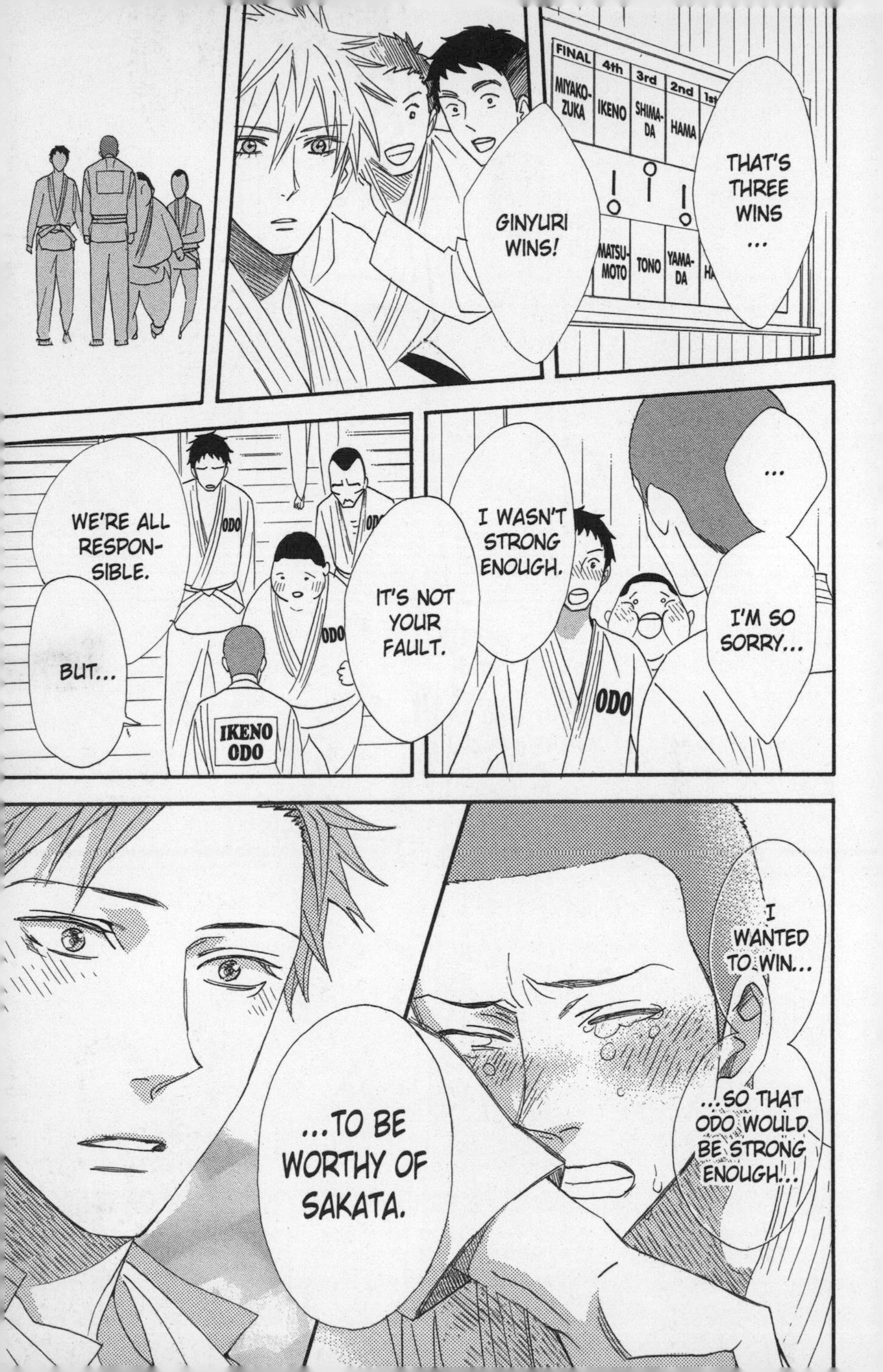
FINAL
4th
3rd
2nd
1st
MIYAKO-ZUKA
IKENO
SHIMA-DA
HAMA
MATSU-MOTO
TONO
YAMA-DA
THAT'S THREE WINS...
GINYURI WINS!
...
I'M SO SORRY...
I WASN'T STRONG ENOUGH.
ODO
IT'S NOT YOUR FAULT.
ODO
ODO
WE'RE ALL RESPON-SIBLE.
BUT...
IKENO
ODO
I WANTED TO WIN...
...SO THAT ODO WOULD BE STRONG ENOUGH...
...TO BE WORTHY OF SAKATA.

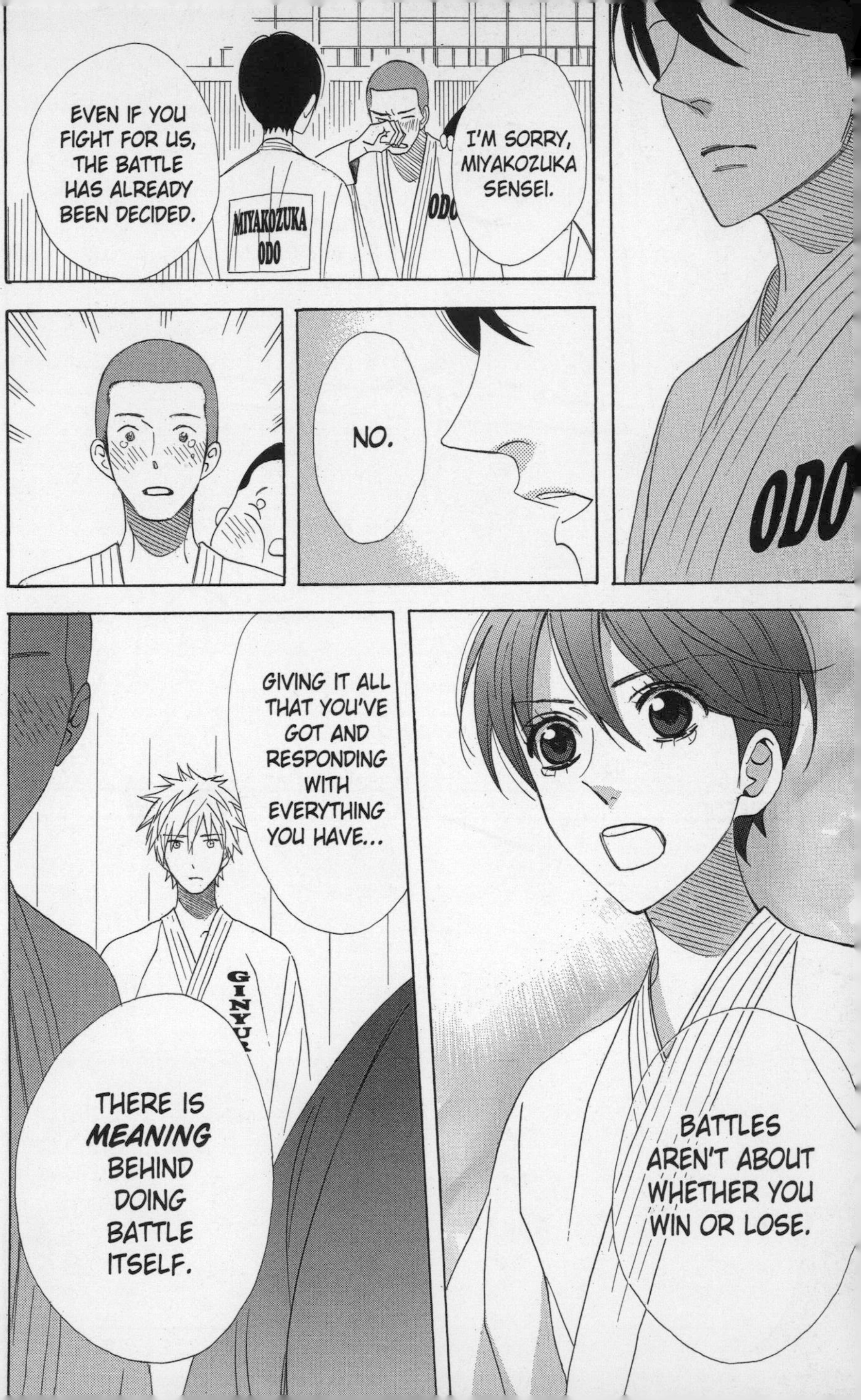
ODO
I'M SORRY, MIYAKOZUKA SENSEI.
EVEN IF YOU FIGHT FOR US, THE BATTLE HAS ALREADY BEEN DECIDED.
MIYAKOZUKA ODO
NO.
BATTLES AREN'T ABOUT WHETHER YOU WIN OR LOSE.
GIVING IT ALL THAT YOU'VE GOT AND RESPONDING WITH EVERYTHING YOU HAVE...
THERE IS *MEANING* BEHIND DOING BATTLE ITSELF.

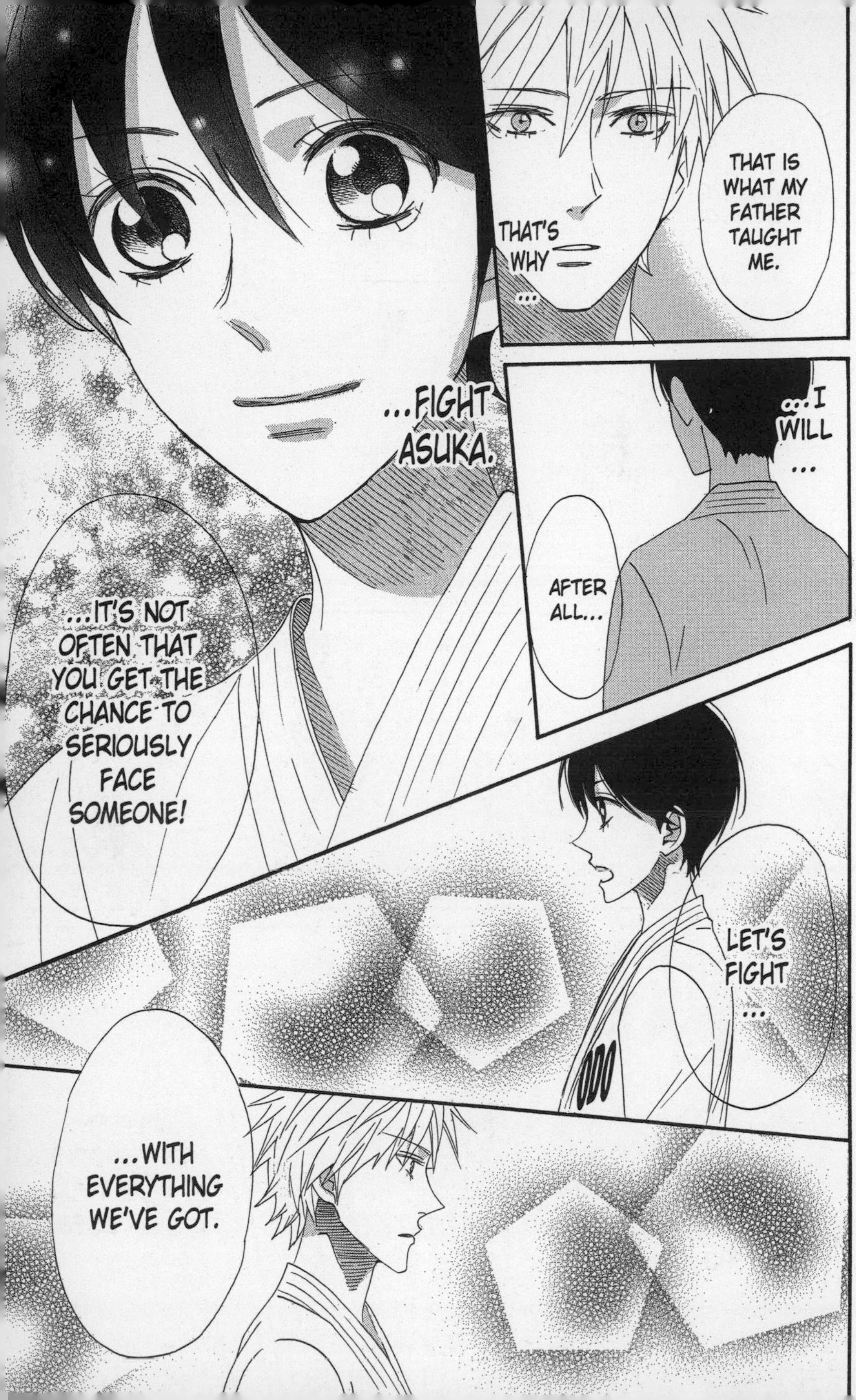
THAT IS WHAT MY FATHER TAUGHT ME.
THAT'S WHY ...
...I WILL ...
AFTER ALL...
...FIGHT ASUKA.
...IT'S NOT OFTEN THAT YOU GET THE CHANCE TO SERIOUSLY FACE SOMEONE!
LET'S FIGHT ...
...WITH EVERYTHING WE'VE GOT.

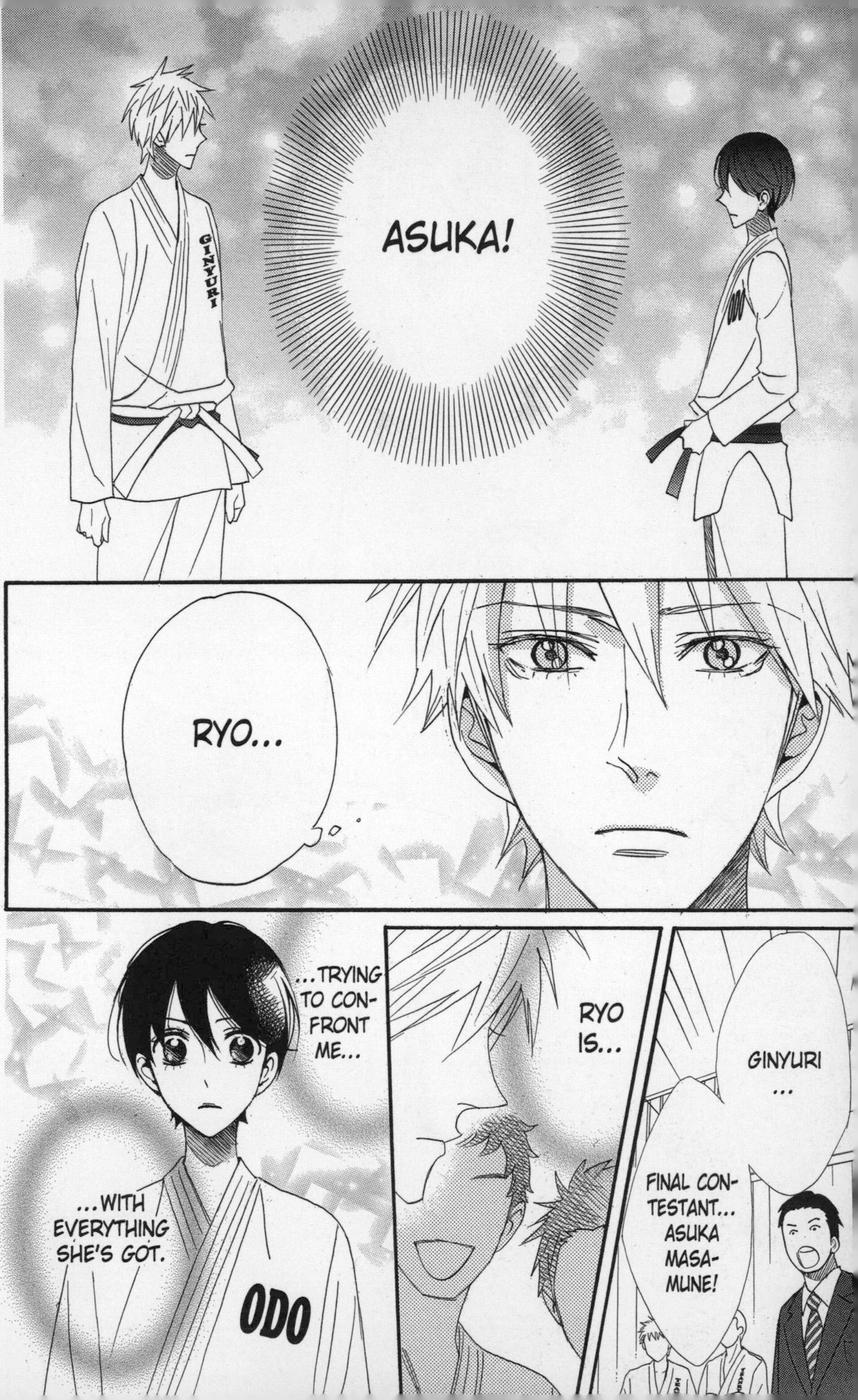
ASUKA!
RYO...
GINYURI ...
FINAL CONTESTANT... ASUKA MASAMUNE!
RYO IS...
...TRYING TO CONFRONT ME...
...WITH EVERYTHING SHE'S GOT.

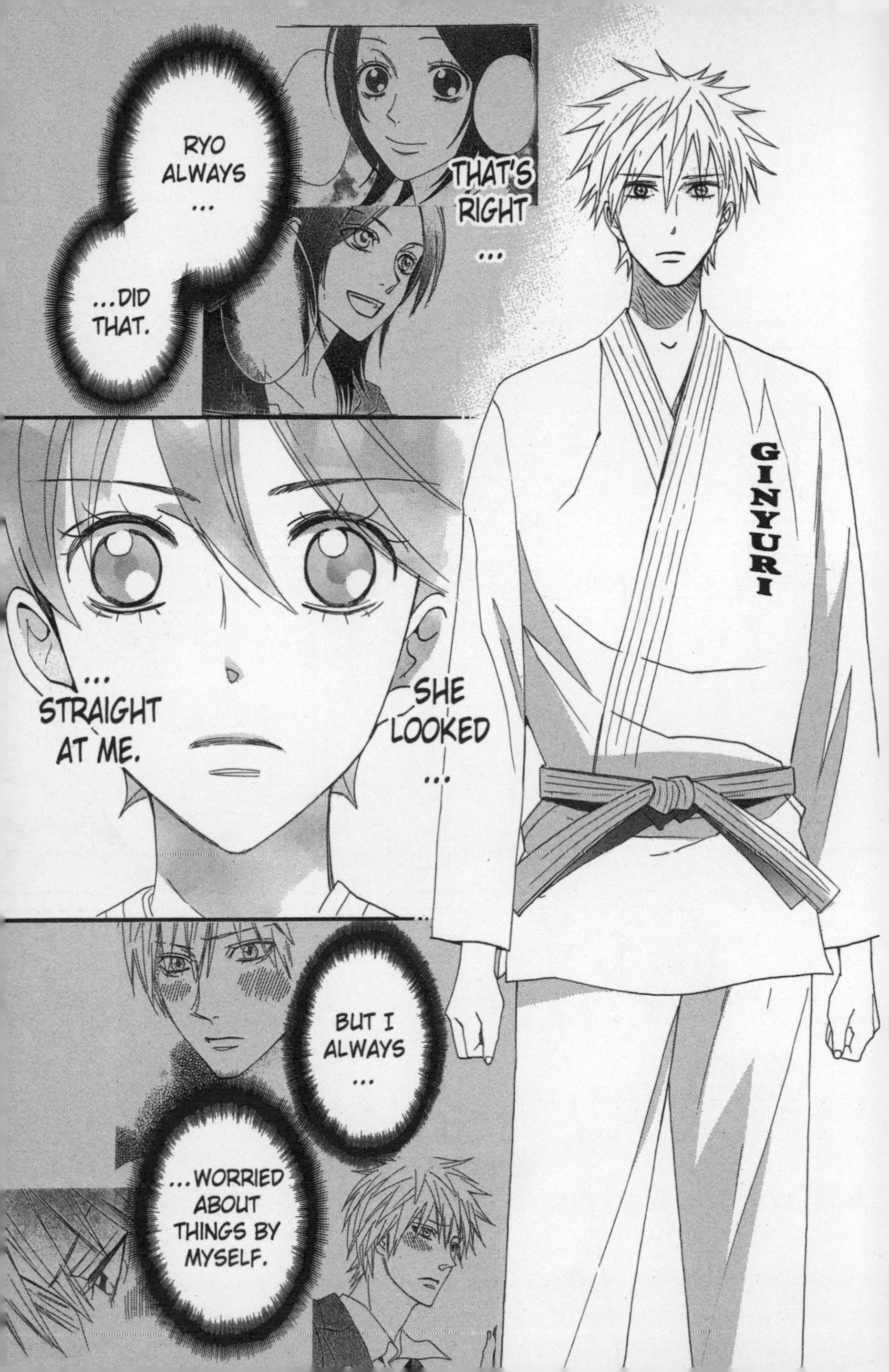
GINYURI
THAT'S RIGHT ...
RYO ALWAYS ...
...DID THAT.
SHE LOOKED ...
... STRAIGHT AT ME.
BUT I ALWAYS ...
...WORRIED ABOUT THINGS BY MYSELF.

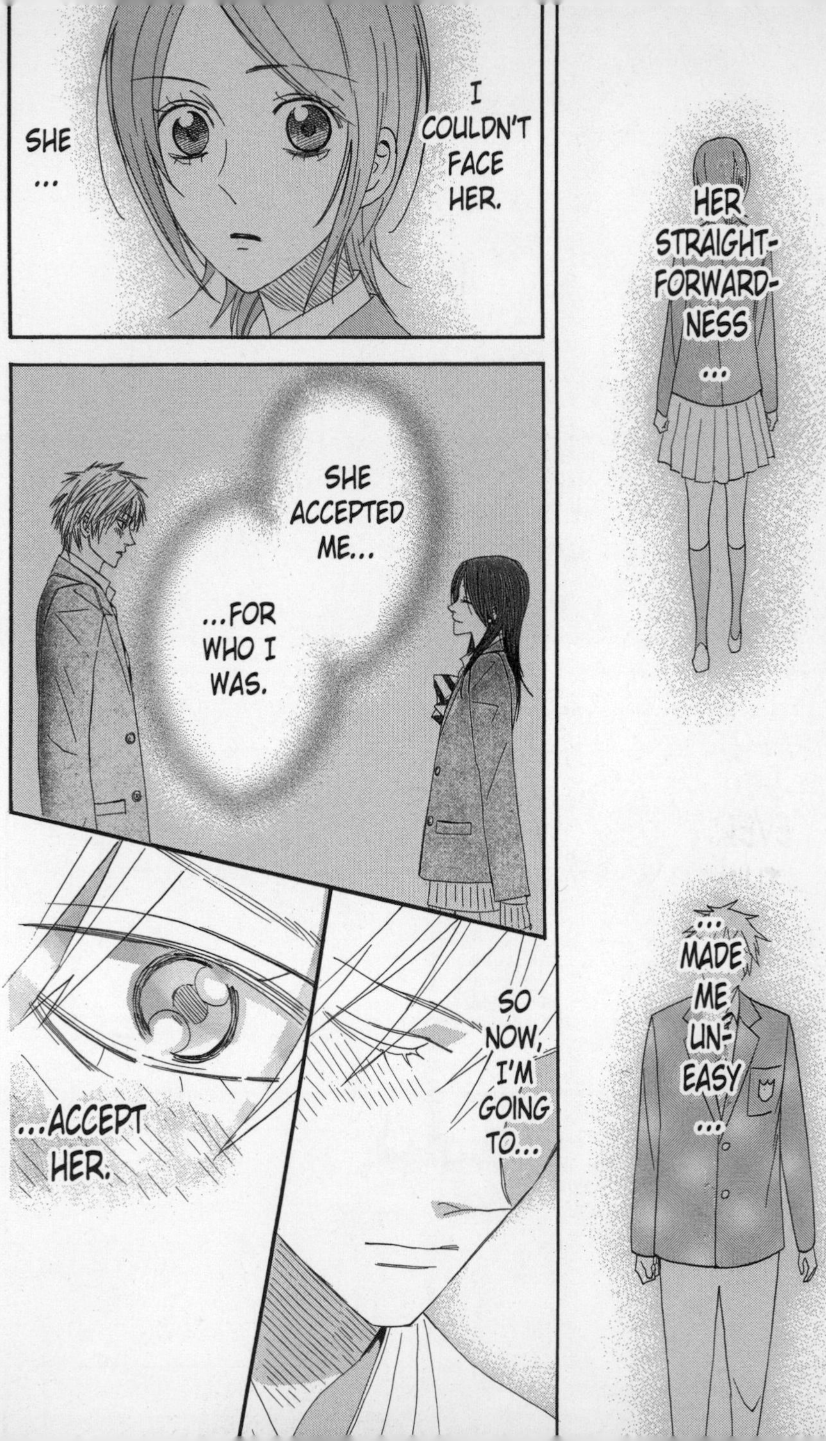
HER STRAIGHT-FORWARD-NESS ...
... MADE ME UN-EASY ...
I COULDN'T FACE HER.
SHE ...
SHE ACCEPTED ME...
...FOR WHO I WAS.
SO NOW, I'M GOING TO...
...ACCEPT HER.

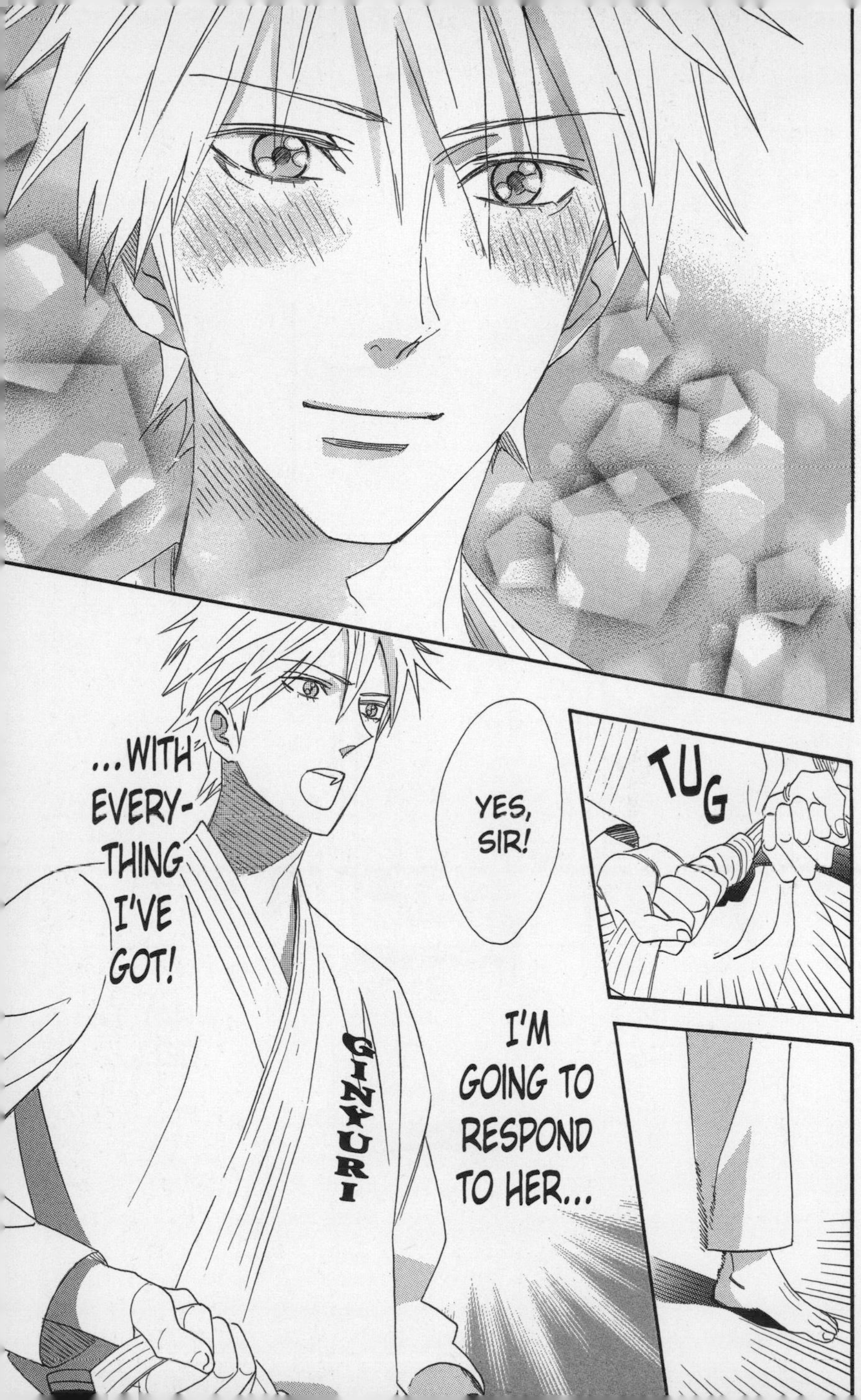
TUG
I'M GOING TO RESPOND TO HER...
YES, SIR!
...WITH EVERY-THING I'VE GOT!
GINYURI

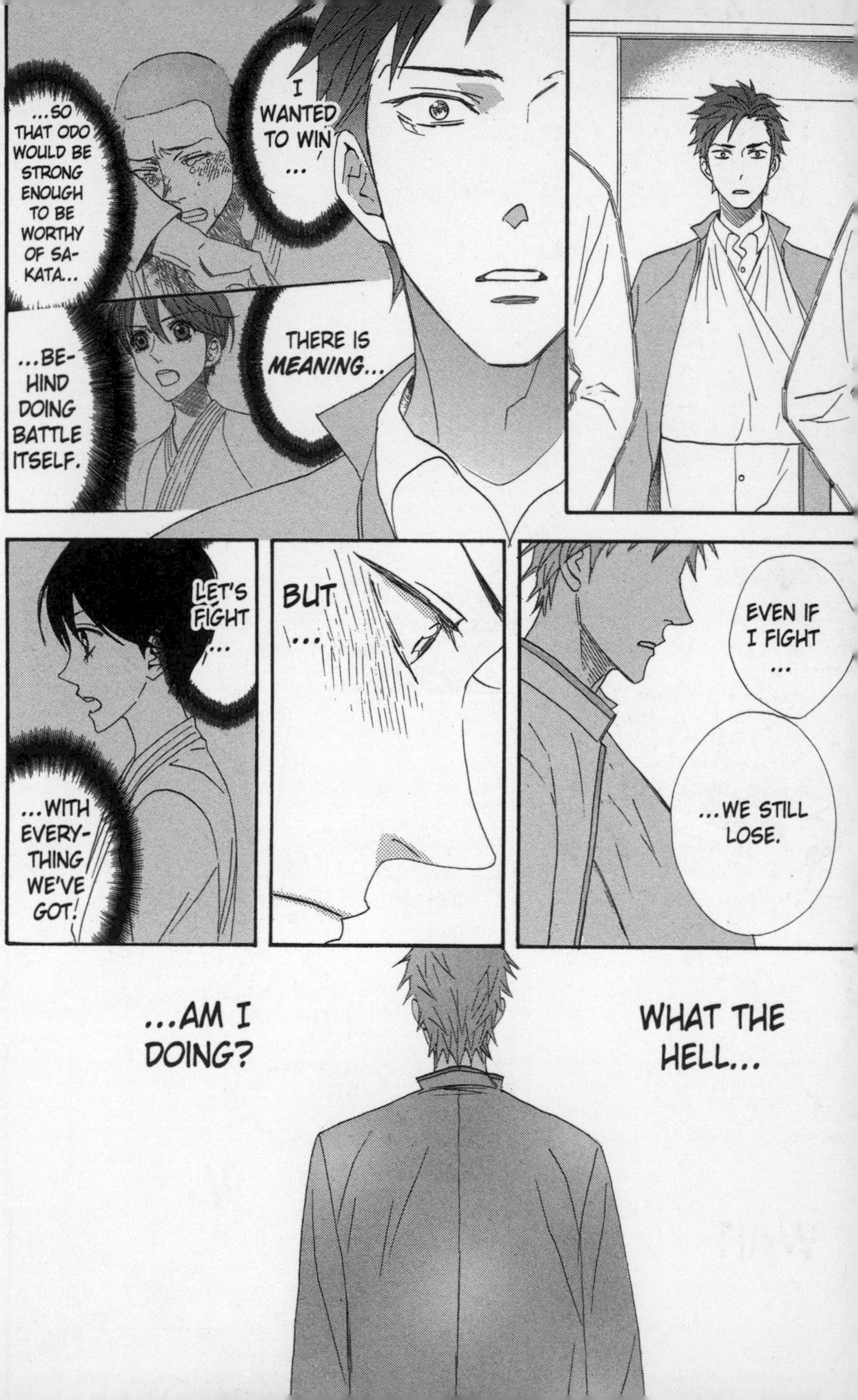
I WANTED TO WIN...
...SO THAT ODO WOULD BE STRONG ENOUGH TO BE WORTHY OF SA-KATA...
THERE IS *MEANING*...
...BE-HIND DOING BATTLE ITSELF.
EVEN IF I FIGHT...
...WE STILL LOSE.
BUT...
LET'S FIGHT...
...WITH EVERY-THING WE'VE GOT!
WHAT THE HELL...
...AM I DOING?

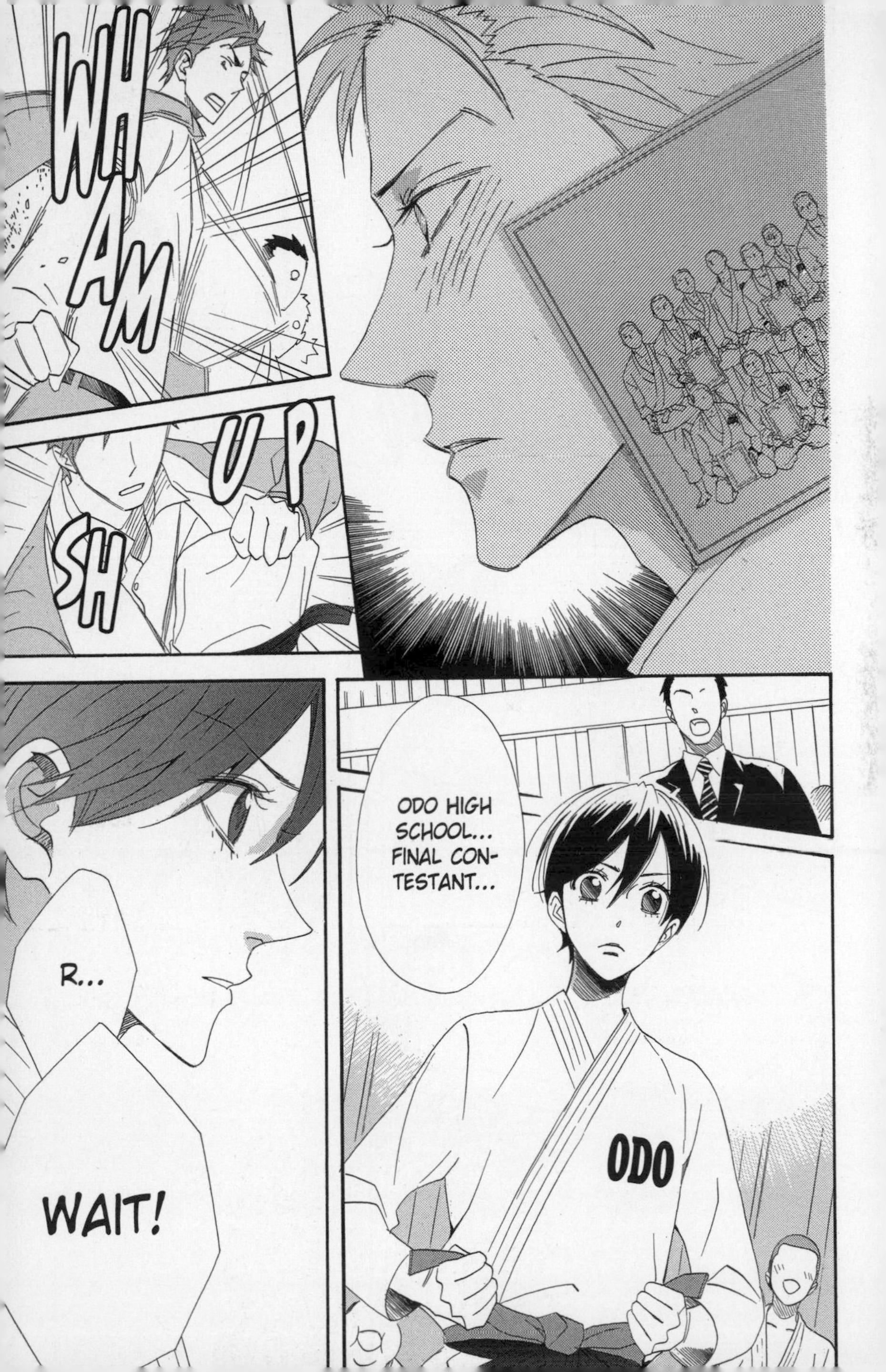
WHAM
SHUP
ODO HIGH SCHOOL... FINAL CON-TESTANT...
ODO
R...
WAIT!

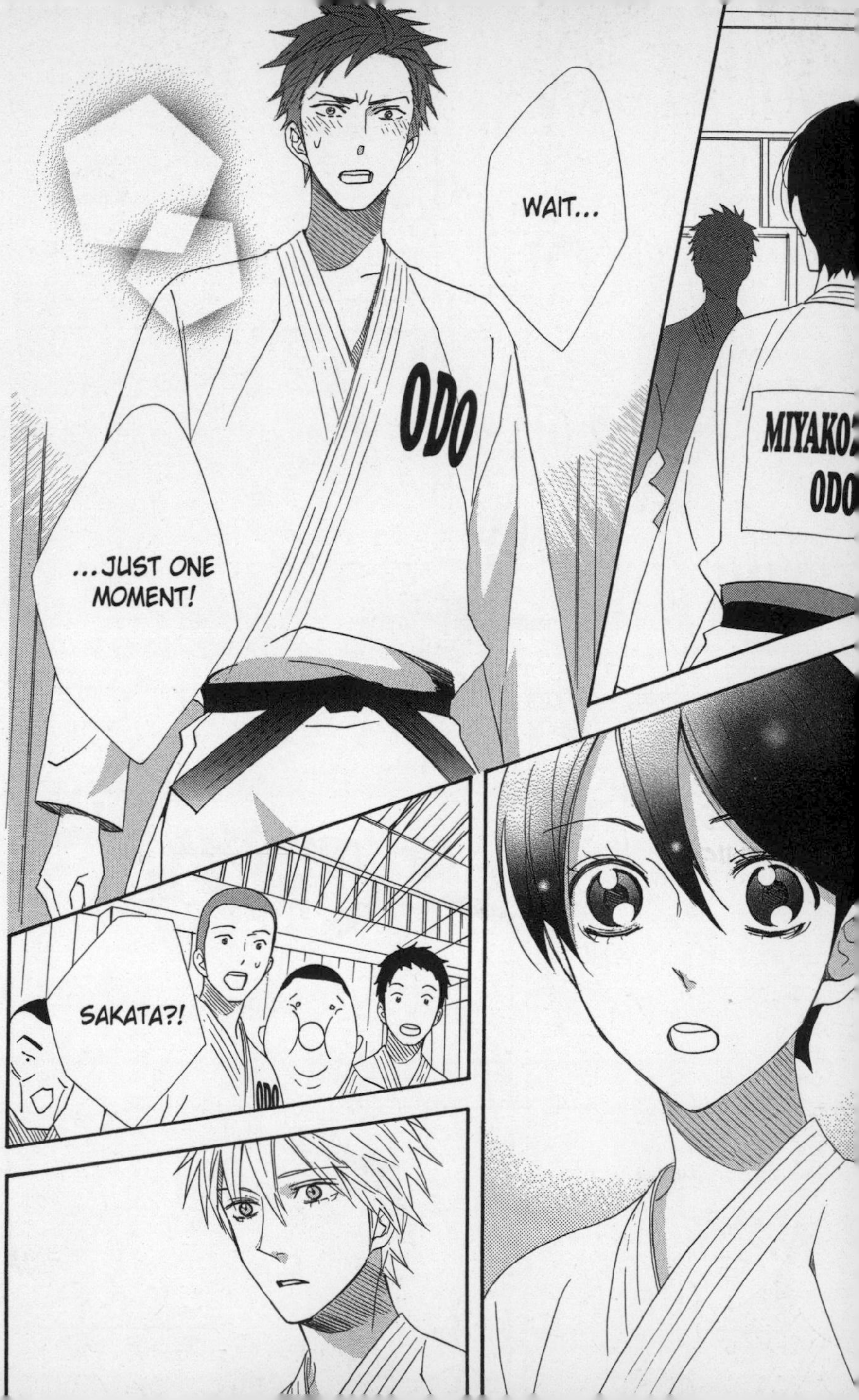
MIYAKO
ODO
WAIT...
...JUST ONE MOMENT!
ODO
SAKATA?!
ODO

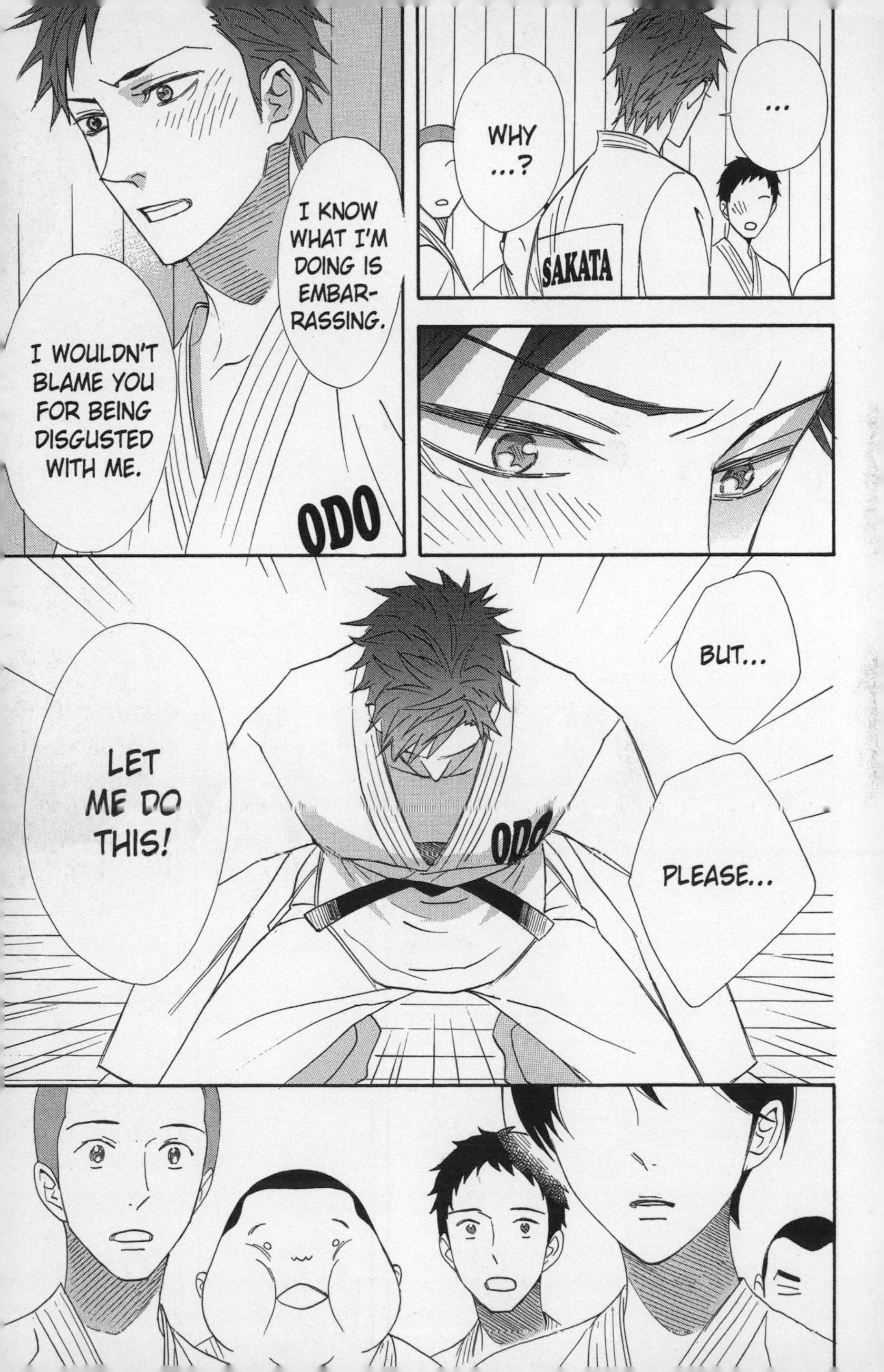
...
WHY ...?
SAKATA
I KNOW WHAT I'M DOING IS EMBAR-RASSING.
I WOULDN'T BLAME YOU FOR BEING DISGUSTED WITH ME.
ODO
BUT...
PLEASE...
ODO
LET ME DO THIS!

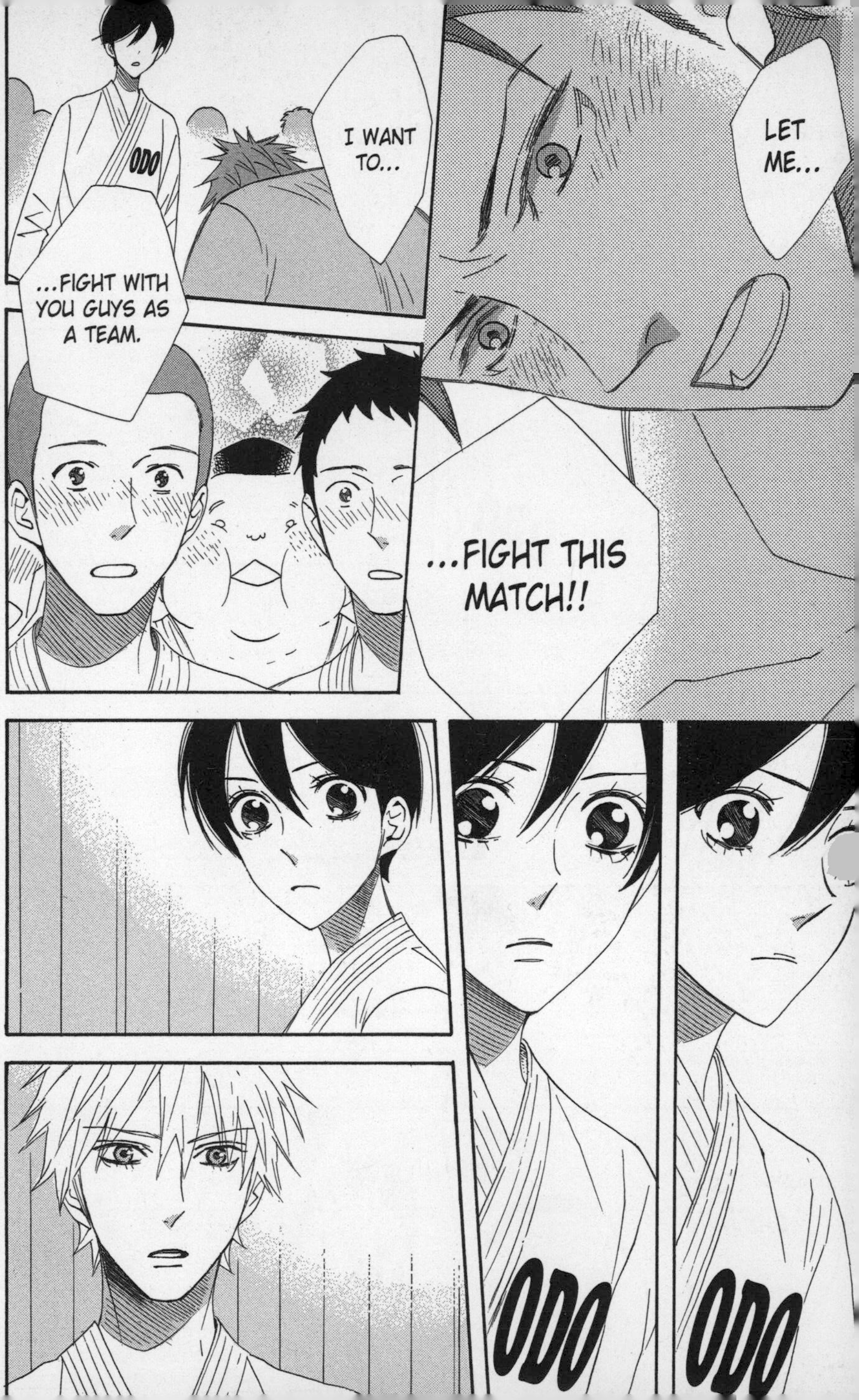
LET ME...
...FIGHT THIS MATCH!!
ODO
I WANT TO...
...FIGHT WITH YOU GUYS AS A TEAM.
ODO
ODO

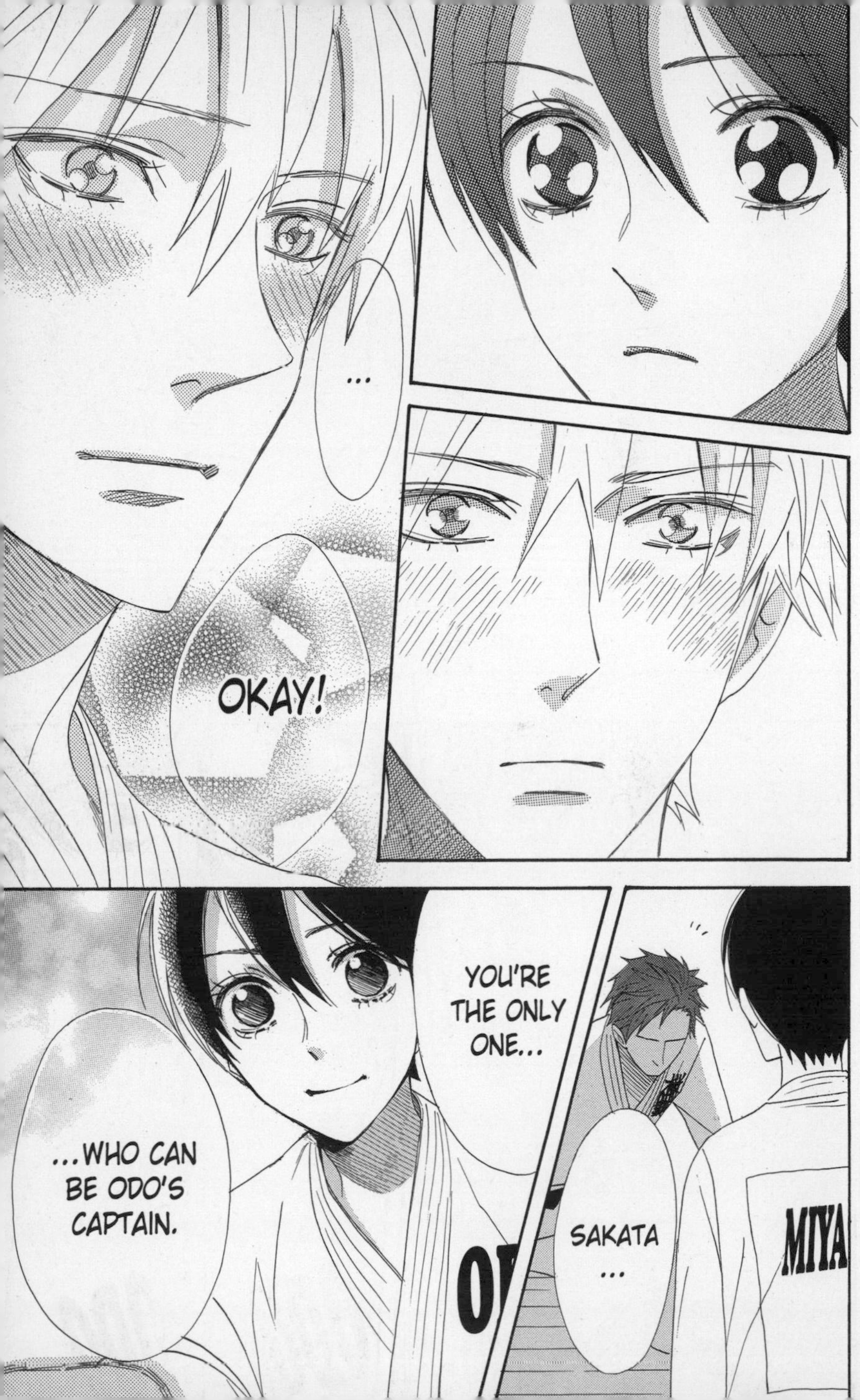
...
OKAY!
SAKATA ...
YOU'RE THE ONLY ONE...
...WHO CAN BE ODO'S CAPTAIN.

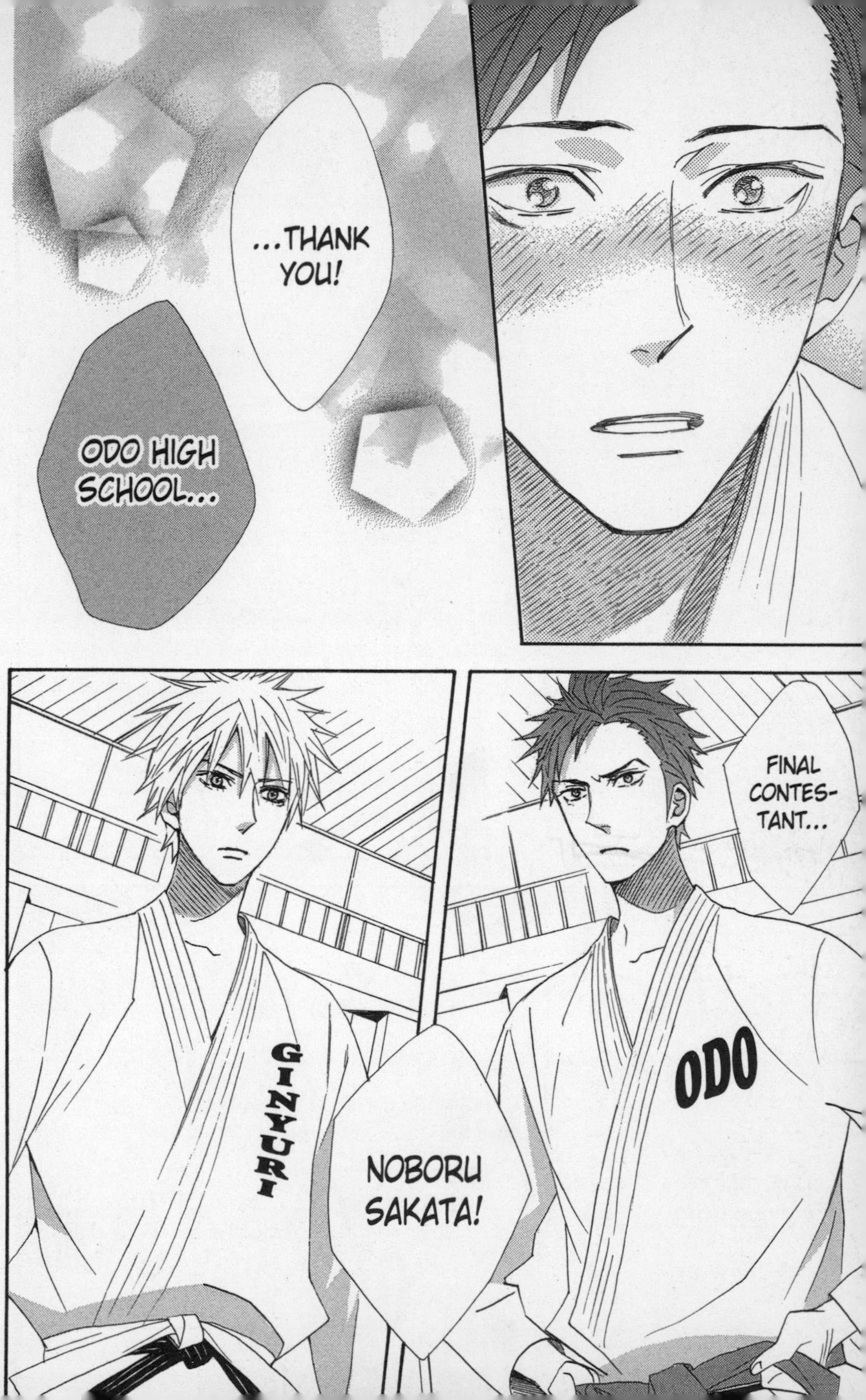
...THANK YOU!
ODO HIGH SCHOOL...
FINAL CONTES-TANT...
ODO
NOBORU SAKATA!
GINYURI

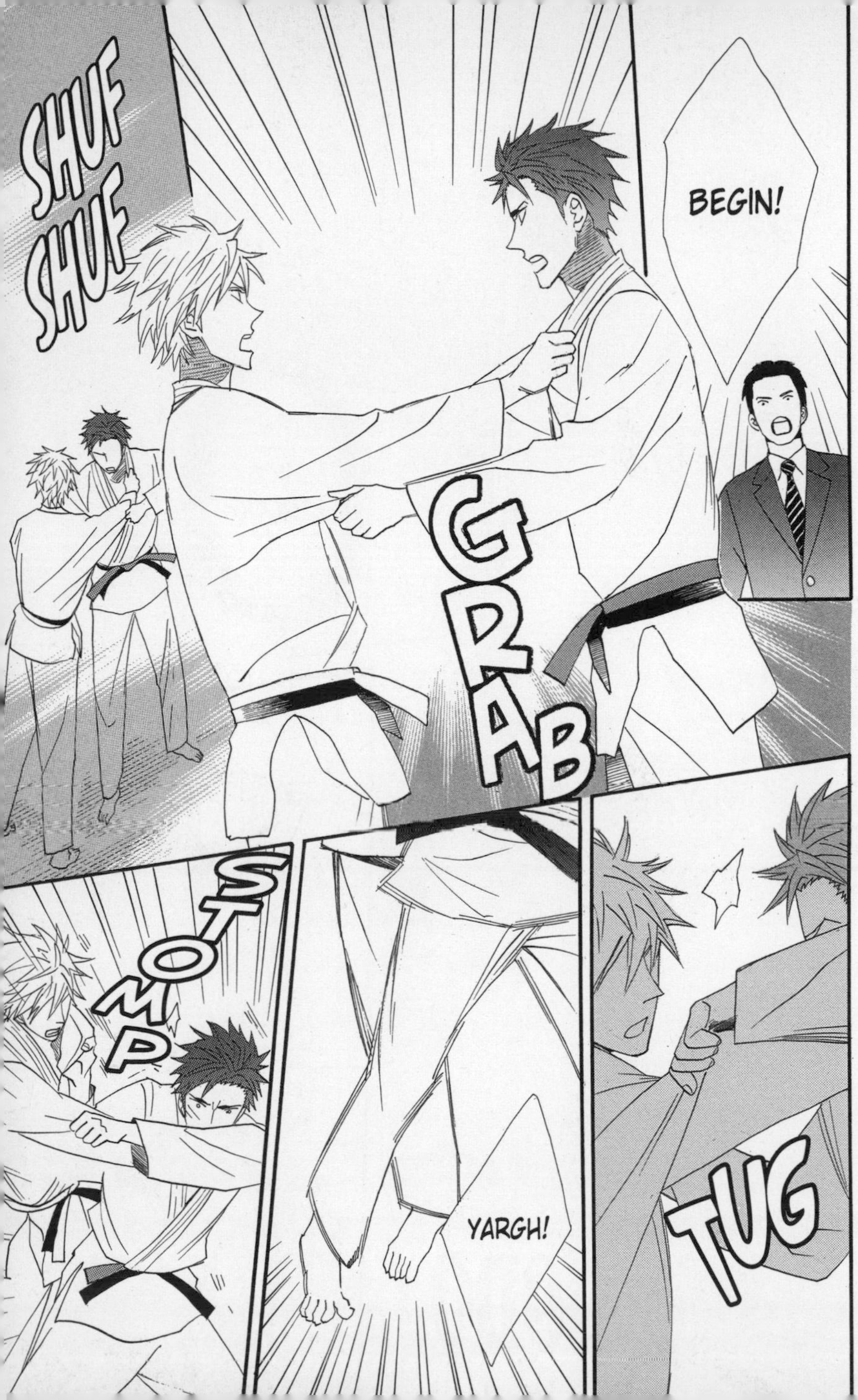
BEGIN!
GRAB
SHUF SHUF
TUG
YARGH!
STOMP

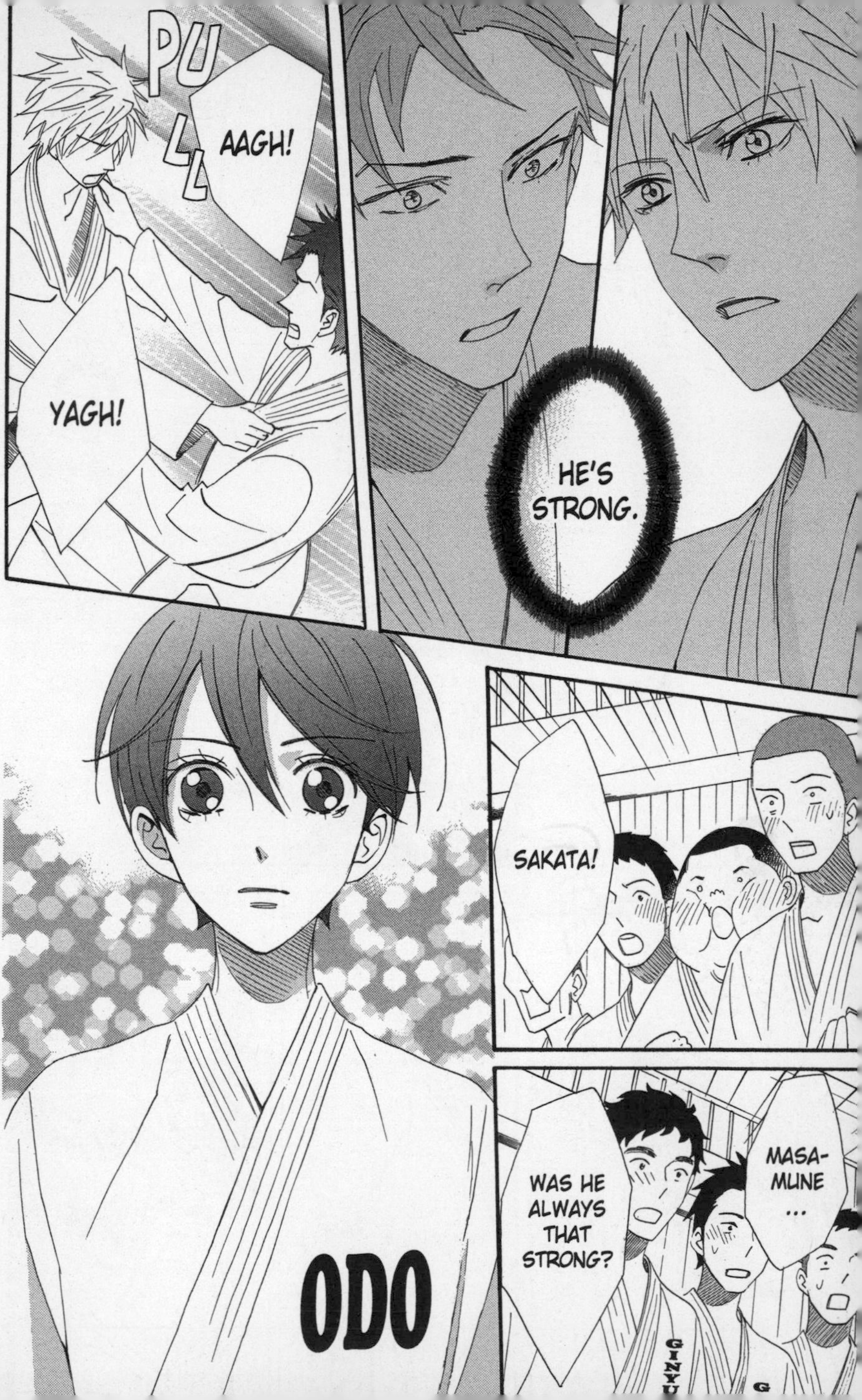
HE'S STRONG.
PULL
AAGH!
YAGH!
SAKATA!
MASA-MUNE...
WAS HE ALWAYS THAT STRONG?
GINYU
ODO

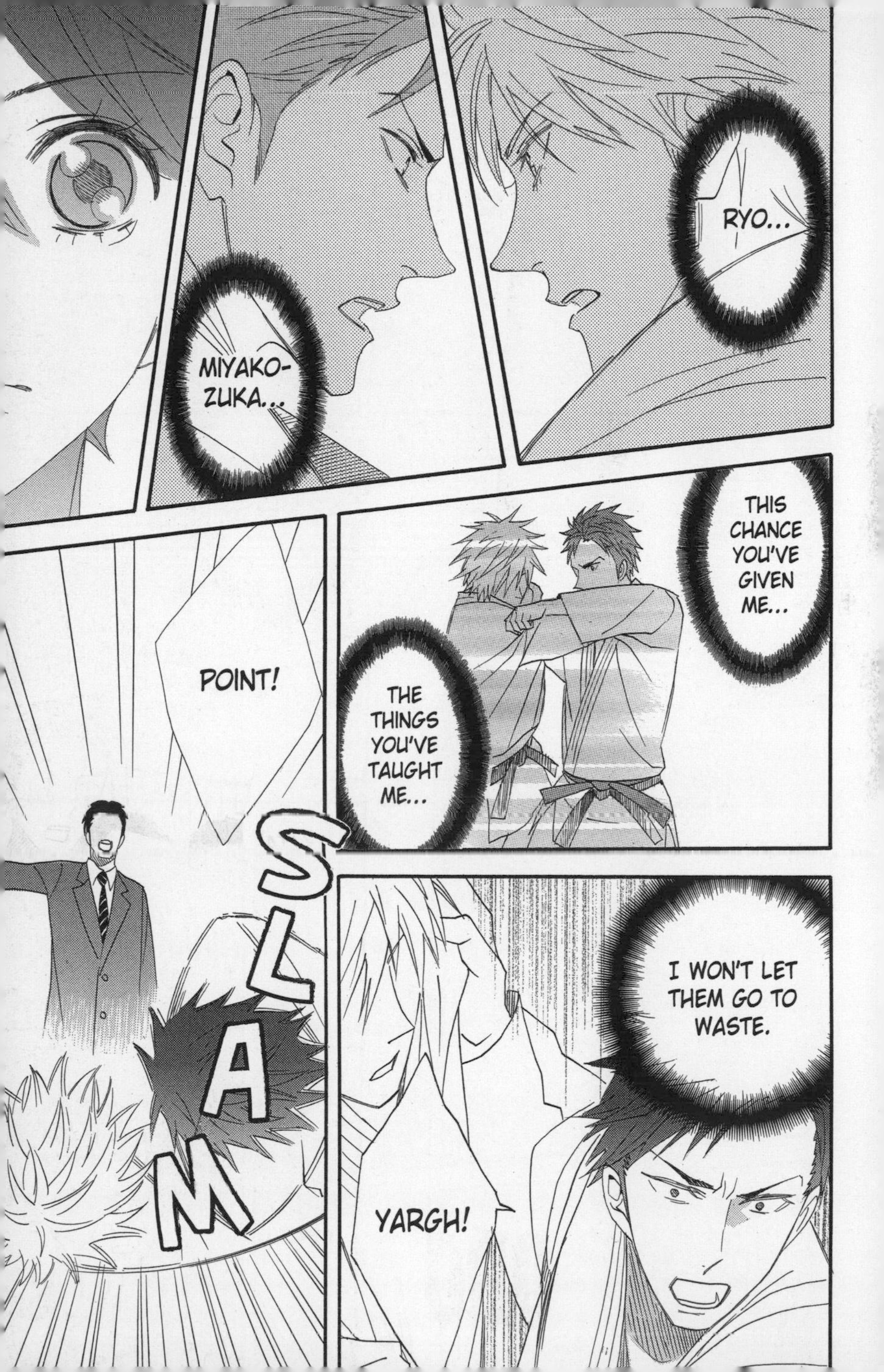
RYO...
MIYAKO-ZUKA...
THIS CHANCE YOU'VE GIVEN ME...
THE THINGS YOU'VE TAUGHT ME...
I WON'T LET THEM GO TO WASTE.
YARGH!
POINT!
SLAM

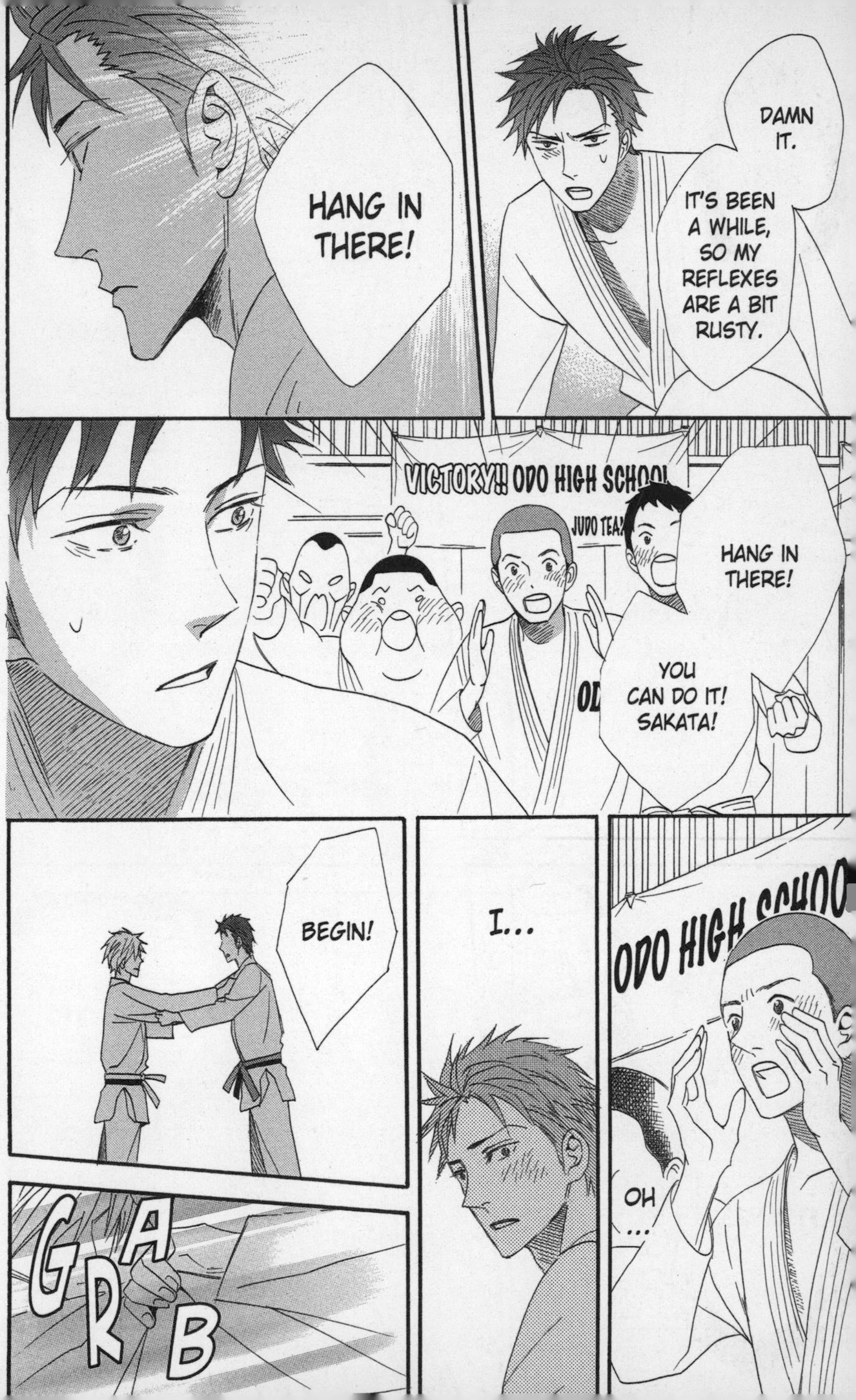
DAMN IT.
IT'S BEEN A WHILE, SO MY REFLEXES ARE A BIT RUSTY.
HANG IN THERE!
VICTORY!! ODO HIGH SCHOO
JUDO TEA
HANG IN THERE!
YOU CAN DO IT! SAKATA!
OD
ODO HIGH SCHOO
OH ...
I...
BEGIN!
GRAB

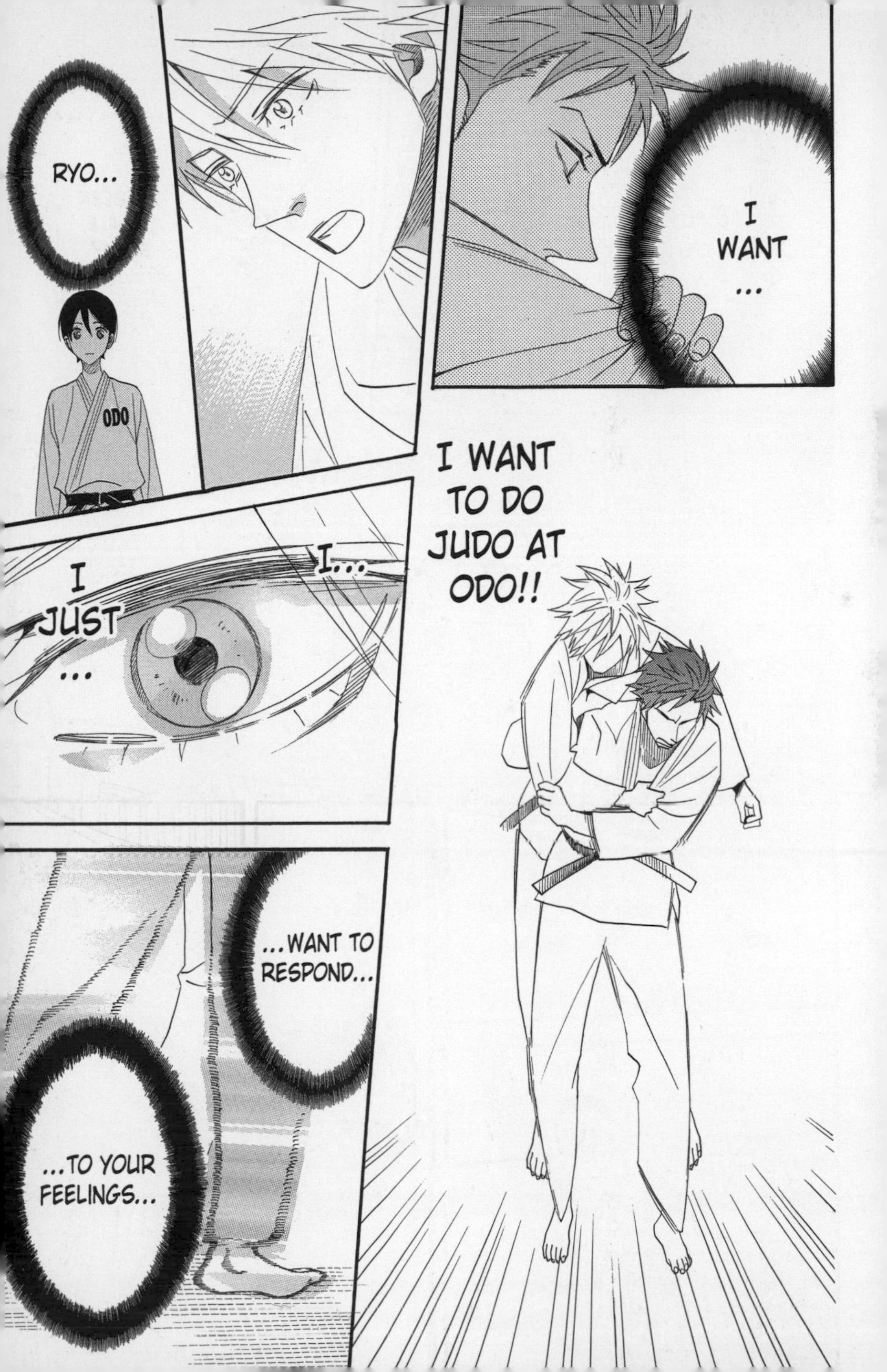
I WANT ...
RYO...
ODO
I WANT TO DO JUDO AT ODO!!
I...
I JUST ...
...WANT TO RESPOND...
...TO YOUR FEELINGS...

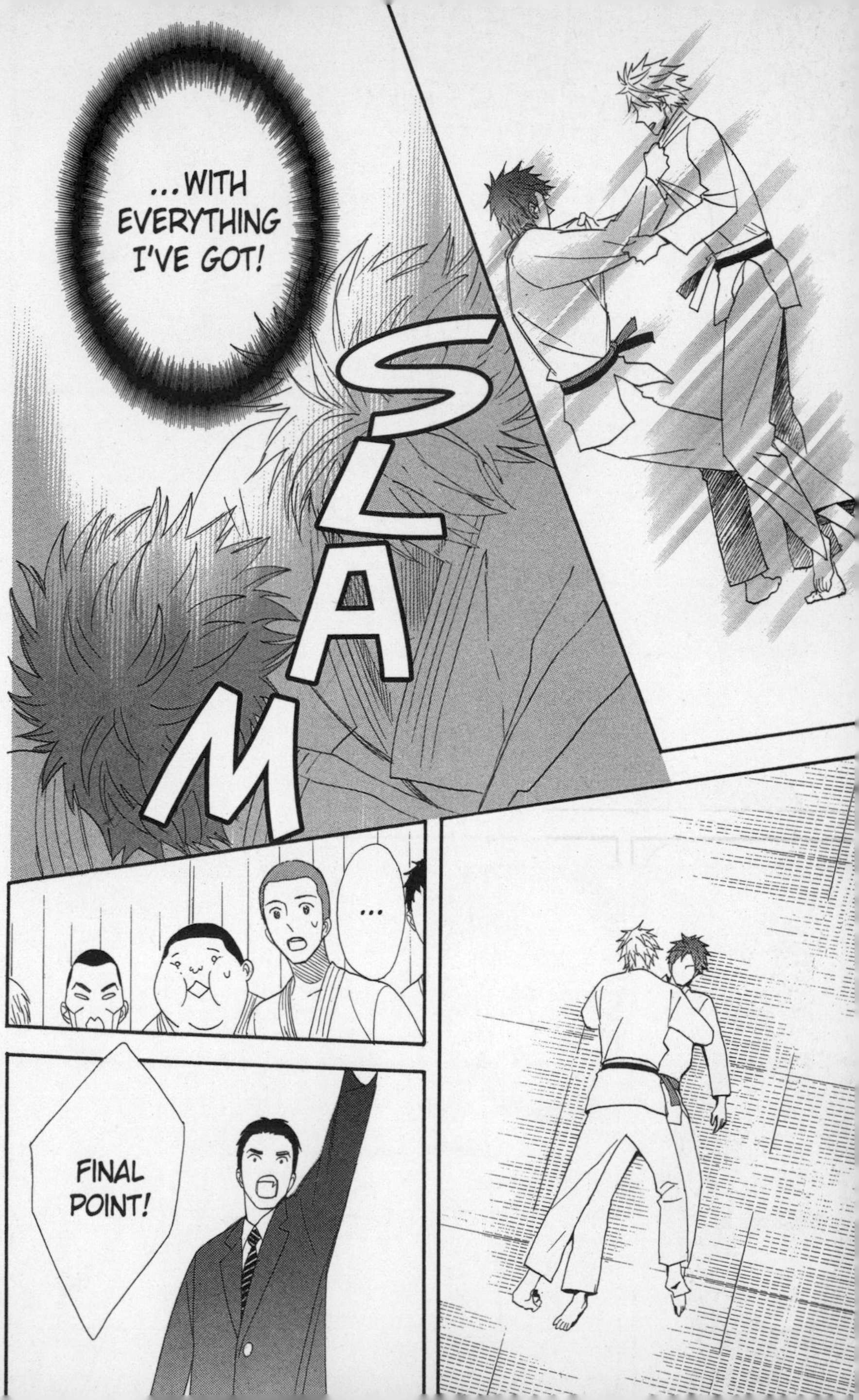
...WITH EVERYTHING I'VE GOT!
SLAM
...
FINAL POINT!

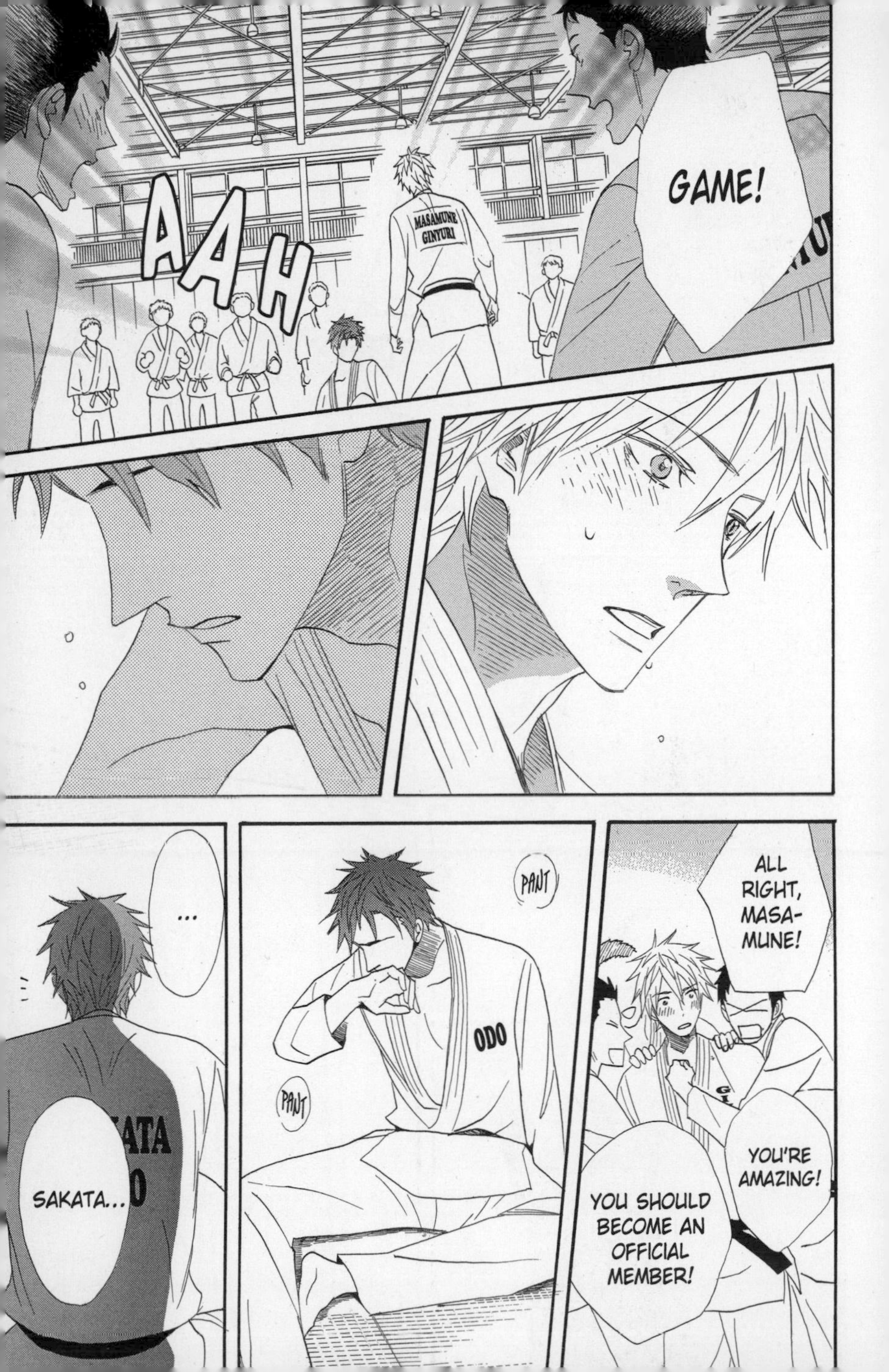
GAME!
MASAMUNE GINYURI
AAH
ALL RIGHT, MASA-MUNE!
YOU'RE AMAZING!
YOU SHOULD BECOME AN OFFICIAL MEMBER!
PANT
ODO
PANT
...
SAKATA...

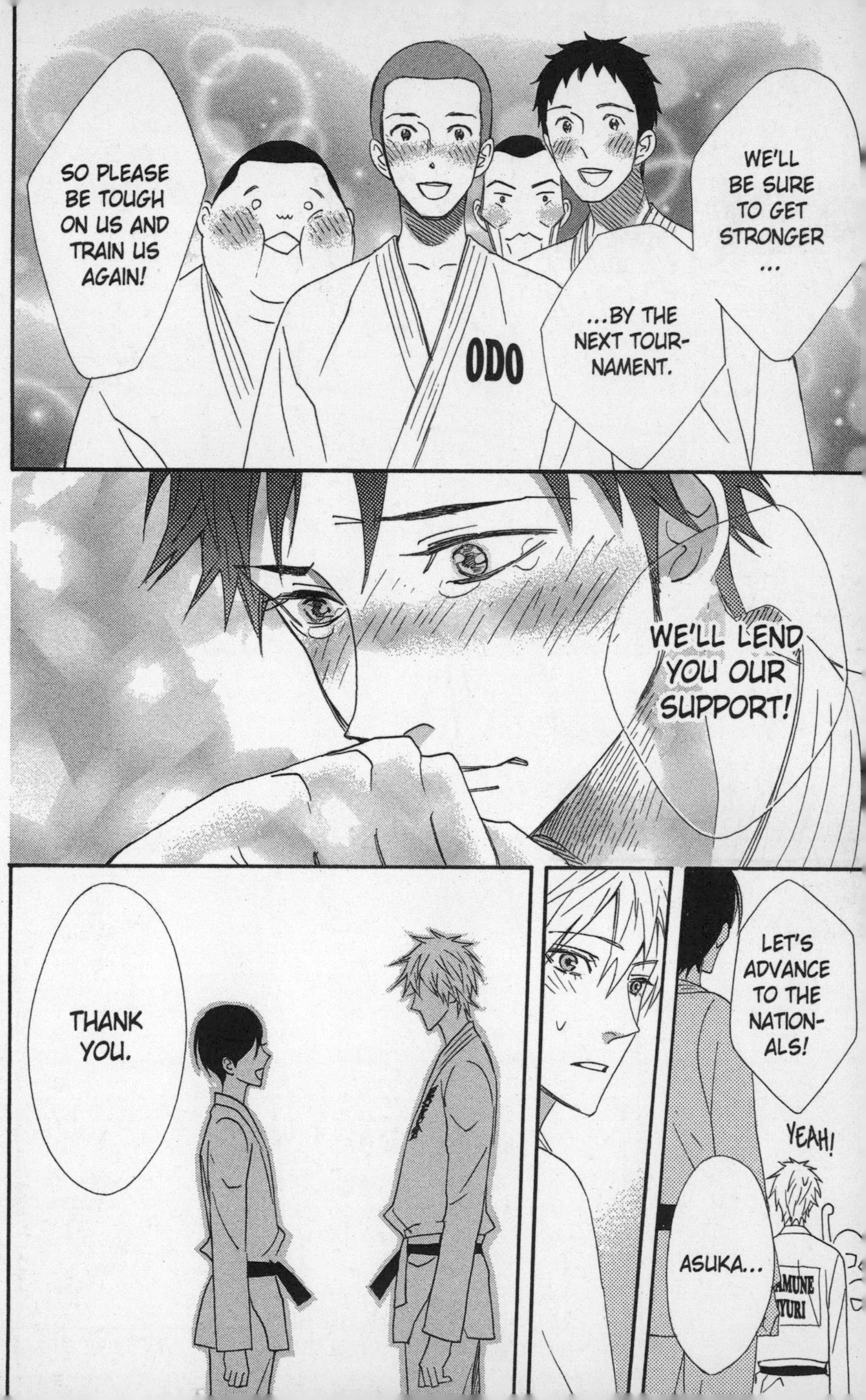
WE'LL BE SURE TO GET STRONGER ...
...BY THE NEXT TOUR-NAMENT.
ODO
SO PLEASE BE TOUGH ON US AND TRAIN US AGAIN!
WE'LL LEND YOU OUR SUPPORT!
LET'S ADVANCE TO THE NATION-ALS!
YEAH!
ASUKA...
THANK YOU.

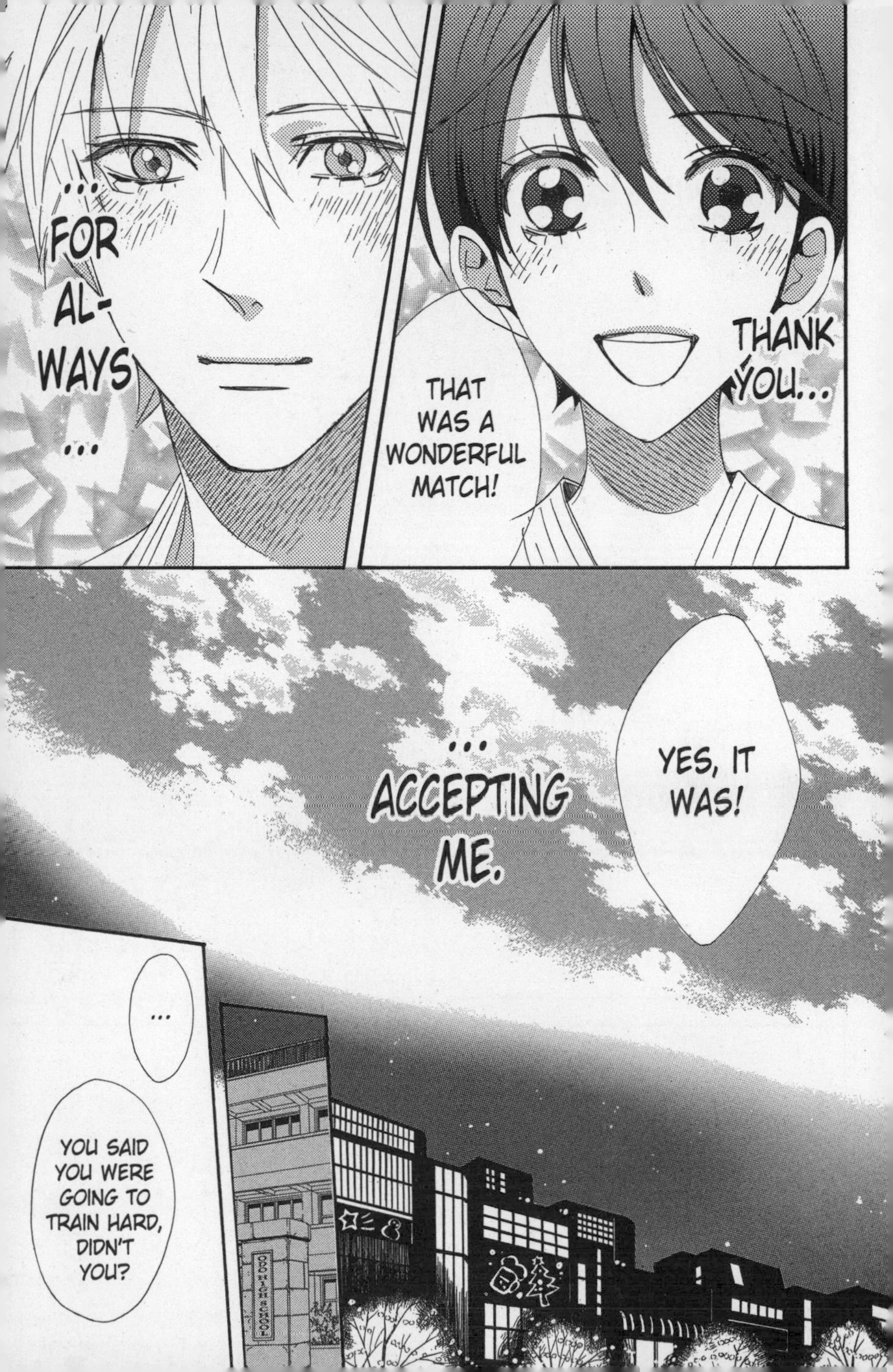
THANK YOU...
THAT WAS A WONDERFUL MATCH!
...FOR AL-WAYS...
YES, IT WAS!
... ACCEPTING ME.
...
YOU SAID YOU WERE GOING TO TRAIN HARD, DIDN'T YOU?

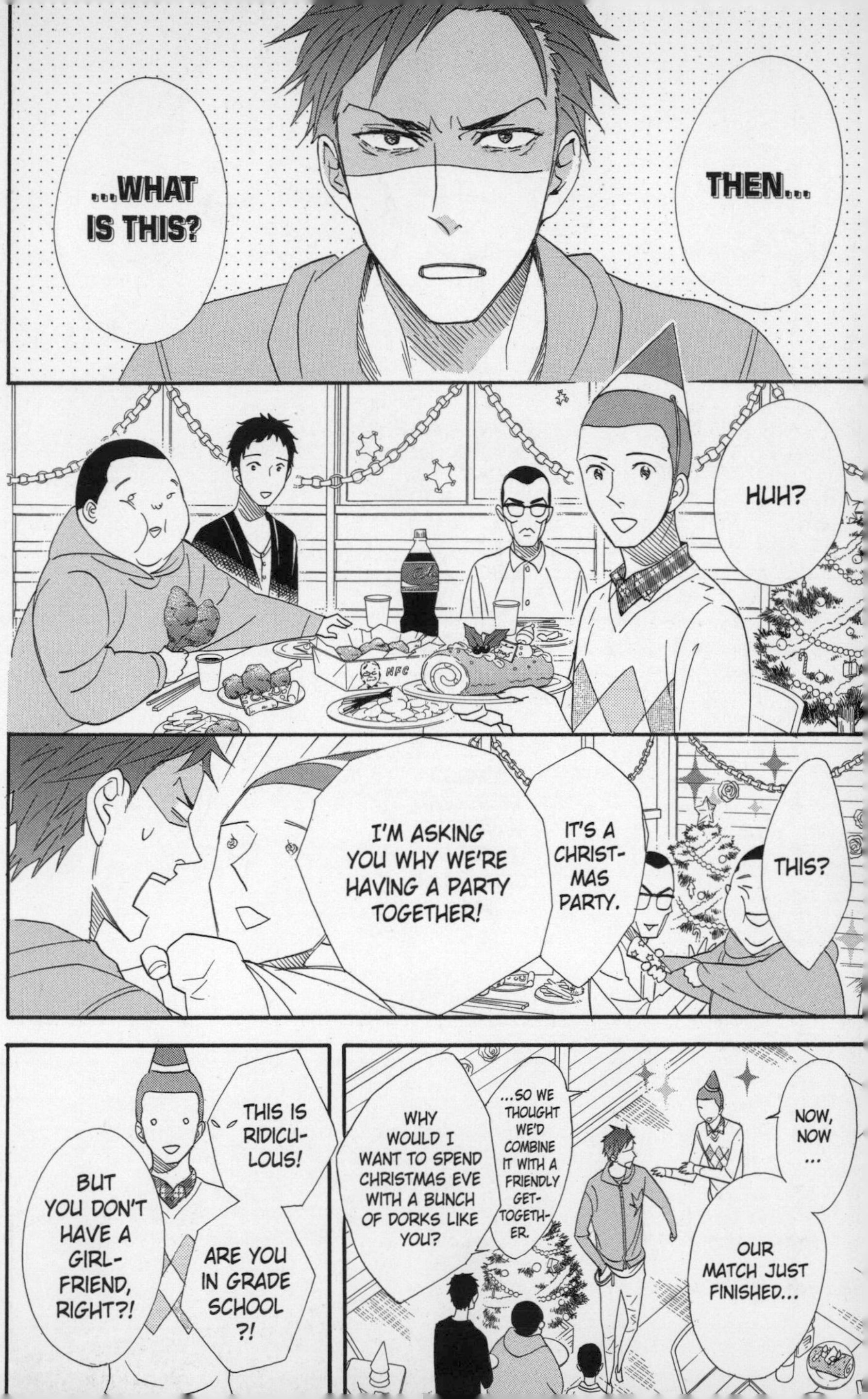
THEN...
...WHAT IS THIS?
HUH?
THIS?
IT'S A CHRISTMAS PARTY.
I'M ASKING YOU WHY WE'RE HAVING A PARTY TOGETHER!
NOW, NOW ...
OUR MATCH JUST FINISHED...
...SO WE THOUGHT WE'D COMBINE IT WITH A FRIENDLY GET-TOGETHER.
WHY WOULD I WANT TO SPEND CHRISTMAS EVE WITH A BUNCH OF DORKS LIKE YOU?
THIS IS RIDICULOUS!
BUT YOU DON'T HAVE A GIRLFRIEND, RIGHT?!
ARE YOU IN GRADE SCHOOL?!

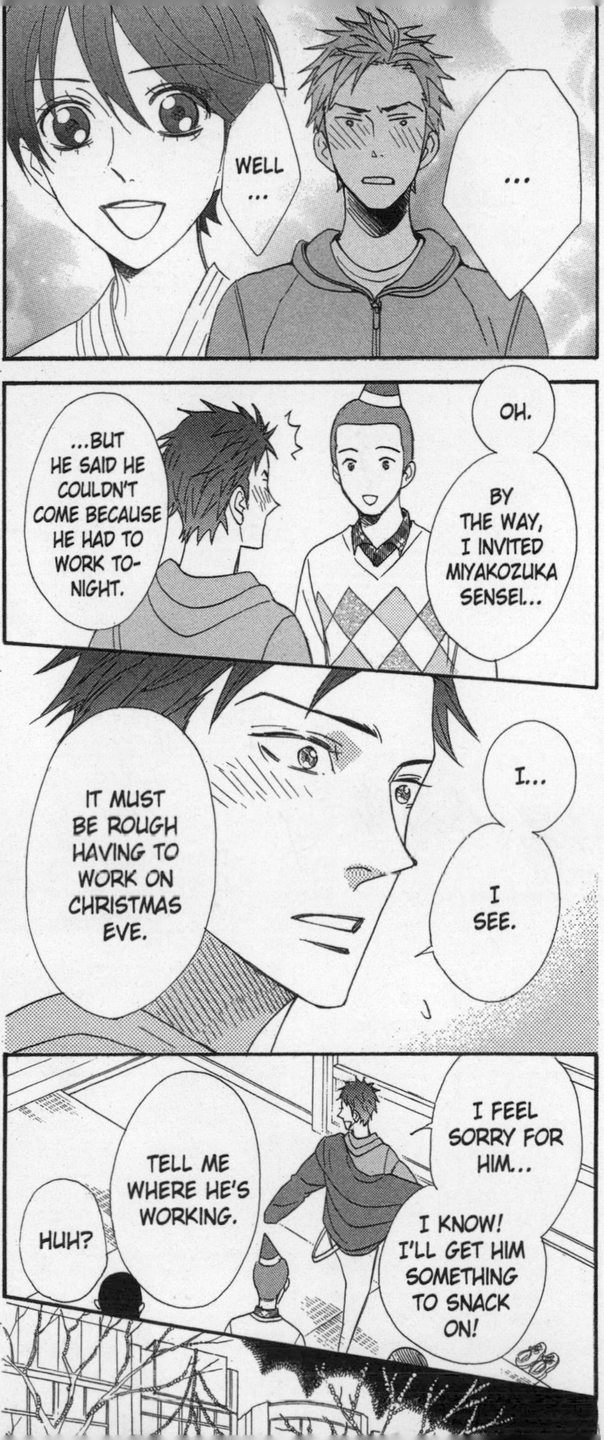
...
WELL ...
OH.
BY THE WAY, I INVITED MIYAKOZUKA SENSEI...
...BUT HE SAID HE COULDN'T COME BECAUSE HE HAD TO WORK TO-NIGHT.
I...
I SEE.
IT MUST BE ROUGH HAVING TO WORK ON CHRISTMAS EVE.
I FEEL SORRY FOR HIM...
I KNOW! I'LL GET HIM SOMETHING TO SNACK ON!
TELL ME WHERE HE'S WORKING.
HUH?

This is a continuation from the quarter column segment earlier in this volume.

Aside from Sakata's hair color changing, one of the judo team members disappears.

When this comic ran in *Hana to Yume*, there were five team members aside from Sakata. But then it became four!

How scary...

Otomen, or rather, my comics in general, change quite a bit between the *Hana to Yume* version and the graphic novel version. Or rather, they're corrected...

There was one more clear mistake, but I left it in as a memento. *(Laugh)*

The hint is Ryo's clothes...

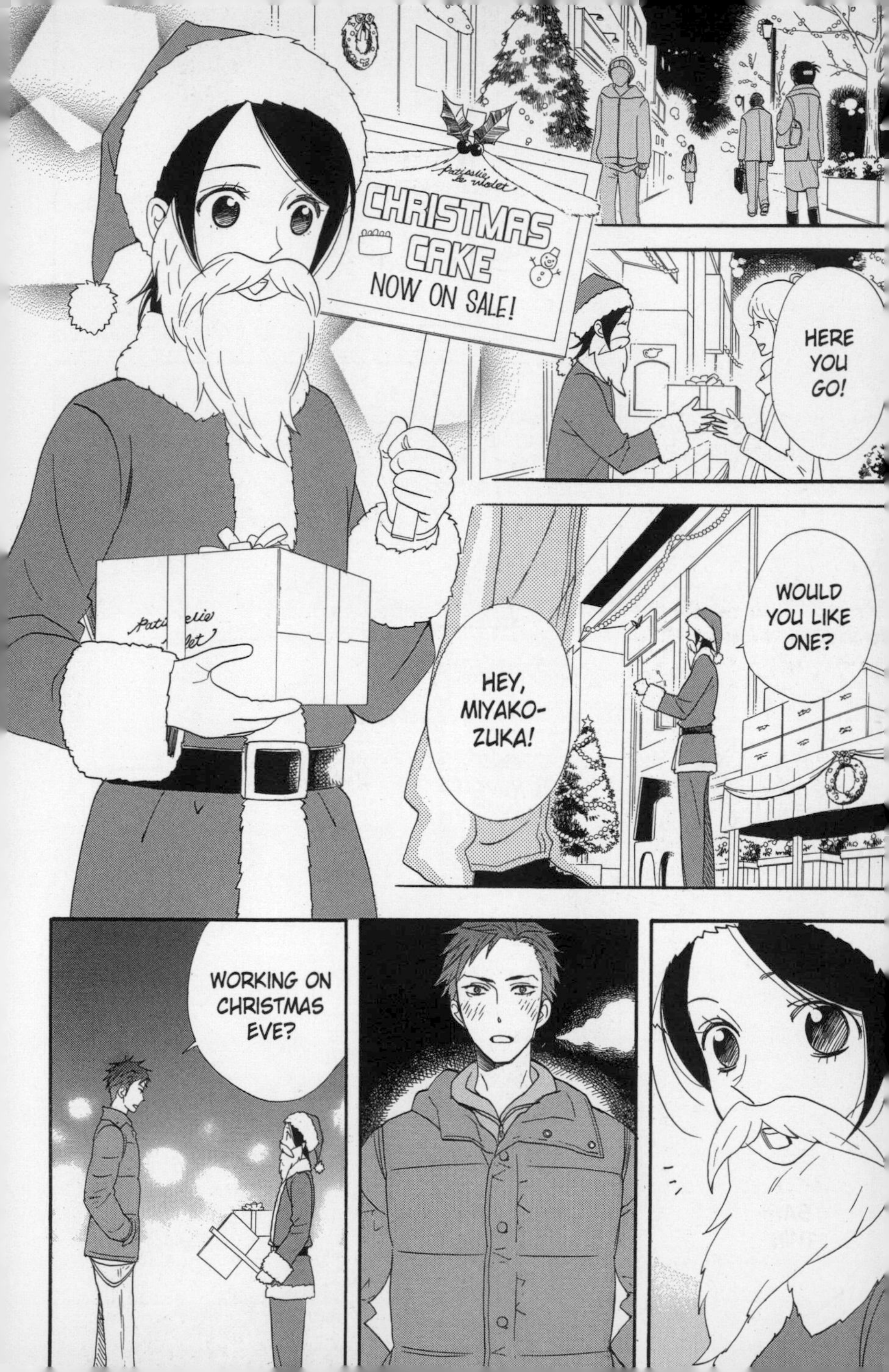
HERE YOU GO!
WOULD YOU LIKE ONE?
HEY, MIYAKO-ZUKA!
CHRISTMAS CAKE
NOW ON SALE!
WORKING ON CHRISTMAS EVE?

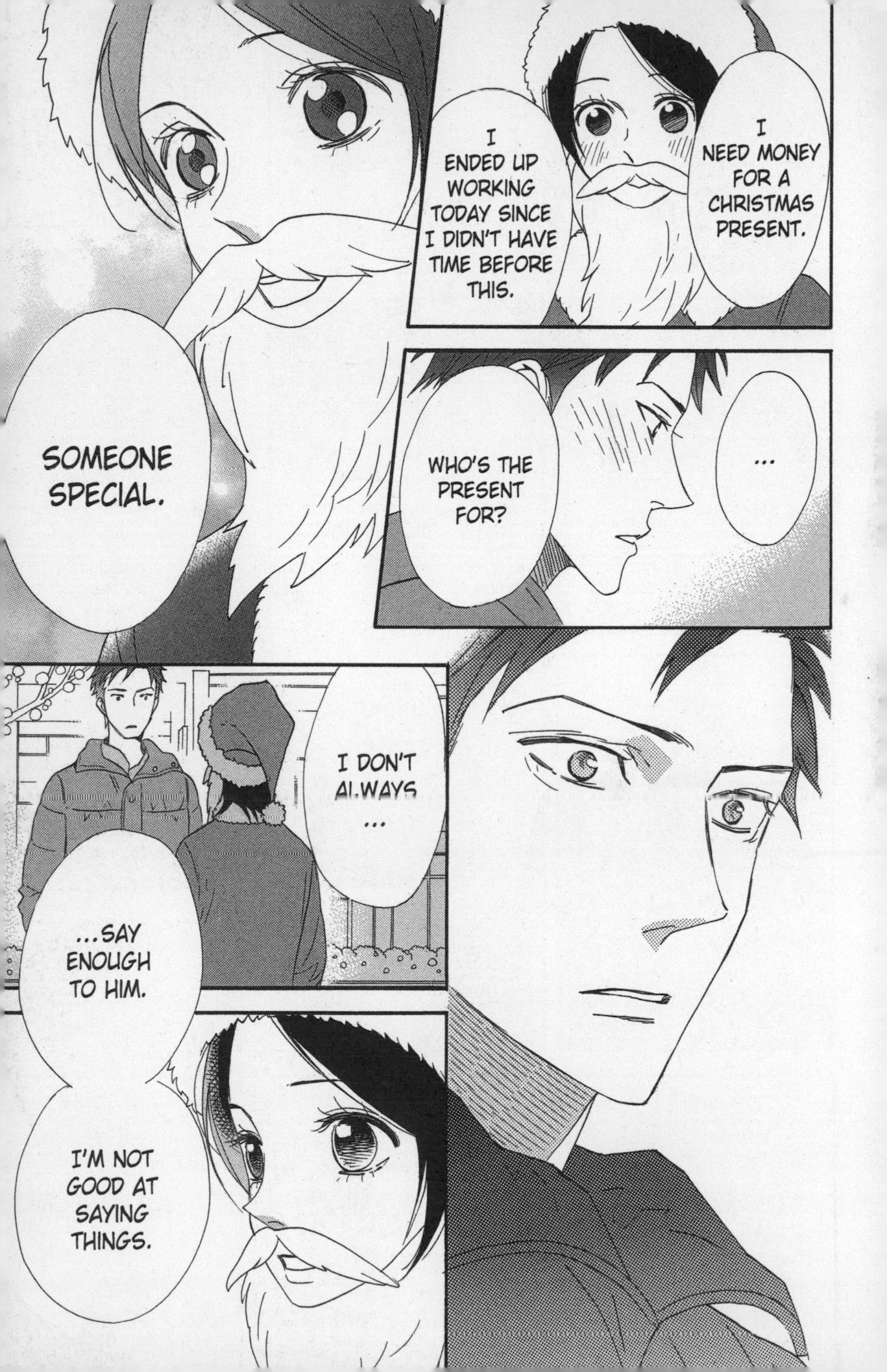
I NEED MONEY FOR A CHRISTMAS PRESENT.
I ENDED UP WORKING TODAY SINCE I DIDN'T HAVE TIME BEFORE THIS.
...
WHO'S THE PRESENT FOR?
SOMEONE SPECIAL.
I DON'T ALWAYS ...
...SAY ENOUGH TO HIM.
I'M NOT GOOD AT SAYING THINGS.

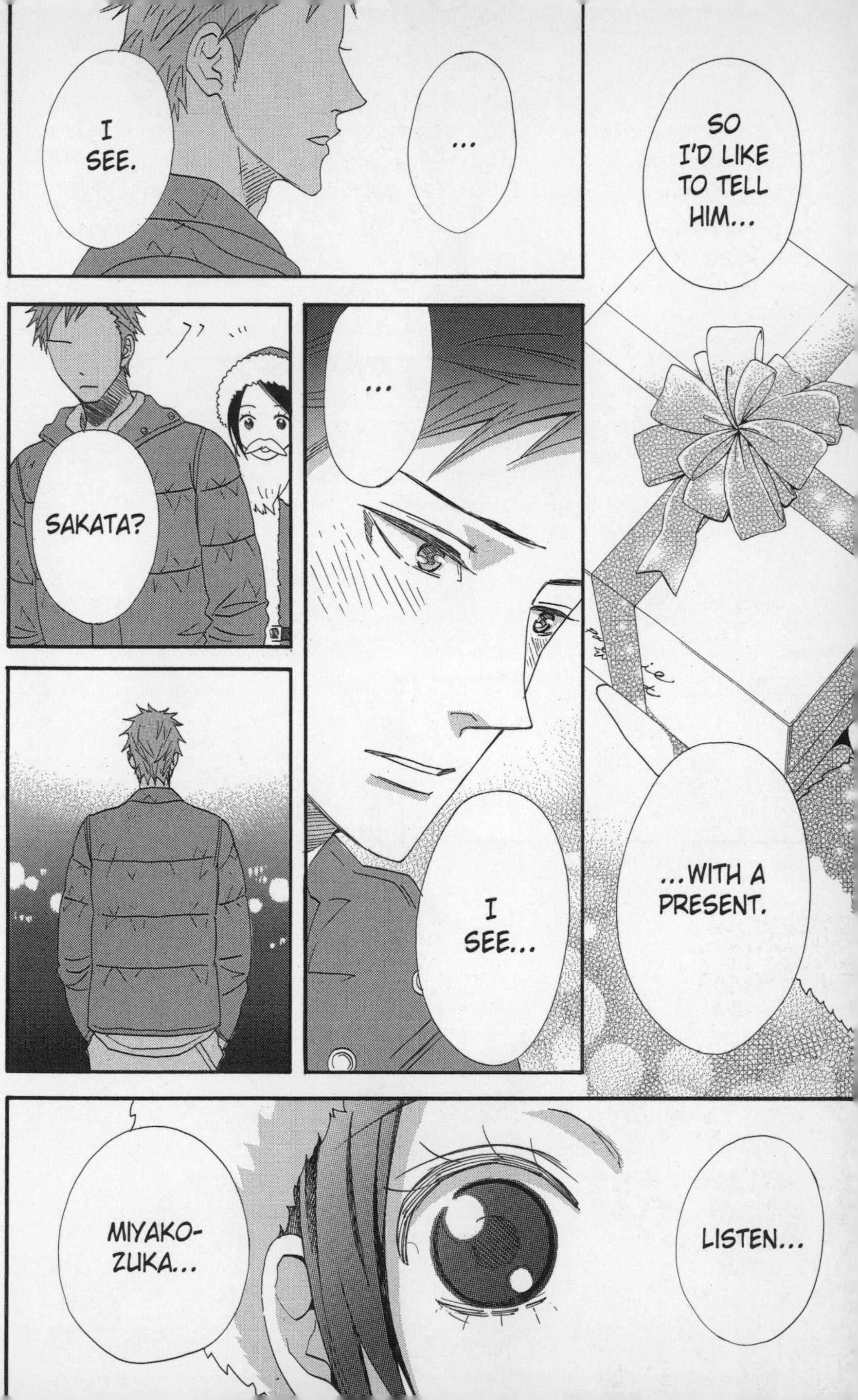
SO I'D LIKE TO TELL HIM...
...WITH A PRESENT.
...
I SEE.
...
I SEE...
SAKATA?
LISTEN...
MIYAKO-ZUKA...

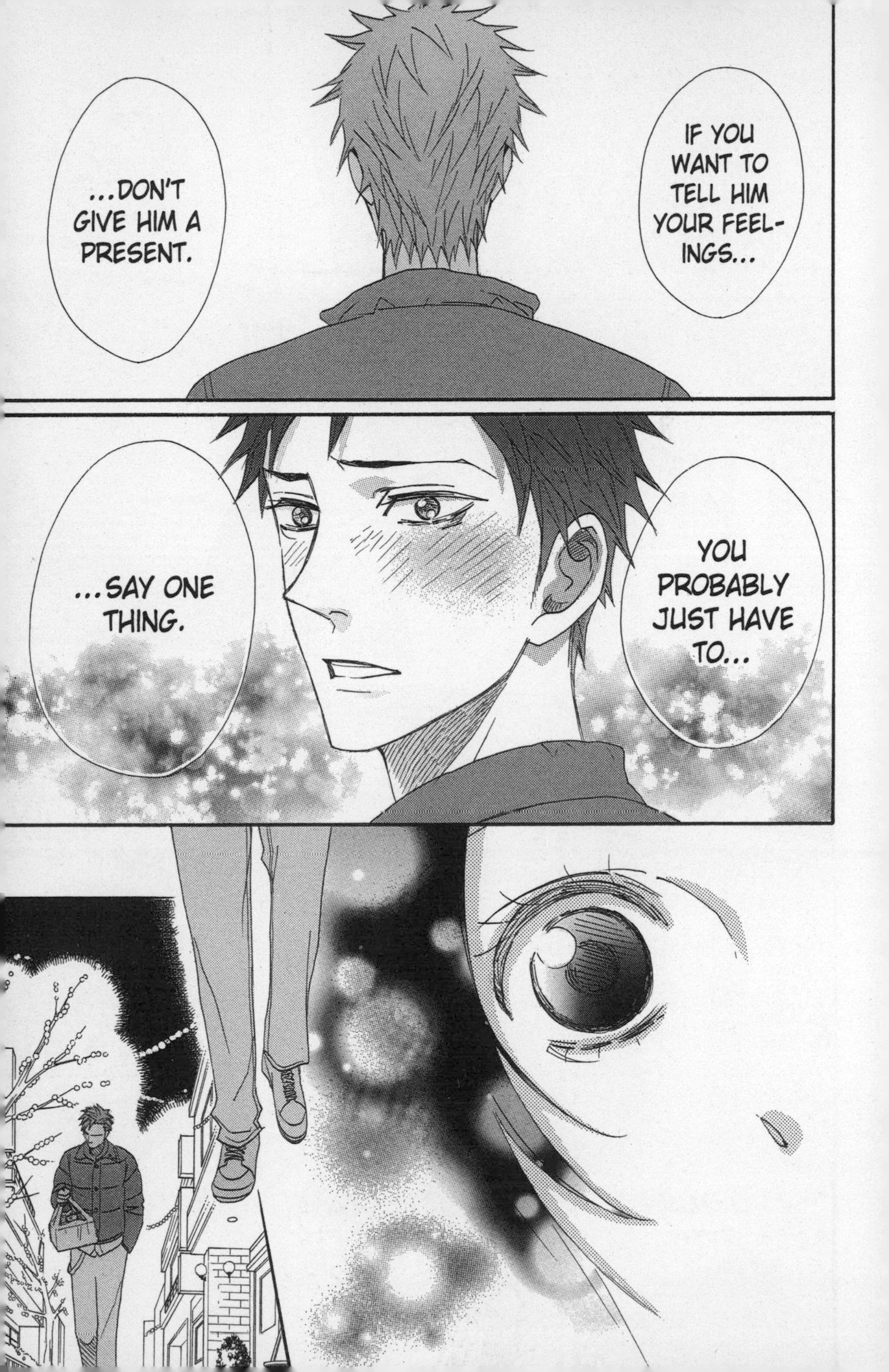
IF YOU WANT TO TELL HIM YOUR FEEL-INGS...
...DON'T GIVE HIM A PRESENT.
YOU PROBABLY JUST HAVE TO...
...SAY ONE THING.

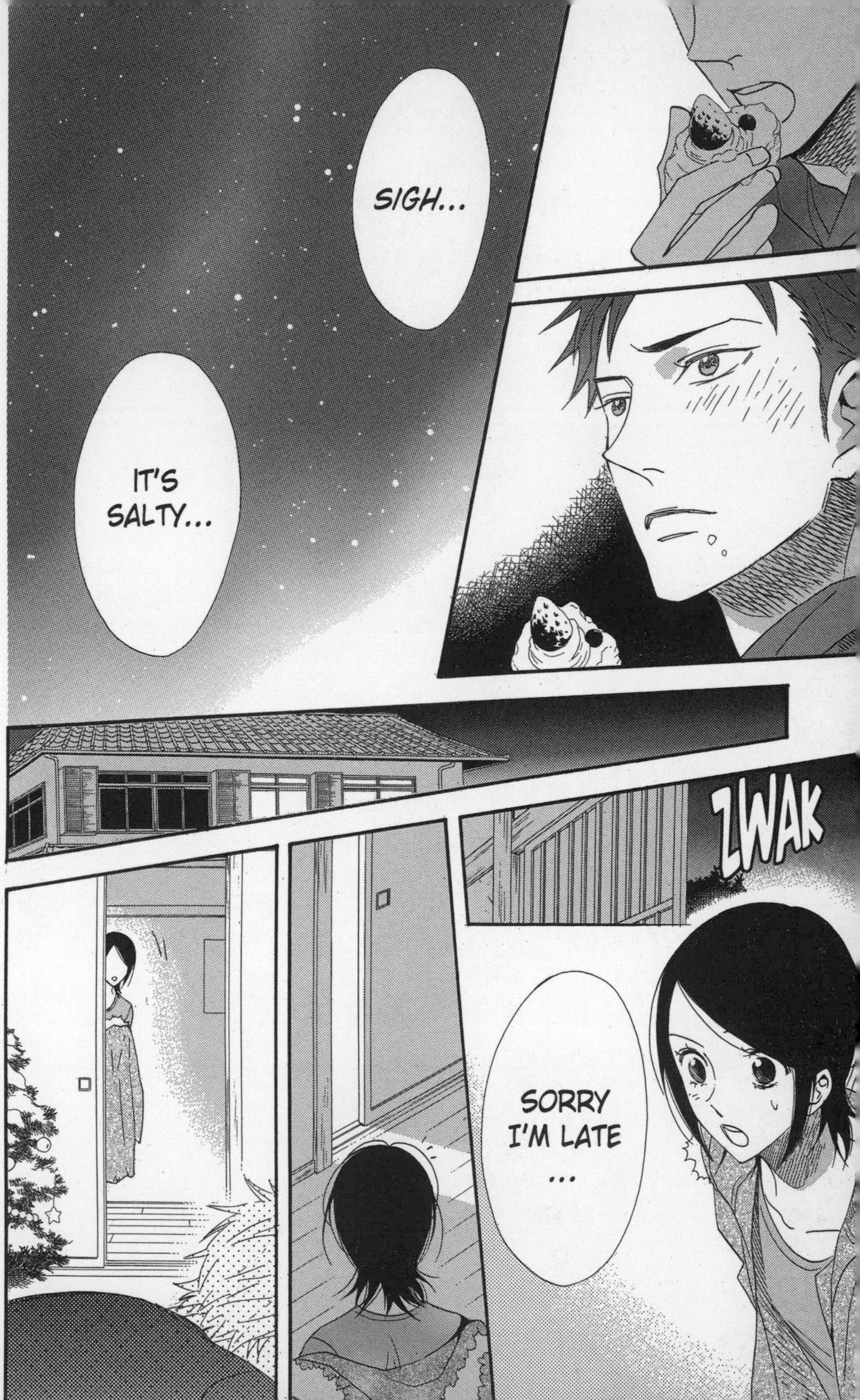
SIGH...
IT'S SALTY...
ZWAK
SORRY I'M LATE ...

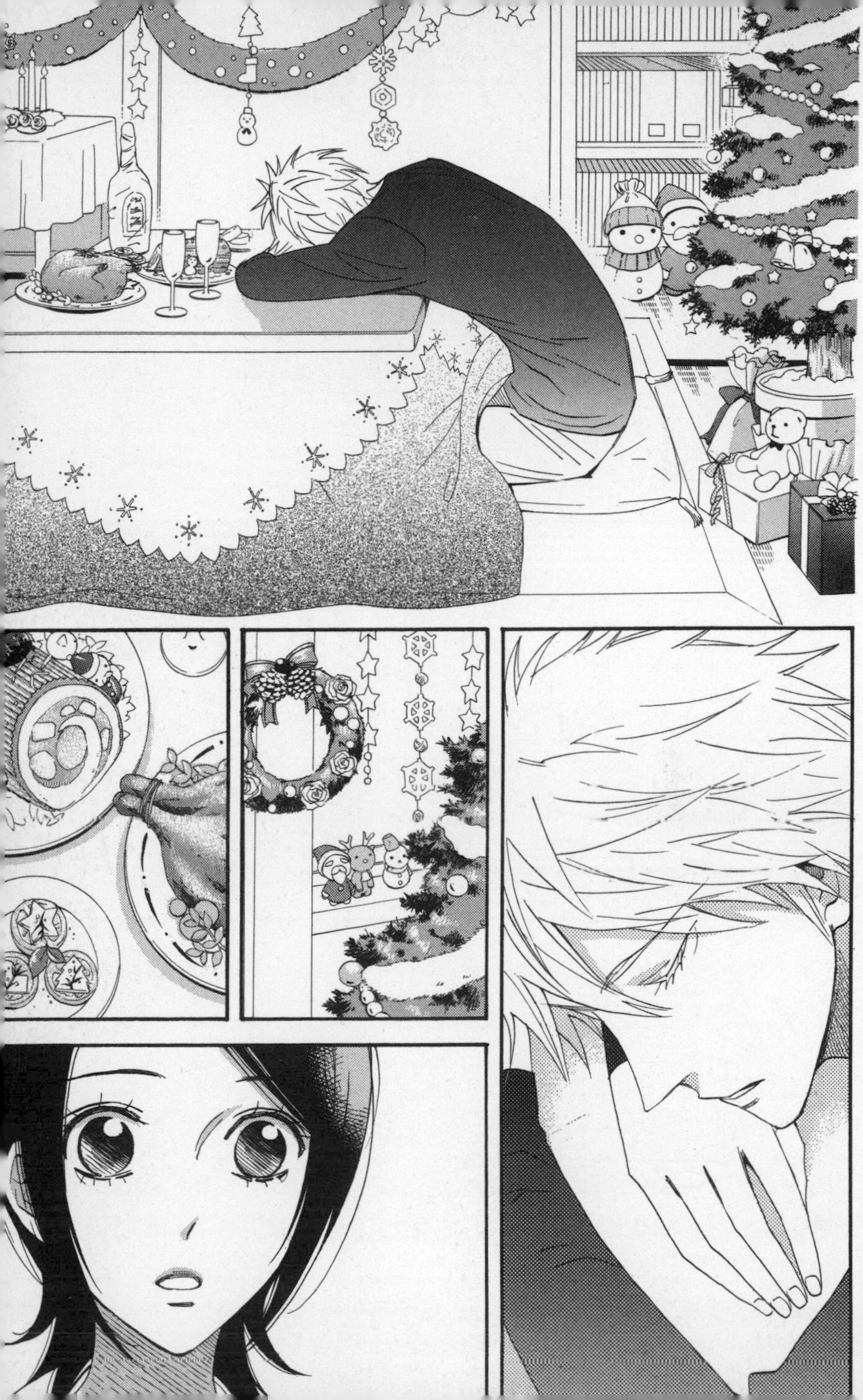

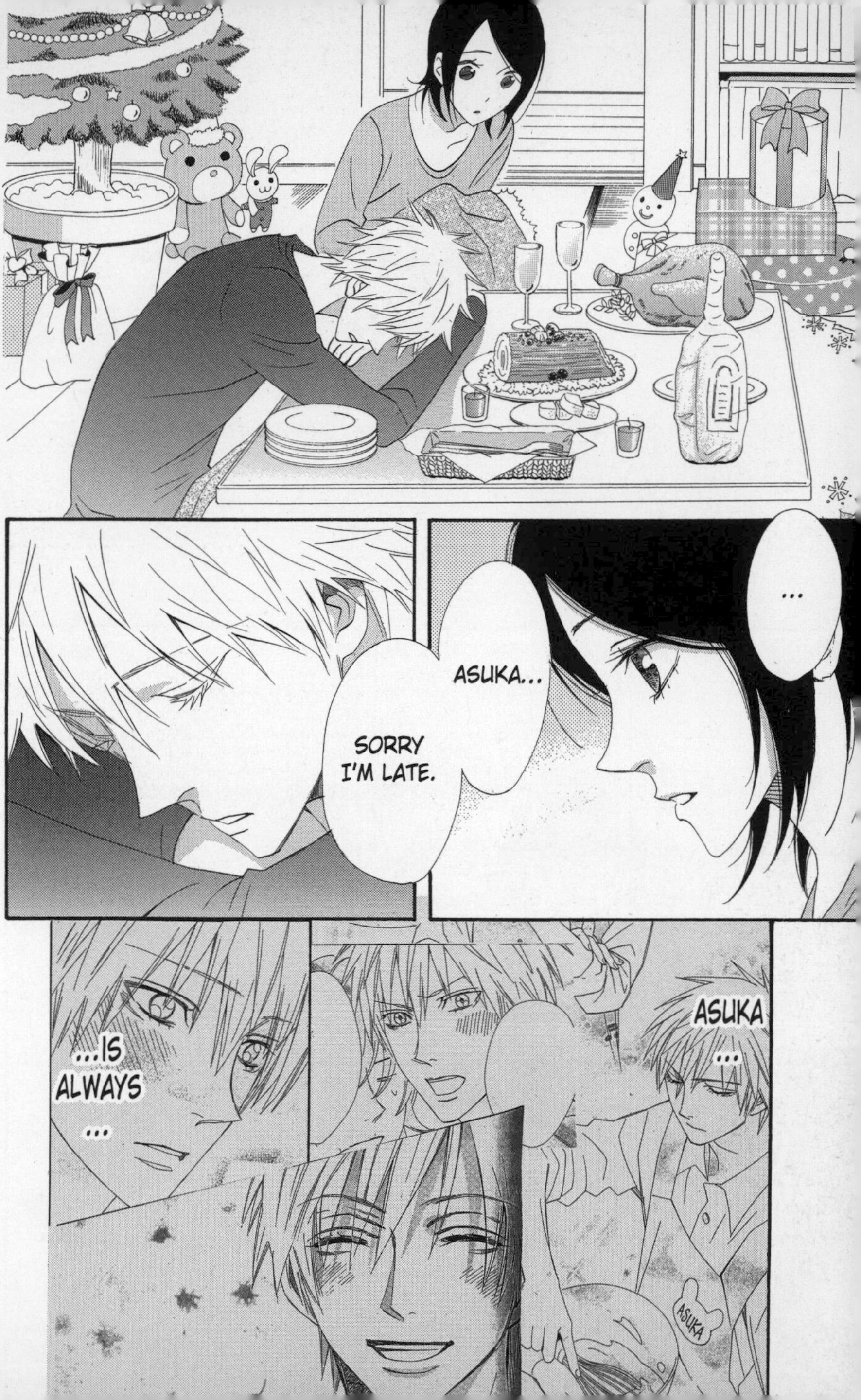
...
ASUKA...
SORRY I'M LATE.
ASUKA ...
ASUKA
...IS ALWAYS ...

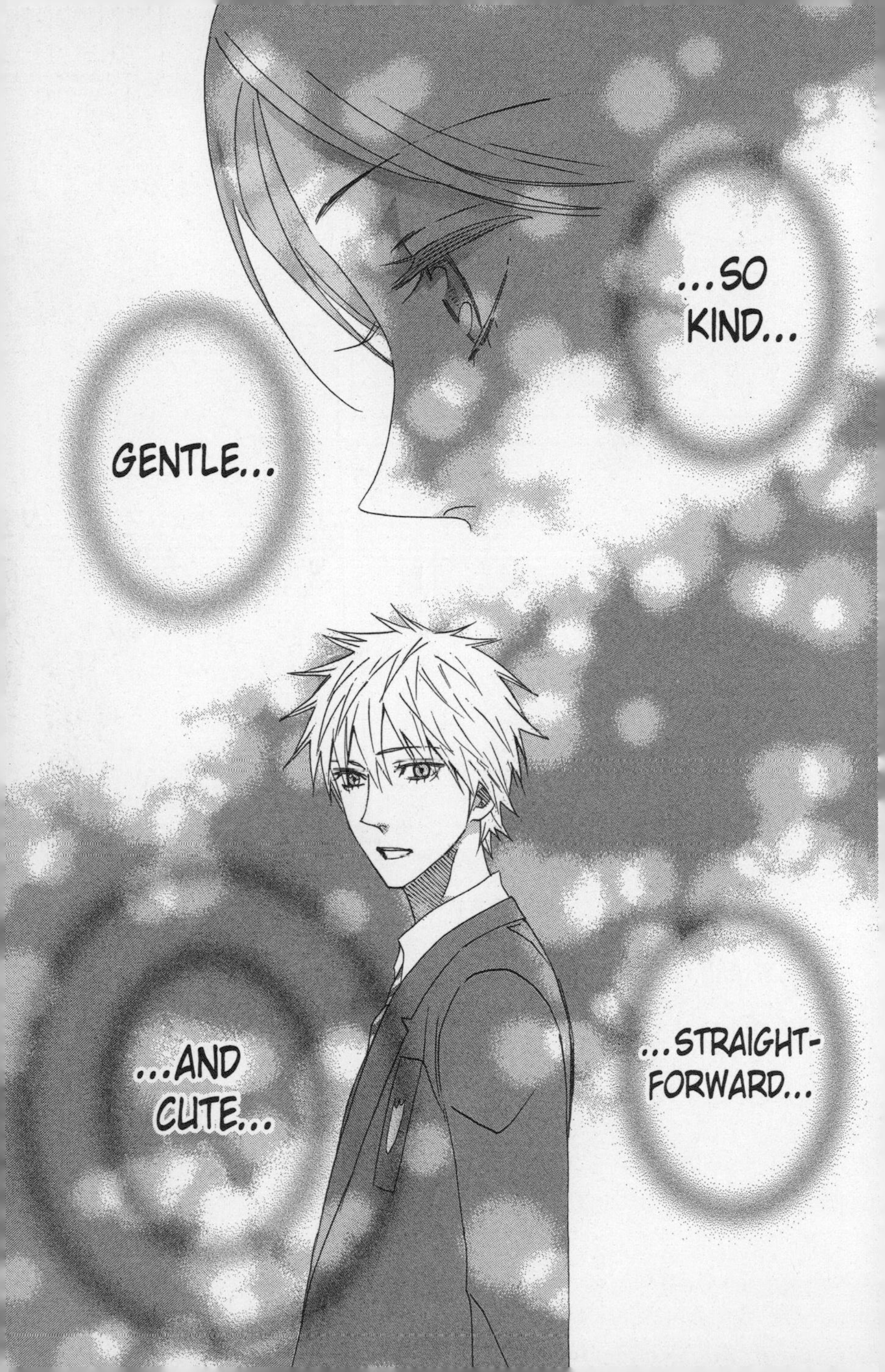
...SO KIND...
GENTLE...
...STRAIGHT-FORWARD...
...AND CUTE...

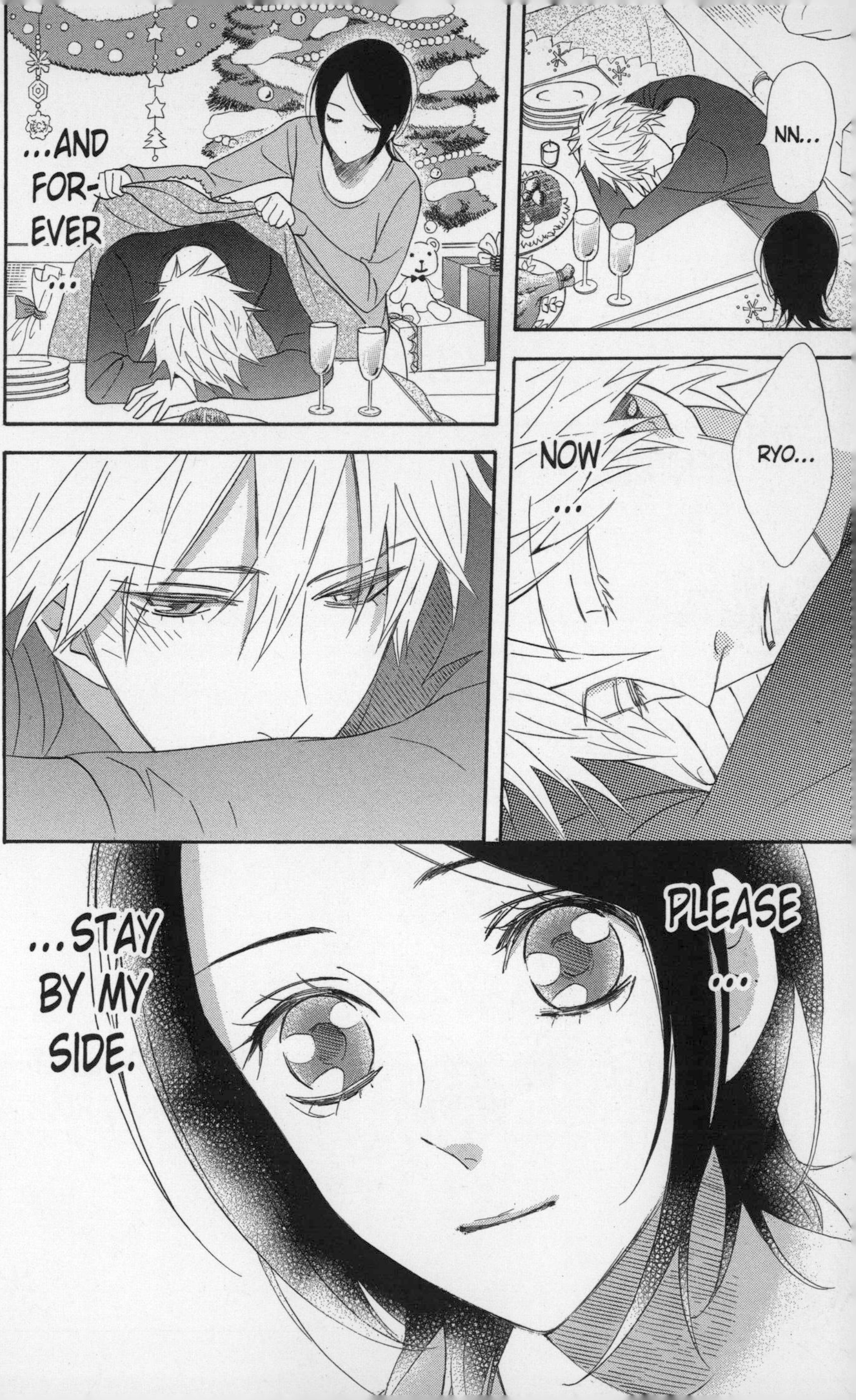

NN...
...AND FOR-EVER ...
RYO...
NOW ...
PLEASE ...
...STAY BY MY SIDE.

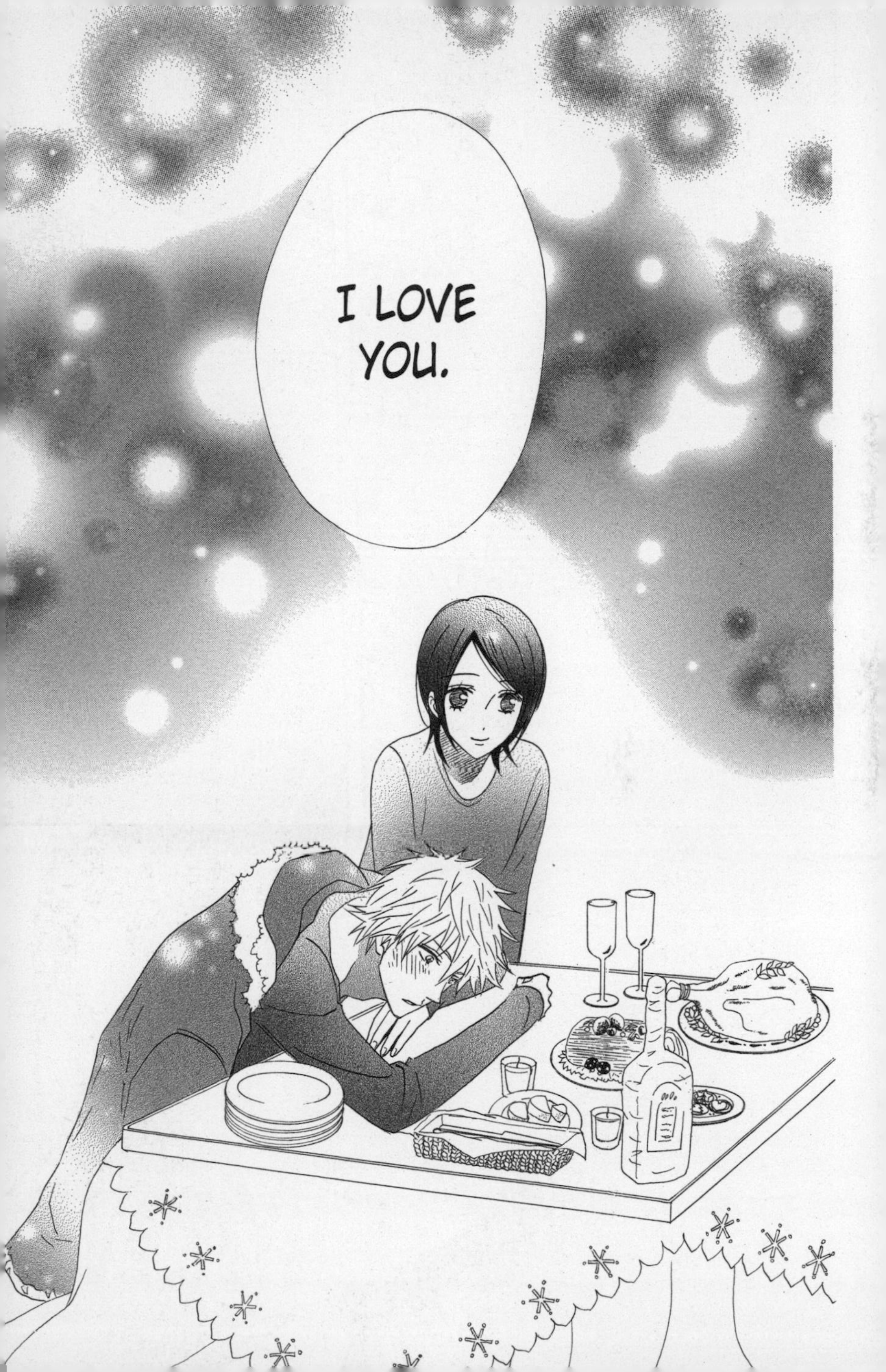
I LOVE YOU.

OTOMEN

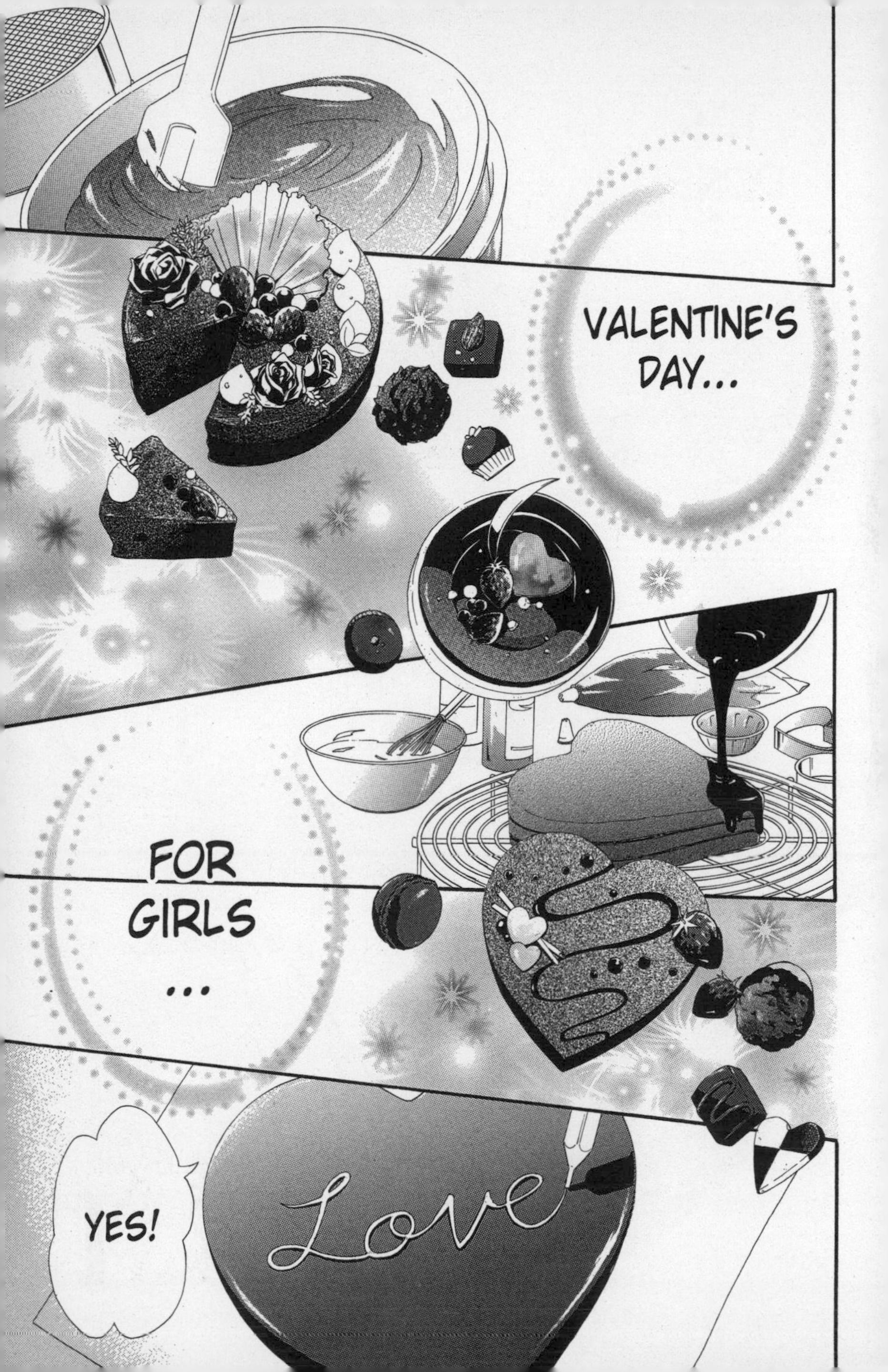
VALENTINE'S DAY...
FOR GIRLS ...
Love
YES!

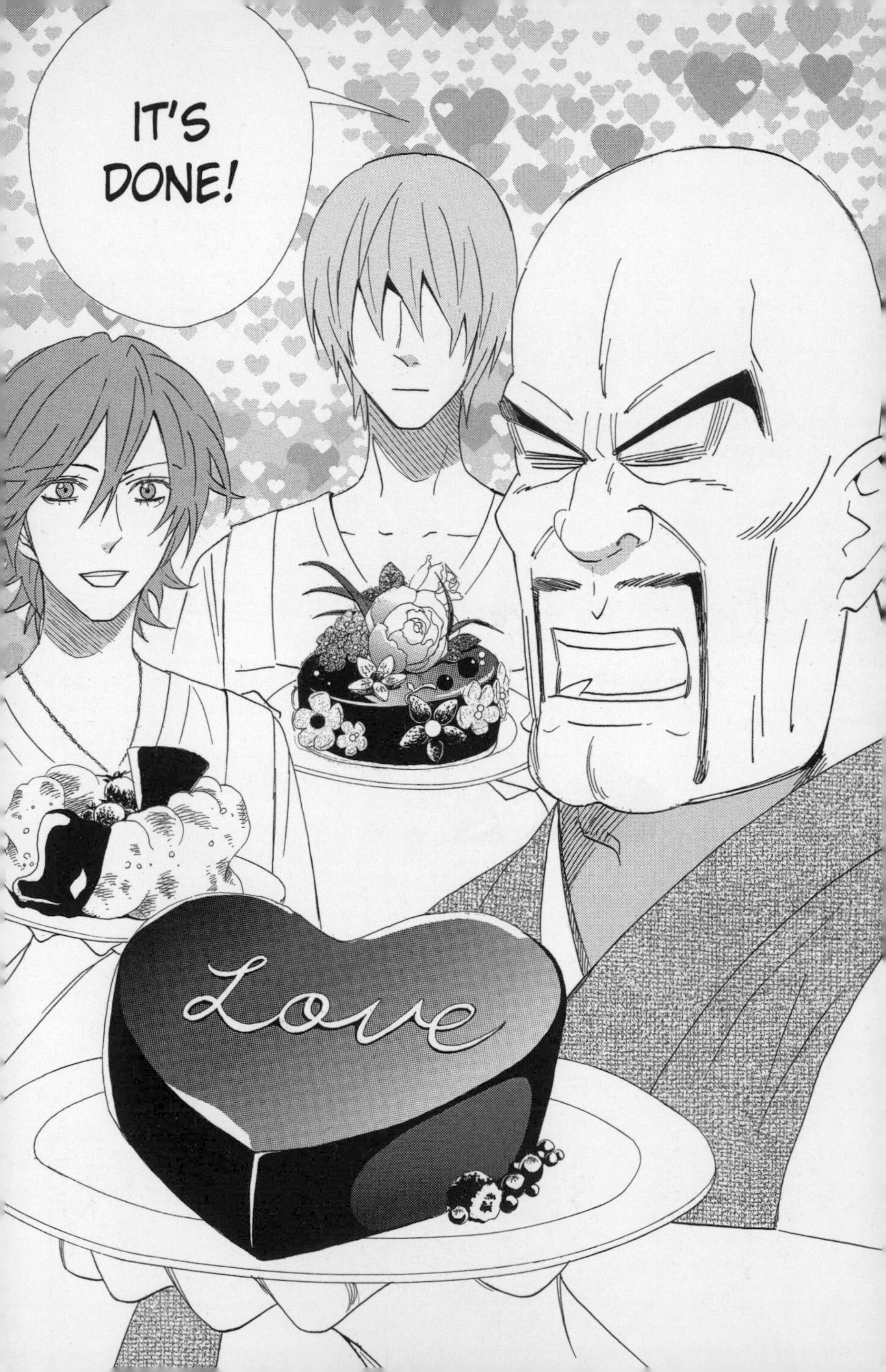
IT'S DONE!
Love

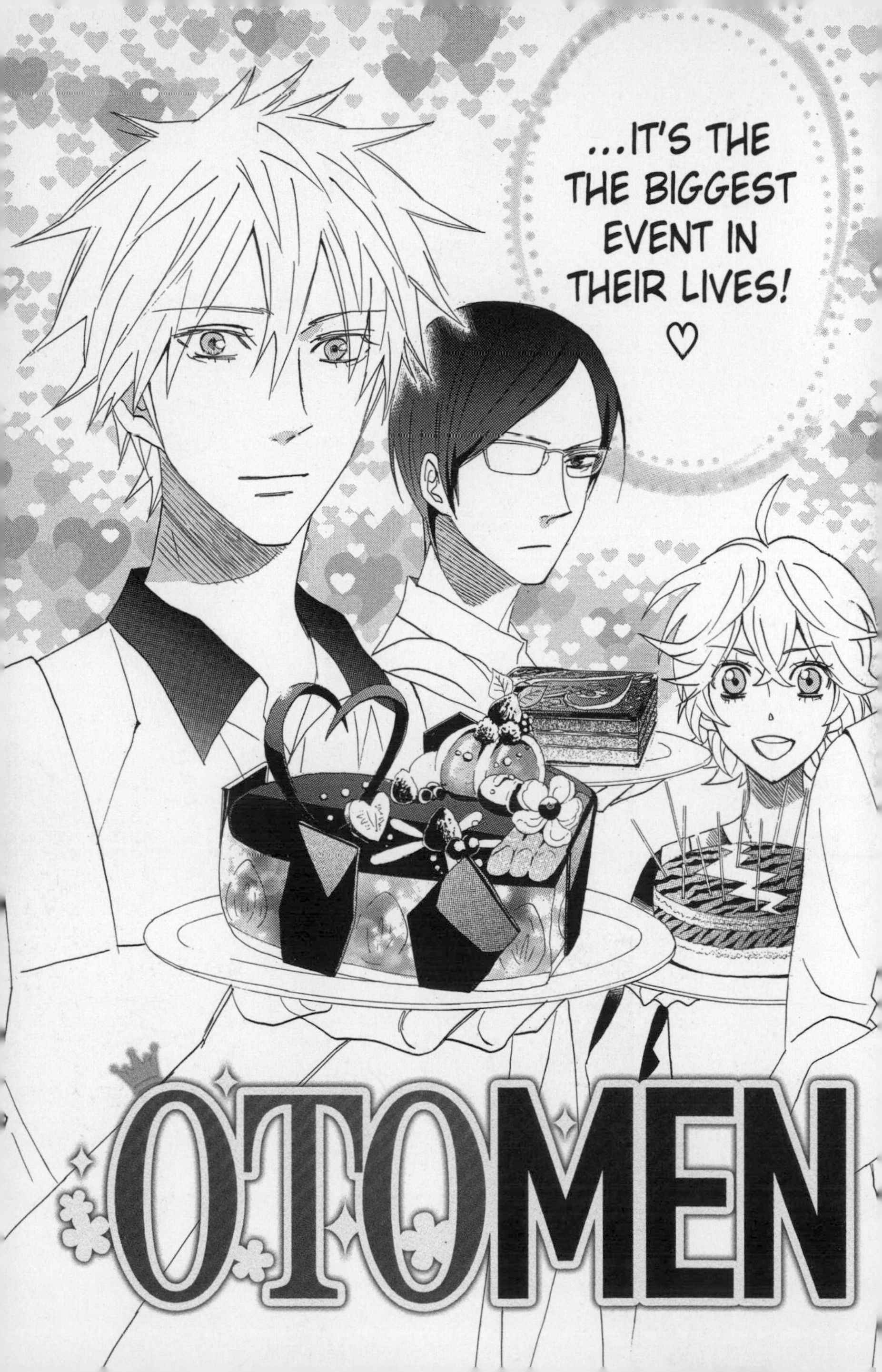
...IT'S THE THE BIGGEST EVENT IN THEIR LIVES! ♡
OTOMEN

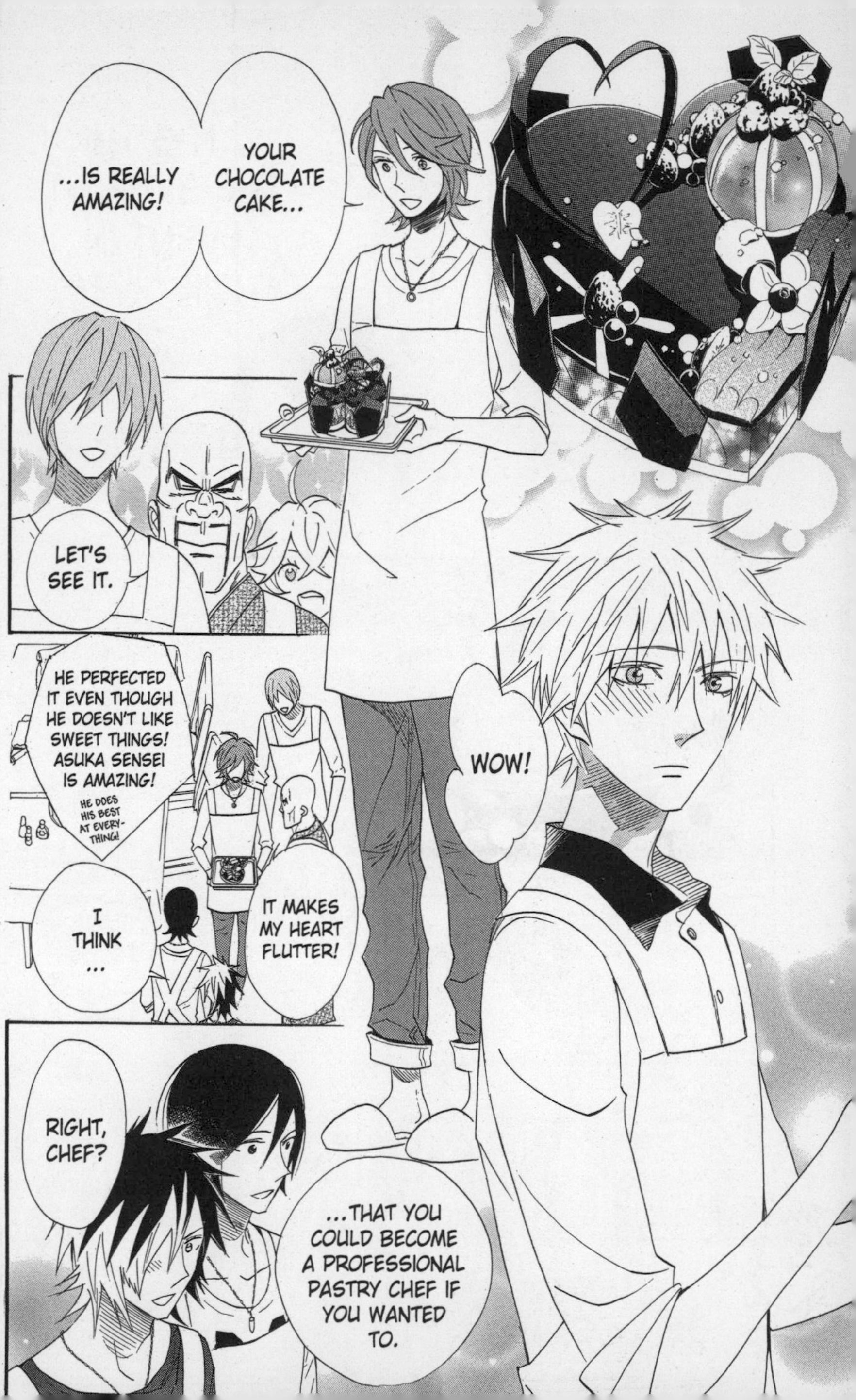
YOUR CHOCOLATE CAKE...
...IS REALLY AMAZING!
WOW!
LET'S SEE IT.
HE PERFECTED IT EVEN THOUGH HE DOESN'T LIKE SWEET THINGS! ASUKA SENSEI IS AMAZING!
HE DOES HIS BEST AT EVERY-THING!
IT MAKES MY HEART FLUTTER!
I THINK...
...THAT YOU COULD BECOME A PROFESSIONAL PASTRY CHEF IF YOU WANTED TO.
RIGHT, CHEF?

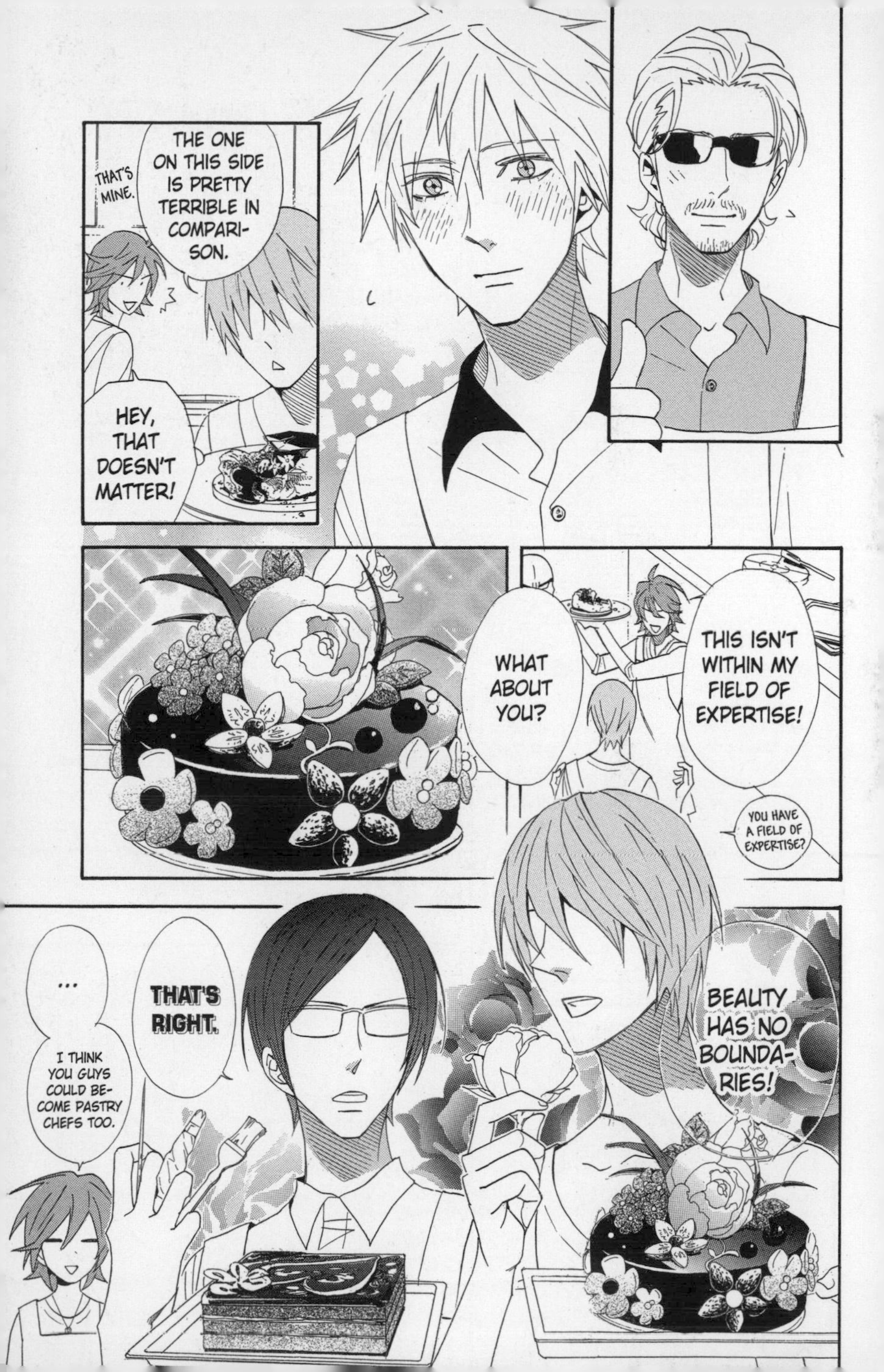
THE ONE ON THIS SIDE IS PRETTY TERRIBLE IN COMPARI-SON.
THAT'S MINE.
HEY, THAT DOESN'T MATTER!
THIS ISN'T WITHIN MY FIELD OF EXPERTISE!
WHAT ABOUT YOU?
YOU HAVE A FIELD OF EXPERTISE?
BEAUTY HAS NO BOUNDA-RIES!
THAT'S RIGHT.
...
I THINK YOU GUYS COULD BE-COME PASTRY CHEFS TOO.

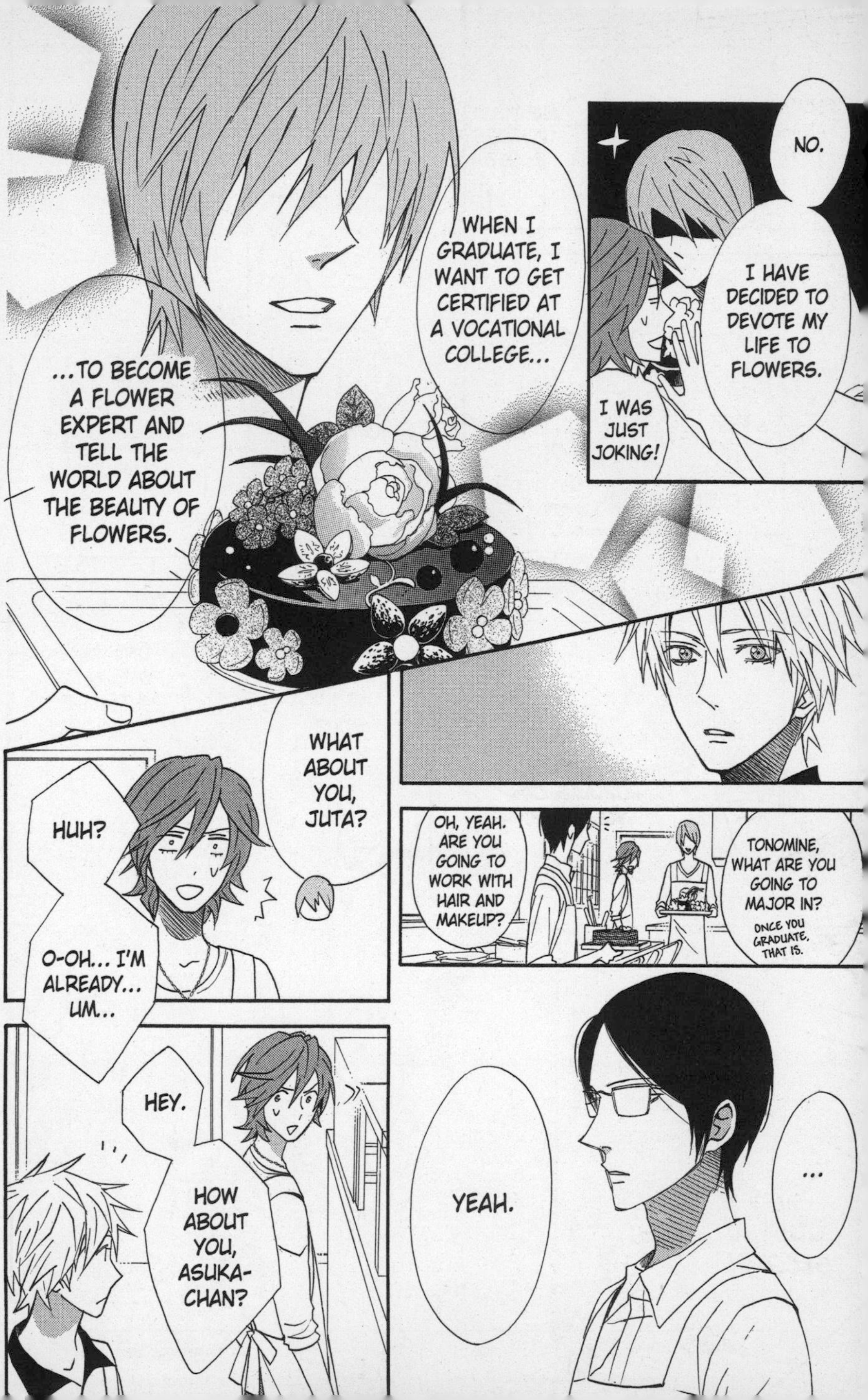
NO.
I HAVE DECIDED TO DEVOTE MY LIFE TO FLOWERS.
I WAS JUST JOKING!
WHEN I GRADUATE, I WANT TO GET CERTIFIED AT A VOCATIONAL COLLEGE...
...TO BECOME A FLOWER EXPERT AND TELL THE WORLD ABOUT THE BEAUTY OF FLOWERS.
TONOMINE, WHAT ARE YOU GOING TO MAJOR IN?
ONCE YOU GRADUATE, THAT IS.
OH, YEAH. ARE YOU GOING TO WORK WITH HAIR AND MAKEUP?
WHAT ABOUT YOU, JUTA?
HUH?
O-OH... I'M ALREADY... UM...
...
YEAH.
HEY.
HOW ABOUT YOU, ASUKA-CHAN?

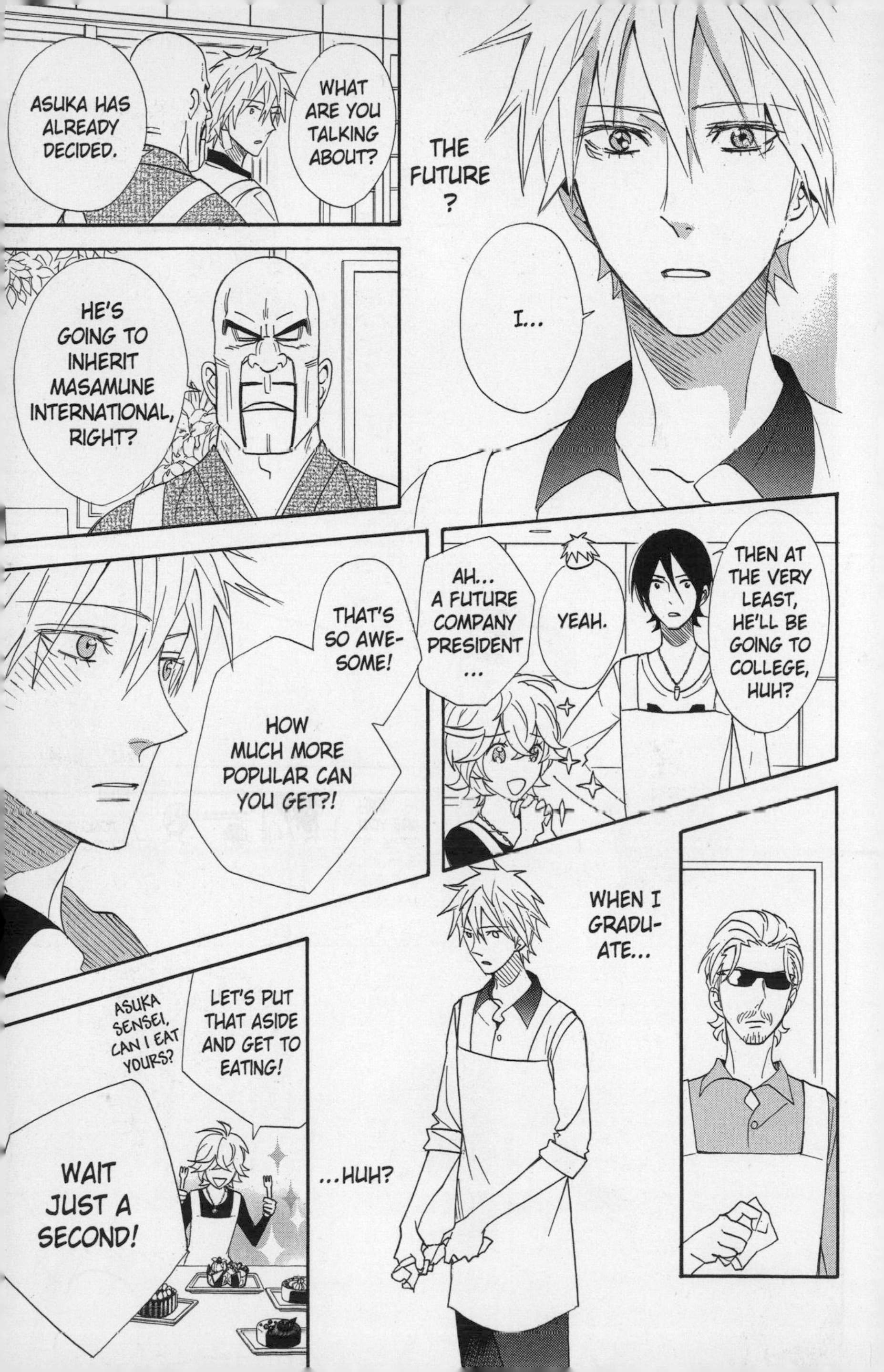
THE FUTURE ?
I...
WHAT ARE YOU TALKING ABOUT?
ASUKA HAS ALREADY DECIDED.
HE'S GOING TO INHERIT MASAMUNE INTERNATIONAL, RIGHT?
THEN AT THE VERY LEAST, HE'LL BE GOING TO COLLEGE, HUH?
YEAH.
AH... A FUTURE COMPANY PRESIDENT...
THAT'S SO AWE-SOME!
HOW MUCH MORE POPULAR CAN YOU GET?!
WHEN I GRADU-ATE...
...HUH?
LET'S PUT THAT ASIDE AND GET TO EATING!
ASUKA SENSEI, CAN I EAT YOURS?
WAIT JUST A SECOND!

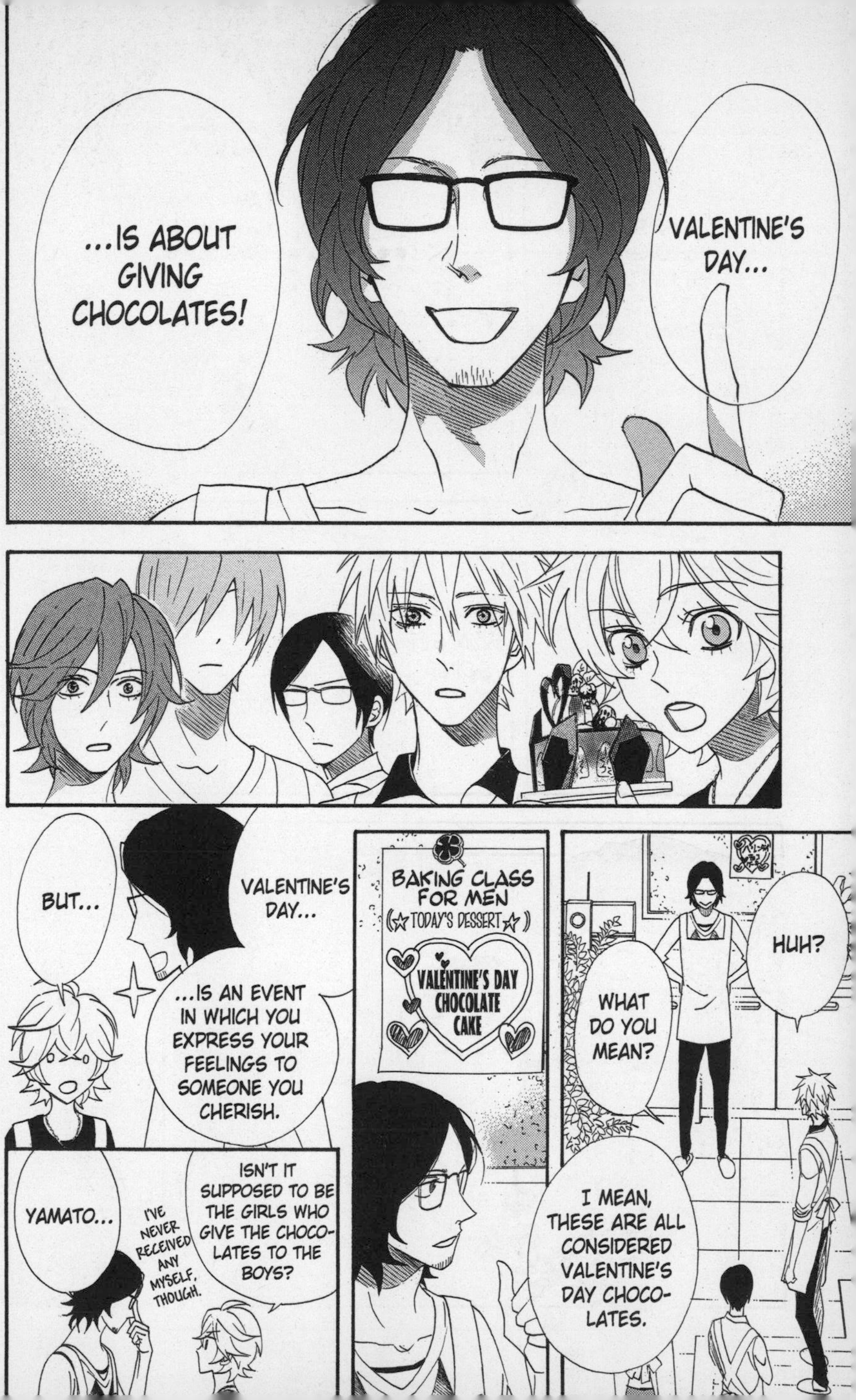
VALENTINE'S DAY...
...IS ABOUT GIVING CHOCOLATES!
HUH?
WHAT DO YOU MEAN?
I MEAN, THESE ARE ALL CONSIDERED VALENTINE'S DAY CHOCO-LATES.
BAKING CLASS FOR MEN
TODAY'S DESSERT
VALENTINE'S DAY CHOCOLATE CAKE
VALENTINE'S DAY...
...IS AN EVENT IN WHICH YOU EXPRESS YOUR FEELINGS TO SOMEONE YOU CHERISH.
BUT...
ISN'T IT SUPPOSED TO BE THE GIRLS WHO GIVE THE CHOCO-LATES TO THE BOYS?
I'VE NEVER RECEIVED ANY MYSELF, THOUGH.
YAMATO...

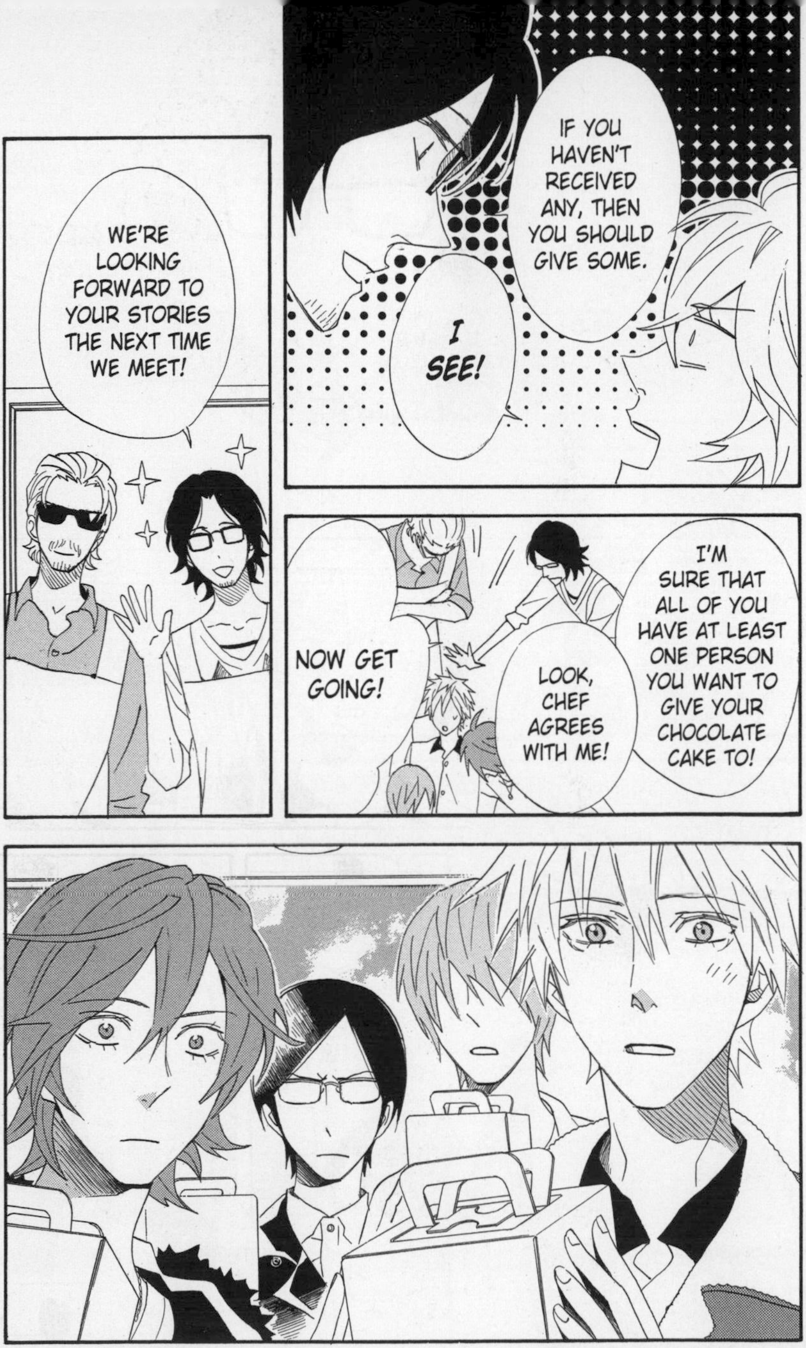
IF YOU HAVEN'T RECEIVED ANY, THEN YOU SHOULD GIVE SOME.
I SEE!
I'M SURE THAT ALL OF YOU HAVE AT LEAST ONE PERSON YOU WANT TO GIVE YOUR CHOCOLATE CAKE TO!
LOOK, CHEF AGREES WITH ME!
NOW GET GOING!
WE'RE LOOKING FORWARD TO YOUR STORIES THE NEXT TIME WE MEET!

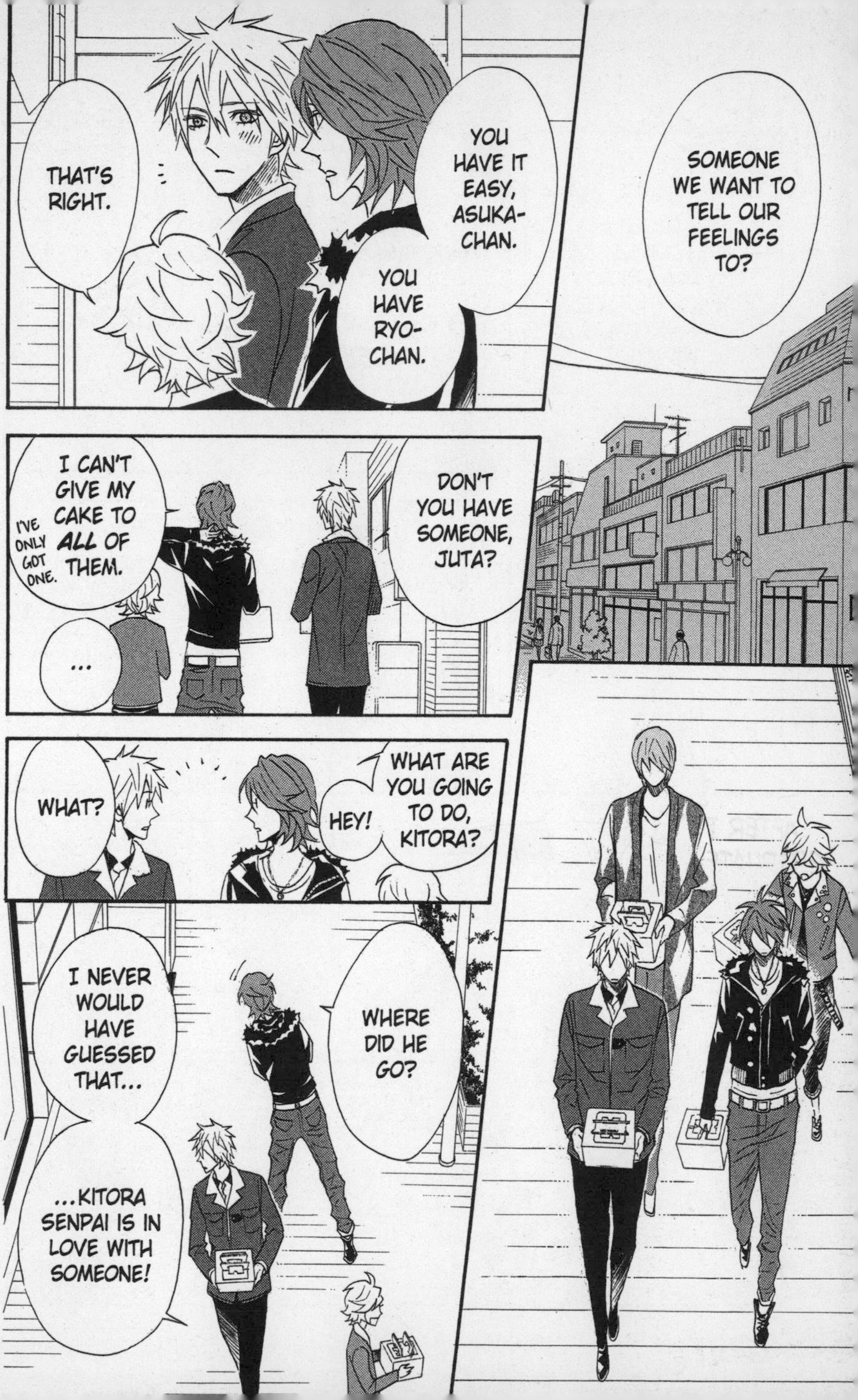
SOMEONE WE WANT TO TELL OUR FEELINGS TO?
YOU HAVE IT EASY, ASUKA-CHAN.
YOU HAVE RYO-CHAN.
THAT'S RIGHT.
DON'T YOU HAVE SOMEONE, JUTA?
I CAN'T GIVE MY CAKE TO ALL OF THEM.
I'VE ONLY GOT ONE.
...
WHAT ARE YOU GOING TO DO, KITORA?
HEY!
WHAT?
WHERE DID HE GO?
I NEVER WOULD HAVE GUESSED THAT...
...KITORA SENPAI IS IN LOVE WITH SOMEONE!

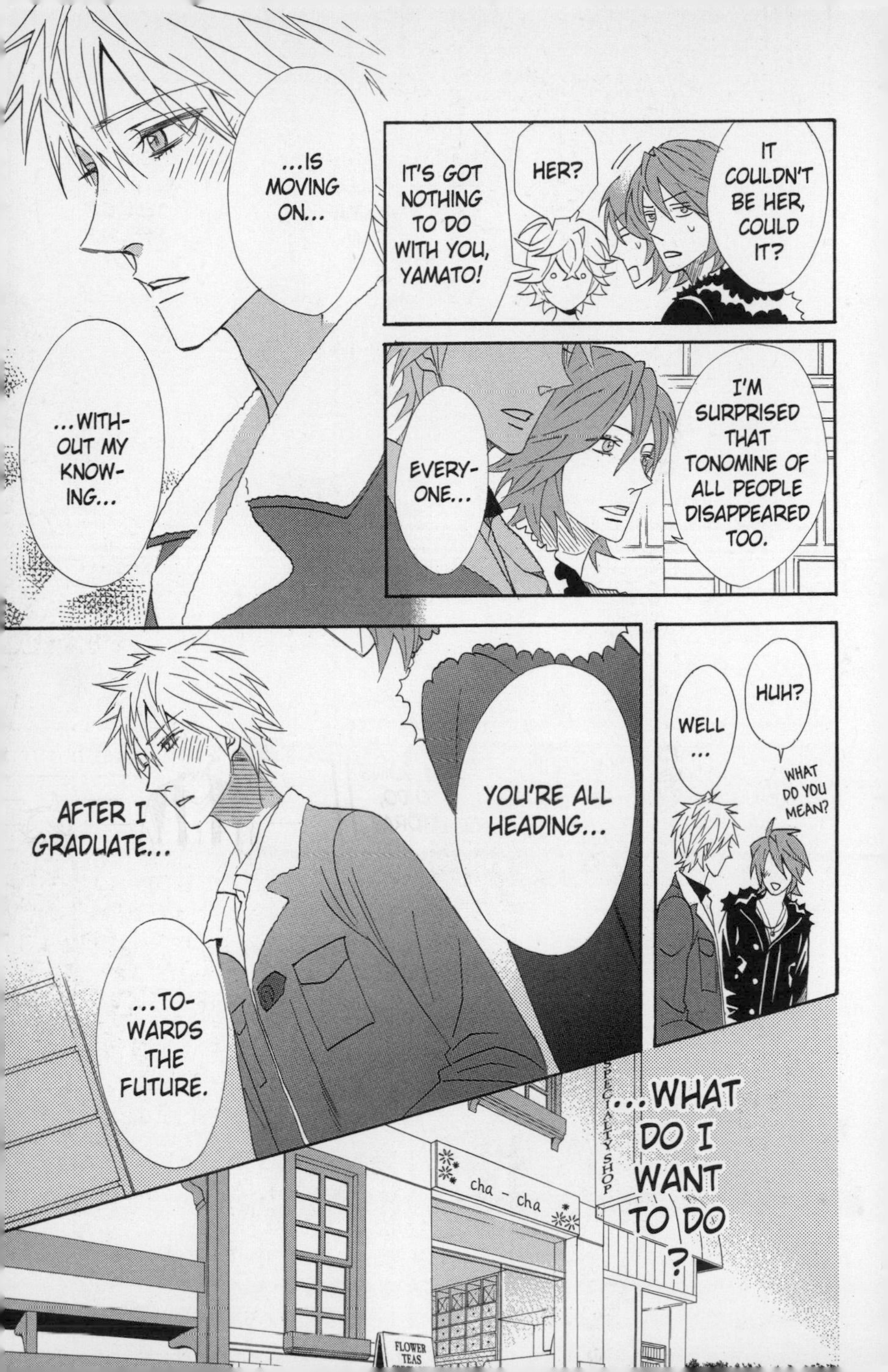
IT COULDN'T BE HER, COULD IT?
HER?
IT'S GOT NOTHING TO DO WITH YOU, YAMATO!
I'M SURPRISED THAT TONOMINE OF ALL PEOPLE DISAPPEARED TOO.
EVERY-ONE...
...IS MOVING ON...
...WITH-OUT MY KNOW-ING...
HUH?
WHAT DO YOU MEAN?
WELL...
YOU'RE ALL HEADING...
...TO-WARDS THE FUTURE.
AFTER I GRADUATE...
...WHAT DO I WANT TO DO?
SPECIALTY SHOP
cha - cha
FLOWER TEAS

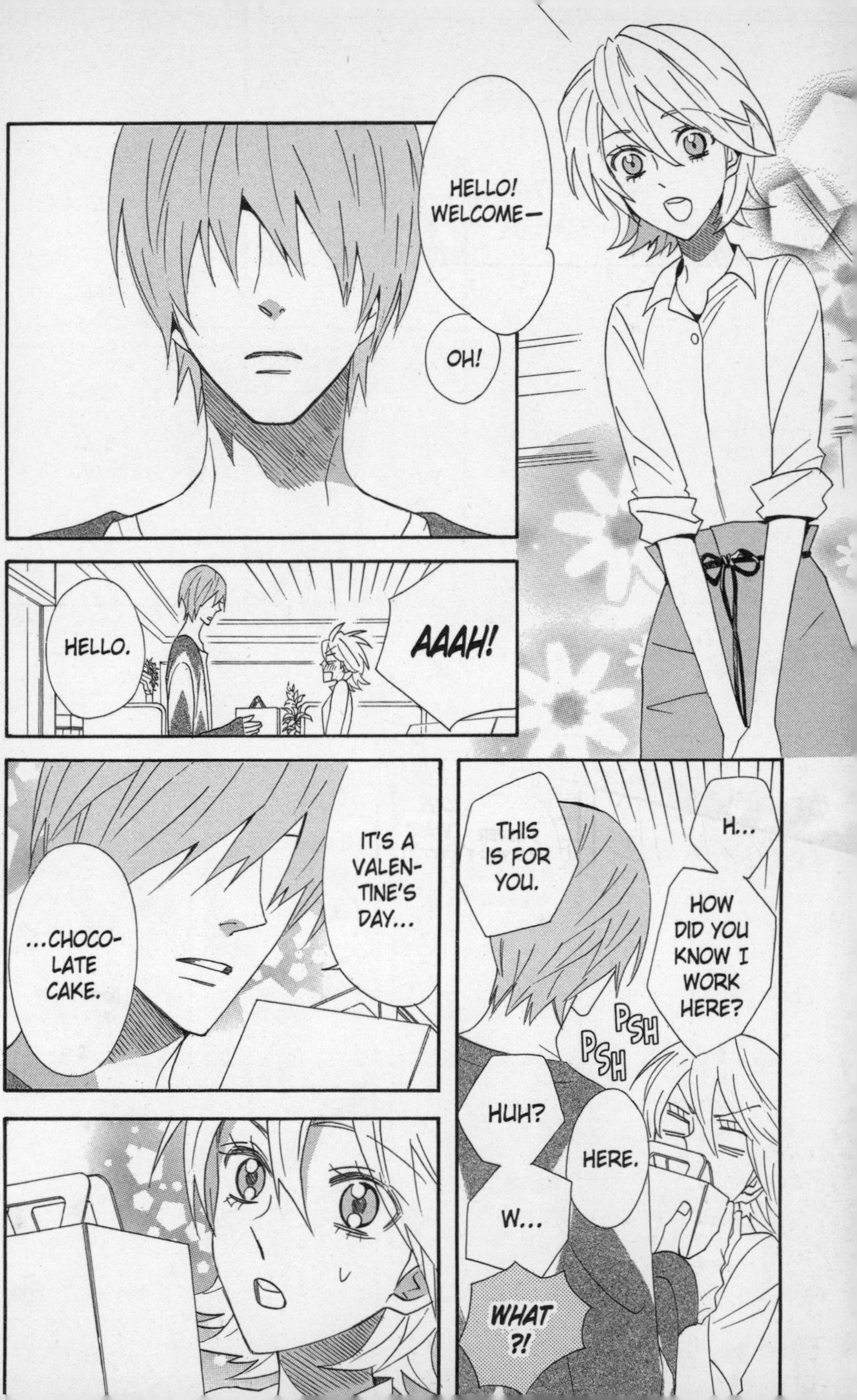
HELLO! WELCOME—
OH!
AAAH!
HELLO.
H...
HOW DID YOU KNOW I WORK HERE?
THIS IS FOR YOU.
PSH
PSH
HUH?
HERE.
W...
WHAT?!
IT'S A VALEN-TINE'S DAY...
...CHOCO-LATE CAKE.

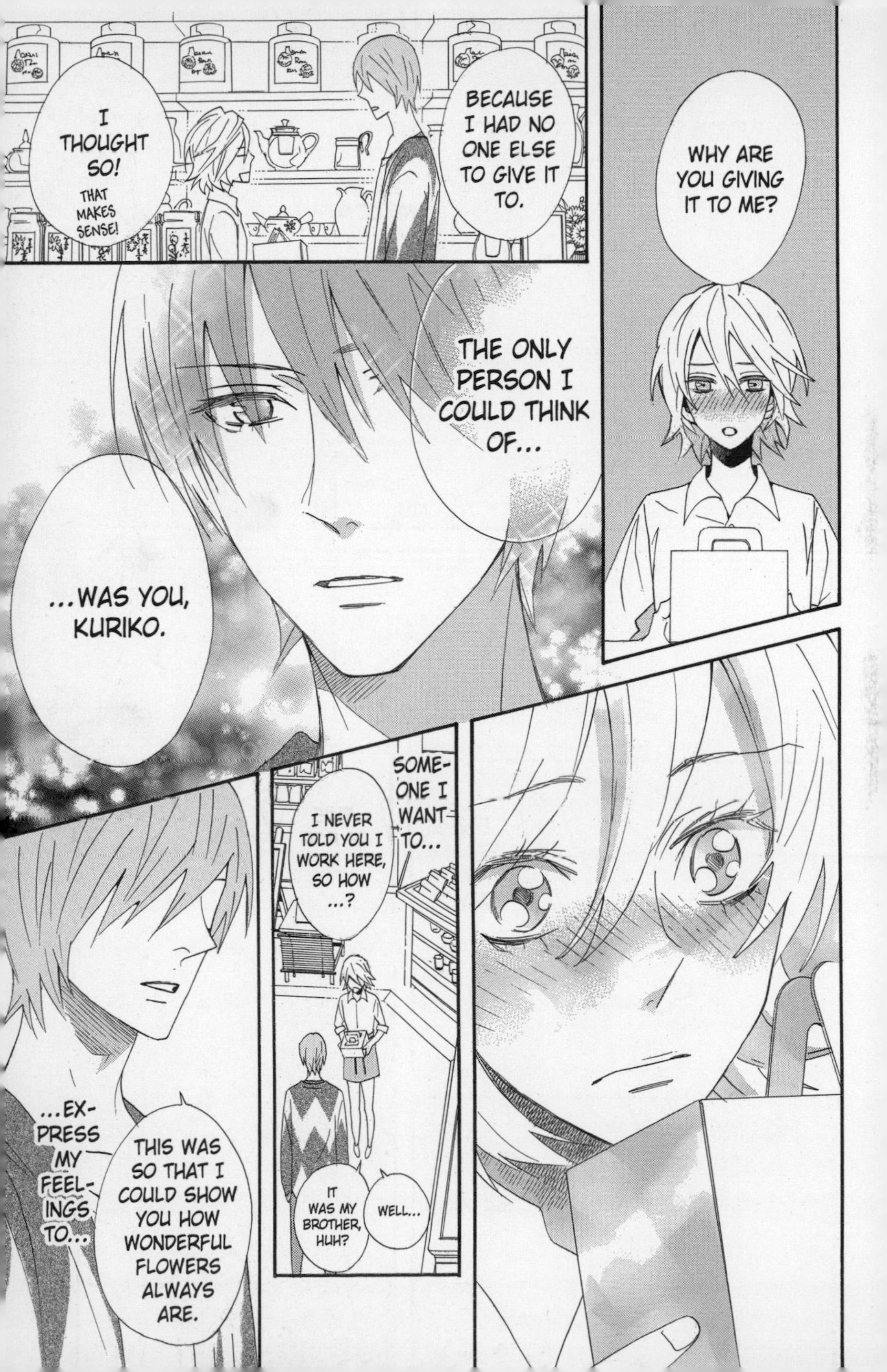
WHY ARE YOU GIVING IT TO ME?
BECAUSE I HAD NO ONE ELSE TO GIVE IT TO.
I THOUGHT SO!
THAT MAKES SENSE!
THE ONLY PERSON I COULD THINK OF...
...WAS YOU, KURIKO.
SOME-ONE I WANT TO...
I NEVER TOLD YOU I WORK HERE, SO HOW ...?
WELL...
IT WAS MY BROTHER, HUH?
THIS WAS SO THAT I COULD SHOW YOU HOW WONDERFUL FLOWERS ALWAYS ARE.
...EX-PRESS MY FEEL-INGS TO...

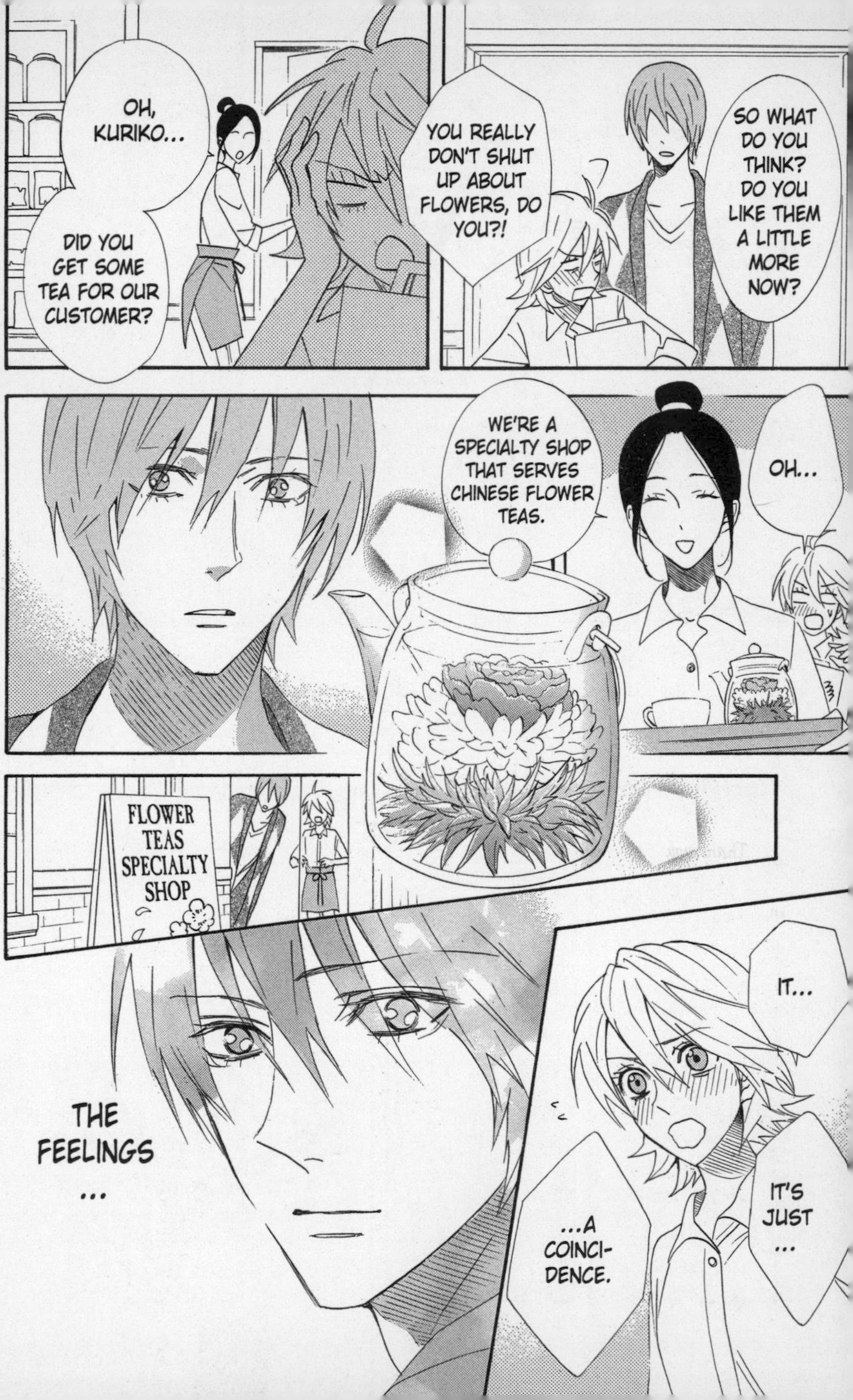
SO WHAT DO YOU THINK? DO YOU LIKE THEM A LITTLE MORE NOW?
YOU REALLY DON'T SHUT UP ABOUT FLOWERS, DO YOU?!
OH, KURIKO...
DID YOU GET SOME TEA FOR OUR CUSTOMER?
OH...
WE'RE A SPECIALTY SHOP THAT SERVES CHINESE FLOWER TEAS.
FLOWER TEAS SPECIALTY SHOP
IT...
IT'S JUST...
...A COINCIDENCE.
THE FEELINGS...

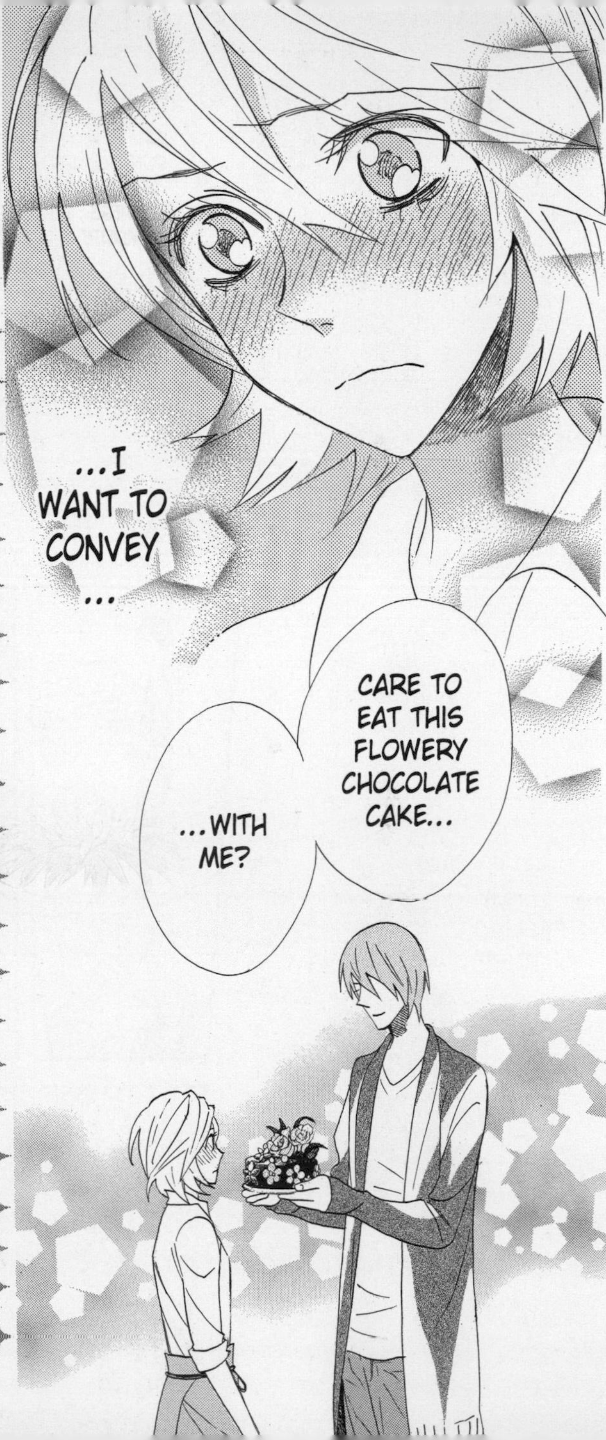
...I WANT TO CONVEY...
CARE TO EAT THIS FLOWERY CHOCOLATE CAKE...
...WITH ME?

Production Assistance:

Shimada-san
Takowa-san
Kuwana-san
Kaneko-san
Sakurai-san
Nakazawa-san
Tanaka-san
Kawashima-san
Sayaka-san
Yone-yan
Komatsu-san

Special Thanks:

Abe-san
My Family
All My Readers

Thank you very much for reading! I hope to see you in the next volume.

By the way, I'm on Twitter. My account name is kanno_aya.

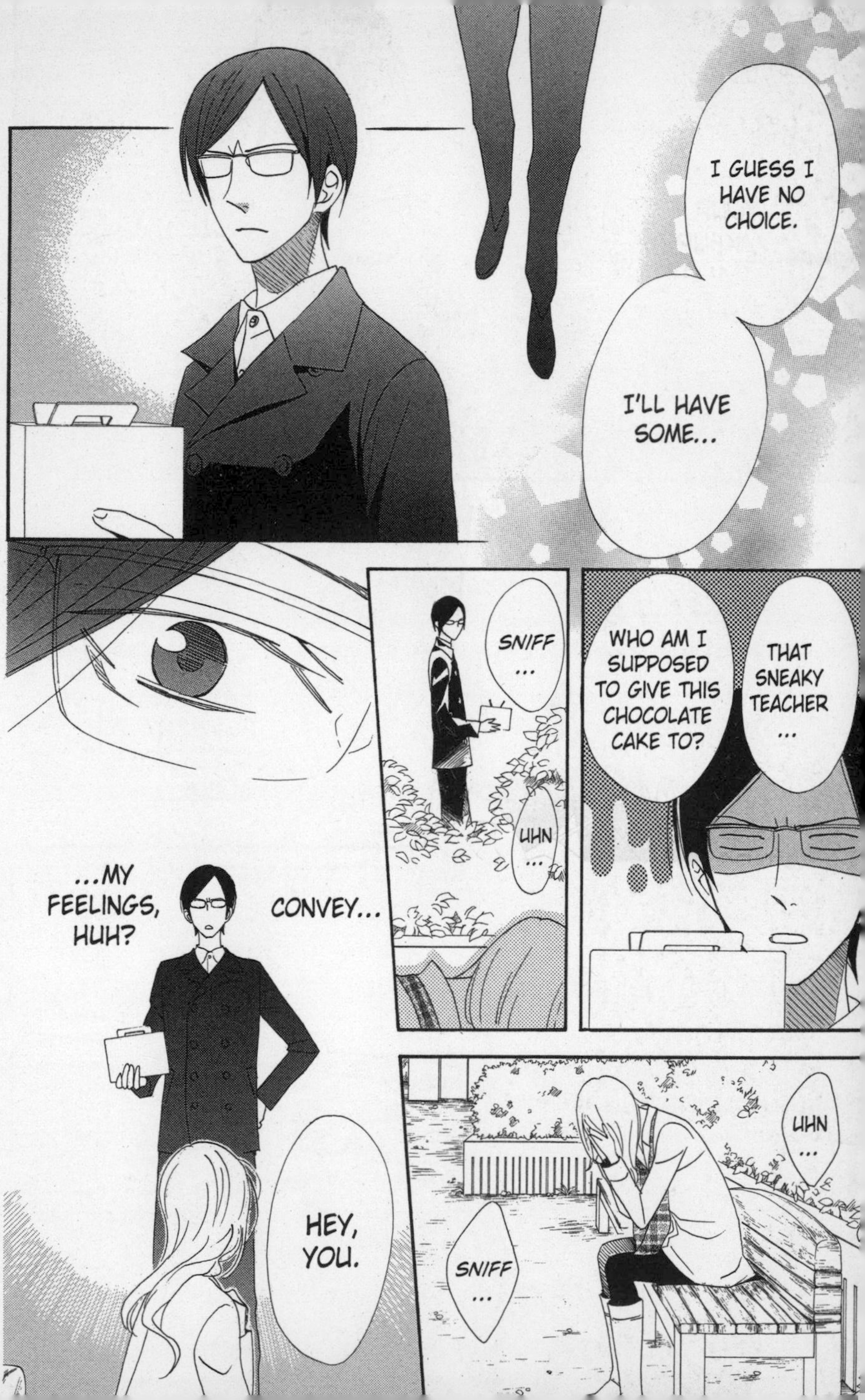
I GUESS I HAVE NO CHOICE.
I'LL HAVE SOME...
THAT SNEAKY TEACHER ...
WHO AM I SUPPOSED TO GIVE THIS CHOCOLATE CAKE TO?
SNIFF ...
UHN ...
UHN ...
SNIFF ...
CONVEY...
...MY FEELINGS, HUH?
HEY, YOU.

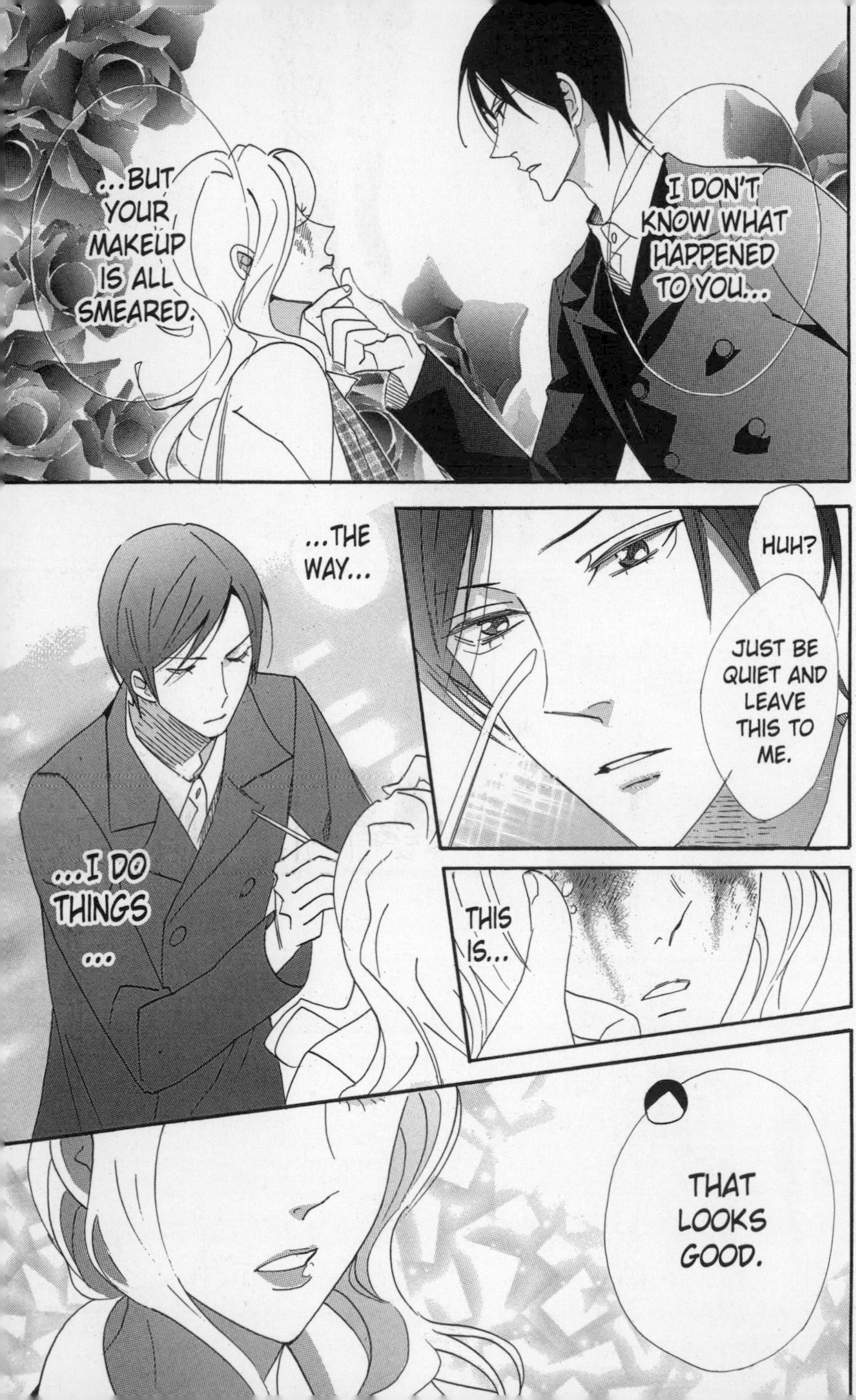
I DON'T KNOW WHAT HAPPENED TO YOU...
...BUT YOUR MAKEUP IS ALL SMEARED.
HUH?
JUST BE QUIET AND LEAVE THIS TO ME.
THIS IS...
...THE WAY...
...I DO THINGS ...
THAT LOOKS GOOD.

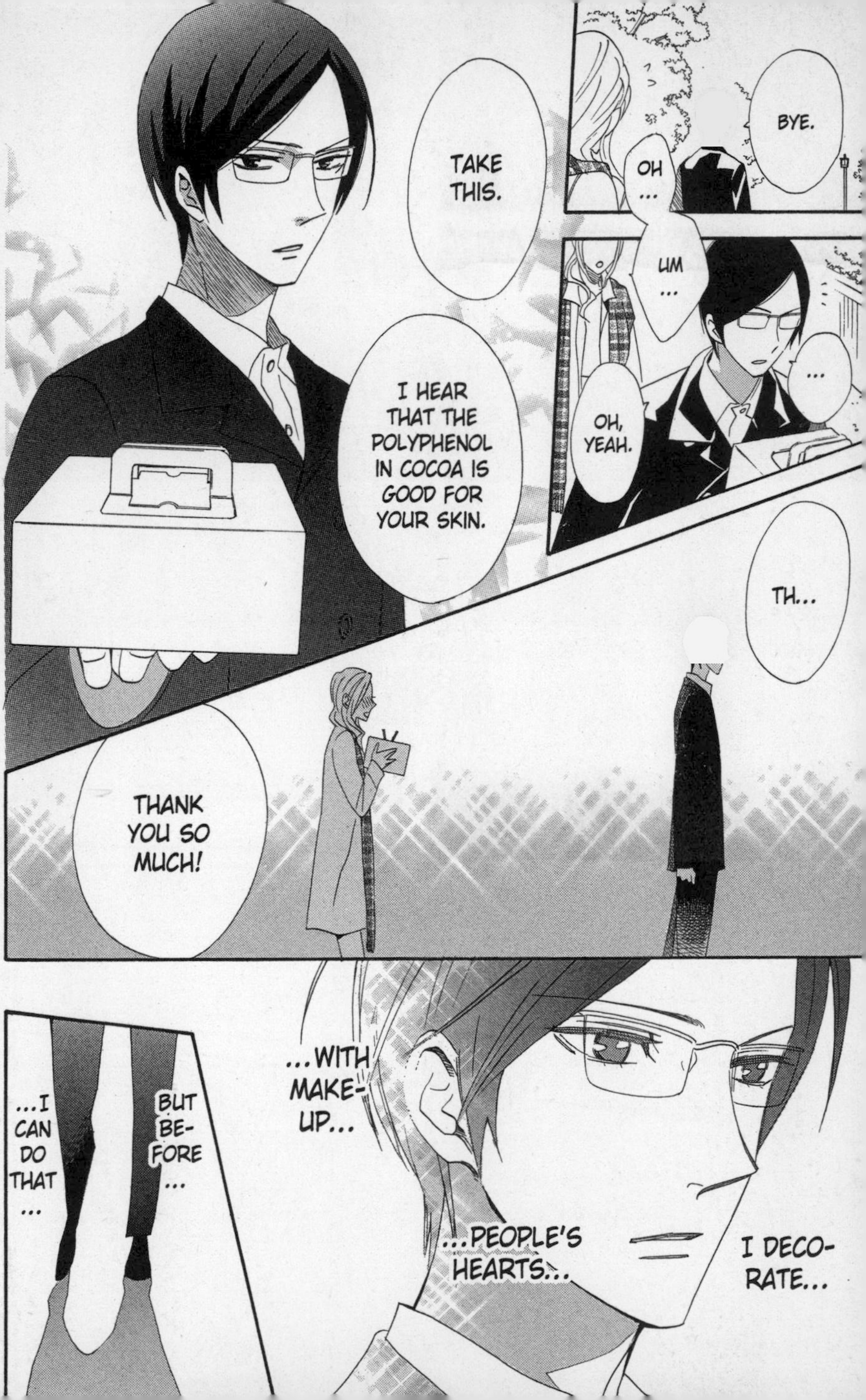
BYE.
OH...
UM...
...
OH, YEAH.
TAKE THIS.
I HEAR THAT THE POLYPHENOL IN COCOA IS GOOD FOR YOUR SKIN.
TH...
THANK YOU SO MUCH!
I DECO-RATE...
...PEOPLE'S HEARTS...
...WITH MAKE-UP...
BUT BE-FORE...
...I CAN DO THAT...

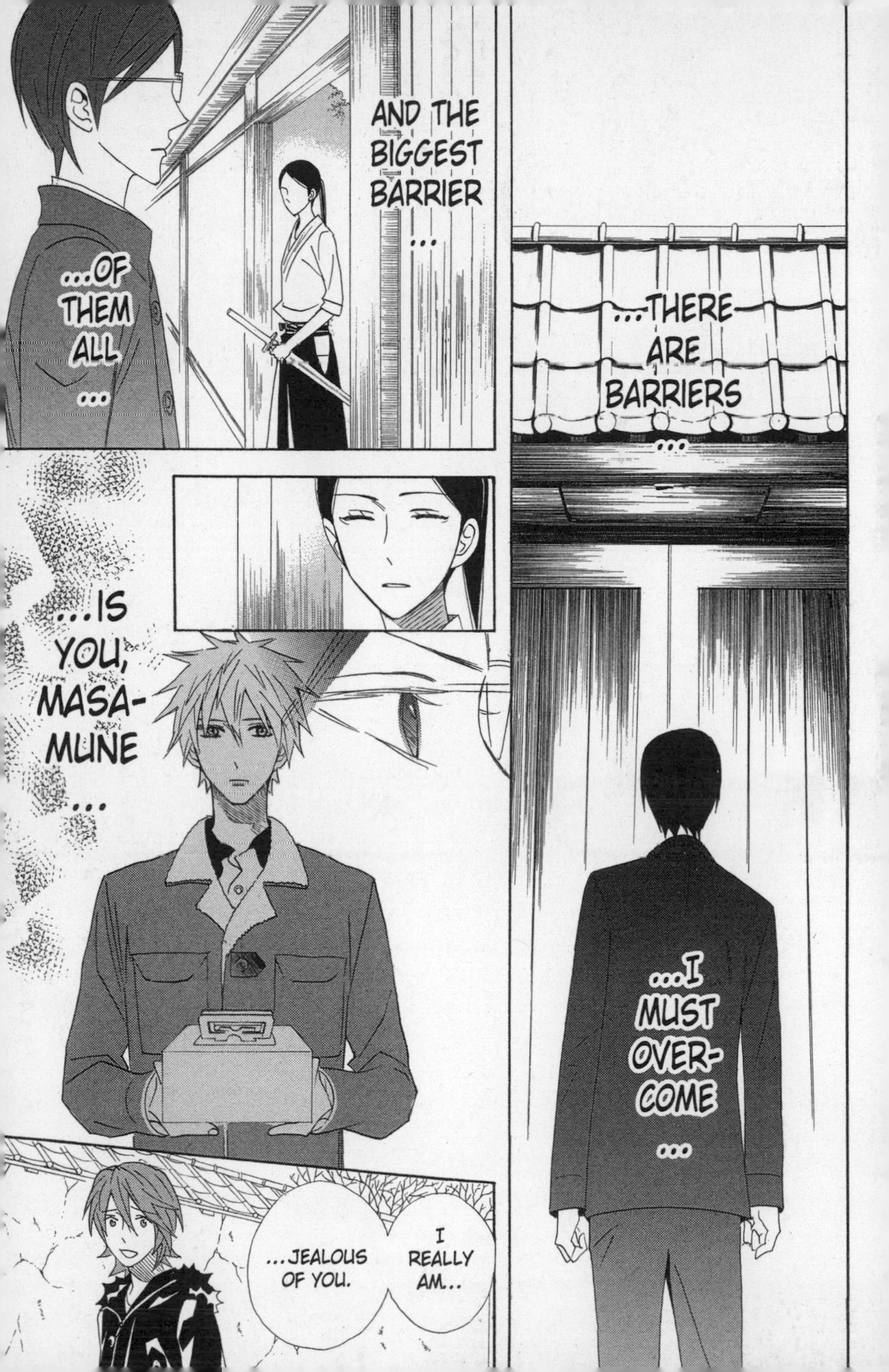
...THERE ARE BARRIERS...
...I MUST OVER-COME...
AND THE BIGGEST BARRIER...
...OF THEM ALL...
...IS YOU, MASA-MUNE...
I REALLY AM...
...JEALOUS OF YOU.

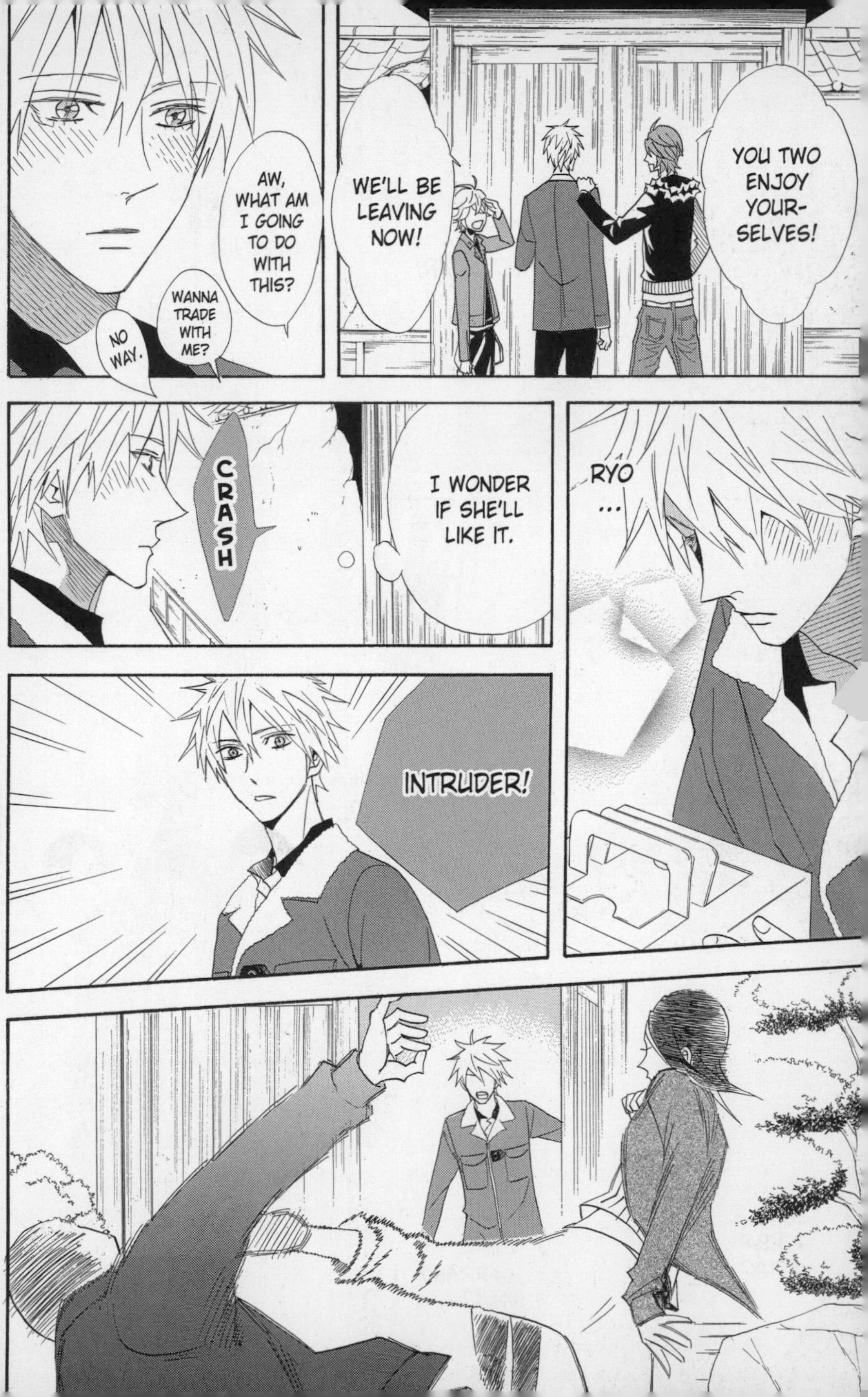
YOU TWO ENJOY YOUR-SELVES!
WE'LL BE LEAVING NOW!
AW, WHAT AM I GOING TO DO WITH THIS?
WANNA TRADE WITH ME?
NO WAY.
RYO ...
I WONDER IF SHE'LL LIKE IT.
CRASH
INTRUDER!

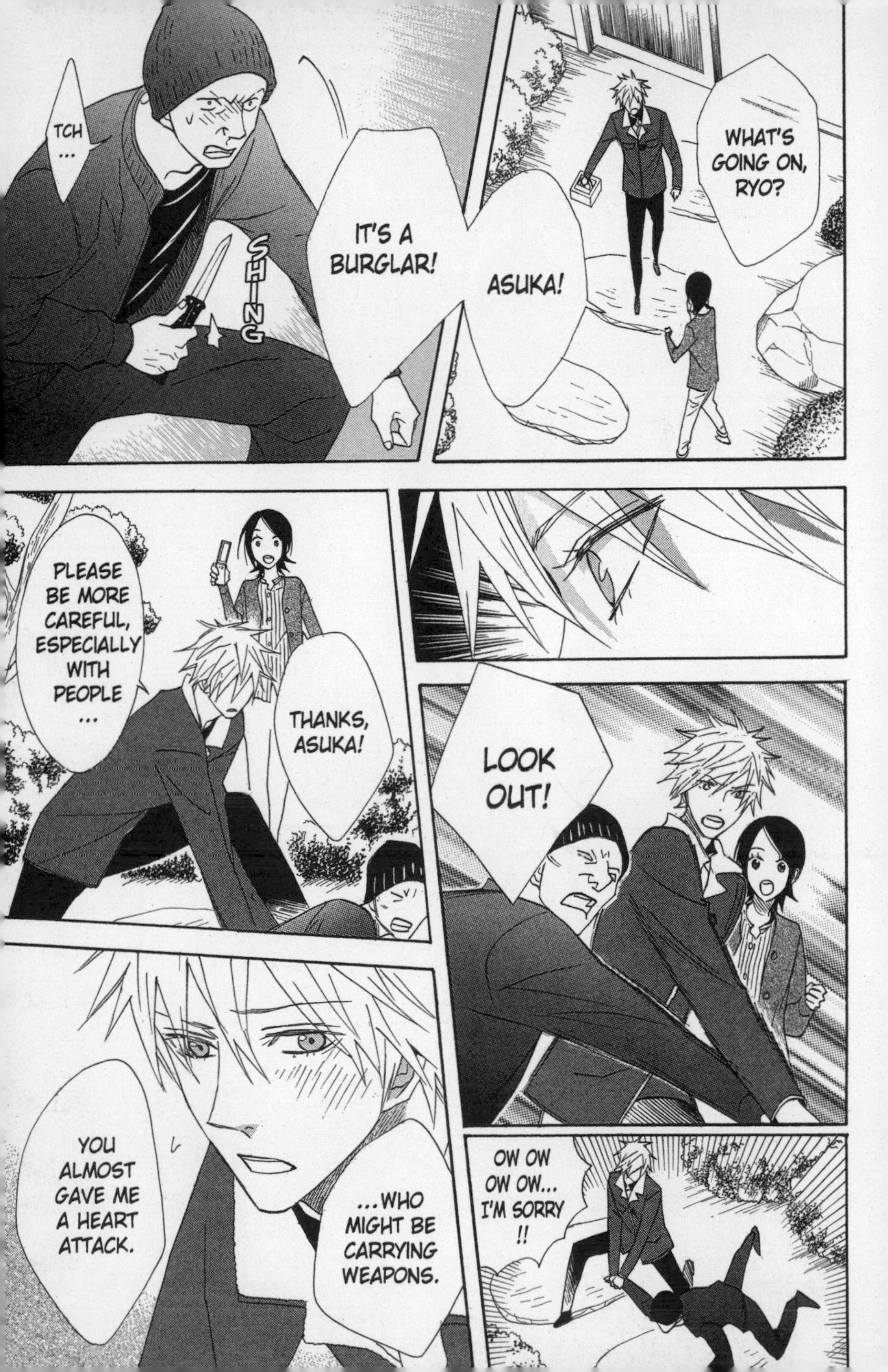
WHAT'S GOING ON, RYO?
ASUKA!
IT'S A BURGLAR!
TCH ...
SHING
LOOK OUT!
THANKS, ASUKA!
PLEASE BE MORE CAREFUL, ESPECIALLY WITH PEOPLE ...
OW OW OW OW... I'M SORRY !!
...WHO MIGHT BE CARRYING WEAPONS.
YOU ALMOST GAVE ME A HEART ATTACK.

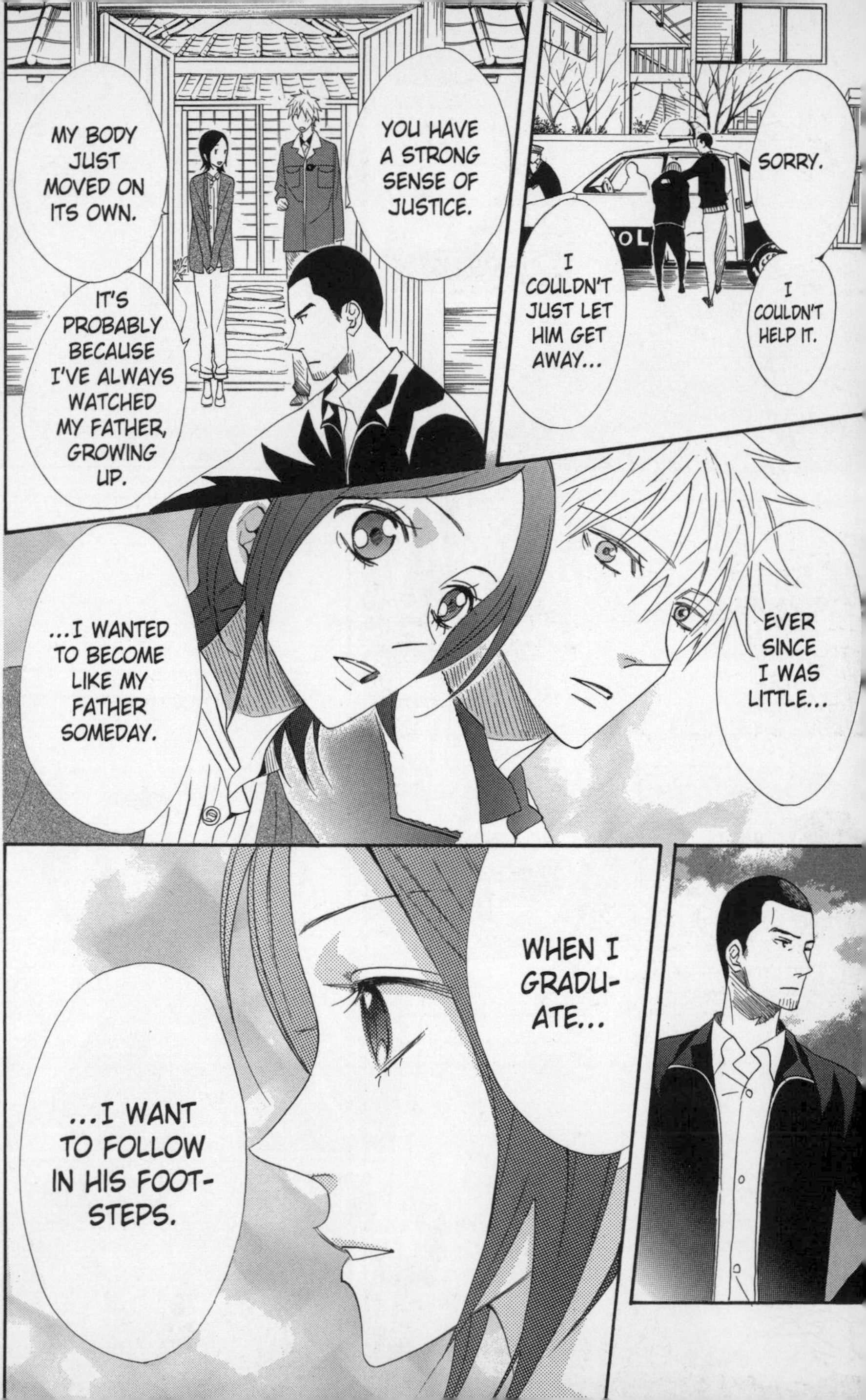
SORRY.
I COULDN'T HELP IT.
I COULDN'T JUST LET HIM GET AWAY...
YOU HAVE A STRONG SENSE OF JUSTICE.
MY BODY JUST MOVED ON ITS OWN.
IT'S PROBABLY BECAUSE I'VE ALWAYS WATCHED MY FATHER, GROWING UP.
EVER SINCE I WAS LITTLE...
...I WANTED TO BECOME LIKE MY FATHER SOMEDAY.
WHEN I GRADU-ATE...
...I WANT TO FOLLOW IN HIS FOOT-STEPS.

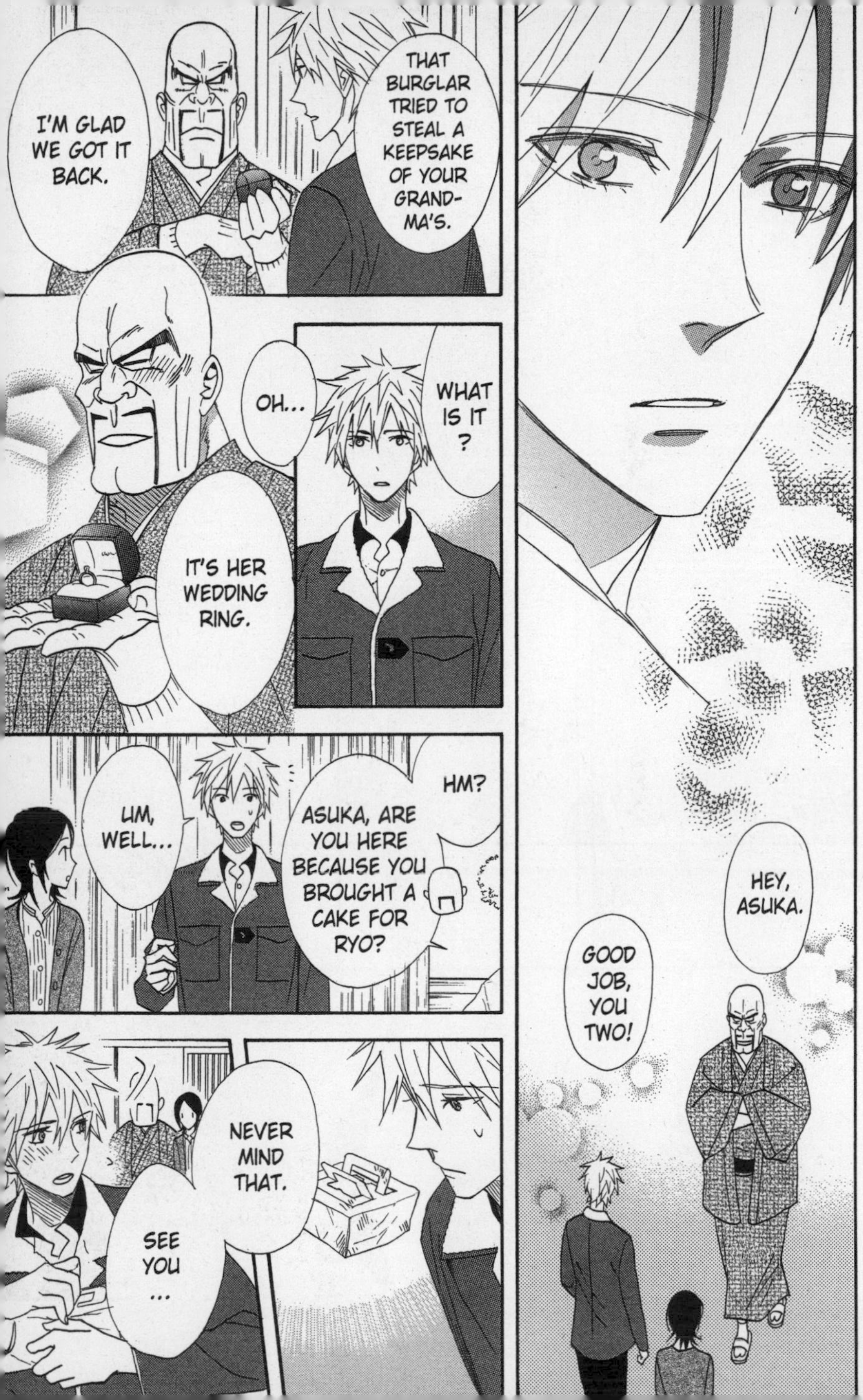
HEY, ASUKA.
GOOD JOB, YOU TWO!
THAT BURGLAR TRIED TO STEAL A KEEPSAKE OF YOUR GRANDMA'S.
I'M GLAD WE GOT IT BACK.
WHAT IS IT ?
OH...
IT'S HER WEDDING RING.
HM?
ASUKA, ARE YOU HERE BECAUSE YOU BROUGHT A CAKE FOR RYO?
UM, WELL...
NEVER MIND THAT.
SEE YOU ...

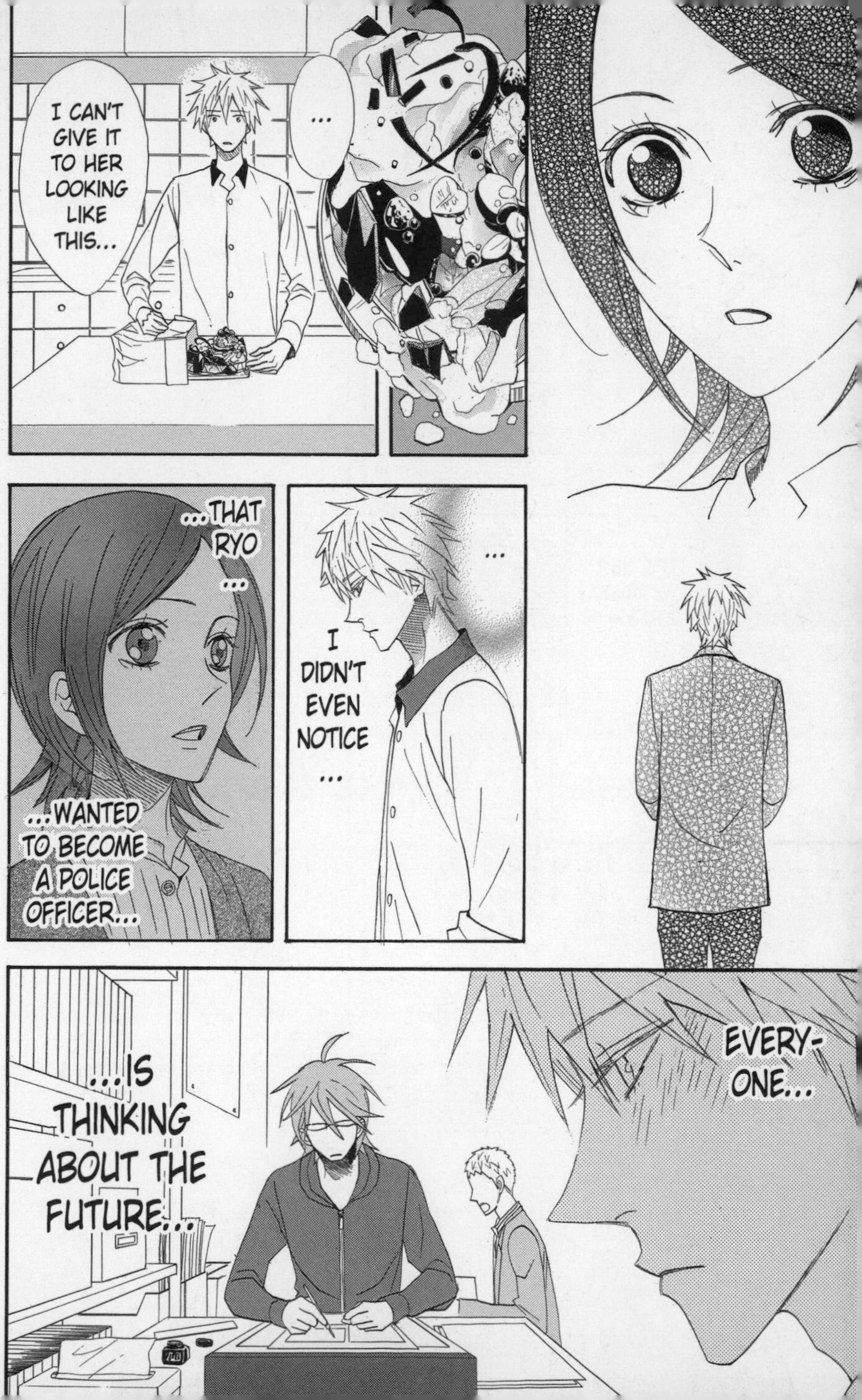
...
I CAN'T GIVE IT TO HER LOOKING LIKE THIS...
...
I DIDN'T EVEN NOTICE ...
...THAT RYO ...
...WANTED TO BECOME A POLICE OFFICER...
EVERY-ONE...
...IS THINKING ABOUT THE FUTURE...

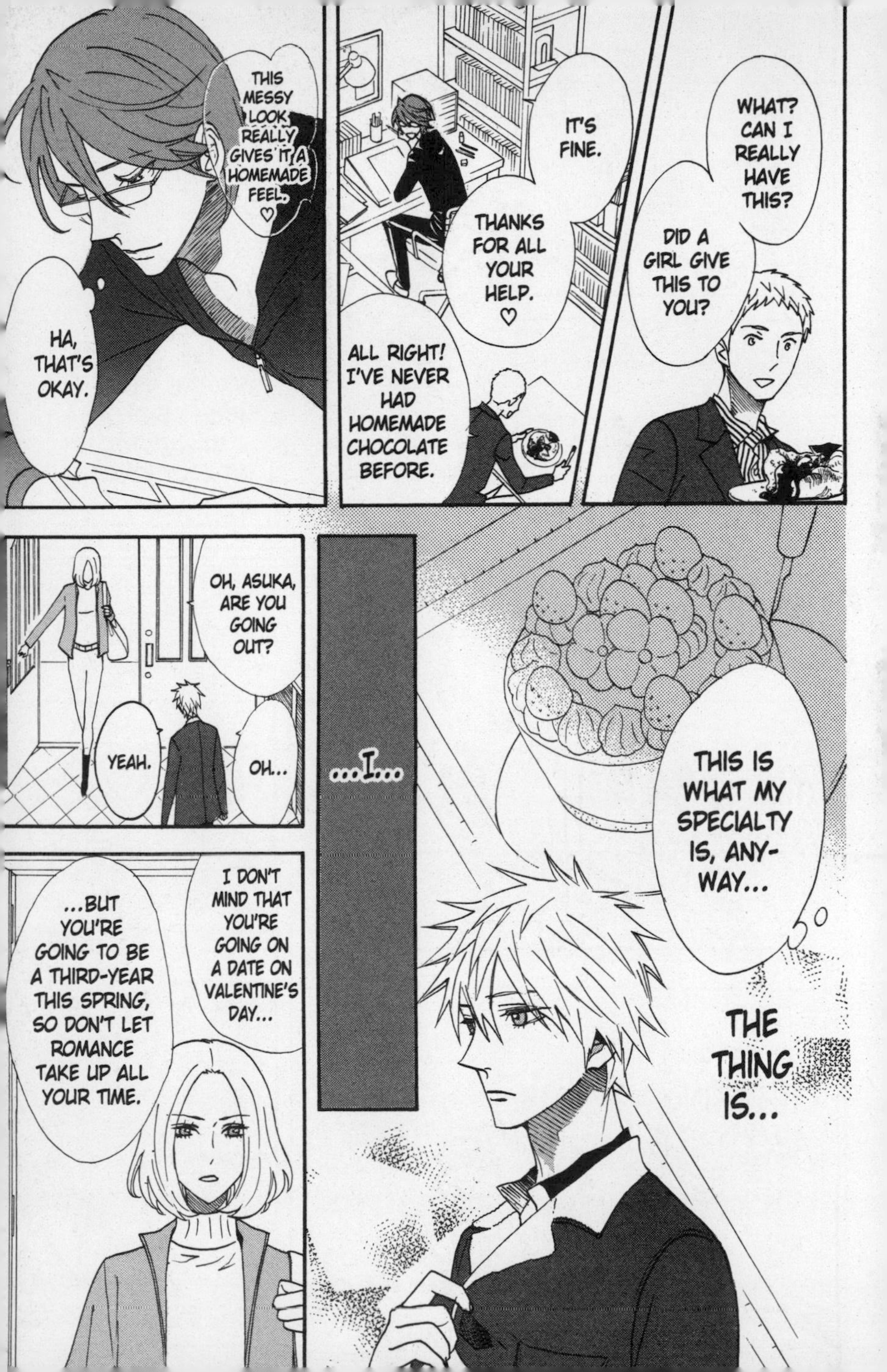
WHAT? CAN I REALLY HAVE THIS?
DID A GIRL GIVE THIS TO YOU?
IT'S FINE.
THANKS FOR ALL YOUR HELP. ♡
ALL RIGHT! I'VE NEVER HAD HOMEMADE CHOCOLATE BEFORE.
THIS MESSY LOOK REALLY GIVES IT A HOMEMADE FEEL. ♡
HA, THAT'S OKAY.
THIS IS WHAT MY SPECIALTY IS, ANY-WAY...
THE THING IS...
...I...
OH, ASUKA, ARE YOU GOING OUT?
YEAH.
OH...
I DON'T MIND THAT YOU'RE GOING ON A DATE ON VALENTINE'S DAY...
...BUT YOU'RE GOING TO BE A THIRD-YEAR THIS SPRING, SO DON'T LET ROMANCE TAKE UP ALL YOUR TIME.

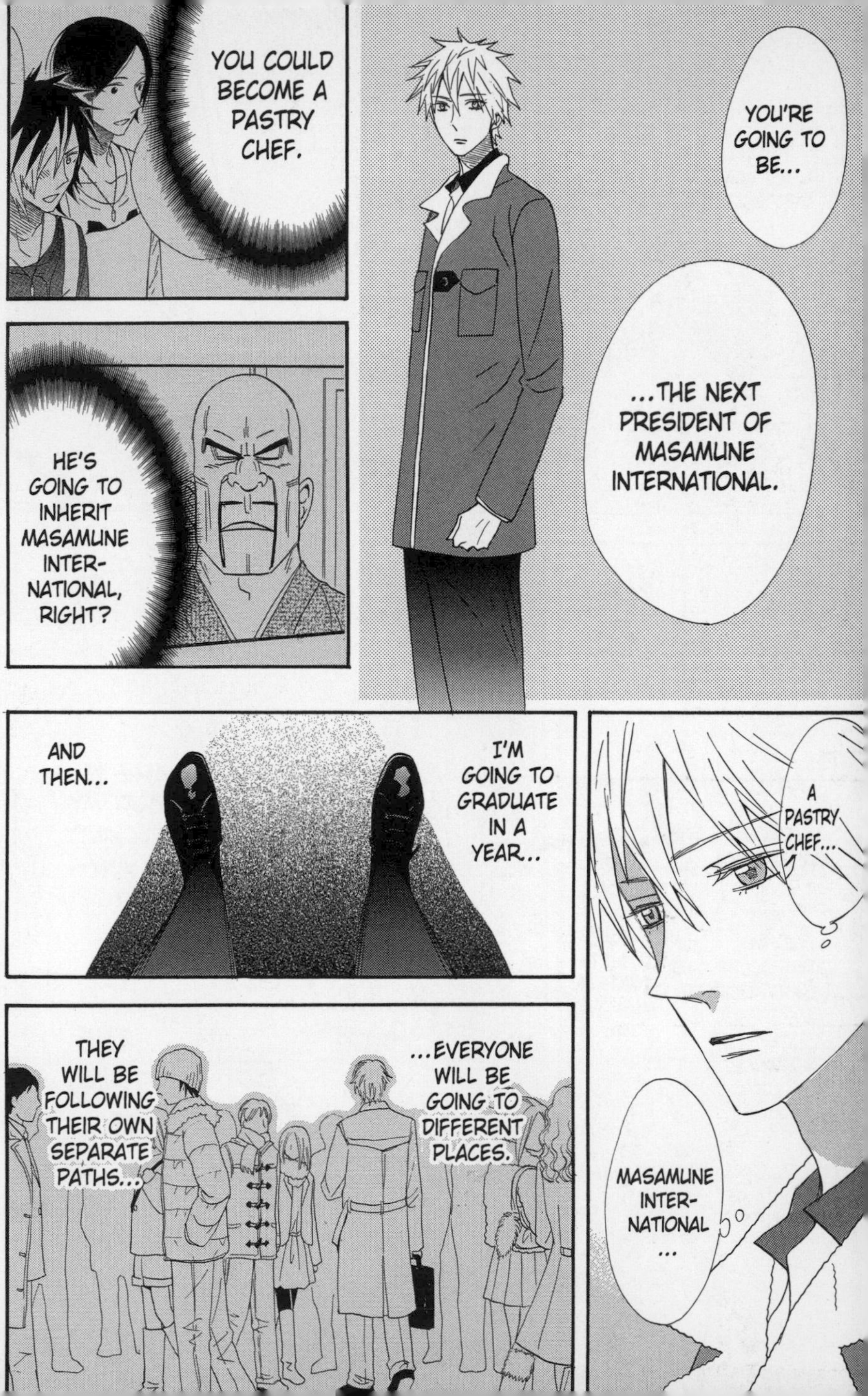
YOU'RE GOING TO BE...
...THE NEXT PRESIDENT OF MASAMUNE INTERNATIONAL.
YOU COULD BECOME A PASTRY CHEF.
HE'S GOING TO INHERIT MASAMUNE INTER-NATIONAL, RIGHT?
A PASTRY CHEF...
MASAMUNE INTER-NATIONAL...
I'M GOING TO GRADUATE IN A YEAR..
AND THEN...
...EVERYONE WILL BE GOING TO DIFFERENT PLACES.
THEY WILL BE FOLLOWING THEIR OWN SEPARATE PATHS...

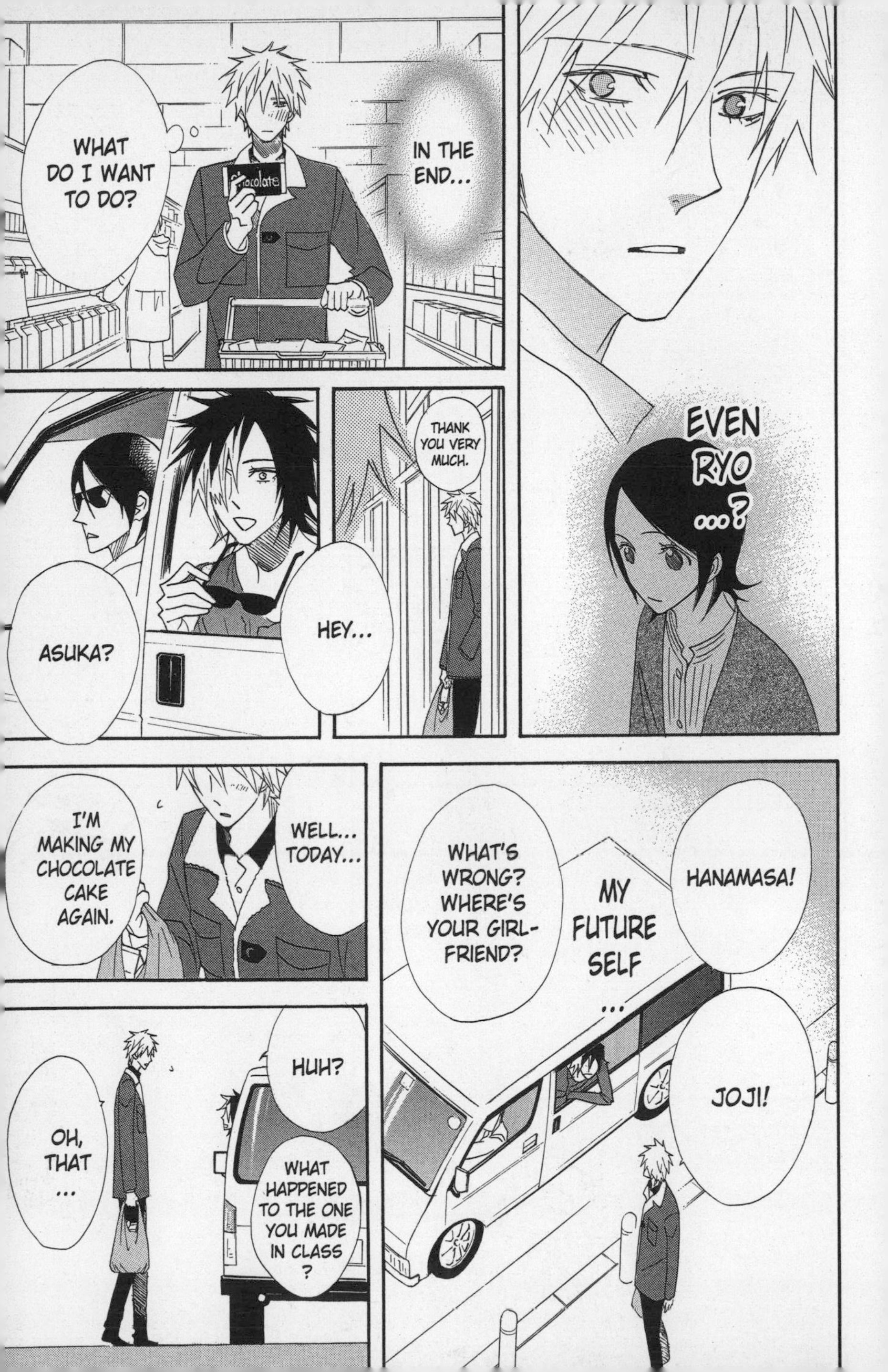
EVEN RYO ...?
IN THE END...
WHAT DO I WANT TO DO?
Chocolate
THANK YOU VERY MUCH.
HEY...
ASUKA?
WELL... TODAY...
I'M MAKING MY CHOCOLATE CAKE AGAIN.
HANAMASA!
JOJI!
WHAT'S WRONG? WHERE'S YOUR GIRL-FRIEND?
MY FUTURE SELF ...
HUH?
WHAT HAPPENED TO THE ONE YOU MADE IN CLASS ?
OH, THAT ...

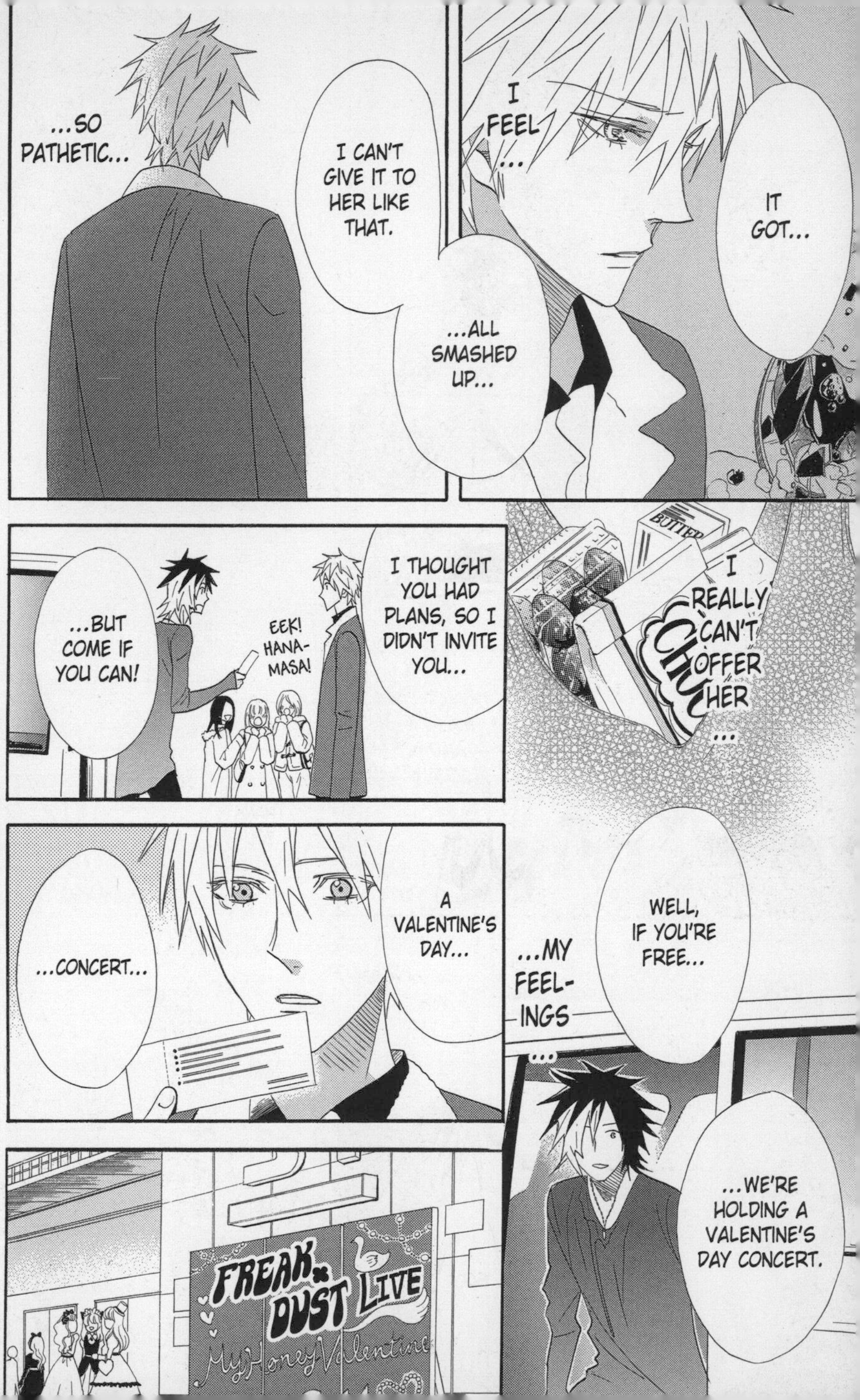
I FEEL...
IT GOT...
...ALL SMASHED UP...
I CAN'T GIVE IT TO HER LIKE THAT.
...SO PATHETIC...
BUTTER
I REALLY CAN'T OFFER HER...
...MY FEEL-INGS...
WELL, IF YOU'RE FREE...
...WE'RE HOLDING A VALENTINE'S DAY CONCERT.
I THOUGHT YOU HAD PLANS, SO I DIDN'T INVITE YOU...
EEK! HANA-MASA!
...BUT COME IF YOU CAN!
A VALENTINE'S DAY...
...CONCERT...
FREAK DUST LIVE
My Honey Valentine

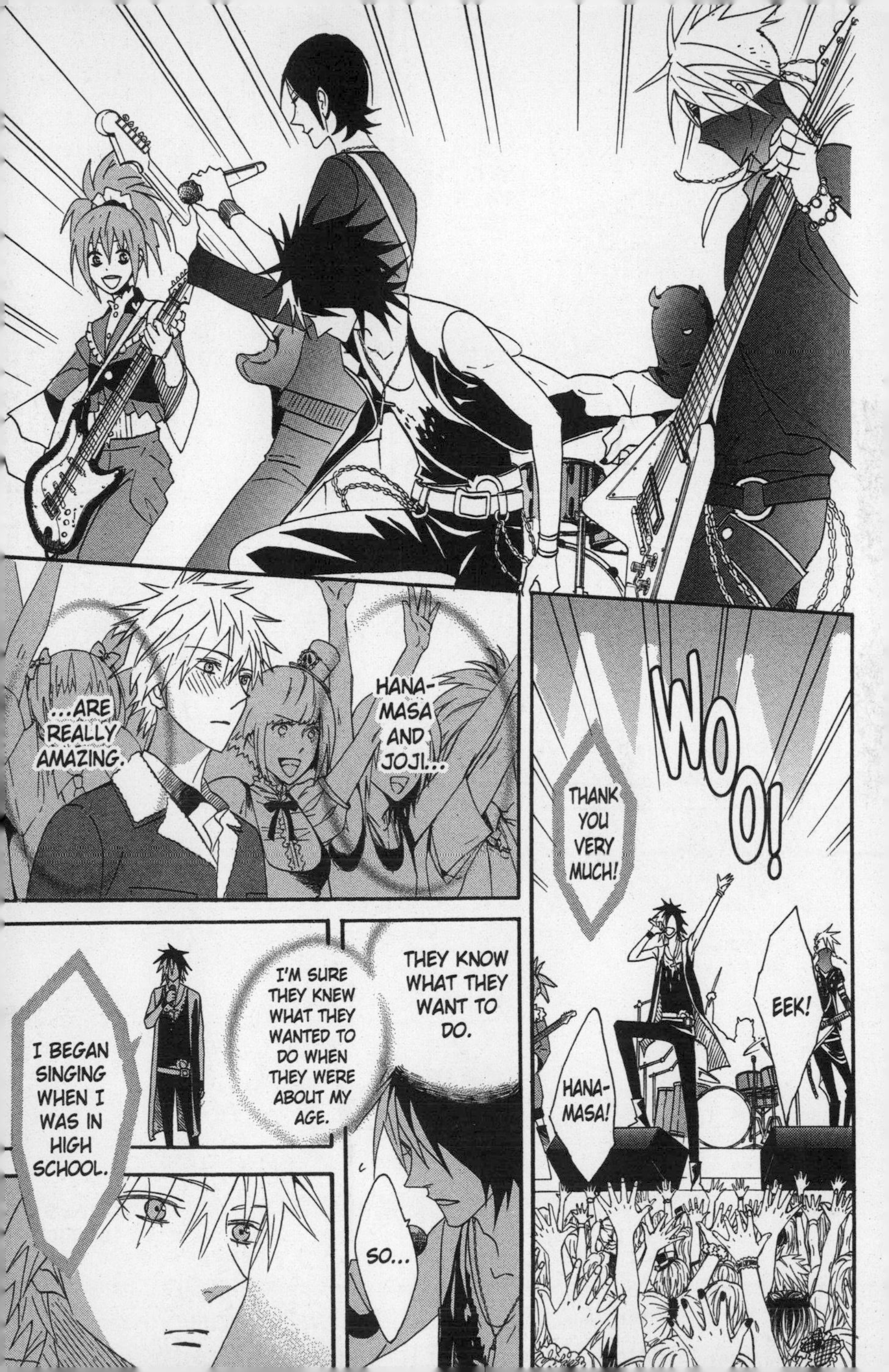
WOO!
THANK YOU VERY MUCH!
EEK!
HANA-MASA!
HANA-MASA AND JOJI...
...ARE REALLY AMAZING.
THEY KNOW WHAT THEY WANT TO DO.
I'M SURE THEY KNEW WHAT THEY WANTED TO DO WHEN THEY WERE ABOUT MY AGE.
I BEGAN SINGING WHEN I WAS IN HIGH SCHOOL.
SO...

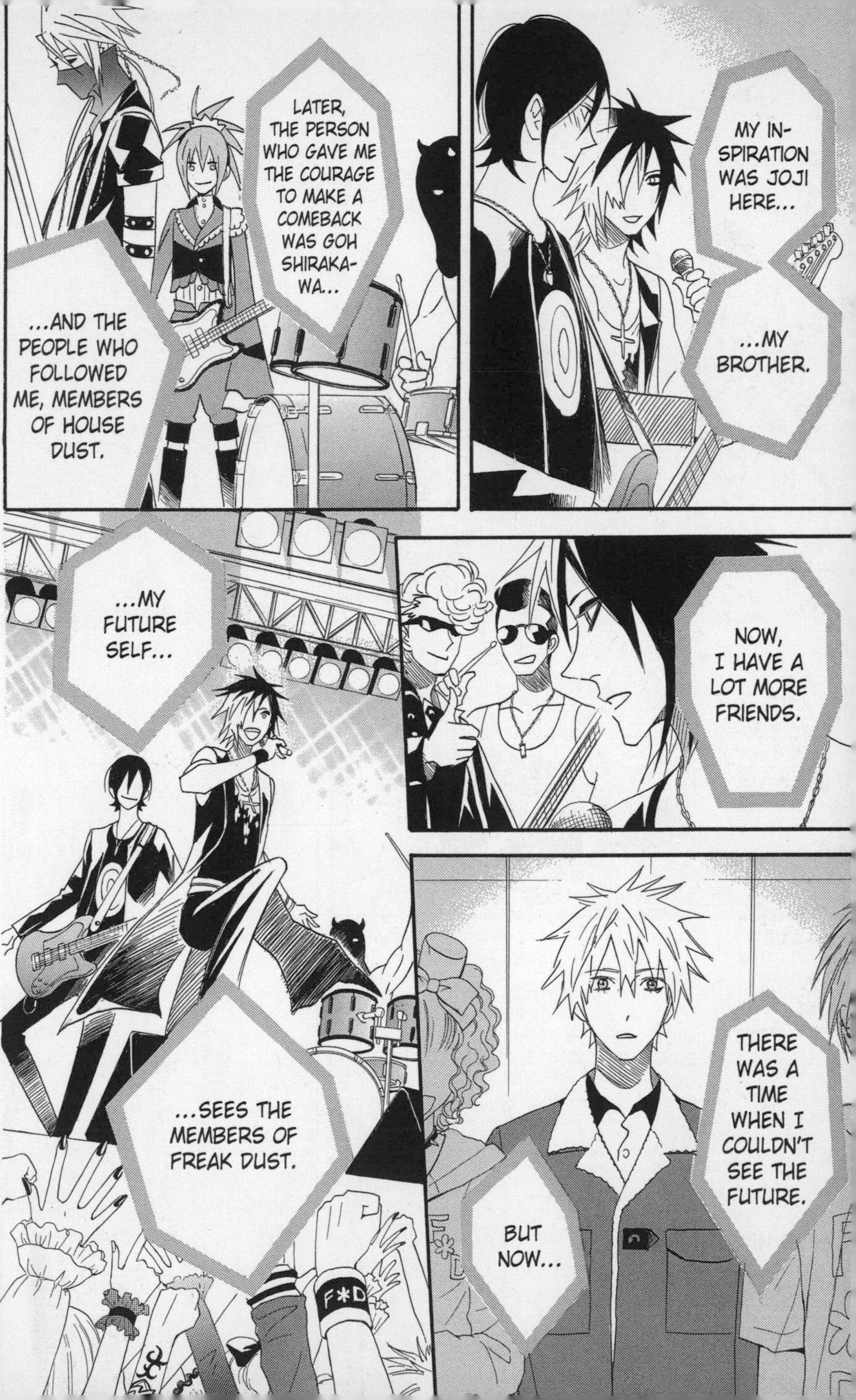
MY IN-SPIRATION WAS JOJI HERE...
...MY BROTHER.
LATER, THE PERSON WHO GAVE ME THE COURAGE TO MAKE A COMEBACK WAS GOH SHIRAKAWA...
...AND THE PEOPLE WHO FOLLOWED ME, MEMBERS OF HOUSE DUST.
NOW, I HAVE A LOT MORE FRIENDS.
THERE WAS A TIME WHEN I COULDN'T SEE THE FUTURE.
BUT NOW...
...MY FUTURE SELF...
...SEES THE MEMBERS OF FREAK DUST.
F*D

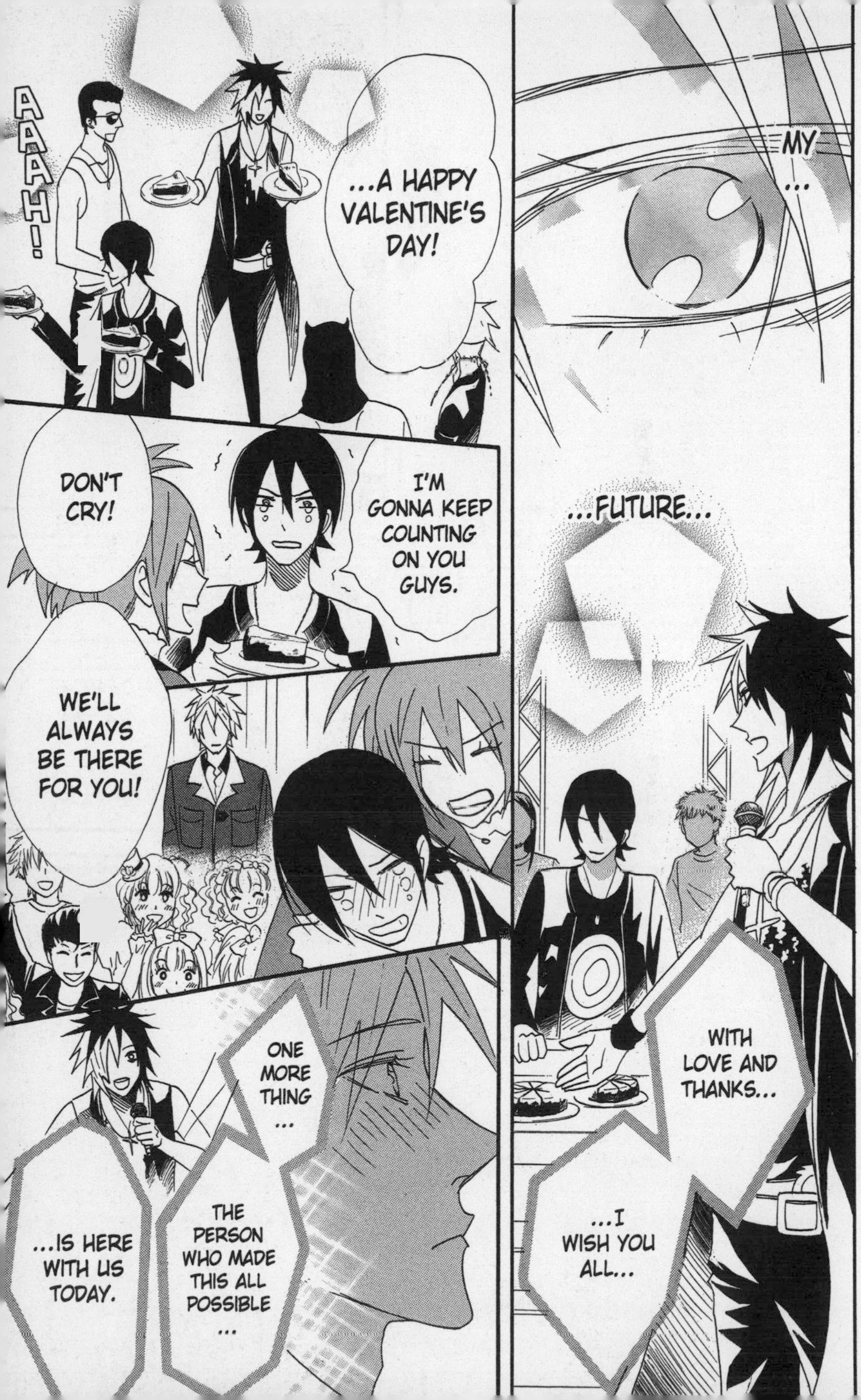
MY ...
...FUTURE...
WITH LOVE AND THANKS...
...I WISH YOU ALL...
...A HAPPY VALENTINE'S DAY!
AAAAH!
I'M GONNA KEEP COUNTING ON YOU GUYS.
DON'T CRY!
WE'LL ALWAYS BE THERE FOR YOU!
ONE MORE THING ...
THE PERSON WHO MADE THIS ALL POSSIBLE ...
...IS HERE WITH US TODAY.

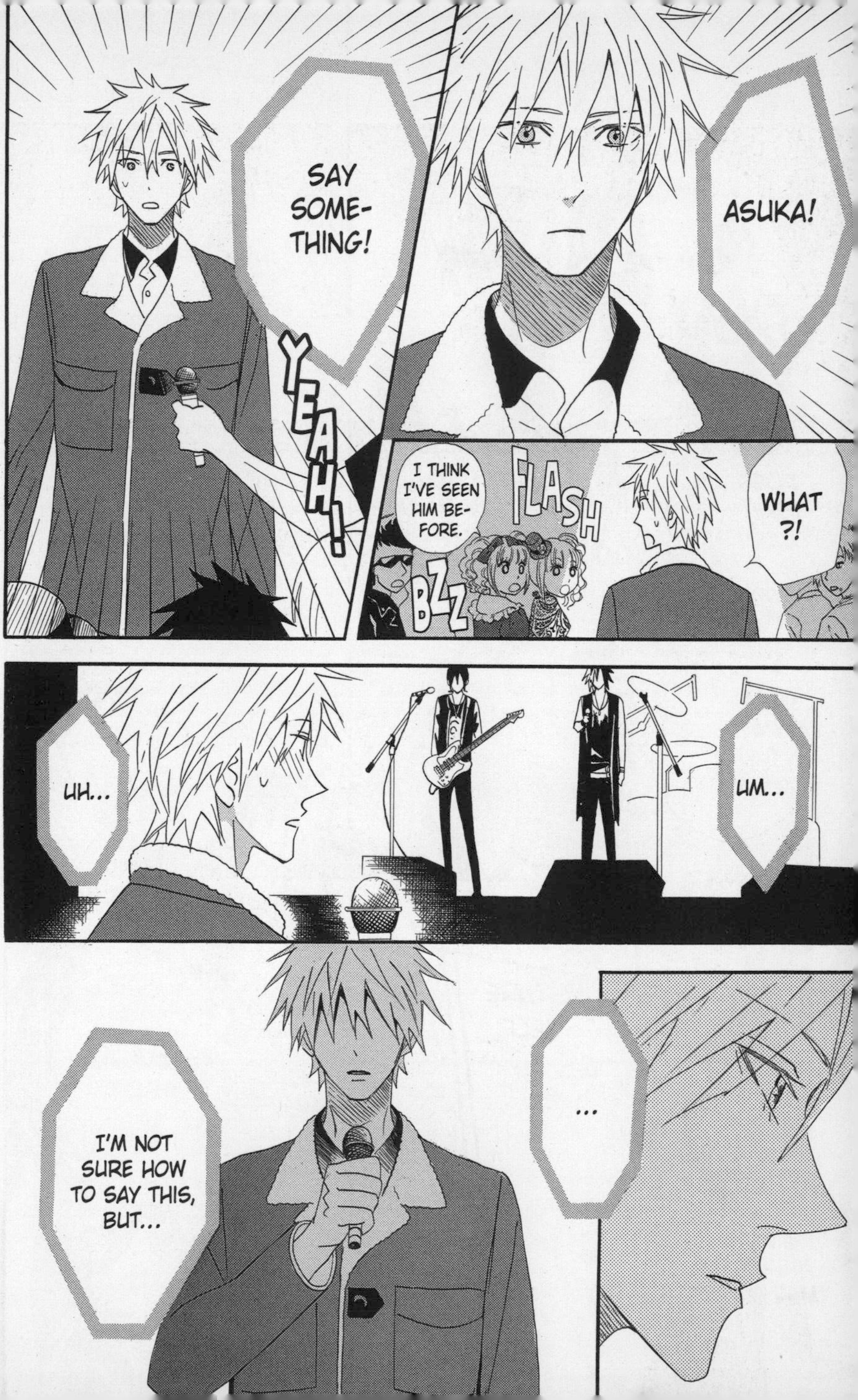
ASUKA!
WHAT ?!
FLASH
I THINK I'VE SEEN HIM BEFORE.
BZZ
SAY SOME-THING!
YEAH!
UM...
UH...
...
I'M NOT SURE HOW TO SAY THIS, BUT...

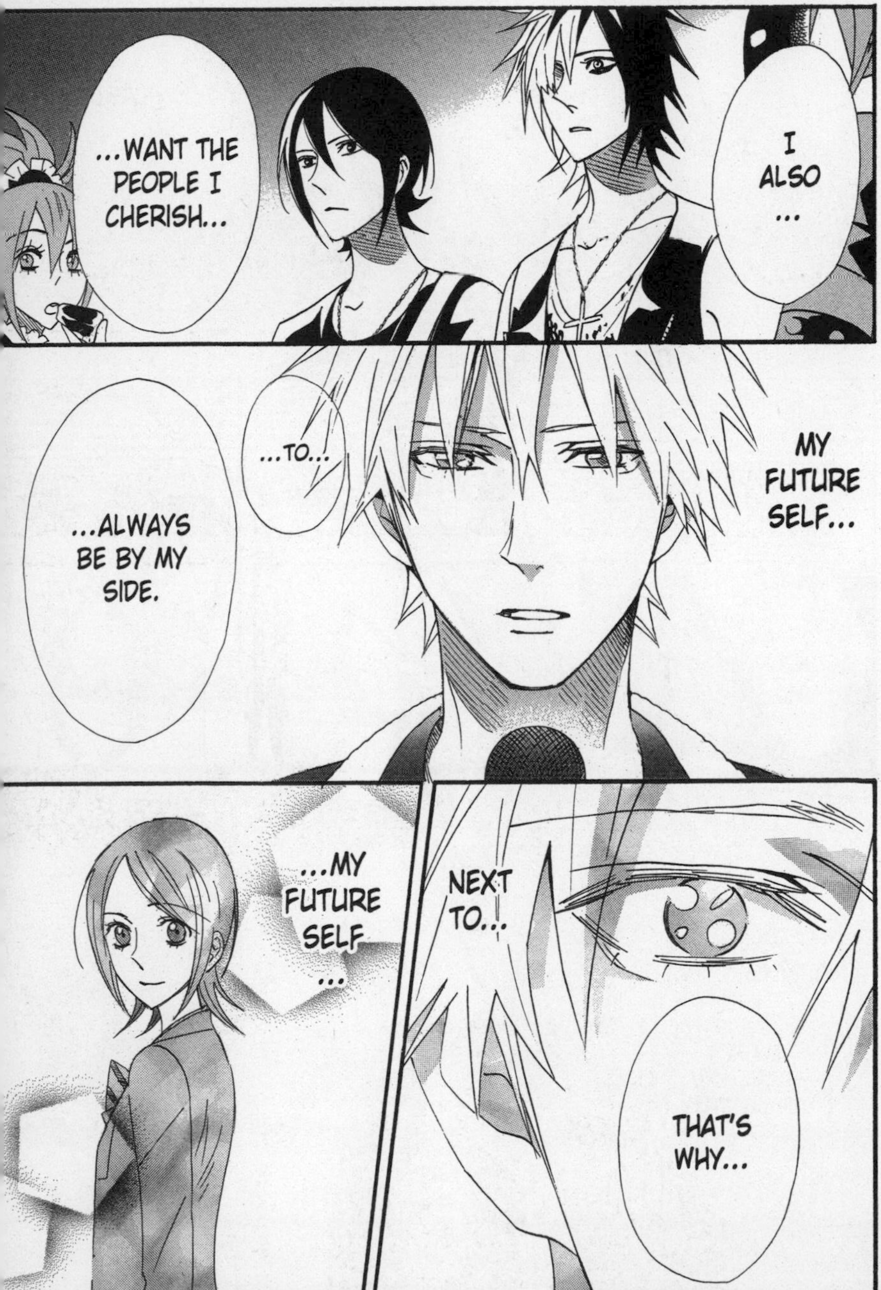
I ALSO ...
...WANT THE PEOPLE I CHERISH...
MY FUTURE SELF...
...TO...
...ALWAYS BE BY MY SIDE.
NEXT TO...
THAT'S WHY...
...MY FUTURE SELF ...

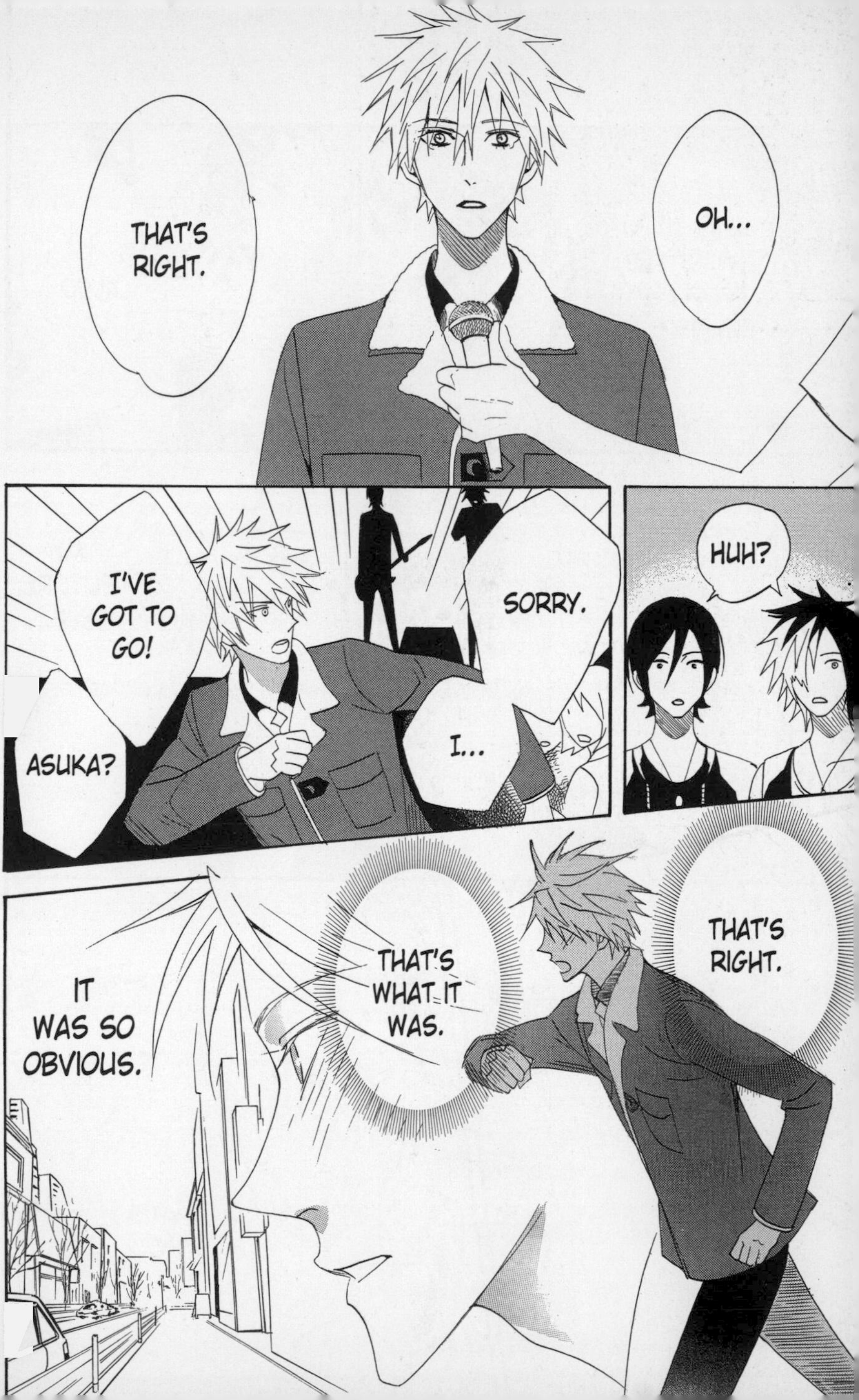
OH...
THAT'S RIGHT.
HUH?
SORRY.
I...
I'VE GOT TO GO!
ASUKA?
THAT'S RIGHT.
THAT'S WHAT IT WAS.
IT WAS SO OBVIOUS.

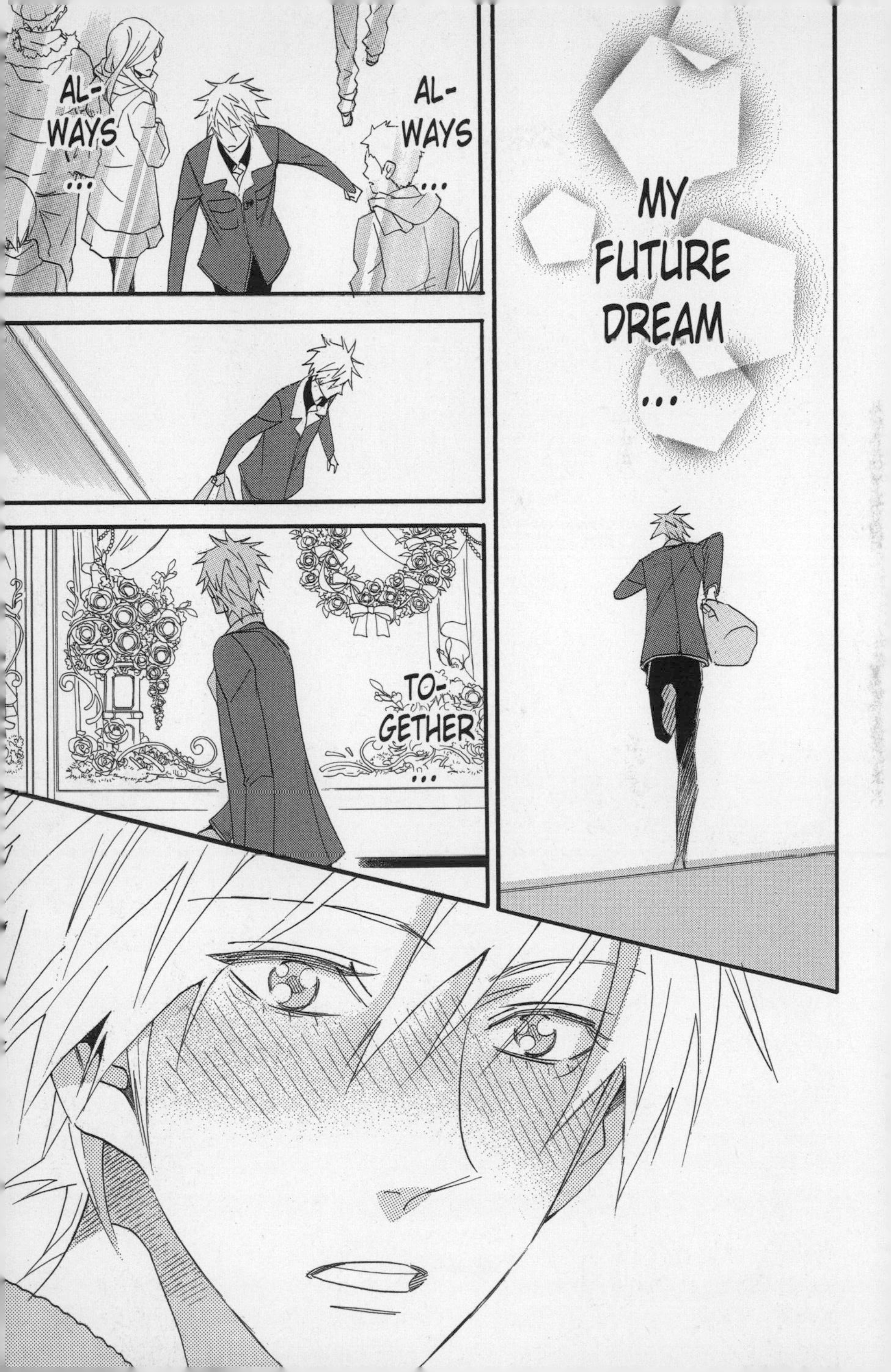
MY FUTURE DREAM ...
AL-WAYS ...
AL-WAYS ...
TO-GETHER ...

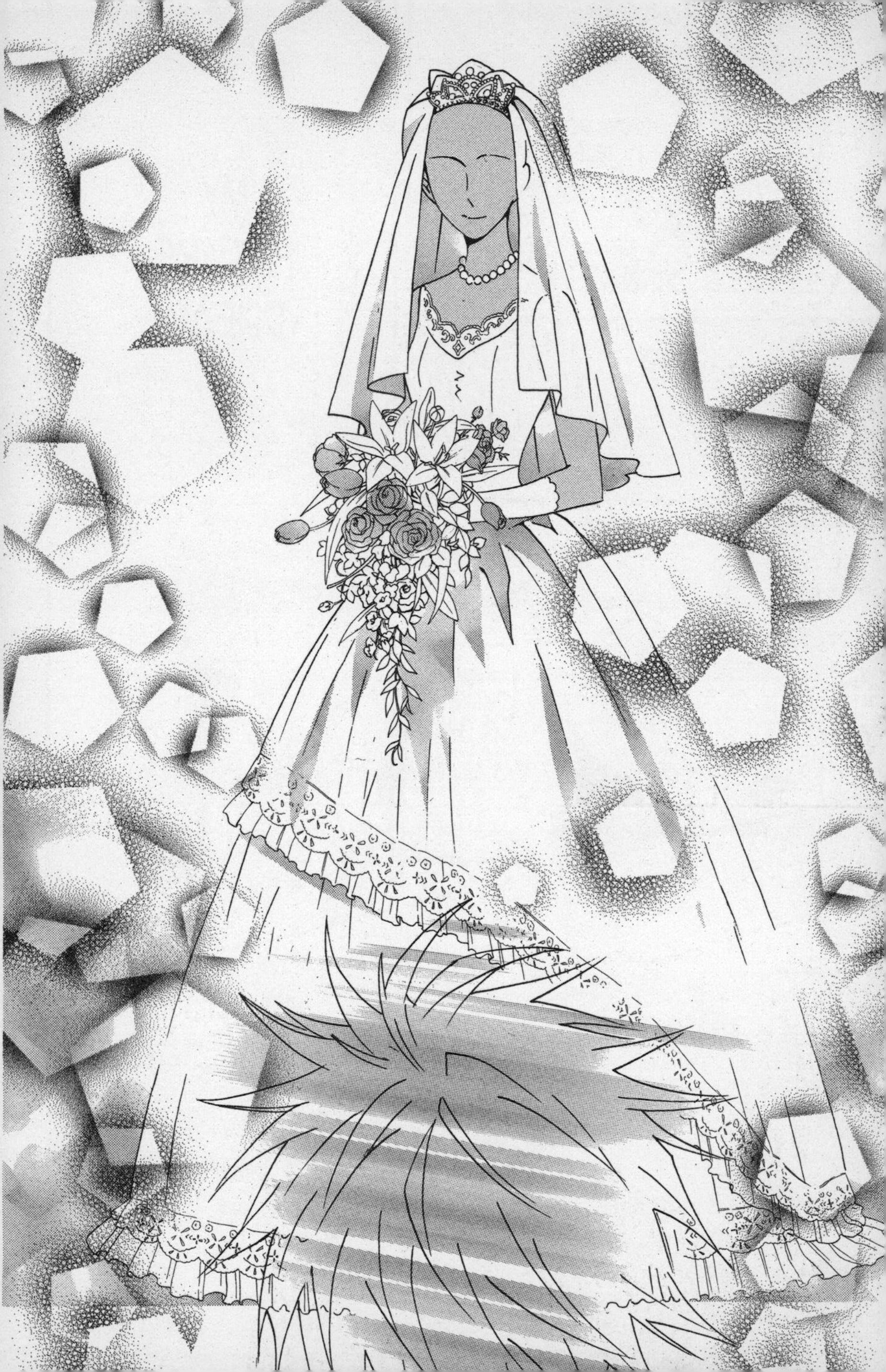

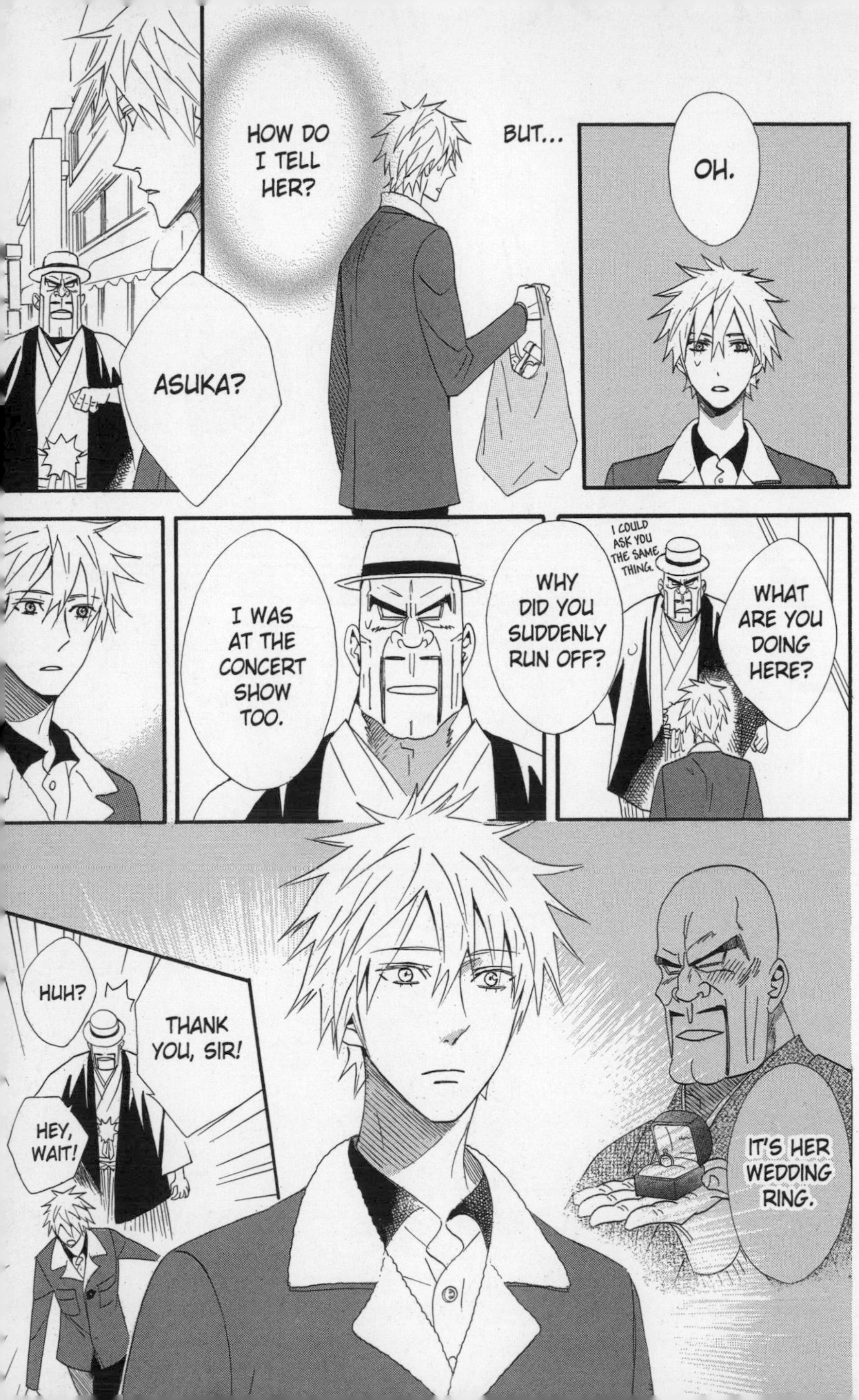
OH.
BUT...
HOW DO I TELL HER?
ASUKA?
WHAT ARE YOU DOING HERE?
I COULD ASK YOU THE SAME THING.
WHY DID YOU SUDDENLY RUN OFF?
I WAS AT THE CONCERT SHOW TOO.
IT'S HER WEDDING RING.
THANK YOU, SIR!
HUH?
HEY, WAIT!

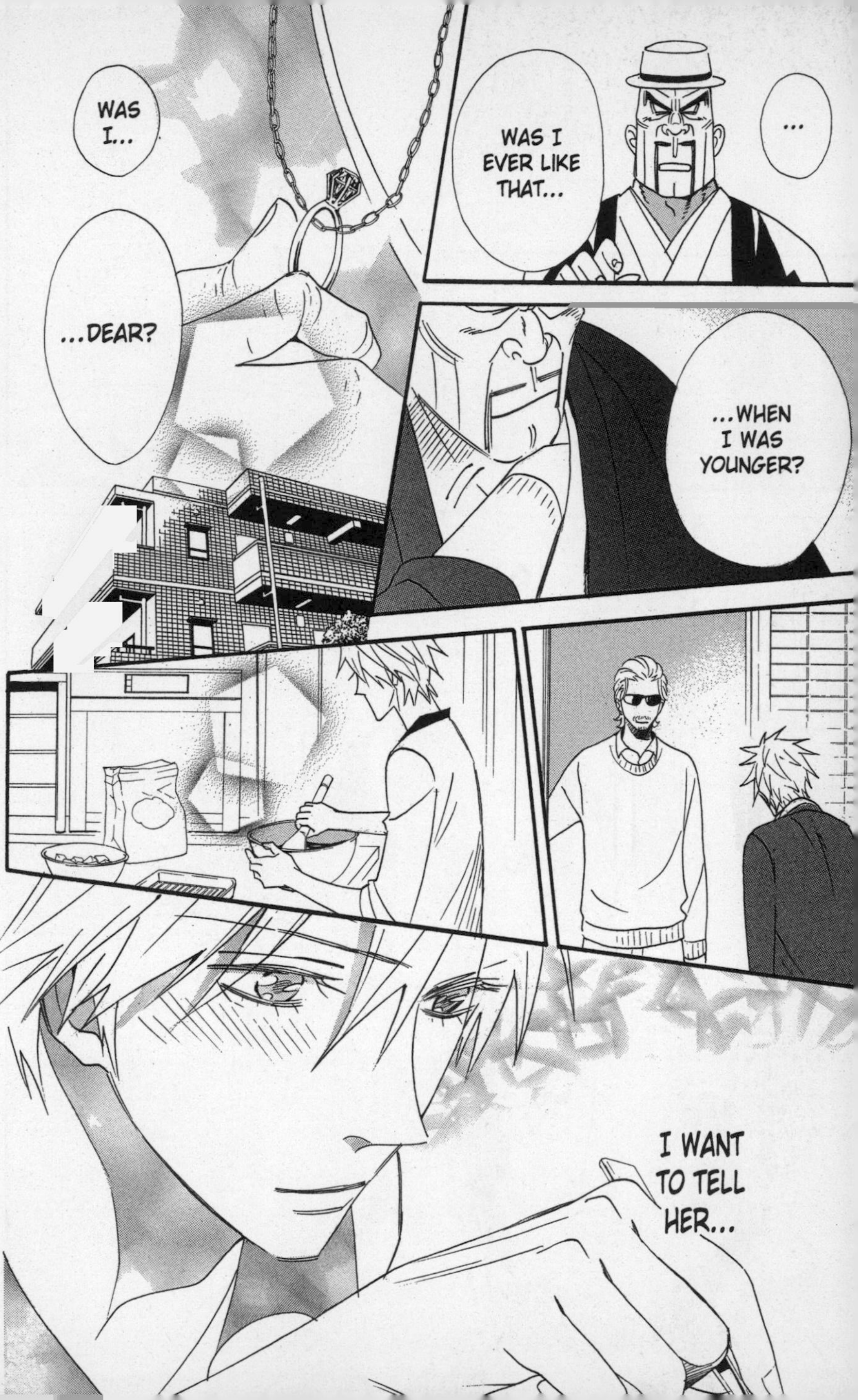
...
WAS I EVER LIKE THAT...
...WHEN I WAS YOUNGER?
WAS I...
...DEAR?
I WANT TO TELL HER...

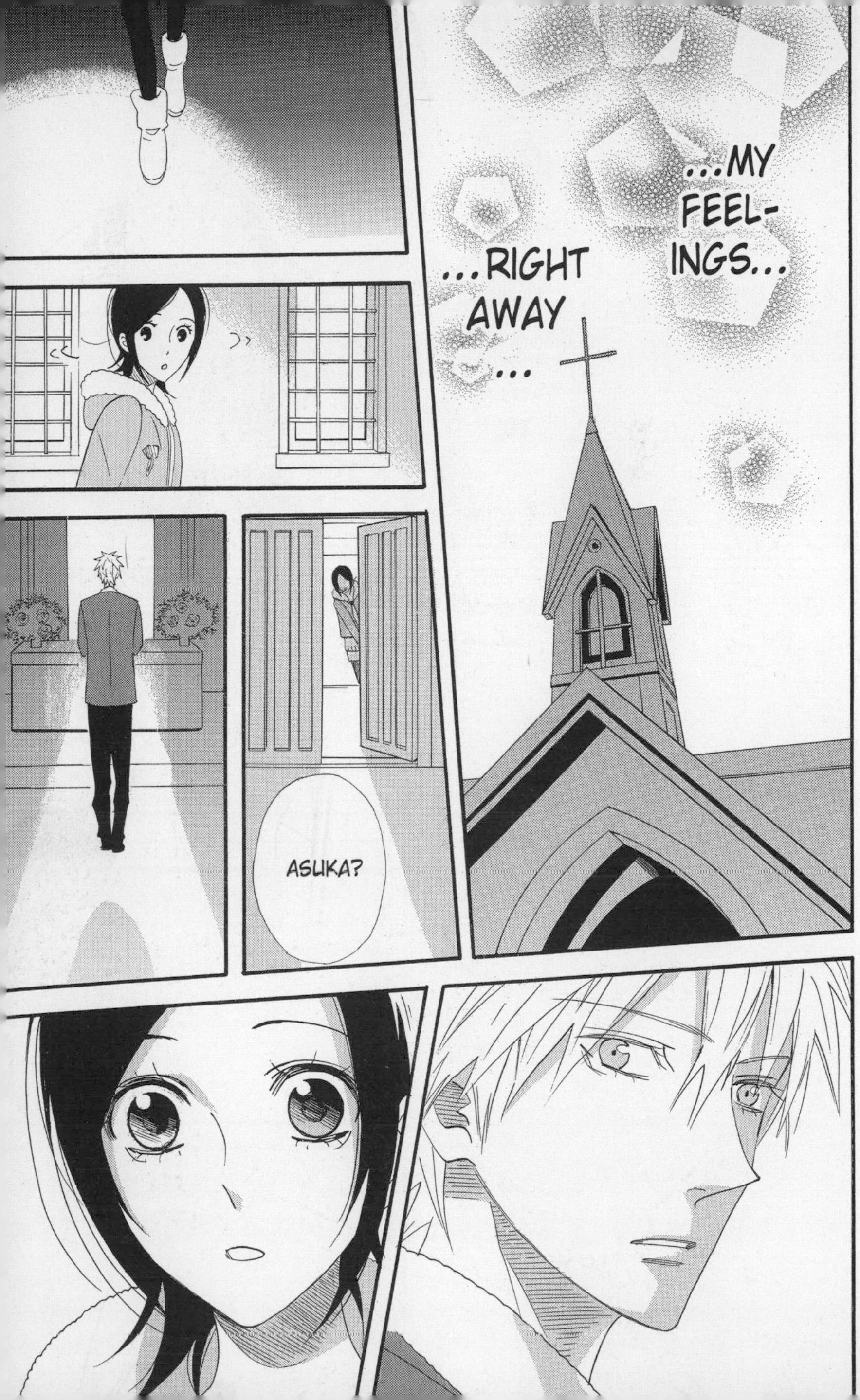
...MY FEEL- INGS...
...RIGHT AWAY ...
ASUKA?

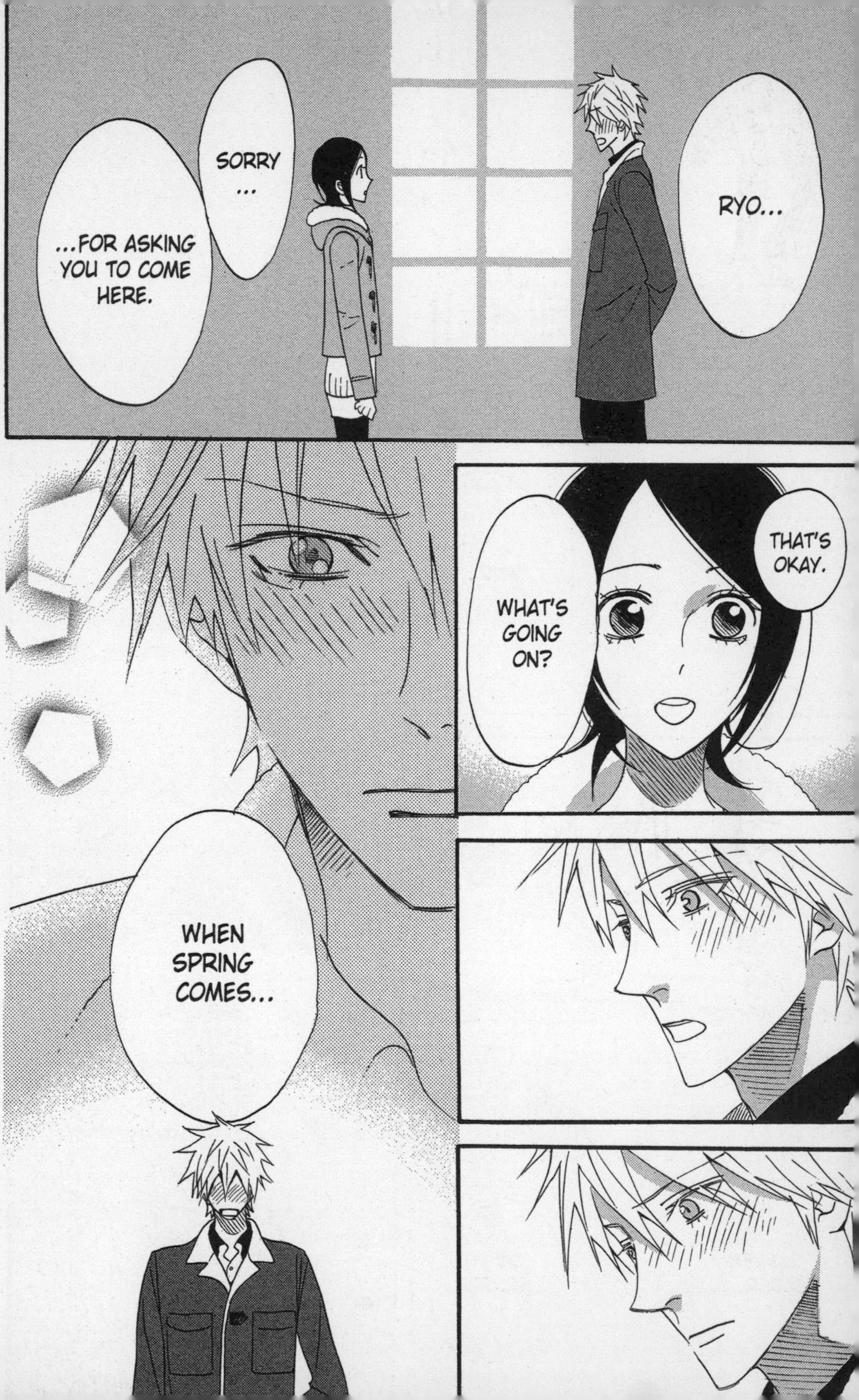
RYO...
SORRY ...
...FOR ASKING YOU TO COME HERE.
THAT'S OKAY.
WHAT'S GOING ON?
WHEN SPRING COMES...

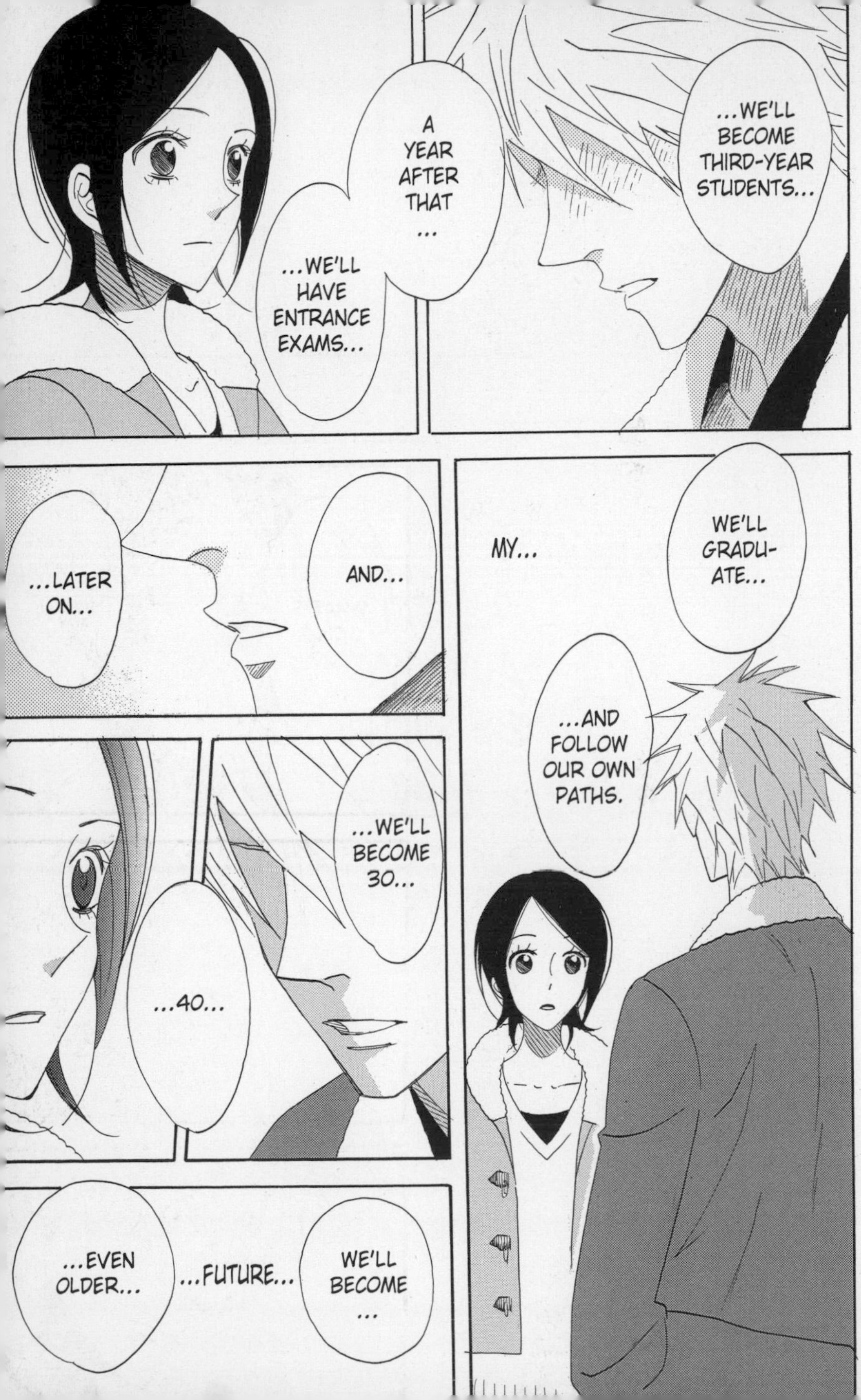
...WE'LL BECOME THIRD-YEAR STUDENTS...
A YEAR AFTER THAT ...
...WE'LL HAVE ENTRANCE EXAMS...
WE'LL GRADUATE...
...AND FOLLOW OUR OWN PATHS.
MY...
AND...
...LATER ON...
...WE'LL BECOME 30...
...40...
WE'LL BECOME ...
...FUTURE...
...EVEN OLDER...

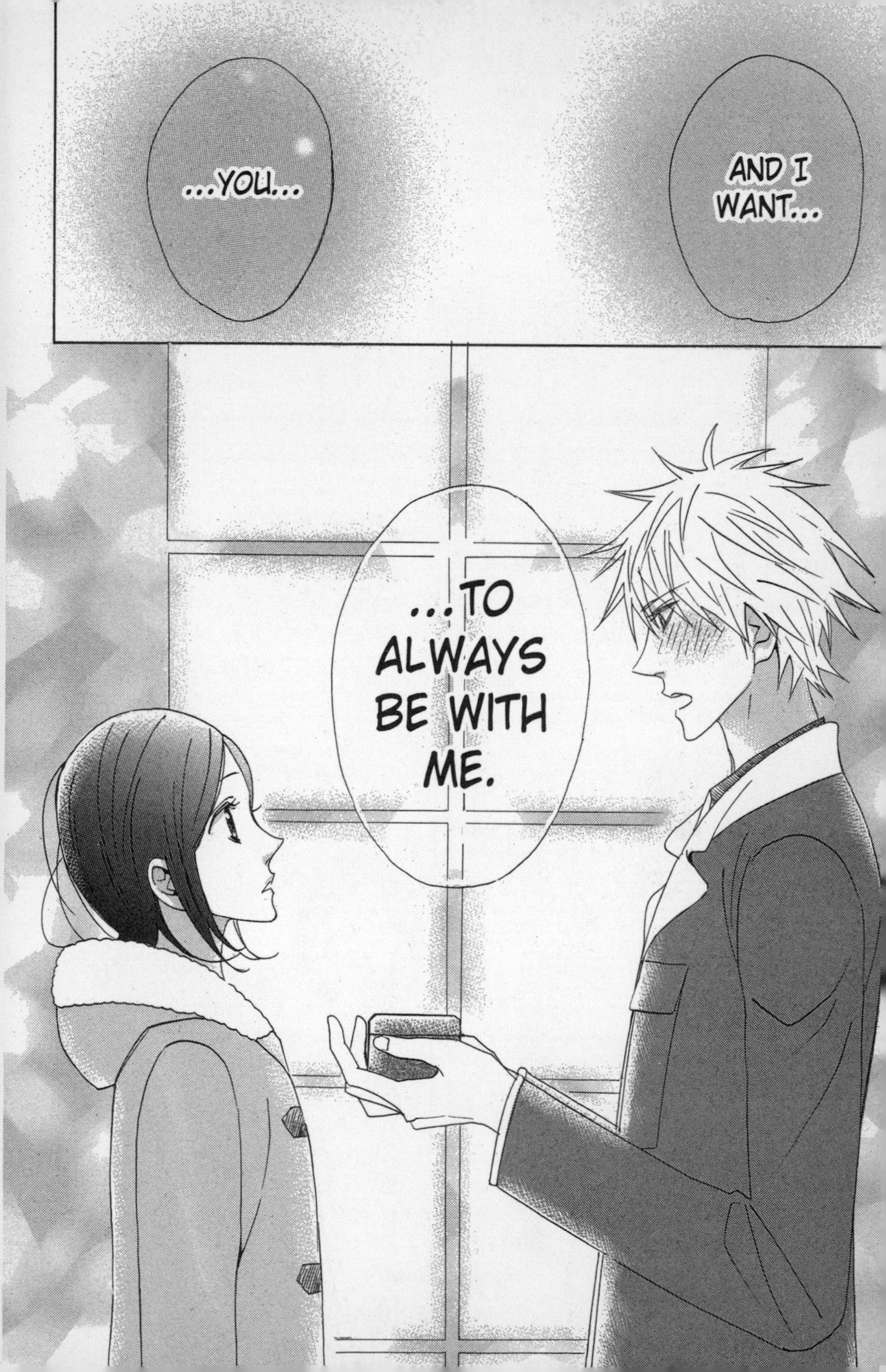
AND I WANT...
...YOU...
...TO ALWAYS BE WITH ME.

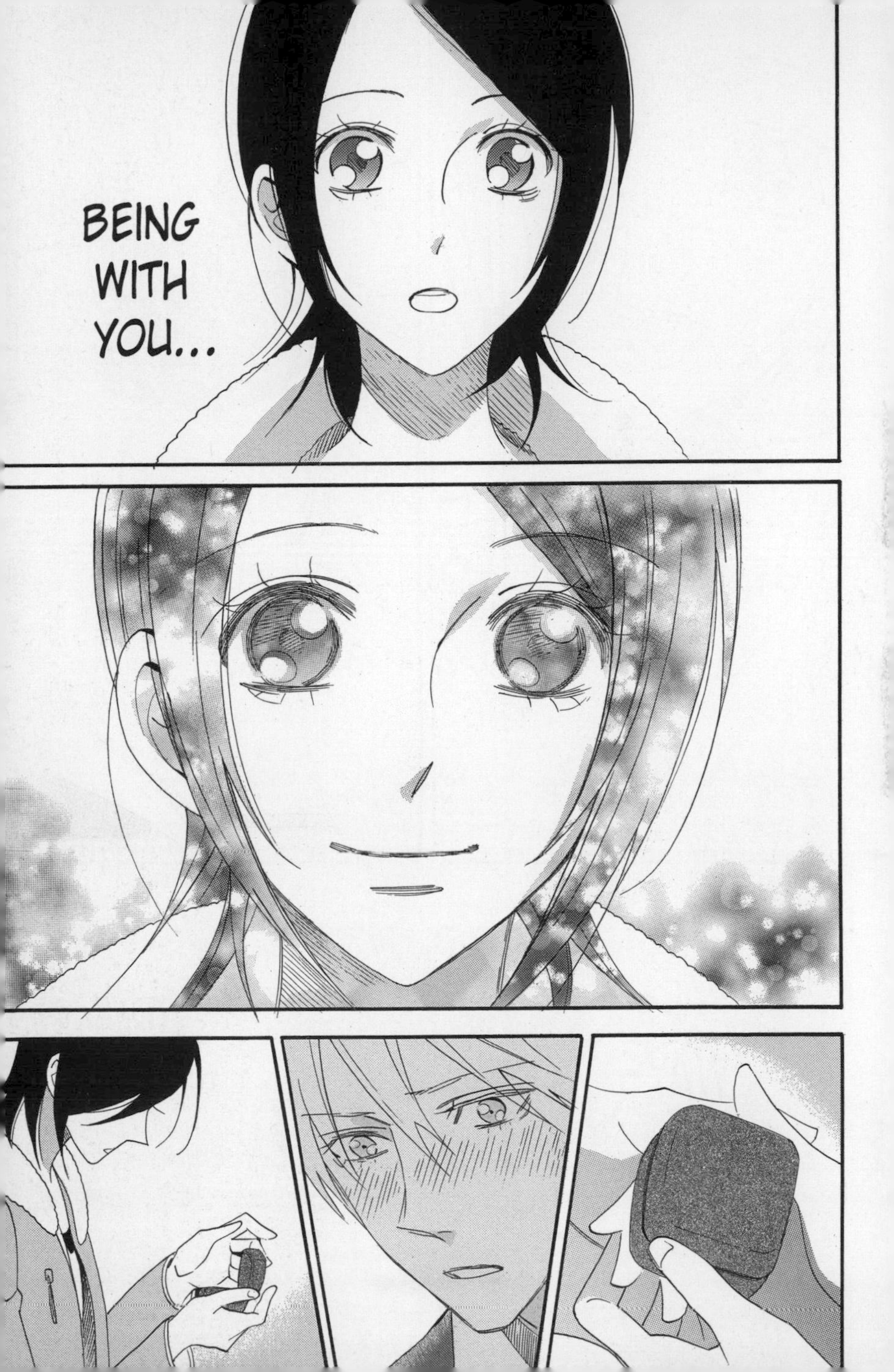
BEING WITH YOU...

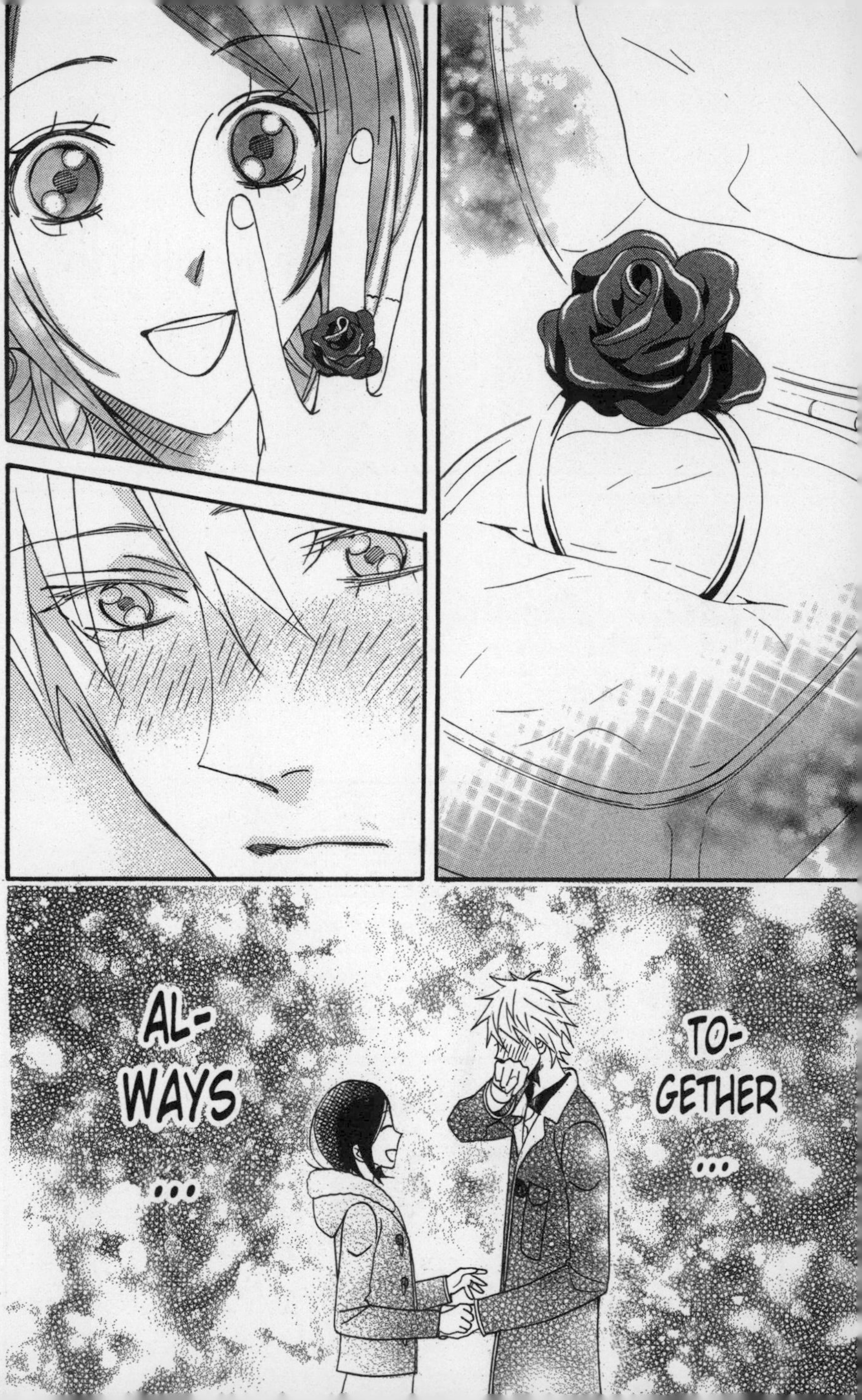
AL-WAYS ...
TO-GETHER ...

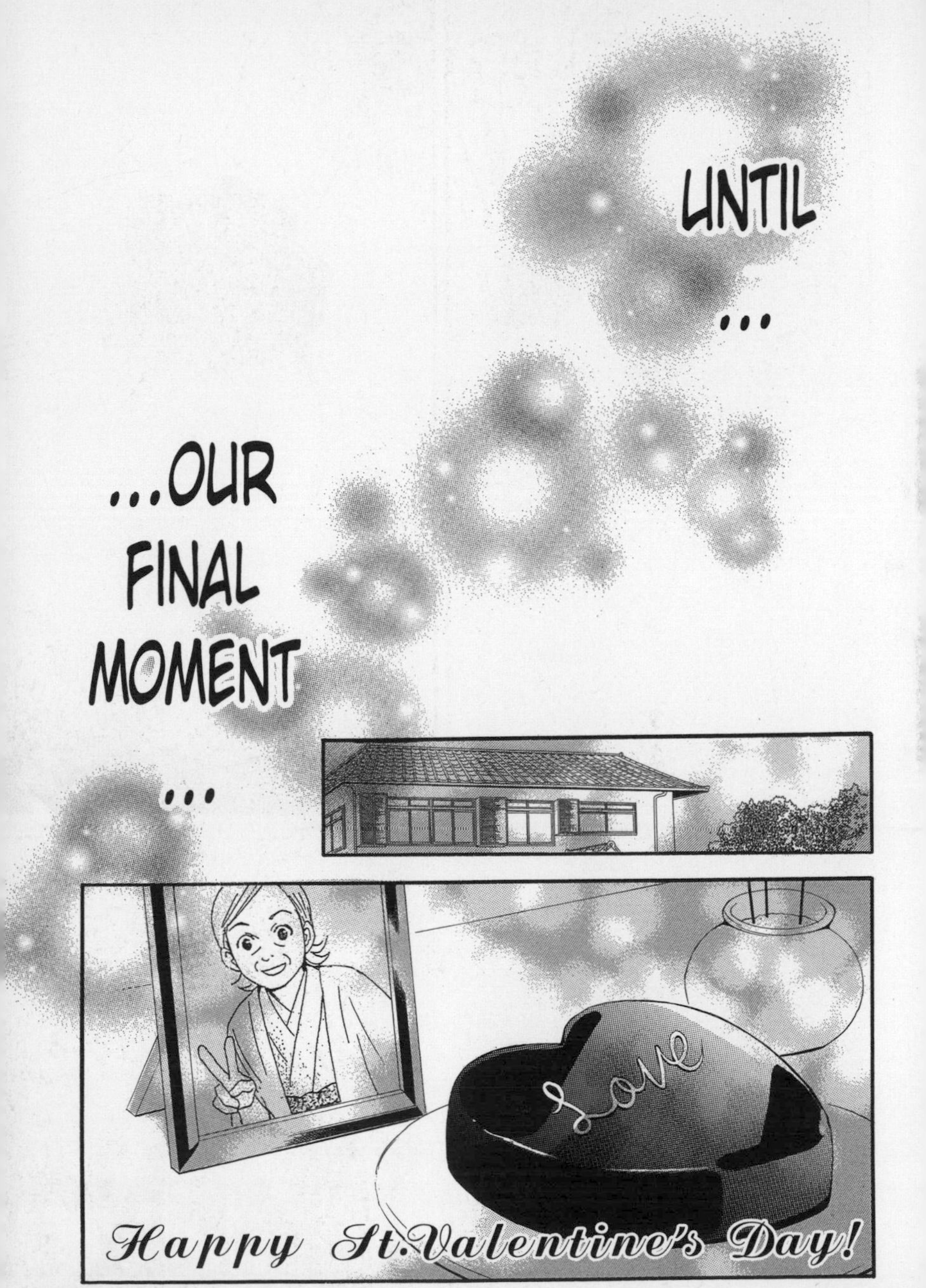
UNTIL ...
...OUR FINAL MOMENT ...
Love
Happy St.Valentine's Day!

OTOMEN 13 / THE END

OTOMEN

Confused by some of the terms, but too MANLY to ask for help?

Here are some **cultural notes** to assist you!

Chan – an informal honorific used to address children and females. *Chan* can also be used toward animals, lovers, intimate friends and people whom one has known since childhood.

Kun – an informal honorific used primarily toward males; it can be used by people of more senior status addressing those junior to them or by anyone addressing male children.

San – the most common honorific title. It is used to address people outside one's immediate family and close circle of friends.

Senpai – used to address one's senior colleagues or mentor figures; it is used when students refer to or address more senior students in their school.

Sensei – honorific title used to address teachers as well as professionals such as doctors, lawyers and artists.

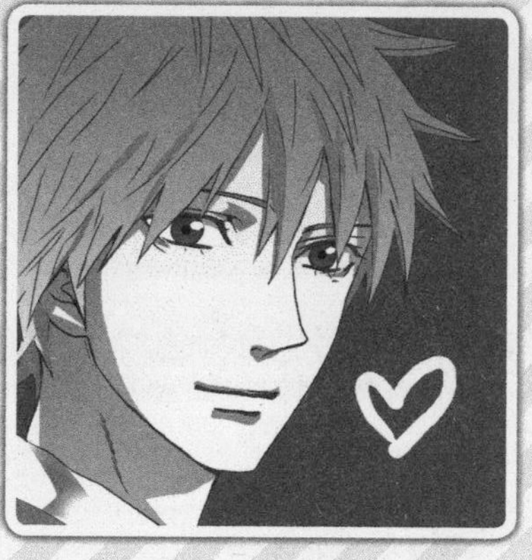

Aya Kanno was born in Tokyo, Japan. She is the creator of *Soul Rescue* and *Blank Slate* (originally published as *Akusaga* in Japan's *BetsuHana* magazine). Her latest work, *Otomen*, is currently being serialized in *BetsuHana*.

OTOMEN

Vol. 13
Shojo Beat Edition

Story and Art by | **AYA KANNO**

Translation & Adaptation | **JN Productions**
Touch-up Art & Lettering | **Mark McMurray**
Design | **Fawn Lau**
Editor | **Amy Yu**

Otomen by Aya Kanno © Aya Kanno 2011
All rights reserved. First published in Japan in 2011 by HAKUSENSHA, Inc., Tokyo.
English language translation rights arranged with HAKUSENSHA, Inc., Tokyo.

Printed in the U.S.A.

Published by VIZ Media, LLC
P.O. Box 77010
San Francisco, CA 94107

10 9 8 7 6 5 4 3 2 1
First printing, September 2012

www.viz.com

www.shojobeat.com

SURPRISE!

YOU MAY BE READING THE WRONG WAY!

It's true: In keeping with the original Japanese comic format, this book reads from right to left—so action, sound effects, and word balloons are completely reversed. This preserves the orientation of the original artwork—plus, it's fun! Check out the diagram shown here to get the hang of things, and then turn to the other side of the book to get started!

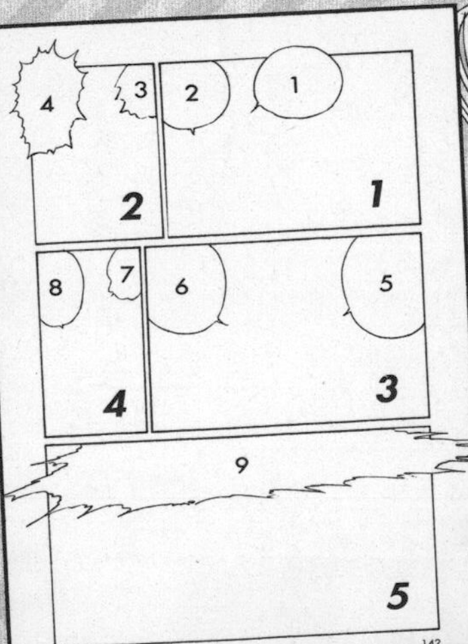
1
2
3
4
1
2
5
6
7
8
3
4
9
5

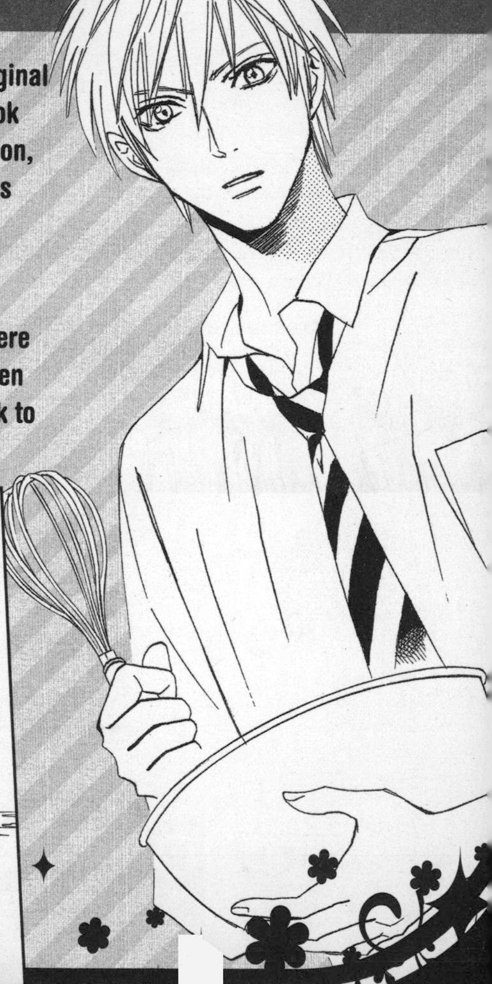